HISTORY OF THE AMERICAN CINEMA

Volume 2

1907 – 1915

Song slide from MY LOVIN' PICTURE MAN (*1910*).

HISTORY OF THE AMERICAN CINEMA
CHARLES HARPOLE, GENERAL EDITOR

2
THE TRANSFORMATION OF CINEMA 1907–1915

Eileen Bowser

UNIVERSITY OF CALIFORNIA PRESS

Berkeley • Los Angeles • London

University of California Press
Berkeley and Los Angeles, California
University of California Press, Ltd
London, England
First Paperback Printing 1994

This edition is reprinted by arrangement with Macmillan Publishing
Company, a division of Macmillan, Inc.

Library of Congress Cataloging-in-Publication Data

Bowser, Eileen.
    The transformation of cinema, 1907–1915 / Eileen Bowser.
      p. cm.
    Originally published: New York : Scribner ; Toronto : Collier
Macmillan Canada ; New York : Maxwell Macmillan International,
© 1990. (History of the American cinema ; v. 2)
    Includes bibliographical references and indexes.
    ISBN 0-520-08534-5 (alk. paper)
    1. Silent films—United States—History and criticism. 2. Motion
pictures—United States—History. 3. Motion picture industry—
United States—History. I. Title II. Series: History of the American cinema ; v. 2.
PN1993.5.U6H55   1994 vol. 2
[PN1995.75]
791.43'0973 s—dc20
[791.43'097309041]
                                    93-41317
                                        CIP

Printed in the United States of America

1   2   3   4   5   6   7   8   9

The paper used in this publication meets the minimum requirements of
American National Standard for Information Sciences—Permanence
of Paper for Printed Library Materials, ANSI Z39.48–1984. ⊛

Cover design by Ritter and Ritter, Inc.

Advisory Board

History of the American Cinema

Charles Harpole, general editor of the History of the American Cinema, is a cinema historian, filmmaker, and consultant. Author of *Gradients of Depth in the Cinema Image* and articles on cinema and mass media, he has written animation for Sesame Street and directed a film in Russia. He has taught at New York University, the University of Texas–Dallas, the University of Georgia, and Ohio State University. He now teaches, writes, and makes films in Florida, where he also helped found the Florida film festival.

The Cinema History Project and the *History of the American Cinema* have been supported by grants from the National Endowment for the Humanities and the John and Mary R. Markle Foundation.

Dedicated to Richard Griffith,
former Curator of the Department of Film
of The Museum of Modern Art, who assigned me
to read the Moving Picture World *in January 1955.*
I have not finished it yet.

Contents

Preface

A theory that explains everything in general explains very little in particular.

— Arthur Schlesinger, Jr., "As Time Goes By, Our Past Is on Film,"
Washington Post, 19 February 1984

*I*f history is the past interpreted for the present, it follows that every generation needs its own history, rewritten with a different emphasis and from new viewpoints. The present history of American film from 1907 to 1915 is much influenced by the revisionist work that began in Brighton, England, in 1978, at the international symposium on "The Fiction Film 1900–1906" organized by the Fédération Internationale des Archives du Film (FIAF). Many of the received ideas about that historical period were challenged in the course of the symposium and the work that followed. We hope that this book, following on the period studied at Brighton, will continue that trend and force us to see freshly this key period of film history.

The Brighton symposium began as a project to look anew at all the films that the world's film archives have been able to collect and preserve and make accessible for researchers. But the films of that period were so different from those which came after that the historians engaged in the project thought it necessary to go further, to find additional sources of information in order to understand what it was they were seeing. Part of the explanation, they believed, was to be found in the differing circumstances of film production, distribution, and exhibition: that is, in the film experience as a whole. Similarly, this second volume of the *History of the American Cinema* is an effort to understand, through a better knowledge of how films were seen and experienced at the time they first appeared to their audiences and of the surrounding circumstances of their production, distribution, and exhibition, and the prevalent cultural and social ideas at the time, just how it was that films and filmmaking were transformed in this period. Film forms changed as drastically in the seven years covered by this volume as at any point in motion-picture history. At the same time, the film business itself changed from a hand-crafted amusement enterprise and sideshow to a gigantic entertainment industry and the first mass-communication medium. One of the goals of this book is to demonstrate that these two phenomena are in certain ways related.

I have made no attempt to catalog the most important films and filmmakers of the period, although many of them are mentioned, together with less important ones. No essays on the significance of David Wark Griffith or THE BIRTH OF A NATION will be found, but the names of the director and the film appear in almost every chapter. My intention is to provide a general background of a kind that will make it difficult for historians more narrowly focused on a single film or filmmaker or production company to assume that a specific quality or usage is unique to that film, person, or company, instead of realizing that it was common to the period. Previously, I have made such assumptions myself, thinking, for example, that the Biograph Company executives were responsible for the curious insistence on releasing David Wark Griffith's first two-reel films one reel at a time, when in fact the entire distribution and exhibition system of the time was predicated on the release of the films one reel at a time.

Acknowledgments

One of the great discoveries of the Brighton project was that the work of reevaluating film history for our generation is greatly helped by film historians working together in teams and groups, by viewing films together, discussing together, sharing information and ideas. My own work has certainly been affected by the film historians associated with the Brighton symposium. The work of Tom Gunning and Charles Musser, whose doctoral dissertations I had the privilege of reading when they were still in progress, has been of particular importance in that regard. On the other hand, the meticulous work of film historian George Pratt, who did not happen to be a part of the Brighton project, has long been an inspiration to me as well. I am especially grateful to Tom Gunning and George Pratt for having generously given time to read my manuscript in draft form and for having provided invaluable comments. John Mercer was also of particular help for his careful copy editing of the second draft. Herbert Reynolds' attention to detail helped me avoid some errors. To Charles Harpole a special acknowledgment is due for having conceived the project in the first place, for making it a reality, and for offering guidance from beginning to end. I am also indebted to the National Endowment for the Humanities and the University of Texas for their support of the project.

My gratitude to the staff at Scribners for the warm encouragement and help of Karen Day and John Fitzpatrick as well as the careful attention of Ann B. Toback, Miriam Rosen, and Emily Garlin.

I would like to thank Richard Oldenburg, Director of the Museum of Modern Art, and Mary Lea Bandy, Director of the Department of Film, for granting me a year's sabbatical to work on this book, and members of the department's staff, who not only made that year possible but also on occasion gave specific help to my research: Jon Gartenberg, Peter Williamson, Anne Morra, Charles Silver, Ron Magliozzi, Ed Carter, Mary Corliss, and Terry Geesken. At the Library of Congress, I received the generous assistance of Barbara Humphries, Cathy Loughney, Pat Loughney, Joseph Balian, and Gillian Anderson. I owe thanks to Christopher Horak of the Film Department of the International Museum of Photography at George Eastman House and to Elaine Burrows and the staff of the National Archives of the British Film Institute; and special thanks to Bill Bowser, for much patience.

EILEEN BOWSER

HISTORY OF THE AMERICAN CINEMA

Volume 2

1907 – 1915

1

The Nickelodeon

The Nickel Madness; the Amazing Spread of a New Kind of Amusement Enterprise Which Is Making Fortunes for Its Projectors.

—Headlines in *Harper's Weekly*, 24 August 1907

*I*t was a time before there were World Wars, but only just before. The Second International Peace Congress was held at The Hague in 1907, and the third one was scheduled for 1915. People were talking about Peace, Rights for Women, Prohibition, Labor Relations, Child Welfare, and Moving Pictures. What had appeared at first as the "moving-picture craze" was bigger than anyone had anticipated. The reactions were bewildered and confused. Many feared the worst: this was getting out of control. America was confronting for the first time the phenomenon known as mass communication. Newspapers and magazines were part of it too, but they did not share in the excitement and apprehension that surrounded the moving image.

All across the country the little store shows known as nickelodeons were doing a gold-rush business in the midst of the economic recession of 1907. In downtown entertainment districts the nickel shows congregated in the same blocks with the herd instincts of overdue city buses. The shows ran continuously from morning to evening. Enterprising young men who could scrape together a little cash to invest in a picture show were getting rich, opening one nickelodeon after another, establishing theater chains or rental exchanges. The warning about the proverbial goose that provided the golden eggs, frequently heard in those days, fitted the situation rather well.

Upper- and middle-class people did not frequent these shows, or if they did, they hoped not to be seen there. At least this was the situation reported a couple of years later. At the beginning of 1909, with change in the wind, a trade periodical editor remembered, "During the past three or four years . . . any person of refinement looked around to see if [he were] likely to be recognized by anyone before entering the doors."[1]

This does not mean that respectable people in 1907 could not see moving pictures if they wanted. For one thing, they could see them at the high-class vaudeville show, since few variety shows lacked a reel or two of moving pictures. They could see them in museums of curiosities, such as the Eden Musee in New York City, patronized by the "upper classes," or in the town halls, or in legitimate theaters between the acts of plays or as Sunday-evening "concerts." They could even see them in churches. In the country or the smallest towns, they had to wait for the touring show to book into the local opera house, or the grange hall, or YMCA, or await the arrival of the old-style black-tent show, which still followed the route of country fairs or circuses, showing films inside its darkened canvas walls. By 1908 or 1909, only the very smallest towns lacked a moving-picture theater of some sort. Where the population was not big enough to support a permanent theater, an exhibitor would do a circuit of several towns, showing films one night a week in each. As one exhibitor wrote to the *Moving Picture World:* "I know a party who makes out well with a circuit of five small towns about the size [six to seven hundred people] you mention. He shows twice a week in the largest one and once a week in the others, does his own singing and entertaining and employs only one expert operator." In many towns, when the first permanent moving-picture show opened, even if it were a nickel house, all classes of people attended.[2]

For the millions of urban working-class people and new immigrants, going to the movies represented not only an affordable amusement but an extraordinary fascination. It is possible that motion pictures have never had such a devoted and enthusiastic audience since these early years. People went night after night, or from one show to another. Frank Howard, a prominent New England exchange man, defined a motion-picture fan as "one that attends one theatre every day, at least once a day, if not two or three times." In 1907 the nickel show was still usually only about half an hour, although competition was already pushing it to greater lengths in some areas. Usually, there was plenty of time to go from one to the next.[3]

Workers in Willimantic, Connecticut, a factory village "where hundreds sleep in cold and cheerless furnished rooms," found warmth and social life at the moving-picture show instead of the saloon. "Men not often seen in the company of their wives on the streets were now taking whole families to the motion pictures night after night," reported the *Willimantic Journal.* The reference to the saloon was no joke in those days of the "Wets" and the "Drys." The saloon provided a gathering place, a social life, and a political center for the blue-collar working man, the foreign-born, and the non-Protestant. It did not escape the attention of the Protestant upper-class reformers that the nickelodeons cut a significant amount of time from that spent in saloons. Nickelodeons were even credited or blamed, depending on the point of view, for putting some of the saloons out of business.[4]

The nickelodeon audience was neither monolithic nor immutable. Perceptions of this audience were mythic even in 1907, and it is difficult to get a precise picture of its constituents. Most discussions of it have centered around the little store show in the entertainment districts of the big cities. When Joseph Medill Patterson, known as "the young millionaire Socialist" in the golden years of American socialism, tells us in the often-cited *Saturday Evening Post* article of 1907 that a third of the spectators were children, we can give some credence to his claim because there are sufficient confirming accounts. Children continued to make up large portions of the audience despite all the efforts of reformers to keep them out and despite the legislation in many cities ruling that an adult must accompany each child. For example, in New York in May 1909 a visitor to the evening show at the Bronx Theater (at Wendover and Park Avenue in the Bronx), located in a working-class neighborhood, found the audience largely composed of children, plus a few adults and a uniformed officer whose job it was to keep order. The children saw Selig's RIP VAN WINKLE with Humanoscope (actors speaking lines from behind the screen) and other pictures, and a lady singing with song slides. At the end of 1910 in a Connecticut mill town, a survey of 350 schoolchildren ten to fourteen years old showed that all but 34 of them attended movies, 183 once a week, 130 twice a week, and 9 every day. Of those 9 daily filmgoers, 6 of them attended an average of 6 days a week, while 3 were there because they had jobs in nickelodeons. Of the 316 who attended the movies, 130 did so without adults, and only 20 went only in the afternoon. There were 75 children who attended on Sunday evenings.[5]

However, I have some doubts about Patterson's statement that "for some reason, young women from sixteen to thirty years old are rarely in evidence, but many middle-aged and old women are steady patrons, who never, when a new film is to be shown, miss the opening." In the afternoon, it might have been true that few young women were seen in the nickelodeons, for they were now flocking to the workplace, in nothing like the numbers of today, of course, but in large enough quantities to bring with them the winds of change. They worked not only in the mills and the factories and the sweatshops, but in the more refined atmosphere of offices, where they filled positions as telephone switchboard operators, typists, and telegraphists. In the new moving-picture industry itself there were to be many positions open to them. The New Woman was enjoying her newfound freedom, and that would have included dropping in at the cafes, dance halls, and nickelodeons after the day's work was done. To be sure, the more refined or conservative young ladies would not be found in such places, but there were a sufficient number of young women present to alarm the guardians of morality.[6]

Patterson continued:

> In cosmopolitan city districts the foreigners attend in larger proportion than the English speakers. This is doubtless because the foreigners, shut out as they are by their alien tongues from much of the life about them, can yet perfectly understand the pantomime of the moving pictures. As might be expected, the Latin races patronize the shows more consistently than Jews, Irish or Americans. Sailors of all races are devotees.

When Patterson speaks of sailors, this indicates that he probably visited nickelodeons catering to transient audiences. Yet if he had observed the nickelodeons on the Lower East Side of New York or Halstead Street in Chicago, he would have found a very high attendance by Jews. H. F. Hoffman reported that Pathé Frères' films were particularly popular in the Jewish ghetto of Chicago because they usually had few subtitles, which could not be read by this audience. The same was true, he said, in Polish and Slavic neighborhoods.[7]

A suburban exhibitor, who appears to have been a considerable snob, complained that the New York exchanges bought films only according to the demands of their best customers, the Lower East Side theaters. They demanded blood-and-thunder melodrama, while exhibitors in Stamford, Connecticut, or Rutherford, New Jersey, or even on 116th Street in Manhattan, could not get the films suitable for their more literate audiences. "The other night," he wrote, "I made an excursion to the vicinity of Essex and Rivington streets, in the very heart and thick of the tenement district." He admitted seeing one scenic film, in poor condition, in this nickelodeon:

> The audience also sat still for one or two high-class films without any fuss, although we are sure they didn't understand what they were looking at any more than they would a Chinese opera. . . . I would have been more comfortable on board a cattle train than where I sat. There were five

hundred smells combined in one. One young lady fainted and had to be carried out of the theater. I can forgive that, all right, as people with sensitive noses should not go slumming. But what is hardest to swallow is that the tastes of this seething mass of human cattle are the tastes that have dominated, or at least set, the standard of American moving pictures (*Moving Picture World*, 23 September, 1910, p. 658).

However, another nickelodeon in the same neighborhood was described by another observer in a 1908 article entitled "Where They Play Shakespeare for Five Cents":

The Herr Professor was telling the story of *Romeo and Juliet*. Standing beside the screen at one end of a long room, fitted up with its metallic ceiling and its rows upon rows of benches, he looked like a veritable Jewish Balzac. The Herr Professor is eager to make of his five-cent theater an educational center among the children and grown people of the lower East Side, and to judge by the manner in which the crowds are flocking through the gaily painted entrance, and by the overflow left standing on the sidewalk waiting for the next performance, there is no doubt that the Herr Professor is meeting with success. He is a graduate of two foreign universities, and has good ideas, no matter how much he may be limited by the business conditions of the moving picture world. The Herr Professor is a theater manager. Evening after evening he receives the tin rolls of films containing the melodrama or classical play that is to form the half-hour's amusement.

Sometimes relying on his own voice, he will fill the hall with his stentorian tones. At other times, fagged out by the constant repetition of the story, he will resort to the megaphone. The audience that flocks to the Herr Professor's Theatre is an interesting mixture of foreigners of all classes. Girls drop in alone, a fact that speaks well for the moral condition of that quarter of town. Boys come in squads. A mother and father and their children count upon an evening's entertainment. But perhaps the most interesting part of this human spectacle is the audience of wan and curious little people who stand outside, unable to afford the luxury costing five cents (Montrose J. Moses, *Theater Magazine*, September 1908, p. 264).[8]

It would be impossible to count accurately the number of nickelodeons existing at any one time. They were constantly going out of business and springing up anew. Most of the available figures do not distinguish true nickel showplaces from every other place where motion pictures were exhibited. Even in the years when the Motion Picture Patents Company extracted a weekly two-dollar fee from each licensed exhibitor, it was difficult to keep track precisely, owing to the constant changes in status of the movie houses. *Variety's* "conservative estimate" was 2,500 nickelodeons for the entire country at the beginning of 1907. In May 1907, the *Moving Picture World* said there were 2,500 to 3,000, and in November, the figure cited by Patterson was "between four and five thousand." By July 1908, an approximate figure of 8,000 was given by an Oakland, California, newspaper.[9]

The nickelodeon at Broadway and Division Street in Camden, New Jersey.

The opera house and the nickelodeon were only a few doors apart on Valley Street in Corning, Ohio, in 1908.

Does this reflect the real growth, or only the variance in estimates? The figures indicate a kind of peak about the end of 1908. Even though many store shows were to go out of business in the following year, there were as many new ones, according to figures supplied by the Motion Picture Patents Company in May 1909. The Patents Company claimed six thousand licensed theaters and two thousand independent, for a total of eight thousand in the United States. The roundness of the figures shows them to be approximate. It is also evident from this information that eight thousand moving-picture theaters included all the kinds of exhibition places, since the Patents Company would have issued licenses to any theater, nickelodeon or not, that wished to use its films. By 1910, the numbers were growing again: the Patents Company records show ten thousand theaters of all kinds in that year. At the same time the population of the United States was about ninety million, or a national average of nine thousand persons for each moving-picture show. By 1914, the figure given by Frank L. Dyer of the Patents Company was about fourteen thousand moving picture theaters in the United States. By this time, the nickelodeon era was over, despite the fact that many nickelodeons still existed.[10]

Perhaps we can get a better feel for these numbers and rates of growth by looking at some individual cities or towns. In Indianapolis, for example, there were twenty-one nickelodeons and three ten-cent theaters in 1908, only three years after the first nickelodeon had appeared there. Each nickelodeon in this city gave a show consisting of one reel of film, which might contain two or three different subjects, and an illustrated song, with the show taking twenty to twenty-five minutes—"except when there is a crowd waiting, then it is speeded up to 15 to 17 minutes." The shows in Indianapolis were open from nine in the morning till eleven at night, which allowed about twenty to thirty shows each day. If you could afford ten cents, you could go to one of the three high-class theaters and get an evening of three or four reels of pictures with live entertainment consisting of illustrated songs, vaudeville acts, and slide lectures lasting from one to one-and-a-half hours. By 1911, the number had increased to seventy-six motion-picture theaters alone, not including regular theaters that changed over to movies during the summer. However, only fifteen of the movie houses remained downtown in 1911, because of the high rents.[11]

In 1908 there were fifteen nickelodeons in Grand Rapids, Michigan, and the exchange that supplied most of them thought this was too many. To survive, they depended on spectators who attended day after day. In 1909 Philadelphia had about 184 "picture parlors," and on Girard Avenue there were five shows in four blocks, the patronage drawn mostly from "poor working class people." However, in September 1908 Sigmund Lubin had opened a high-class theater on Market Street in Philadelphia, which he modestly called "Lubin's Palace," "unquestionably the largest and most elaborate moving picture theater in the world," seating eight hundred spectators. In 1909, Rochester, New York, had seventeen shows for a population of 200,000.[12]

Chicago, probably the biggest moviegoing town of all in those days, had 407 picture houses in 1909 for a population of slightly over two million, or approximately one nickelodeon or theater for each 5,350 people. In New York City there was one for each 11,250 people. By October 1912, there were said to be 732 exhibitors in Chicago, 650 of them showing moving pictures exclusively. At the end of 1913, however, the Chicago License Bureau listed only 550 moving-picture theaters.[13]

The number supplied by the *Moving Picture World* for New York City in 1908 was 300 to 400, for a population of over 4.5 million people. Robert Allen found only 123 motion-picture exhibitions listed in *Trow's Business Directory* for Manhattan in the 1908 edition, exclusive of the vaudeville theaters. The large numbers of nickelodeons clustered in the borough of Brooklyn may account in part for the discrepancy, and the *World's* figures may have included all types of exhibition places. It is also very likely that some store shows never got listed in *Trow's*, as they were a very fly-by-night business in 1908. Coney Island saloons, with no show license, gave film shows for free and gained their profits from the sale of drinks.

City ordinances similar to those in New York governing the size of nickelodeons existed in many other cities, but somehow in New York they were more restrictive or took longer to change. Film historians have mistakenly understood the New York City limit of 299 seats as a regulation of the common show license under which nickelodeons operated (the trade press of the time made the same error), but in fact this was a condition of the building codes and fire laws. The March 1911 report of Raymond B. Fosdick to Mayor Gaynor made it clear: "Licenses for picture houses may be of two kinds, dependent not upon the seating capacity, but wholly upon the kind of performances." The ordinance was changed in 1913 to permit movie theaters to have 600 seats according to changes in the building codes.

New York remained far behind the rest of the country in building new and more expensive moving-picture theaters, as well as in upgrading other exhibition conditions. The dominant theatrical interests were a likely factor in holding back growth. The Motion Picture Patents Company said in May 1909 that there were then only half as many motion-picture theaters in New York as had existed the previous December. If these rather startling figures are accurate, it must have been the Patents Company itself that was responsible for cutting down its own potential market by threatened or actual litigation against the use of unlicensed projection machines. There were a lot of Patents Company replevin suits in the first months of 1909, whereby licensed films in unlicensed theaters were seized. By 1910, however, the *Moving Picture World* reported about six hundred picture shows in Greater New York.[14]

It seems no city can be taken as typical. New England was different from both the Midwest and New York. In every region and every major city there were slightly different situations that still have to be studied before we have a comprehensive picture of the nickelodeon era.

Russell Merritt's study of Boston nickelodeons and Robert Allen's research on Manhattan store shows, together with the contemporary accounts in periodicals, newspapers, and the trade press, reveal some of the variants in locations and trace the expansion. In large cities nickelodeons tended to group themselves at first in the already-established amusement districts, right next door to the high-class vaudeville and legitimate theaters in many cases, and expanded into higher-class residential areas and suburbs as time went on, moving away from the overcrowded tenement districts that at first provided the largest source of customers.[15]

The Boston situation studied by Russell Merritt differed in several ways from that found in other major cities. Boston was then still considered the cultural capital of the country and tended to look down its patrician nose at common amusements. The census figures of 1910 show almost three-quarters of a million people, yet in that year Boston had just twenty moving-picture theaters, or one for approximately each 33,500 persons, compared to New York's 11,250 and Chicago's 5,350. Nor were these nick-elodeons in the sense of the admission price, as almost all of them charged ten cents from the day of their opening. Russell Merritt concludes that "nickelodeons were seldom a nickel," but in fact, elsewhere in the country they almost always were, until the little store show finally vanished in the mists of time. Intense competition held the admission at a nickel even though the length of the show kept increasing, in-cluding more films and more vaudeville acts. When theaters were built with greater seating capacity, they often retained the five-cent admission because they could give fewer shows during a day but still make the same income at the box office. This situation eventually contributed to driving the small theaters, dependent on rapid turnover, out of business. Regular vaudeville theaters charged much more than the nickelodeons, and moving-picture exhibitors tried to increase admission prices when they increased the number of films and vaudeville acts in their programs. But it was not easy to do that if the local competition offered the same for five cents. In Denver, for example, known as "the Nickel City of the West," exhibitors were still trying to raise prices with only partial success at the end of 1914. Small theaters in the mountain district of Tennessee, open only one or two nights a week and still charging five cents in 1915, were being forced to close because they could not pay the war tax when it was increased from $25 to $50 a year.[16]

Lary May, in his study of social changes reflected in the movies, *Screening Out the Past*, begins by remembering Henry Seidel Canby's *The Age of Confidence*, in which Canby "saw one apt symbol for that change in his home town, the center of local society, the opera house, had been turned into a movie theater open to all."[17] The idea of movies as a potent device for the democratization of American society was extremely popular with social theorists: in their view, the movies were going to teach the foreign-born to adopt the values of the established social system of native-born white Protestant culture. That meant order, discipline, hard work, responsibility for others, and strict sexual control. It meant preserving the family.

There was some selection, before 1909, of high-class films for the shows catering to the middle-class and the refined: scenic films and educational films sprinkled judiciously with comedies and the classics of literature. As Charles Musser has dis-covered, the lecture tours of Lyman Howe and Burton Holmes were approved, and in the case of Howe even supported, by church people who considered amusements frivolous or immoral, because these kinds of shows were deemed educational. In fact, the same films were being shown in both kinds of exhibition places, with the most vulgar subjects omitted in the higher-class halls and a reduced amount of educational films selected for the nickelodeons. The propriety of moving-picture shows had more to do with exhibition venues and methods than the moral quality of the films being shown. The reformers and uplifters tried to increase the educational value of films in the nickelodeon after 1908, but as we will see in chapter 3, audiences often rejected such films.[18]

The trend was for these two exhibition systems, serving the high-class theaters and the nickelodeon, to come closer together. Within a few years just about everybody outside the large cities was going to the same theaters, seeing the same films, and sharing in the communal experience: people of all classes, and the whole family. As Canby had observed, the opera house was once the place for high society, the well-to-do, and the upward-striving middle class. Now, the opera house was turned into a movie theater and the whole town attended. To be sure, they did not always

Opening night at the Rex Theater, Hannibal, Missouri, 4 April 1912. The balcony was reserved for blacks.

mix in the same sections within the theater (wherever moving picture theaters were large enough to have "sections"). A variety of admission prices ensured a separation of classes, as in the legitimate theaters. The division of audiences into separate theaters may have lasted longer in cities, where the little neighborhood theater and the movie palace downtown charged different admission prices.

The "democratization of America" was not all that easy. In many parts of the country, blacks had to sit up in the balcony. A brave "colored woman" who refused to sit in the balcony of the Victoria Theater in Rochester, New York, in 1913 lost her suit to defend her civil rights. It should be noted that "Italians and the rougher element" were also expected to sit in the balcony in that theater. "In the South the colored brother is given to understand that he must flock by himself or there will be trouble, but in the North the case is different and every now and then there seems to be an organized effort on the part of the negroes to make as much trouble as possible." The *Moving Picture World* editor who reported this reminisced about his own experiences:

> In Washington a number of years ago we broke into the theatrical business as usher in the balcony of one of the theaters. There they had a Section D for the colored patrons, and the box office man sold D to all colored applicants, but now and then a negro would hire a white boy to buy his tickets for him and turn up with seats in the white sections. In such a case the usher was instructed to drop the tickets on the floor and use a couple of D tickets with which he was provided. It was not strictly

honest, perhaps, but it met guile with guile, and something of that sort was necessary in a low-price house (*Moving Picture World*, 4 October 1913, p. 147).

Despite the efforts of Progressives, some of them former Abolitionists, working to integrate the former slaves and their offspring into American society, and some black Americans struggling for equality, the unconscious, easy acceptance of prejudice and its stereotypes by the majority of Americans can be seen in hundreds of films throughout the whole period of silent film, including the most famous example, THE BIRTH OF A NATION, in 1915.

There were certainly some communities where the races mixed freely. There were also theaters wholly owned by blacks and catering to the black clientele, 214 of them in America in 1913, according to the head of the black-owned and -operated Foster Photoplay Company of Chicago, William Foster.[19]

By 1907, there were enough of the cheapest, shabbiest kind of nickelodeon to alarm the responsible citizens and social reformers. They knew something unusual was going on, even if they didn't know they were confronting a small social revolution. Many of the inner-city nickelodeons, such as those on "Motion Picture Row" on East Fourteenth Street in New York City and on Halstead Street in Chicago, were undeniably dark and smelly and crowded and noisy. The audiences were loud and enthusiastic. The Jewish and Catholic immigrants from eastern and southern Europe showed less restraint in their emotions than the native-born white Protestants, and they jabbered in languages that were strange to Anglo-Saxons. There was the odor of poverty and the unwashed, to which was added, on damp days, the smell of wet wool. The "hawker" called out to the passersby, mechanical music blared out, and the manager-owner would lounge around the entrance, counting his nickels, watching the competition next door or across the street. The moving pictures would run from two to ten minutes each, and there would be several films on the program. If there were a crowd out front waiting to spend its nickels, the manager might decide to shorten the program, either by speeding up the cranking of the projector or by dropping a film from the program.

According to the alarmists, pimps and white slavers waited outside the nickelodeons to offer to pay the way in for young women: perhaps this did happen sometime, somewhere, but it is difficult to separate the hysteria of the yellow press from the self-protecting statements of the moving-picture trade. The fear is symptomatic of the changing lifestyles of young women, no longer totally under the control of the Victorian family structure. Films about white slavery enjoyed a vogue, in the name of reform, but their exploitative nature was soon recognized, and in the end they added to the pressure for censorship.

In fact, the darkness inside and the enthusiasm of the unwashed poor who made up the patronage was something unknown and fearful to those outside. However, the high-minded idealists of the time saw instead the potential for uplifting the masses in these stygian holes. The unsightly conditions existed chiefly in the slum areas. Even in 1907, some of the store shows, in other parts of the city, and especially in small towns, were entirely respectable.

Who were the people running the profitable nickelodeon business? Nickelodeon owners and managers came primarily from the same kind of background as the majority of the spectators; the blue-collar workers, the immigrants, large numbers of them Jew-

The Princess Theater in St. Cloud, Minnesota. The Italian spectacle film, THE FALL OF TROY (CADUTO DEL TROIA) was released in the United States in 1911.

ish. Many of them did not share the middle-class Protestant culture of the producers in the pre-1907 era. (Sigmund Lubin, the successful Philadelphia producer, was the exception: the single Jewish immigrant among the heads of the Motion Picture Patents Company.) These nickelodeon owners and distributors were to form the nucleus of the independent movement against the licensed producers, and eventually, the same people founded the new production companies that would dominate the industry: William Fox, Carl Laemmle, Adolph Zukor, Marcus Loew, the Warner Brothers.

The "operators," as projectionists were then called, were the first segment of the new industry to organize into unions. It is hardly surprising that they did so quickly, because the new entrepreneurs of show business, the nickelodeon managers, were often hiring young, untrained boys at low wages to work seven days a week where Sunday-closing laws permitted, from early morning to late at night, at a trade that required hard work and professional skill. They, the bosses, were among the last of the various components of the industry to organize in order to control competition and bring some order to their business. They were intensely competitive, struggling to get a foothold and survive.

In many cases, the owner of a nickelodeon had started out as a one-man show, running the projection machine himself as well as collecting the nickels and delivering narrations for the films and singing between the reels. But competition (and after 1908, uplift movements) demanded something more of the performance. The operator had to crank the machine by hand all day long, keeping an eye on the varying speed, the focus, and the amount of light, and nurse the worn and torn perforations through the sprockets. He had to trim his carbon lights, make repairs and cuts to the film, and display slides for the singer or the lecturer, or announcement slides, which he sometimes made himself. To be good at his profession, he needed to have an understanding of electricity and the laws of optics, and he needed to be a mechanic, in order to repair the projection machine when it broke down. Often he was expected to go and pick up the reels for each day's show, either at the film exchange or at the railway station, returning the ones already used, and he had to see that the day's show was in good enough repair to go through the machine twenty or more times. An underpaid projectionist in Fergus Falls, Minnesota, complained:

> I will say that all they asked of me was to get the films from the express office, put out the advertising matter, sweep out, dust the theater, and once a week wash off the tile front; build the fires and see that everything was ready for the show; meet the vaudeville people when we had them, and wait on them; ship back the films and do any electrical work required about the place, as well as operate the machine. . . . The requirements here are to run one reel of film and then an illustrated song; another reel and a second song without stopping. The operator is required to thread the machine while running the song slides and they even wanted me to re-wind the first reel while running the second, so as to stop only one minute to adjust the carbons at the close of the show. . . . For this work they paid me the handsome sum of $12 per week, but as the theater changed hands April 1, I was dismissed in favor of an $8 eighteen-year-old boy, who never ran a machine in his life until last year, and then only as a helper (*Moving Picture World*, 29 April 1911, p. 953).

It was due to the operator's grave responsibility in case of fire that cities began to require licensing of projectionists. Fire was always a danger when films were released on highly flammable nitrate stock, and before fire safety regulations were enacted and enforced, there were many disasters or near-disasters. In New York, the new law of 1910 licensing projectionists required applicants to be U.S. citizens, which promptly threw out of work a lot of immigrants who had already become highly skilled. After considerable agitation, that part of the law was finally revised, but by that time many of the foreign-born projectionists had moved to other cities.[20]

The music of the nickelodeons was performed by live musicians as well as by all kinds of wondrous mechanical pianos, organs, and orchestras, such as "The Wurlitzer Automatic Orchestra" or "The Piano-Orchestra." Musicians or mechanical substitutes entertained at intermissions and usually performed simultaneously with the pictures, very often with little relevance to what was on the screen. There is evidence of a few nickelodeons without any music at all, but these existed only for lack of means to employ a pianist or even a scratchy phonograph, except for an occasional place where a manager preferred to hear just the sound of his own voice explaining the pictures. From Evansville, Indiana, in 1911, Thomas Bedding reported that "the manager of the Lyric does not seem to believe in music, but he lectures while the picture is on the screen." The New England reporter for the *Moving Picture World*, known as "Henry," claimed that after visiting theaters in his part of the country from 1907 to 1910, he had never heard a self-playing piano in use in any of them: "The houses now are using, as they did since their opening, a pianist and trap-drummer, while a few have full orchestras." In this as in other ways, New England's practice was not typical of the whole country. Elsewhere, mechanical music-players were very popular. In 1912, when the musicians began to organize into unions and had to strike to get recognition, mechanical music-makers were more welcome than ever to the managers.[21]

Accounts of attending the nickelodeons are filled with stories of inappropriate ragtime that accompanied the tender love scene or the melancholy death scene. Ragtime, much used in the variety show, was all very well in the days when films were either actualities or comedies, as almost all films were before 1907, but the feeling of discordance grew as the melodrama gained ground. The use of ragtime was also deplored by the reformers, because it was not considered respectable music for the middle class. In practical terms, after 1907, the distribution system made it nearly impossible for a musician to be prepared for what he or she was to play. Where there was a daily change and a continuous show, the first show of the day must have been quite different from the last ones, when the accompanist had become familiar through repetition with the task at hand.

The high-class show houses and the touring exhibitors such as Lyman Howe had well-rehearsed teams of people behind the screen, making sounds, and mechanical sound-effect devices, but in the little nickelodeon sometimes the most that could be afforded was the pianist. The drummer with his set of traps providing sound effects was generally the next employed after the pianist, if the budget allowed for two musicians. Both of them, but especially the drummer, soon found they could amuse themselves and the audience by providing deliberately inappropriate sound effects and drum rolls, making comedies out of heavy melodramas. Tender love scenes and tragic death scenes could easily be made to provoke laughter with a drum roll, a falling body could become slapstick with a sound effect, and a kiss could be empha-

The spring floods of 1913 in Hamilton, Ohio, canceled the Jewel Theater's showing of Vitagraph's RED AND WHITE ROSES.

sized with smacking sounds. Probably many of the films deserved this treatment, but once they started on this course, the musicians could also ruin a very good film and frequently did. The critics, who in those days more frequently saw films with audiences than at private screenings, reported the totally different effect the same films could have when seen with or without competent and appropriate accompaniment.[22]

The lone musician, or the piano player together with the drummer, could, with some practice, improvise for each new film that came along. They soon learned to anticipate the love scene, the comic chase, the death scene, or the race to the rescue. But how did the hardy band of musicians known as the orchestra in the bigger theaters manage to improvise? Not very well, according to some accounts.

Vitagraph began to send out prepared music scores with its "films de luxe" in October 1909, and the Edison *Kinetogram* began to give suggestions for music for some specific films in the same month. It was not until 1911 that regular columns of advice for musicians appeared in trade periodicals.[23]

It was a poor show house that did not supply a singer between the reels, while the projectionist threaded up the one projector. The tradition of singing with illustrative slides was much older than the nickelodeon: it was a popular part of the variety show. There were businesses devoted to producing the slides, much like the ones producing the moving pictures. Fred J. Balshofer "posed the players and photographed illustrated slides for . . . popular songs of the day" for the Shields Lantern Slide Company in New York City before going to work for Sigmund Lubin in 1905. The young Norma Talmadge posed for song slides before she went to Vitagraph and became a movie star, as did some others.[24]

While other non-film elements of the performance changed or faded away, the illustrated-song slides remained in most theaters as late as 1913, and even later in some. Only with the rise of the feature film did the performances begin to disappear, or rather, to be subsumed in the song film, which continued into the twenties and thirties with the "bouncing ball" audience-participation films. Bigger magazines on projection machines, or in the better houses, two projection machines, made it possible to avoid the waits for changing the reel, and filling these blanks in the program while the reel was changed had been the practical function of the singer.

There were other reasons, too, for the illustrated song performance to last as long as it did. Music publishers paid for singers to appear in the nickelodeons in order to promote their latest songs. This entertainment was often free for the exhibitor, at least in larger cities. There were also many popular song artists available from the touring variety shows, which offered a rapidly shrinking market for their talent in the face of the advancing motion-picture theater. In small towns, there was also a pool of home-style talent to draw on, not only singers, but pianists and other musicians. In the days before radio and television, family music performances were more frequently a part of home entertainment, and refined middle-class sons and daughters were taught to perform at home and at church and community gatherings as part of their social graces. When the singer at the motion-picture show sang the chorus, the audience was frequently invited to join in and happily did so. They were accustomed to being asked during the old variety show and they continued to participate in the community singing long after the song slides were replaced by the song film. The communal factor was always to be an important element of the moviegoing experience.[25]

Do You Know the Keynote of

 **SUCCESS ??**

Give your people something different from your Competitors

Namely, Songs that you don't hear everyday at every place you come

We make the **"DIFFERENT KIND OF A SONG"**

Songs which are the HITS of some of the leading publishers of N. Y.

But at the same time it is FRESH and NEW

not MURDERED by all M. P. Theatres, when you get it

Now if you want
Your people to come **AGAIN and AGAIN** You had better
Look over this list

an convince yourself that the songs we advertise here are new and up-to-date

AND DEMAND THEM FROM YOUR EXCHANGE

Dearest - -	Pub. by Music House of Laemmle	
I think I hear my Country Calling	"	"
Don't Say Good by	"	"
I'll build a fence around you	- -	Mills
Since I've been going with you	- -	Remick
Outside of that you're all right	- - -	Nybo
Gee But it's great to meet a friend from your home town		"
Lou Lou - - -	Seymour Furth Mus. Co.	
In One Girls Heart	- -	Head Mus. Pub. Co.

Price $3.00 Per Set

EXCELSIOR SLIDE CO.

138 East 14th Street - - New York City

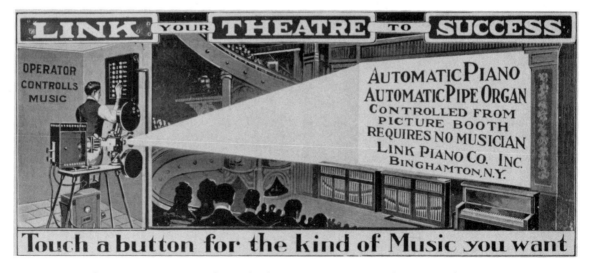

Advertisements sent to the Oxford Opera House, Oxford, New York, in 1911.

Posing for song slides was a profession that might lead to a movie career. Lillian
"Dimples" Walker, sitting on the piano, and Anita Stewart, among the pots and pans,
became Vitagraph stars. Alice Joyce, in the clamshell, was a model for the illustrator
Harrison Fisher before becoming a Kalem star.

So ubiquitous was the singer with slides that it was common for new theaters during the period or older ones undergoing renovation to install elaborate little alcoves on either side of the screen for the singer to stand in while performing. As the period 1908–1913 was dominated by the practice of the "daily change"—a new show every day—the music publishers complained that it was impossible to have song "hits." A song, like the pictures, was apt to be presented for just one day at any one theater before moving on to another. By October 1912, the *Moving Picture World* reported that while the illustrated song was holding on in popularity, the supply of songs and slides was being too quickly exhausted; there was always the danger, warned the writer, that in such a case vulgarity might creep into the show.[26]

The vaudeville act was not quite as ubiquitous as the illustrated song, but in some sections and during some periods nearly all nickelodeons included it.

There must have been an enormous quantity of unemployed performers available, because the nickelodeons had taken much of the audience away from the low-priced variety shows. On the other hand, a stage manager noted in 1911 that while there was scarcely a one-night-stand theater in America making a profit, the motion picture, "which has emptied the galleries and balconies, has driven the medium-priced companies off the road, has established vaudeville houses in towns that could not otherwise support them." The storefront shows did not have stages or space for elaborate scenery, so the vaudeville they offered had to be simple acts with one or two performers and not much in the way of scenery and props. This was the type known as "small-time vaudeville." The acts were of the kind that, in big-time vaudeville, were played in front of the curtain while the more elaborate sets were changed. Only the theaters and opera houses and halls where variety shows had played across the country since the eighties (many of which were soon to be turned into motion-picture theaters) could provide the facilities for big-time vaudeville and an audience used to paying higher admission prices. Later on, the existence of these theaters provided a venue for motion-picture road shows and special showings of the long feature film, outside the normal exhibition system.[27]

In nickelodeon days, where rapid turnover of the audience was important, the variety acts had to perform over and over again at very frequent intervals. It was an even harder life than these performers had lived in the old days, playing "two a day." Although at the height of the "daily change" fever for movies the variety act was often held over for as much as a week, it would rarely stay in the same place longer than that. Managers who insisted they had customers coming back every day never quite explained why their public had to see a new film but were willing to see the variety act several times.

The Progressives who wanted to uplift the industry and educate the masses in attendance at the nickelodeon deplored the vulgarity of the variety show and campaigned actively to get rid of it. From their point of view, all these distractions had to be removed from the motion-picture theater if the picture was to really influence its audience. The motion-picture producers shared their mission, but did not articulate their other major objection, namely that vaudeville stood in the way of expanding the market, because the exhibitor who used it needed fewer films to fill his program. However, reformers and producers alike encouraged the educational lecture in the nickelodeon as uplift for the lower classes and as an attraction for the "better classes." The educational lecture appealed to American notions of higher culture, and there was a long-standing tradition of attending lectures on all kind of subjects: literary, historical, philosophical, and most popular of all, travel topics, with slides. Even in New York's Lower East Side ghetto, the weary tenement-dwelling immigrants, exhausted from long hours of labor in the sweatshops, dragged themselves to evening lectures they only half understood in the hope of improving themselves.[28] Thus Herr Professor in the Lower East Side nickelodeon in New York City lecturing on Shakespeare was to be praised for his efforts. He also served as manager of the theater and therefore did not demand an extra salary. The poorer nickelodeons could not afford to hire a lecturer, either for the purpose of educating the audience or to speak along with the film to explain what was going on. Some lecturers in the moving-picture theaters had a high reputation and were billed as an attraction on the posters out front. Some doubled as the "talker" with the film.

By 1907, the convergence of the nickelodeon's demand for product, the popularity of the story film, and the new immigrant audiences from different cultures that now filled the nickelodeons in major cities resulted in a crisis in film narrative. Earlier methods of narration were inadequate for the growing complexity of the stories that producers were attempting to relate. There were complaints about a lack of clarity. One way in which this crisis (to be discussed in more detail in chapter 4) manifested itself was in a renewed demand for someone talking along with the film to explain what was going on: the "showman-narrator," or lecturer. For the same reason, there were new experiments with mechanical synchronization of sound with film. The Cameraphone opened in Baltimore on 27 April 1908. In May the Theatrephone was announced: this was said to be a device to synchronize disks with moving pictures, which was going to be used to present *Hamlet* and other plays and operas. The French company Gaumont sent its new "talking and singing" motion-picture machine to Savannah, Georgia, in the summer of 1908, along with two technicians to install it. This was called the Chronophone, and by October it was playing New York. A month later, there were three mechanical sound systems on the market: Gaumont's Chronophone, the Cameraphone, and the Synchroscope, which was something Carl Laemmle was promoting. Troupes of actors, such as the one called Actologue, traveled with films on the road, speaking the lines from behind the screen, for films such as COLLEGE CHUMS, THE COUNT OF MONTE CRISTO, and EAST LYNNE. Another such troupe appeared under the name of Humanovo, organized by Adolph Zukor, future founder of Paramount Pictures.[29]

Both the sound systems and the professional actors as "talkers" behind the screen were expensive, of course, and appeared only in vaudeville houses, opera houses, or the bigger theaters, not with the small storefront show. In the smaller operations, the owner, his wife or his child, or the singer, or the piano player could be pressed into service to talk along with the film. Managers without the means to hire a "talker" would post in the lobby the synopses sent out by the film's producers in the form of printed bulletins. For this reason, Biograph's one-page *Bulletin* was considered more desirable than the other companies' multiple-page house organs, and eventually the others followed Biograph's example. Similar demands for aids in understanding films would be renewed in 1913, when the arrival of the multireel feature film again created a crisis in film form. The silent film was very rarely silent, and a kind of search to replace the missing sounds continued throughout this period in the form of talkers, lecturers, synchronized records, live or canned music, or live or mechanical sound effects. The search for visual equivalents of speech and sound led to new styles of film construction, as described in chapter 4.

As long as vaudeville remained a part of the presentation, the varied program of the nickelodeon reflected the pre-1907 concept of the "show." This concept never really disappeared throughout the silent period, in the sense that live playlets and ballets and pantomimes preceded the main feature in the biggest movie theaters through the twenties. But the time came when these extras, the illustrated song, the vaudeville act, and the educational lecture, were dropped in the nickelodeon and the ordinary theater. This was the time when the motion picture assumed its new role as the carrier of dreams and illusions of reality.

2

A Game of Freeze-Out

There was a time—it was the golden age—when the merchant of films or apparatus did his business directly with the consumer; he knew him. The business took care of itself because the offering was equal to the demand. The dizzy growth of the industry in the course of these last years has changed this happy state of things. The customers have multiplied to such proportions that the manufacturer would need a magic power to know them all.

—Georges Dureau, *Ciné-Journal*, no. 1, 15 August 1908

*I*n 1907 a nickelodeon manager got films wherever and however he could. The problem was to get enough of them. Nothing prevented an exhibitor from purchasing films directly from the producers, but this was not very practical for a program that changed twice a week or even daily. Why continue to buy films that would be shown only a limited number of times? It made more sense to rent them from distribution exchanges that purchased them from the producers. Some of the rental exchanges were organized by nickelodeon owners, or former owners, who had accumulated a collection of films. It was a logical step for a supplier of lantern slides and optical goods, such as George Kleine in Chicago, to add a stock of films for rent or sale. In other instances, the producers set up separate branches to handle rentals: this was the case with the Vitagraph Company and the Lubin Company, for example. Any exchange that could get hold of enough films to keep a number of exhibitors supplied week in and week out was making good money as well. William Swanson, one of the most successful of the exchange men to enter the business in 1907, said he soon achieved an income of $20,000 a week.[1]

While exhibitors in 1907 might run films made at any date, showing them as many times as the public still wanted to see them, and indeed had to take any films they could get their hands on, the fact is that audiences were so motion-picture crazy that they were going repeatedly and wanted new subjects all the time. Films, like vegetables, were a perishable product. If an exhibitor only had old films, the customer might go down the street to see something new. Of course, this would not have been possible in the smallest towns with only one show, but the cities with their rows of nickelodeons were the largest consumers and represented the significant market for determining business practices.

The system by which the exchange would make up the program that the theater showed began in this chaotic period. The exhibitor who lived far from exchanges, as was often the case in the West, as William Swanson explained, had to take what was shipped, and there was not much opportunity to choose. Among those who lived near exchanges and collected and returned films "over the counter," there were those who did not care much anyway. They just sent over the projectionist with the previous day's reels with orders to get some more. Others, who did care enough to try to select, would get the best films only if they were good customers, or went into the back room to give a bribe to the booking man. Film quality was not always so much a matter of content or style as of condition: given the shortage of product that existed, a good film was the one that was not all scratched up ("rainy") and whose perforations and splices would still hold up in projection. Among the many conditions that the producers said they wanted to correct was the showing of seriously scratched, dirty, torn prints with images that danced drunkenly on the screen. Their concern was couched in terms of "the good of the industry," an expression that can usually be understood as "the good of ourselves." What worried producers the most, I suspect, was that some rental exchanges and exhibitors were making a higher degree of profit on their investment than those who actually manufactured the product.

The production of films in America in 1907 was still a handcrafted amusement industry, trying in vain to keep up with the rapidly expanding market. There were only about 1,200 films of one reel or less, mostly less, released in the entire United States in that year, and only about 400 of them were made in America. Most of the others were French, with the largest number coming from Pathé Frères. This was not much to feed thousands of hungry nickelodeons. Production had to be expanded to meet the demand if the new industry were to flourish and become stable. Some people still considered motion pictures a temporary craze, while others saw a vast future. But expansion was delayed by the fights for control of the industry. Edison's production even slipped back from its previous output during 1906 and early 1907. Nonetheless, in the United States, until the production-distribution-exhibition systems stabilized, there was some reluctance to invest greater capital.[2]

In 1907 there was a serious economic recession. That did not stop people from going to the nickelodeons in ever-increasing numbers, but it did give pause to the production companies, with their investments in this new enterprise, and even some alarm to the Empire Trust Company, which was a major lender to the American Mutoscope and Biograph Company. During that summer, the bank sent Jeremiah J. Kennedy, a civil engineer from Brooklyn who seems to have specialized in administering all kinds of companies (perhaps his profession was really acting as a troubleshooter), to look into the affairs of Biograph. He stayed, and before long he became the leading force in organizing the entire motion-picture industry. During these years Kennedy never gave up his positions in various other businesses, and it is clear that he was a very energetic man. Said Richard Hollaman of the Eden Musee: "A more resourceful, aggressive, persevering and point-getting man I have never met. . . . He is certainly one century plant."[3]

The previous decade's legal contenders now settled into two hostile camps. The latest court decisions had in effect held all the motion-picture cameras in use to be infringing Edison's patents, with the notable exception of the Biograph Company's camera. The Edison Company instituted a new round of lawsuits or threatened suits for infringement against several of the production companies, and then moved ahead to negotiate a settlement by offering each major company a license to use Edison's patents. They began their negotiations with Pathé Frères of Paris. This was logical, as Pathé had been the dominant producer on the world market for a long time and still held what was by far the largest part of the American market in 1907. Once Pathé fell into line, Edison business manager William Gilmore and Edison lawyer Frank Dyer figured, the others would certainly agree to the same terms. Pathé Frères was the one company that would have had the resources to challenge the Edison claims, a challenge later made and won by others. But Pathé did not contest. In Europe, of course, Edison's patents had no effect, but that had not stopped Edison from seeking to hamper Pathé's American distribution. Until licensed by Edison in December 1907, Pathé imported only positive prints; after that, it brought in negatives and printed the positives in America. It seems on the face of it that Edison must have agreed to freeze out much of Pathé's foreign competition on the American market, as that is in fact what happened, giving Pathé a decided advantage in what was the world's biggest market. French producers reported in October 1909 that for 5 prints reserved for France and 40 for Europe, 150 would be ordered by the United States.[4]

It was Edison's actions that had resulted in giving over the American market to the foreign competition around the turn of the century. Now the Edison Company's new schemes would lead to the American film industry's gaining control over all foreign competition, including Pathé Frères. In 1907, 60 percent of the subjects released on the American market were of foreign origin, but by the last six months of 1909, foreign productions represented less than 50 percent of films released and the percentage was declining. The goal of overcoming foreign competition was never openly discussed, yet it was surely in the minds of Edison and his colleagues. Later, industry spokesmen made a virtue of the fact that the dominance of foreign films had ceased. European films, it was claimed, failed to express the moral values of the native product. But at the time the plot, if plot it was, began, the values expressed in films the world over were scarcely distinguishable. In the beginning the universality of the film medium was particularly evident: the same kinds of subjects and styles appeared the world over. It could be argued that some French films portrayed actual nudity, while American films showed pretended nudity (actresses wearing flesh-colored leotards), but the risqué spirit was the same.[5]

Patent litigation was a regular method of business for Edison, as it was for George Eastman and many others. It was common business practice, and it evidently seemed proper to Edison. There is a confident self-righteousness in his statements about his patents. He had a habit of patenting everything in sight, without having successfully invented all of the devices he claimed. Eventually he did lose suits based on some patents. But then, as now, the small businessman did not have the resources to fight endless legal battles even if he might win them in the long run. He had to go along with the greater power or face financial ruin. In any case, the latest court decisions made it appear that Edison held the strong suit, and most companies were not prepared to contest. Everyone was tired of the costly lawsuits.

Once Pathé fell in line, most of the producers followed. Vitagraph, Kalem, Lubin, Méliès, Selig, and Essanay joined Pathé to form the Edison Licensees. Biograph held out, as did George Kleine. Here is where the history begins to get a bit complicated.

Edison, Vitagraph, Selig, Lubin, Biograph, and the two French firms, Pathé Frères and Georges Méliès, were all film-production companies founded in the first few years of the industry. Now they were the old-timers, the establishment. Pathé, as we have noted, was the giant producer, not only in America but all over the world. In terms of the number of film subjects released (which is not an indication of the copies sold, as Charles Musser has demonstrated in his study of Edison records), Vitagraph was by far the largest of the American producers in 1907, Lubin and Selig

The Biograph Company studio was in this brownstone building at 11 East Fourteenth Street in New York from 1906 to 1913.

the next largest, with Biograph and Edison the last. It is amusing to note that from the viewpoint of 1913, Frank Dyer of Edison remembered Biograph in 1907 as being the largest domestic producer and Edison's active competitor. I suppose he was actually thinking of other aspects of their rivalry, or of an earlier time.[6]

At the end of 1907, both Kalem and Essanay were still small and unimportant production companies. The Kalem Film Company was founded early in 1907 by two men who had been with Biograph from its early years: Samuel Long, who had been in charge of the laboratory, and Frank Marion, responsible for scenarios and production. Twenty percent of the capital came from George Kleine, the Chicago exchangeman who started out as a dealer in lantern slides and optical goods. Kleine was named president of Kalem, although he was based in Chicago and Kalem was in the New York area. Two Biograph actors were soon persuaded to join Kalem, Sidney Olcott as director and Gene Gauntier as leading woman and, after a short time, the company's scriptwriter. The first Kalem production was THE RUNAWAY SLEIGH-BELLE, released in the spring of 1907. According to the memoirs of Gene Gauntier, Kalem's owners felt a sense of achievement in being accepted as an Edison licensee. Charles Musser says that the inclusion of Kalem among the licensees was designed to appease Kleine, because the Edison Company wanted to exclude mere importers of film, such as the Kleine Optical Company, from the group. When Biograph and George Kleine decided to fight Edison's group, it became necessary for the Kalem owners to buy out Kleine in April 1908 in order to avoid conflict of interest.[7]

The Essanay Film Manufacturing Company, a Chicago firm, also claimed existence from the beginning of 1907, but the first Essanay release, called AN AWFUL SKATE, did not appear until 31 July of that year. Essanay was founded by George K. Spoor, who was a thirty-three-year-old former theatrical road-show manager turned movie exhibitor, and Gilbert M. "Broncho Billy" Anderson, formerly of Edison and Selig, who was to be director, scriptwriter, and leading actor. The name was formed from the initials of the two men, "S" and "A," just as Kalem's name came from the initials of its three founders, Kleine, Long, and Marion. According to the Edison plans,

D. W. Griffith as an extra in FALSELY ACCUSED! *(Biograph, 1907). The future director is the man at left helping to put up a sheet to serve as a motion-picture screen for showing evidence in a murder trial.*

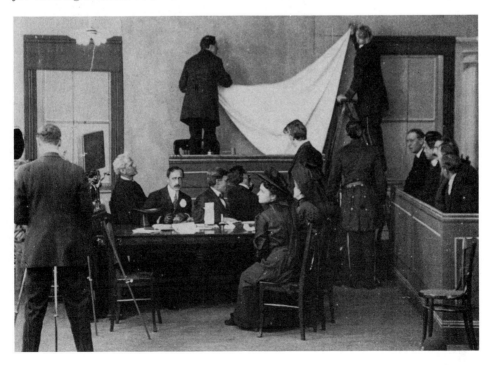

Essanay, as the newest and least important company, was to be given a license only if Biograph failed to join, in which case the licensees would need to be strengthened.[8]

Georges Méliès of Paris was a prestigious producer, but the amount of film he turned out in his handcrafted production system, while amazing in its way, was negligible when compared to that of a big production factory like Pathé Frères. The Méliès imports would not provide any serious competition for them. The Edison license was granted to the Méliès Company through its U.S. representative, Georges's brother, Gaston.

As for George Kleine, he not only was an importer of foreign-made films but also had served as the Chicago agent for major American companies such as Vitagraph and Edison. According to the testimony of J. Stuart Blackton and others, he was one of the leaders of the scheme to organize the industry under the Edison patents, going back and forth between the Chicago producers, the Edison Company, Pathé, and Eastman Kodak and organizing the meeting of manufacturers in November 1907 at the Hotel Astor. When the Edison interests decided that Kleine Optical could be licensed but sought to limit its imports to only two brands of foreign films, Kleine joined forces with the other side, becoming a Biograph licensee. It was said that Kleine performed a diplomatic role, trying to bring the sides together. But Kleine, as one of Biograph's licensees, was in a weak position as far as Kleine Optical Company was concerned. He had already lost the Chicago agency he once held for the leading American producers. A memorandum of a proposed agreement of 29 July 1908, from Dyer of the Edison Company to Marvin of the Biograph Company, had

Office of the Georges Méliès Company in New York

its terms been accepted, would have given Kleine the right to import 5,000 feet of film a week, while the other Biograph Licensees would be allowed to import only 2,000 feet a week. Kleine ended up with less in the final settlement of the disputes.[9]

Following the decisions of the courts that the Biograph camera was the only one not to infringe Edison's patents, the Biograph Company was unwilling to join as anything less than equal partner with Edison, sharing fifty-fifty in the royalties. Biograph strengthened its position by buying the rights to the Latham patent in early 1908. This was the patent covering the so-called Latham loop, which prevented the film from breaking in the projector (this loop still exists in all projection systems), and it was said to apply to cameras as well until later lawsuits denied the claim. The loop was not essential in the days when films were less than 100 feet because there was not enough tension built up in that short a length to break the film. But much longer films, several hundred feet or even a thousand, were already in use by this time. Jacques J. Berst, Pathé's American manager, admitted that he published articles in the trade papers during that year of open warfare saying that "the Latham patent was of no value . . . but, in fact, I knew very well it was not true." On 21 March 1908 Biograph also signed an agreement with Armat Moving Picture Company, complicating the question of the Armat-Jenkins patents. Biograph could sue Edison and Edison could sue Biograph, and nobody would win, especially not the exhibitors or the exchanges. Frank Dyer had run up against a man with a bigger bluff than himself: Jeremiah J. Kennedy.[10]

A committee composed of potential Edison-licensed manufacturers (including for the moment Biograph, Kleine, and the other importers who would later join the Biograph licensees) called the exchange owners together at a conference in Pittsburgh on 16 November 1907, where they formed the United Film Services Protective Association, with William Swanson as president. Their program consisted of the following points:

1. Renters will purchase film only from the licensed producers and importers;
2. Films will not be duped (*i.e.*, copied);
3. Films will not be sub-rented (*i.e.*, rented to another exchange);
4. Films will not be sold secondhand (*i.e.*, not to another exchange);
5. Used film will be returned to the producer.[11]

The stated purpose of the policy was to get rid of the old, worn prints that the producers felt were giving the industry a bad name. A more important reason was not articulated, however: to ensure that more profits came back to the producers and less to the distributors and exhibitors. This program, proposed by the producers and accepted by the distributors, was ratified at a meeting held in Chicago on 14 December 1907, but here the attempt to organize the whole industry collapsed because Biograph held out.

Biograph's output alone was not yet sufficient to fill a program for the exchanges. To give Biograph more strength on the market, they issued their own licenses to importers of foreign films: Kleine Optical Company; Williams, Brown, and Earle; the Charles E. Dressler Company (the film interests were identified with Isaac W. Ullmann); and the Great Northern Company, representing Nordisk Films of Denmark.[12]

On 8 February 1908, at a meeting in Buffalo, the Edison forces managed to get most of the exchanges to go along with them and sign allegiance to the producers under the Edison patents. At this meeting the organization of distributors shortened its name to the Film Service Association, frequently further shortened to the acronym FSA. There is conflicting testimony on qualifications for membership in this ostensible federation of exchanges that was actually controlled by the Edison forces. It seems that the producers could join but could not become officers. In any case, some producers—Vitagraph, Lubin and Essanay—maintained separate exchange arms, and these were entitled to membership.[13]

In a trade advertisement of 14 March 1908, H. N. Marvin and J. J. Kennedy of Biograph announced, "We were urged to join the Edison-Pathé combination but we refused. . . . We will protect our customers." War was now declared. All the efforts to organize and stabilize the industry were as yet without much result. Biograph and the group of importers licensed by that company still sold prints outright, to exhibitors or exchanges. This made it possible for them to continue to do business even though Edison had most of the exchanges locked up. Under the Edison license agreements and the rules of the Film Service Association, film was supposed to be returned to the manufacturer, but in fact this was not enforced. The return was postponed because production was not yet high enough to allow the exchanges to get by on the new films alone. During this time, however, the Edison licensees paid their royalties for the use of the patents. Still the largest producer, Pathé Frères paid between $17,000 and $18,000 to Edison during 1908.[14]

At the 11 July 1908 meeting of the FSA, a price system was established according to the day of release, which infected the whole distribution-exhibition complex with the disease of release date for the next several years. Only films shown on the first day at the first hour of release were truly "fresh" and valuable, like so many eggs fresh from the hens. After that, the price and therefore the value, went down. After thirty days, films were practically useless and became known as "commercial."

On 27 August, 1908 Kleine received a telegram from J. J. Kennedy of Biograph: "Edison Company reports that aggressive price cutting of your Philadelphia representative is likely to embarrass final negotiations with Edison Licensees. We recommend moderation in this respect; negotiations proceeding satisfactorily." Kleine obeyed promptly by getting rid of the Philadelphia exchange altogether, a branch that had opened just a few days earlier. By 23 September 1908, Kleine had signed a new contract with Gaumont for 2,000 feet a week, and with the signing of the Patents Company agreement, he was limited to this amount plus 1,000 feet from Urban-Eclipse each week.[15]

There were meetings of the producers all during that summer and fall of 1908 to try to reconcile the differences and bring the Edison and Biograph groups together. The meetings extended to Europe: George Eastman was in negotiation with the European producers, who were trying to organize along the lines of the Edison licensees. They were encouraged by Eastman because he presumed there could be a recognition of Edison's patents, which were unprotected in Europe, but Pathé would not cooperate with that scheme. It was in Eastman Kodak's interest to be involved in whatever organizing was done in Europe since at this point its biggest market was there.[16]

In November, Blackton of Vitagraph was in Paris meeting with Pathé Frères and Nordisk (Great Northern), the Danish firm, working on an alliance of French producers. This also came to nothing, but it makes one wonder if a defection from the

Celebrating the creation of the Motion Picture Patents Company, New York, December 1908: From left to right: Samuel Long (Kalem), Albert Smith (Vitagraph), George Scull (Edison), George Kleine (Kleine Optical), Thomas Edison, Frank Dyer (Edison), Sigmund Lubin, Harry N. Marvin (Biograph), J. Stuart Blackton (Vitagraph), Frank Marion (Kalem). Figures at extreme left and behind Frank Dyer's shoulder may be Jeremiah J. Kennedy, Jacques Berst, or Gaston Méliès.

Edison combine was being considered by Pathé and Vitagraph. There is some support for this theory in the office that Pathé had opened in New York, rumored to be a rental exchange that would provide films to the independents. It was announced in September that Pathé decided against doing this. Perhaps research among the Pathé papers in France will one day clear up these mysteries, but in any case, the U.S. producers finally came together. Everyone could see that the industry could only be organized if Edison and Biograph agreed.[17]

At last, Frank Dyer gave in and granted parity to Biograph. The Motion Picture Patents Company was formed and its rules took effect on the first of January 1909. The Patents Company was a holding company for the patents belonging to all the producers. There were sixteen patents involved, coming from Edison, Biograph, the Armat Company, and Vitagraph and covering the issues of the film stock, the cameras, and the projectors. The Patents Company issued licenses, on the payment of royalties, to producers, distributors and exhibitors. Stock shares in the Patents Company were held equally by Edison and Biograph, except for those few needed to qualify the directors, and were kept by the Empire Trust in order that neither could sell without the other's knowledge. The scheme was a clever attempt to avoid the antitrust laws. The licensed producers who did not share in the profits as directly as

Edison and Biograph must have resented their domination, and indeed, there were signs of rebellion at one time or another. But outwardly all was peaceful. No one actually bolted ranks until the Patents Company was ordered disbanded by the federal courts. The Patents Company licensed the same production companies from the beginning to the end of its existence, with the exception of the belated addition of Kinemacolor in 1913 (see chapter 13), and Méliès' American production company.[18]

At the time of the founding of the Patents Company in December 1908, the name of Georges Méliès appeared in the trade papers among the new licensees, but shortly thereafter, it disappeared from the list. It seems that Gaston Méliès, who was something of a rascal, had recently ceased sending back both money and reports to his brother in Paris and, trading on the Edison license granted in both their names to obtain financial backing, had set up his own production company in the United States. How much Georges knew and when he knew it are still in dispute, as is the date when Gaston stopped sending any money. Nevertheless, in the fall of 1908, Gaston persuaded the Edison Company to reissue the Méliès license in the name of this "Georges Méliès Company" and to acknowledge his partners James Lodge and Lincoln J. Carter. The company never produced films but did have a couple of Georges Méliès' French productions to distribute. Lodge and Carter, meanwhile, had secretly sold controlling stock in the company to one Max Lewis, who owned a chain of independent exchanges. This sale went against the terms of the agreement with Edison and certainly would not have been permitted to any licensed manufacturer of the Patents Company.

Claiming ignorance of these dealings, Gaston sided with the Patents Company when they refused to deliver the license that had actually been signed with all the others on 18 December. By sticking with the Patents Company members in the lawsuit that followed, Gaston got his reward in the form of a license to produce (still in the name of Georges Méliès) in the United States, about six months after the founding of the Patents Company. The other "Georges Méliès Company" eventually lost its suit against the Patents Company. It was many years before Georges Méliès was to find out what had happened with his brother and his money, and for many years the two branches of the family did not speak. Gaston Méliès set up his studio in south Brooklyn under the direction of Wallace McCutcheon, who had been chief director of Biograph when David Wark Griffith arrived there late in 1907. The first production of the American Méliès company was THE STOLEN WIRELESS, released on 13 October 1909. Later the company became known as "G. Méliès," to distinguish it from Méliès Star Film, the French firm.[19]

The further maneuvers of the Patents Company scheme to control the motion-picture industry are well illustrated by the involvement of Eastman Kodak, the leading supplier of raw stock for the industry and a key player in this game of freeze-out. The same day that the Motion Picture Patents Company came into being, an agreement was signed between the Patents Company, Edison, and Eastman Kodak, under which Eastman Kodak became the exclusive supplier of raw stock to licensed producers in exchange for ceasing to sell to anyone else. There was a minor exception or two, permitting the sale of raw stock for scientific use, for example, but nothing of economic importance. The agreement also provided that Eastman Kodak would collect royalties from the producers on behalf of the Patents Company for the use of the film patents. This last provision was considered of major importance by the Edison people because it protected the Patents Company from the antitrust laws. It was possible for Eastman to call a halt to the exclusivity clauses of the contract with sufficient notice, but they would still have to continue collecting the royalties for the Patents Company.[20]

That Eastman's involvement, together with that of Pathé, was crucial to the settlement is shown by a letter of 23 November 1908, from Marvin of Biograph to Kleine in Chicago, informing him that settlement was near but that the negotiations were delayed pending the return of George Eastman to the United States. Eastman would certainly have been better off with an open market for its product: the major producers had to have the raw stock, and Eastman was, for practical purposes, the only manufacturer in the country and by far the most important one in the world. However, the Patents Company agreement gave the company a guaranteed market, and Eastman Kodak would have faced a lawsuit based on "contributory infringement" if it sold to nonlicensed producers. Judging by the methods being used to organize the industry, it seems very probable that the Patents Company promised to try to freeze out the stock manufactured by Lumière in France and Ansco in Germany. Marvin's letter to Kleine in November 1908 provides some evidence for this: "I believe your best possible interests will very soon lie in the direction of the highest possible tariff on imported goods." Indeed, it is difficult to see how it would not have been against Kleine's interest as an independent importer. As a Patents Company licensee, however, Kleine would soon be able to import negatives and make his own prints in the United States with Eastman Kodak stock purchased locally, as Pathé Frères did. This meant less footage on which to pay duty.[21]

It was inevitable that the Patents Company would use all its power to prevent independents from obtaining a regular supply of raw stock, and for a period of time they were partly successful. Eastman Kodak was not willing to lose any established customers and had insisted on supplying Biograph as well as the Edison group the previous year. In the course of the negotiations Eastman worked toward the goal of making sure that every producer of any importance was a member of the Patents Company. There would be a number of attempts to produce and market raw stock in the United States during the years of the independents' struggle against the Trust, but no serious and lasting rival to Eastman Kodak emerged.

By 14 February 1911, the independent market had become a significant one, and the power of the Patents Company was beginning to weaken. On that date, the original agreement was amended to permit Eastman to sell to the independents, with only a small financial advantage for the licensed producers. In 1913, by the time the Patents Company was under legal attack from the United States government, Eastman Kodak was having its own legal problems. The case of the Rev. Hannibal Goodwin's prior claim to the process of manufacturing film stock was finally settled out of court, at a cost of $5 million. In the long run, however, Eastman Kodak survived its troubles and the Patents Company did not.[22]

When the second annual meeting of the Film Service Association was held in January 1909 at the Imperial Hotel in New York, some sixty to seventy-five members found themselves presented with a new license agreement that had provisions quite similar to the old one, although it was not an agreement with Edison. Rather, it was with the Motion Picture Patents Company, and this time it had teeth in it. In effect, the FSA was out of business, although it continued an ineffectual existence for another year, primarily as a fraternal business association, for sociability and exchange of information. In any event, there was no longer anything for it to negotiate: its members accepted the terms offered by the Motion Picture Patents Company or they were finished. This included the president, William Swanson, who almost lost his film-exchange business, but, survivor that he was, he left the FSA and started up again, becoming one of the leaders of the independents.

One hundred and fifty exchanges signed up with the licensed group, but by July of 1909 there were only about one hundred licensed exchanges in the United States. About six thousand theaters paid two dollars a week each to the Patents Company for a license, while two thousand or more remained independent. As was to be frequently pointed out by the independents over the next few years, many of these exhibitors had purchased projection machines with no strings attached. They owned them. Now, the Patents Company said that in order to use the machines they would be obliged to pay two dollars each and every week that they remained in business. Otherwise, they would be sued under the patents held by the Patents Company. In practice, the collection of the two-dollar fee proved onerous, and the Patents Company assigned this task to the licensed exchanges that dealt with the exhibitor. In time, the exchanges simply added it on to the price of the contract, and in the

Assembling prints scene by scene in the Biograph laboratory in Hoboken, New Jersey. This was women's work.

competition for customers, it mostly "disappeared" as far as the exhibitors were concerned.[23]

Even as the exchanges and exhibitors were signing up, there were the rumblings of an independent movement of protest, which will be detailed in a later chapter. For the year 1909, though, the basis of an organized industry existed, and now the producers could confidently go forward to invest in expansion, with new and enlarged studios and laboratories, with increased production staffs, and with new assembly-line production methods. Now there could be a standardized product, easily marketed and consumed. Now they could turn out the sausages with enough regularity to satisfy the omnivorous nickelodeon customers.

Each producer had a set releasing day or days every week and a set number of reels to release. For the most part the exchanges contracted by standing order for their output and established a contract to supply a regular service to their customers. Exhibitors could get a variety of service contracts. First-run houses signed up for the first day of release of each film from the licensed producers. They knew from the trade periodicals which films they would get on any date. Most nickelodeons settled for a smorgasbord, getting one film absolutely fresh, one a day old, one a week old, one over thirty days, and so forth. Poor nickelodeons, or ones that had no nearby competition, could do just as well with a program composed entirely of "stale" films. The exchanges negotiated the price for the service separately with each exhibitor, and struggled, often in vain, to keep their customers from competing with each other by showing the same films at the same time. The exhibitor's service price was about the only part of the system that was not standardized. The exchanges paid a fixed price per foot for the films they purchased from the licensed producers. They would buy one print or more, depending on the popularity of the brand. At first they were compelled to buy at least one of everything because of the product shortage.

Asked why there should be a fixed price for films that had variable production costs, J. J. Kennedy explained in 1914 that "it would prevent a regular supply being issued" if there were negotiations and separate orders for each subject. Instead, the price represented an average of such production costs. Asked if the standing order system took away the incentive to improve film quality, he maintained that if a producer increased "average quality" there would be an increase in the average number of copies sold for each picture.[24]

The system fell apart to some extent as intense competition led to unethical practices. The exchanges had the power of life and death over exhibitors, because without the regular supply of films delivered promptly and reliably, the nickelodeon could not survive. Exchanges could force exhibitors to pay kickbacks, they could threaten to put an exhibitor out of business if he or she did not take their service, they could set up their own theater to which they would give preferential treatment. In some areas, exchanges combined interests and would not allow an exhibitor to change from one to another without paying a penalty price increase. At least these were the reasons Kennedy gave for proposing, at the end of 1909, that the licensed producers should establish their own exchange system.

The early attempts to organize the industry were made by people who conceived of it purely as a business with a product to sell. They emphasized its uniformity and standardization and freshness. They wanted to popularize brand names, not individual items. The very names they used indicated the state of mind they brought to the

How films were distributed to the nickelodeons.

business. They were manufacturers, and the product they manufactured was made in a factory. Most of the companies had the word "manufacturing" in their official name: the Edison Film Manufacturing Company, the Vitagraph Film Manufacturing Company, the Lubin Manufacturing Company. The American Mutoscope and Biograph Company was nearly the only one not to include it, probably because they considered their name to be too long already. They dropped the "American Mutoscope" part of it in the spring of 1909, as they had ceased to produce Mutoscopes for the most part, and they then became the Biograph Company. In any case, most of the companies eliminated "manufacturing" from their names within a few years, reflecting a change in attitude toward the moving picture. The same shift in attitude explains the gradual change from "manufacturer" to "producer."

The major producers in 1907 were for the most part respectable businessmen. Not all had impeccable backgrounds: for example, some years earlier the partners in Vitagraph had been part of the cheap vaudeville circuit, or appeared in carnival shows. However, that unfortunate fact could be overlooked now that Blackton, Smith, and Rock were well-established citizens, heads of a successful business. And if a part of the wealth of the respectable producers came from a disreputable source— the dirty, dark, and smelly nickelodeons showing risqué entertainment—in a hypocritical Victorian society, that fact too could ordinarily be ignored. But the growing numbers of nickelodeons began to make it difficult to ignore. The entertainment business was on its way to becoming a major industry. By 1915 it would be claimed (with considerable exaggeration, we now think) to be the fourth-largest industry of the entire United States.

These same producers were good Progressives, committed to the imperialists' responsibility toward the underprivileged classes. They believed that the unfortunates must be educated and learn to share the same value system as the middle classes. In the Philippines, where America was engaged in its virgin experience with colonial responsibility, Progressives urged that motion pictures should be selected with the aim of educating the savages and lifting them upward toward civilization, through "this universal language." What actually happened at the far end of the distribution line was that the Philippine "savages" usually had to make do with the worn and scratched prints of the less uplifted period before 1908. The same imperialist ideals informed the movement to uplift the poor and foreign-born working classes living in the inner-city ghettos.[25]

These attitudes were less true of the exhibitors and exchange men. In the group that succeeded at the highest level, buying more theaters, establishing theater chains, or groups of exchanges, were those who came from the poor, little-educated, and foreign-born working class, rising on the euphoric tide of a new country full of opportunity if one were only willing to work hard. The records do not tell us much about those who failed at this get-rich-quick scheme of the nickelodeons and what might have happened to them. Those who found success and became tycoons were highly competitive and less interested in organizing than the producers.

Allowing for the differences in the cultures from which they came, the two groups nonetheless shared some of the same value systems with regard to progress in America and success in business. The fundamental difference was that the producers were able to agree to cut down competition among themselves in order to organize their group into a productive system, and that gave them the ability to lead the industry in the directions they thought best, for the industry and the audience and for them-selves. Perhaps it was only their organizing of the chaotic nickelodeon business that made the movie "craze" last long enough to become a major industry—at least that is what they believed. Perhaps the medium was so powerful in its potential that it would have survived anyway, in some other form. But the big problem in 1907 from a business point of view had been the lack of stability, the uncertainty of a source of supply for films, which made it a risk to invest a lot of money in the business. By 1909 that problem was nearly resolved, but in the meantime the fledgling industry faced another danger: reform movements.

3

The Recruiting Stations of Vice

In my opinion, nothing is of greater importance to the success of the motion picture interests than films of good moral tone.

—Thomas Edison, *Moving Picture World*, 21 December 1907

*I*n 1909, summarizing the history of the Motion Picture Patents Company in the first six months of its existence, the *Moving Picture World* indicated that "for three or four years prior to December last the moving picture business occupied in public esteem a position so offensive, so contemptible, and in many respects so degrading, that respectable people hesitated to have their names associated with it." A few months earlier, the *World* claimed that "many men . . . apologized for their business in their social life."[1]

A similar picture was given by Albert J. Gillingham, an exchange manager in Michigan who testified for the defense in the Motion Picture Patents Company case. When he entered the business in 1906 or 1907, he declared:

> I am frank in stating that when you told a man you were in the motion picture business, if you would happen to meet a gentleman on the train or anywhere, he would naturally look, and ask what it was. It was looked on with disfavor, as all store shows previously had been shows of an undesirable character. Mostly fake shows. Shows that were showing monstrosities, or had displays outside with a hand organ or a sick monkey. Something of that order (*US* v. *MPPC* 4:2214 [December 1913]).

His comment suggests an additional source for the nickelodeon's poor reputation: perhaps it can not be altogether blamed on the moving-picture show itself, but carries over from an earlier kind of cheap amusement.

It must, of course, be acknowledged that the nickelodeon's notoriety was not a problem everywhere. Frank J. Marion of Kalem, for example, reporting on a tour of the Northwest, said that exhibitors there were men of higher standing in their communities, and patrons included the best class of people in town. Nevertheless, throughout the whole period, the moving picture suffered attacks from the pulpit and from the yellow press. Opportunists found it a way to get public attention, and juvenile delinquents discovered it was useful to claim that they got the idea for wrongdoing from having seen it in a movie. Dr. Anna Shaw, a feminist reformer, was quoted as saying: "There should be a police woman at the entrance of every moving picture show and another inside. These places are the recruiting stations of vice." Magistrate Frederick B. House declared that "95% of the moving picture places in New York are dens of iniquity . . . more young women and girls are led astray in these places than any other way." The feverish nature of these statements may be credited in part to the fear that young women were becoming too independent and free of restraints in post-Victorian society.[2]

One of the avowed goals of the newly organized industry was to clean it up. In Progressive America, people believed that all kinds of improvement were possible and inevitable. They were dedicated to winning the battles for women's suffrage, prohibition, organized labor, and world peace, and the battles against child labor, tuberculosis, and the household fly. With confidence and sincerity, the Motion Picture Patents Company's licensed producers assumed their mission to improve the motion-picture industry and its customers at the same time. To uplift, ennoble, and purify was good business too. Progressive idealism did not conflict with their ideas of how to expand the market. To broaden the base of the audience, to bring in the middle class, to make the movies a respectable place of entertainment for women and children, as Tony Pastor had done for vaudeville a decade or two earlier, it would be useful to educate and uplift the immigrant masses and urban poor, who had made movies successful in the first place. The raw and ignorant could be pushed aside, of course, but that would not only violate the sense of responsibility of the privileged to the less fortunate, it would also limit the market in the other direction. As the New York Motion Picture Company advertised: "Our productions please rich and poor alike, / Whether it be a Reginald or just an ordinary Mike."[3]

The exhibitors, or at least the urban ones, were more likely to have come from the same class as their audiences, and their motives for uplift sometimes included the goal of their own social improvement. For that reason, once successful with a store show, they often opened their new, improved theaters in the better neighborhoods, deserting the public that helped make them rich in the first place. The "descriptive talker" of the Auditorium Theater in Dayton, Ohio, bragged, "We cater to the better classes—just as many diamonds to be seen in our audience as at any other theater."[4]

Social workers believed that the motion-picture shows could be a useful influence on the poor and working class, but the places had to be looked after. In the early summer of 1908, the Kansas City Franklin Institute assigned a settlement worker to investigate the films being shown in the nickelodeons. As a result, charges were brought against one house and complaints made on specific films elsewhere. The Institute's spokesperson explained that "it is not the object . . . to suppress the motion picture shows, for these are the amusement places of the poorer classes." Jane Addams of the famous Hull House in Chicago undertook to show moving pictures in the settlement house in the belief that they could attract and elevate the poor. In 1908 the Fifth Avenue Baptist Church, where John D. Rockefeller was a prominent member, supported the Armitage Chapel at 745 Tenth Avenue in New York City, which ran a moving-picture entertainment every Tuesday evening. The admission fee was one cent; the average attendance was about 250 children, and the goal was to provide a counterattraction to the many nickelodeons in the neighborhood. Charles Musser has shown how Lyman Howe cleverly enlisted the church people on his side by getting them to sponsor his "high-class moving picture shows" in their towns in order to raise funds for some worthy local cause. One of the key rules of the Edison group of licensed producers during 1908 was that films could be supplied only to exchanges that were members of the Film Service Association. But this policy could be abrogated in the name of uplift: religious subjects were available to any renter or exhibitor who wanted them, whether licensed or not. Seidel, "the Socialist Mayor," told the Milwaukee Ministerial Association that instead of complaining that children were being debased by nickelodeons, they should compete with them by arranging educational and moral motion-picture shows in the schools.[5]

Optimists imagined that a new audience for the legitimate theater was being created—a comforting thought for theatrical entrepreneurs whose business was suffering from the loss of the audience for the cheap seats. The People's Institute in New York ran a Children's Theatre, "educating new generations to an appreciation of the drama that will make for broader minds and more desirable citizenship," and the *New York Dramatic Mirror* called for a five-cent theater for a working-class audience, in order to educate the masses. The *Dramatic Mirror* was speaking of the legitimate theater, not movies. But impresario Al H. Woods announced that in the 1908–1909 season all of his fifteen theatrical companies would carry a motion-picture outfit: "I am going to give them the whole thing, melodrama, vaudeville and moving pictures," he promised. Joseph Medill Patterson, meanwhile, declared, "The nickelodeon is . . . developing into theatergoers a section of population that formerly knew and cared little about the drama as a fact of life."[6]

One of the most immediate and practical ways to change the atmosphere of the nickelodeon was the lighted theater. Uplifters didn't like to imagine what might be going on in those dark holes. It was decreed that the light should be sufficient to read a newspaper while the movie was going on. Unfortunately, there was a lack of knowledge of lighting techniques, and many projections were ruined by light reflecting on the screen: on the other hand, reputations were saved. There was a suggestion that the popular open-air theaters of summertime brought in a higher class of people, those who had hesitated to visit the darkened nickelodeons. The descriptions of new moving-picture theaters in those years nearly always mentioned the brightness and quality of the lighting. In Chicago lighted theaters were required by city ordinance, and in New York the License Bureau advised exhibitors that they must keep theaters lighted "so that persons in the audience are at all times visible." In September 1910 a *World* reporter visiting the Comet at Third Avenue near Twelfth Street in New York's Lower East Side tenement district approved the lighting conditions there. He wrote that there was enough diffused light to read by, yet the screen was bright. Men, women, and children filled the hall. He also approved the ventilating system and reported that an usher wandered the aisles spraying a sweet-smelling liquid. (Advertisements for these deodorizing sprays can be found in the pages of the trade periodicals.) Unfortunately, he added, they ran "junk" films—a Vitagraph and a Selig missing their titles, recognized by their trademarks on the sets and believed to be a year old.[7]

Among the other methods of upgrading the milieu of the moving-picture show were the addition of restrooms, nurseries for babies, ushers, refreshments, luxurious decorations, and furnishings, as well as the elimination of the garish posters and the noisy barker and blaring music outside.

Another goal was the elimination of the vulgar vaudeville act. As already noted in chapter 1, the producers of motion pictures urged its total removal from the movie houses, ostensibly for the improvement of the show, but their motives must have included the desire to expand the market for their own product as well. An act that was heavily billed all over the Keith and Proctor circuit in the spring of 1911 gave the uplifters a burning example of the kind of vulgar vaudeville they wanted to get rid of. This popular vaudeville act reflected the public's avid interest in the new flying machines: the house lights were all turned out and a girl sang a song about a flying machine while seated on an airplane outlined with electric lights, suspended on a long crane over the audience, dangling her legs and screaming playfully when someone grabbed her feet or stole a garter.[8]

At the same time, however, many exhibitors found that vaudeville attracted the much-desired patronage of the middle class at a higher admission price. There were cases where exhibitors complained they could not get enough high-class films and needed vaudeville if they were to keep their public. The problem was that the nickelodeons could normally employ only small-time acts and had no real stage. At certain times and in some places competition was so keen that if some theaters persisted in offering both vaudeville and pictures at five cents admission, the other theaters had to do the same to survive.

In October 1909, with the reform movement of the Patents Company well under way, the *World* admonished exhibitors that "the moving picture is just at that stage of its career when the support of the better classes is gradually being extended to it. Their support will come surely and largely enough in due time if repellent influences are sternly suppressed." Sternly suppressed they must be, and the licensed producers would undertake the work of suppressing the exhibitors if they did not take care of it themselves.[9]

It was not only the physical conditions of the nickelodeons that upset the reformers. It was the moving picture itself. The films being shown in the little store shows and in the high-class vaudeville theaters of 1907–1908 were for the most part the same. Although the Edison Company had made some social-interest films and there were still a great number of travel and actuality films to be seen, many reflected the entertaining and amoral spirit of the pre-reform era. They seemed to be acceptable as long as people saw them in the vaudeville house. Now, with moving pictures becoming extraordinarily popular almost overnight, these amusing little films were somehow deemed not suitable for the great masses of people who filled the nickelodeons.

What was so objectionable? For one thing, the domination of French films. "The foremost French makers," declared the *Moving Picture World* in 1908, "maintain a fine standard of excellence, but they owe it to American taste to eliminate some features. The frank way in which marital infidelities are carried on in Paris though a lame moral is sometimes worked in at the end, the eating of rats and cats, the brutal handling of helpless infants, do not appeal to the American sense of humor." *Variety*'s reviews of French films reflect a similar prejudice: AT THE SEASHORE was acted "with an abandon of manner and dress not found on this side"; AVENGED BY THE SEA was "simply morbid and gruesome, one of a kind which should never be taken, let alone placed on the market"; and as for THE NIGHT WATCHMAN, "Europe may like that sort of thing, we don't—and don't want to." Looking back from the vantage point of December 1913, an exhibitor testified that foreign films "four or five years ago" were "horrible, immoral." He indicated he had given an order not to show any foreign pictures in any of his theaters. In 1910, the *World* printed a letter from Washington, D.C., criticizing the Pathé film SCENES OF CONVICT LIFE (AU BAGNE,

MARRIED FOR MILLIONS *(Biograph), released 29 December 1906. Vulgar slapstick comedy was disapproved of by the reformers.*

1907, directed by Ferdinand Zecca) as unsuitable for family audiences. Almost any slapstick comedy film, French or not, if three or more years old, would have risked being found unsuitable after uplift set in.[10]

One 1907 film that belongs in spirit to the earlier decade is Biograph's THE MODEL'S MA (April 1907). The model's mother gives instructions to the artist that her daughter may not pose unclothed. The artist pushes the mother out of the studio, and the girl poses clothed as instructed, but the artist paints her as nude, arousing the ire of the mother when she returns. What is actually shown on the screen was not objectionable even then (there is not, in fact, any nudity in this film), but of course it was a naughty joke, fit for music halls or smokers. Vitagraph's THE BOY, THE BUST, AND THE BATH (July 1907) shows a mischievous boy who sets up a plaster bust of a woman in the boardinghouse bath, fooling a whole series of would-be voyeurs, including a minister. It is great fun but a little improper. Such films rapidly disappeared from the production of the Patents Company licensees, or at least from their catalogues.

By the beginning of 1909, the *Moving Picture World* would propose the following as subjects to be barred from the screen: the inside of prisons, convicts, and police stations, considered to be too morbid; contemporary sensational crime; anything to offend any religion; lingering over murders and executions; piling horrors on horrors; comedies that depended on the degradation of people or their defects.[11]

Lubin's THE UNWRITTEN LAW, released in 1907, was already being suppressed in various cities by summer 1908. The film was made while the sensational case of Harry K. Thaw's shooting of the noted architect Stanford H. White was filling the daily press with lurid stories of the dissolute life of the rich and famous. The first trial for murder either was still in process or had ended in a hung jury when THE UNWRITTEN LAW was first released. A second trial in 1908 resulted in an acquittal for Thaw on the grounds of insanity. The film, however, showed the acquittal more or less on the grounds of justifiable homicide. In it, Thaw is supposed to have been driven temporarily insane because his wife, the beautiful ex–chorus girl, told him that White had seduced her some years before their marriage. There was nothing very lurid about THE UNWRITTEN LAW, but it gained notoriety from the continued attention of the yellow press to the case. In fact, the film itself quickly became old-fashioned, owing to the rapidly changing cinematic styles of the period, but films linked to current events were always guaranteed a big audience, and this particular event continued to be in the public eye for a long time, thanks to the shenanigans of Harry K. Thaw, his very wealthy mother, and his wife. As a result, the film remained in circulation for several years in those places where reform did not have such a strong hand. In addition, Thaw's wife and son both enjoyed film careers a few years later on the basis of her notoriety.[12]

"What excuse can be offered for showing such subjects as the 'Gunness Murder Farm' and the exploits of notorious robbers, outlaws and murderers?" was the rhetorical question posed in the *Moving Picture World* in August 1908, during the time that the Motion Picture Patents Company was being organized. A year later, the showing of a film about the murder of the missionary Elsie Sigel by a Chinese was banned in Bayonne, New Jersey, but this film was still going strong elsewhere in 1911. No matter how much reform, there was always a nickelodeon struggling to survive in the kind of neighborhood that found sensational subjects an attraction.[13]

Films based on acknowledged cultural masterpieces in other media were positive proof that producers and exhibitors were uplifting and educating the audience, providing that an audience could follow them. As we noted in the first chapter, and will discuss in more detail in the next, a crisis in film narrative had presented itself by 1907–1908, when longer and more complex stories were being attempted with methods that often could not make them clear to the audience without someone to explain the meaning of the scenes. The reviewer for the *World*, who considered the Pathé Film d'Art production LA MORT DU DUC DE GUISE to be superb, nevertheless admitted that the audience at the Orpheum in Harlem, where he saw it, could not seem to follow it and received it somewhat coldly. On the other hand, such films were thought to attract the "better classes" to the theater. They might be bored once they got there, but they need not be ashamed to say they went.[14]

France's cultural-uplift program for the moving picture was exemplified in the Film d'Art productions, but the United States, too, could reach for high art by turning to classics of stage, poetry, and literature. Some attempted Shakespeare: Kalem made AS YOU LIKE IT in 1908; Vitagraph did JULIUS CAESAR, RICHARD III, ROMEO AND JULIET, and MACBETH in 1908 and KING LEAR and A MIDSUMMER NIGHT'S DREAM in 1909; and Selig filmed THE MERRY WIVES OF WINDSOR in 1910. Thanhouser, an independent company, made its share of Shakespearian productions and many other classics, then tackled Ibsen: THE LADY FROM THE SEA, PILLARS OF SOCIETY, and A DOLL'S HOUSE in 1911. Vitagraph produced THE BRIDE OF LAM-

MERMOOR, from Sir Walter Scott, in 1909, and Edison did FAUST in the same year. Essanay's version of Dickens' A CHRISTMAS CAROL was in time for the holiday season in 1908; Edison's version came in 1910.

Dickens, Jules Verne, Leo Tolstoy, Nathaniel Hawthorne, Robert Browning—nothing was beyond the reach of aspiring producers of the silent, one-reel film. And if there was much out of reach of the film forms the producers knew, and much out of reach of the mass audiences, that was to change. Meanwhile producers and exhibitors could demonstrate that the motion-picture show was an appropriate place for children and that they were bringing high culture to the masses. Many an enterprising exhibitor arranged with a teacher to have children study the subject of a film in the classroom in advance of its coming to the theater. At least those children would know what the film was about, even though its narrative systems were unable to make the story clear.

The trade periodicals, in support of the industry's uplift movement, had much to say about the use of educational films in the theaters. Beginning with the issue of 12 March 1910, the *World* offered a weekly column called "Education, Science and Art and the Moving Picture." Later, the concept was narrowed to include only educational films, as we understand the term today, but in the beginning there were scarcely enough of these to occupy a weekly column. The first topic was THE HOUSEWIFE AND THE FLY, an educational film about the diseases spread by the common fly. An English production distributed by Kleine, this film was widely shown. Similar films dealing with the prevention of tuberculosis, popularly known as consumption or the white plague, which was the leading killer of the day, and the dangers of unpas-

The prestige of the classics: Vitagraph filmed ROMEO AND JULIET in New York's Central Park in 1908.

teurized milk and flies in the household were shown in conjunction with educational campaigns by local organizations, and this greatly helped the reputation of the exhibitor as a responsible citizen in his or her town. Process films—pictures showing steel manufacture or textile weaving or any modern manufacturing process—were frequently produced in this period, too, and were admired as highly educational, although I don't know whether they were as widely seen. There was a tradition of audience interest in the manufacturing processes that predates the movies, as illustrated by the model coal mine and breaker with which Lyman Howe toured in the nineteenth century.[15]

In 1910 travel lecturer Burton Holmes could draw a crowd of "fashionable people" to Carnegie Hall at prices of $2 and $2.50 ($1 in the gallery), with only scenics and one or two Pathé comedies, but no melodramas. A nickelodeon exhibitor complained because Holmes was showing the very same pictures that he, the exhibitor, had shown earlier at five cents, yet the nickelodeon exhibitor could not get his exchange to stock the scenic pictures anymore. The educational film, like the high-culture film, created an air of respectability and gave a satisfying feeling of improvement. Nonetheless, this does not mean that audiences enjoyed them, and finally, they rejected them. The testimony of exhibitors and exchange men in the suit of the government versus the Motion Picture Patents Company in 1913–1914 gave ample evidence of that rejection. Exchanges kept a small supply of such films on hand for schools, churches, and prisons, but the owners were unanimous in saying that these films were not wanted by the theater audiences. Despite this lack of interest, George

A frame enlargement from CHILDREN WHO LABOR *(Edison, 1912). Produced by the Edison Company in cooperation with the National Child Labor Committee. Directed by Ashley Miller.*

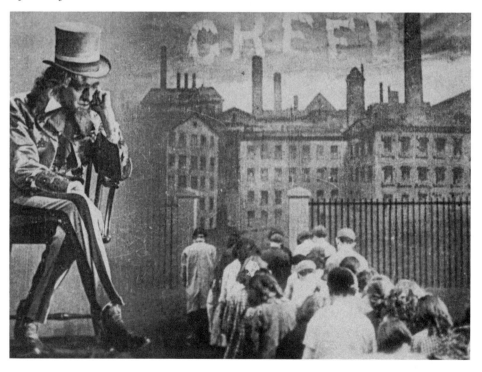

Kleine chose to specialize in distributing the educational film. He evidently found enough profit in it, or was sufficiently determined to uplift his audiences, to publish a series of distribution catalogues, beginning in 1909, dedicated to the educational film. Since there weren't enough scenics and actualities and documentaries available to satisfy him, he included dramas of a specially refined nature, those based on literary classics, and even comedies, to make it possible for a high-class theater, a church, or a school to fill a regular program without fear of offending members of the audience.[16]

Meanwhile, determined producers bent on uplift learned to sugar-coat the educational pill by enclosing the lesson in a drama with a moral. The Edison studio made a regular practice of producing films in cooperation with various welfare organizations and institutions, such as THE RED CROSS SEAL (December 1910), one of the films made each year in cooperation with the American Red Cross campaign; THE AWAKENING OF JOHN BOND (December 1911), on slumlords and tuberculosis; THE CONVICT'S PAROLE (May 1912), suggested by legislation sponsored by the governor of Oregon; THE CRIME OF CARELESSNESS (1913), in cooperation with the Children's Motion Picture League of Greater New York, on the subject of factory safety; and SUFFER LITTLE CHILDREN . . . FOR OF SUCH IS THE KINGDOM OF LABOR (August 1909) and CHILDREN WHO LABOR (February 1912). Thanhouser added to these films about child labor with THE CRY OF THE CHILDREN (April 1912), which was based on a poem by Elizabeth Barrett Browning and gained the endorsement of Theodore Roosevelt. Biograph made such melodramas as FOR HIS SON (January 1912), on the evils of using cocaine in soft drinks, and THOU SHALT NOT (April 1910), on the white plague, in which a couple break their engagement rather than risk passing on the dread disease. Such films disguised their educational purpose in little dramas or melodramas just like the others being shown in the nickelodeons, and thus would be more easily accepted by an audience.[17]

"I heard a minister say, as he left the theater here after seeing [THE SALVATION ARMY LASS, Biograph, 1909], that's a better sermon that I could ever preach," reported the *World* reviewer.[18] The popular melodrama, or everyday drama, preaching a moral, became the most successful genre of film for satisfying the needs of uplift. The more it became expressive, the more it could draw on the emotions of the audience, the more successfully it could fulfill the function of a teacher or a preacher. The desire for uplift gave a strong impetus to this genre in 1909, while the slapstick comedies of the earlier period were suppressed. The cheerful vulgarity and amorality of these films were no longer suitable. For those such as David Wark Griffith, with experience in the touring companies that played live melodrama from one end of the country to another, the time was ripe.

"This is culture, this is refining, this is educational," a reviewer wrote about Griffith's A WREATH OF ORANGE BLOSSOMS in 1911. By 1913 two towns that had forbidden the establishment of moving-picture theaters in their exclusive neighborhoods, Montclair, New Jersey, and Wilmette, Illinois, gave in and withdrew their objections.[19]

Further evidence of the uplift movement can be found in the increasing number of women as exhibitors. In a time when few females could be found in managerial positions, women managing moving-picture theaters were welcomed because it was felt that they brought with them a refining influence (female ushers in the theaters performed a similar function). Mrs. Clement, manager of B. F. Keith's Bijou in

The moral melodrama: A CONVICT'S SACRIFICE (1909), directed by D. W. Griffith for the Biograph Company. Stephanie Longfellow, Gladys Egan, Henry B. Walthall, James Kirkwood.

Title frame from CHILDREN WHO LABOR (Edison, 1912).

Boston, told the *World* in 1910 that her show appealed to a cultured audience. Since, in her opinion, the films alone had not reached a high enough artistic standard, she continued to believe in including lantern-slide lectures, one-act plays, and music. She also approved of high-class vaudeville. She objected to not being able to select films on the open market and thus not being able to stimulate, by her selection, the production of better films.[20]

Although no statistical study of women in exhibition is yet available, it is easy to find the names of female managers just by looking at random in the pages of the *World* at the end of 1912 and again at the end of 1913. Miss Flo Peddycord, for example, owned the Bell Theater in Buchanan, Michigan. She had filled, in her seven or eight years in the business, all the roles of work around the theater, including projectionist. Mrs. Mary McNamara was an exhibitor in Milwaukee. Mrs. Anna M. Mozart ran the Mozart Theater in Los Angeles, a high-class place charging ten to twenty-five cents and running special features for a week, with music supplied by the mechanical Photo-Player Orchestra (she played operatic concerts on it). Miss Jean Oster, manager of the Princess in Cleveland, Ohio, alas for the cause of female uplift, got swept up in Mayor Baker's crusade and arrested for showing an uncensored film, AURORA FLOYD (Thanhouser, December 1912). Mrs. E. J. Streiving of the Crystal Theater in Decatur, Illinois, and Mrs. Musa Reese of the Aereo Theater in Charleston, Illinois, were among the exhibitors attending a Peoria convention. Others included Mrs. R. L. Beck of Dunlap, Iowa, and Mrs. S. J. Brown of the Phoenix Theater in Neola, Iowa. Women exhibitors were apparently more common in the Midwest than elsewhere.[21]

The archetypal image of home and family: HOME, SWEET HOME *(Mutual, 1914), directed by D. W. Griffith. Blanche Sweet and Henry B. Walthall.*

However, uplifting an audience was not an easy task. At the 1913 Motion Picture Patents Company trial, Fred Jeffreys, an exhibitor, explained:

> In lower Jersey City, there is a class of people there who like things that are, well, savoring of great excitement and action. They like cowboy pictures, and hold-ups, and bandits, and things of that kind. . . . They have heard of someone named Napoleon. . . . They know he was a Frenchman, but they would not want to know anything more about him. Then, there are people who like things classy, so to speak. They like to see the Fall of Troy, or Romeo and Juliet, or Richard the Third. . . . Not these pikers where I am now. They want something of every-day life, something not too deep for them.

"Every-day life out West, you mean?" asked his examiner. Jeffreys responded:

> Yes, and right down East, too. This "Mother" gag goes a long way with them. If they can get that stuff, there is a little cry in between. The scrubwomen sit down, and they have a very fine evening's entertainment out of the modern prodigal's return homeward again, and all that stuff. The exhibitors know that, the exchange men know it, the producers know it (*US* v. *MPPC* 3:1832 [November 1913]).

Then there was the threat of censorship. On Christmas Eve 1908, Mayor McClellan closed all the nickelodeons in New York City, and the reverberations were heard across the land. With legal help, the exhibitors obtained an injunction and quickly reopened, but they were "in fear and trembling and all taking special pains to set their house in order and present programs that would not be out of place at a Sunday school entertainment." The official reason given for the closing was poor safety conditions, but it was well understood that the real impetus was the supposedly poor moral condition of the darkened rooms and the kinds of films shown in them.[22]

The court injunction that immediately reopened New York's nickelodeons was obtained from the liberal-minded Judge Gaynor, who was a candidate for mayor in the next election. His action gained him the votes of all motion-picture men and he continued to be a friend to the industry during his terms in office, encouraging city ordinances that were helpful to the business. The leader of the protesting exhibitors, the one who gathered them together to fight Mayor McClellan's actions, was William Fox, who, a year later, could be found fighting all alone against the takeover of the exchanges by the General Film Company.[23]

At the end of January, following the attempt to close the nickelodeons, there was a meeting of clergymen at the Marble Collegiate Church in New York to organize the fight to obtain Sunday closing laws for the city. They asked the Jews to help them, but it is not recorded whether any did so. Sunday-closing laws were a topic of warm interest throughout the period. Such laws were local and varied all over the country. Where Sunday movie showings were permitted, exhibitors took pains to show particularly educational films and hired lecturers for that showing even if they could not afford them the rest of the week. While some of the clergy made a reputation by denouncing the immorality of moving pictures, others, more truly capturing the spirit of their times, saw the potential for uplift and took to showing films inside their churches. Here, they were only following a tradition established by Lyman Howe's "High-Class Moving Pictures" in the previous decade. Such showings increased church attendance, and the producers tried to make suitable films for the purpose. In fact, the showing of films inside churches became too successful in some towns, and the local exhibitors complained. Most churches did not have to follow the same rigorous building codes and fire protection laws as moving-picture theaters did.

When the People's Institute in New York City announced its plans in March 1909 to establish a board of censorship, the trade periodical *Moving Picture World* was caught off guard. In rather abrupt language, it editorialized, "Let the People's Institute mind its own business." This was a bit hasty. The Institute included a very distinguished body of people with a concern for the city's welfare, people whose views were the very epitome of the Progressive attitude. Among the members of the Institute's board were some of the most important society figures, along with big-name reformers, and even such a literary light as Mark Twain. As for the new Board of Censorship, members included Charles Sprague Smith of the People's Institute, the Reverend Walter Laidlaw of the Federation of Churches, Thomas L. McClintock of the Society for the Prevention of Crime, Gustave Straubemiller and Miss Evangeline Whitney of the Board of Education, Mrs. Joseph Price of the Public Education Association, Miss M. Serena Townsend of the Women's Municipal League, the Rev. G. W. Knox of the Ethical Social League, Howard Bradstreet of the Neighborhood Workers' Association, Mrs. Josephine Bedding, John Collier, and Albert Shields.[24]

The organized film industry had decided, not for the last time, to work for self-censorship in order to avoid the hard realities of legal censorship. They had always maintained that a legal censorship would open the way for political corruption, and they now announced a plan to work hand-in-hand with the People's Institute. In fact, the Motion Picture Patents Company even gave the new Board of Censorship some small financial support, which later had to be withdrawn to avoid any appearance of self-interest. They agreed to submit all their films to the board and to not release any films unless approved by it. The independents were also invited to participate in the self-censorship, although, not being in the "club," they were likely to join in more slowly. If their headquarters were far from New York City, then the decision to submit their films for "censorship" was a cost factor. When all of the Patents Company producers had agreed to submit to the self-censorship, the name of the new institution was changed to the National Board of Censorship.

To avoid local censorship, the title "Approved by the National Board of Censorship" could be attached to a film. Some examples of this approval may be found on surviving copies of films such as Lubin's THE ALMIGHTY DOLLAR (July 1910), UNCLE PETE'S RUSE (IMP, October 1911), and THE RIVAL BROTHER'S PATRIOTISM (Pathé American, May 1911), and as late as TESS OF THE STORM COUNTRY (Famous Players, April 1914), although the Board had lost much of its power by then. More commonly, one finds, after June 1912, the Pennsylvania censor's certificate.

The Board of Censorship met at their offices at 80 Fifth Avenue for the first time on 25 March 1909 and sat through 18,000 feet of film, an undertaking of six hours during which sections were ordered cut out of several films. The Motion Picture Patents Company established its own Board of Censorship to sit with them. I don't know how long they kept up this dual board, which may have been intended as window dressing to show its independence from the National Board, but since references to a separate Patents Company board soon disappear, I think they must have given it up as unnecessary duplication of effort. Among other films at that first marathon session, they saw D. W. Griffith's moral melodrama THE DRUNKARD'S REFORMATION. I assume they found it satisfactory.[25]

Sometime that summer the Board of Censorship rejected one of Griffith's films completely, and it was never released. Called THE HEART OF AN OUTLAW, it still survives in the Museum of Modern Art film collections in the form of the original negative, which the Biograph Company retained even though the film was not to be released. THE HEART OF AN OUTLAW does not seem much different from many others of its time. It includes infidelity and a rather high number of shootings, and toys with the notion of incest. But these awful events are not shown in an exploitative fashion, and the film has a moral resolution of sorts. The plot problems that writers faced in turning out these one-reel melodramas one after another could never have been resolved without a generous use of such motifs, and the decisions of the Board did not make them disappear.[26]

On the other hand, the Board apparently approved a Vitagraph production released in November of that same year, FROM CABIN BOY TO KING, which shows a prolonged torture scene that seems a little shocking even today. Pirates who have shanghaied a newsboy to serve as cabin boy brand him with a skull on his chest. During the execution of this deed, the boy's head hangs down from the table backward, facing the camera, and he registers extreme pain. One can be fairly sure that this film was also submitted to censorship, because all the Patents Company members were pledged not to release any films without Board approval.

Most of the comments on films in that period criticized excessive violence and lawlessness. Sexual excesses were seldom noted, and films against the establishment were very rarely criticized, although the latter tended to be the sole reason for censorship in European countries. Pathé Frères and other foreign producers were quick to observe American tastes and morals, and as the American market was the biggest (for the foreign producers who were allowed to distribute in the United States), the films sent here would be those that they knew to be acceptable. At an April 1909 session, the Board looked at 25,000 feet of film produced by Pathé, which represented for that company a month's supply. No subject was rejected. On other occasions, after this promising beginning, Pathé subjects were censored. Either the Board became stricter or Pathé less vigilant in what it imported.

Different times and different individual judgments make it clear why people oppose censorship. The National Board of Censorship (which has been known as the National Board of Review since 1915) claims that the organization was never really in favor of censorship. But the truth is that the socially conscious liberals of that day saw nothing wrong with the National Board of Censorship name until the group was no longer able to serve its original purpose. They were good Progressives, and they were serious in their wish to clean up the movies. Censorship was not a dirty word until it became official. The National Board established a fine reputation for reasoned and intelligent censorship, while local police in various cities made general fools of themselves. But after a trial of a few years, exhibitors, who had to face the sometimes unreasonable forces of respectable society in their towns, found the National Board of Censorship to be powerless, and some of the exhibitors even led the movement for legal censorship.

By June 1914, censorship was considered the crucial issue for the National Exhibitors' Convention held in New York City. "A year ago," it was noted, "local censorship, by the police of various towns and cities, was the only form of regulation the exhibitor had to meet." Major Funkhouser, of the Chicago police, responsible for censorship in that city, had gained a certain fame by such actions as banning a film demonstrating the hesitation waltz, the turkey trot, and the tango. It wasn't so much the dances, he said, as that young people would be led to go to dance halls where liquor was sold, to try them out. Major Funkhouser's censorship was decidedly erratic. An advertisement of that time claimed that another film had been accepted by him: "This film teaches a deep moral lesson. Passed by the Chicago Board of Censors." The film was HENRY SPENCER'S CONFESSION, made with the cooperation of Henry Spencer himself, who was the slayer of Mrs. Mildred Rexroat and nineteen other victims. I don't know this film, but surely the notorious THE UNWRITTEN LAW was considerably milder.[27]

By June 1914, laws for state censorship existed in Pennsylvania, Ohio, and Kansas, while Massachusetts and Connecticut had already taken some action toward similar legislation. The ability of the National Board of Censorship to handle the problems had been challenged by the state legislators. Many importers and distributors of foreign feature films were simply ignoring the National Board, and their more sensational features had aroused the nation to the need for some kind of censorship. Since the National Board of Censorship had no legal powers, some saw it as useless. Nor was it only foreign films that gave trouble. In late 1913 a *World* editorial called the six-reel THE STRANGLERS OF PARIS a "Powerful Argument for Censorship," "reeking with the depiction of crime." The film, based on a Belasco stage production, was "well-made" by the Motion Drama Company of New York, but the *World* urged that "the producer should destroy the negative and swallow the cost."[28]

Pennsylvania had been the first state to have censorship laws, in 1912; Ohio and Kansas followed in 1913. Censorship in Ohio was achieved at the urging of M. A. Neff, who was president of the Ohio Exhibitors' League at the time and the first president of the Exhibitors' League of America. Over the loud protests of many other exhibitors, he managed to get the Ohio law on the books, for what he argued were reasons of self-defense. Many local censor boards were springing up or threatening to, and certainly one board was easier to deal with than many. He soon came to regret that move openly, however. After two months of censoring, Ohio was under injunction to stop, because of a lawsuit begun by the Mutual Film Corporation, and when Mutual lost that case, the producers promptly took it to the U.S. Supreme Court. Nevertheless, these local efforts to stop legal censorship failed, and censorship laws continued to spread to other states.[29]

The majority of exhibitors were still in favor of the National Board of Censorship, and where local censorship existed in reasonably intelligent form, as they felt it did in New Haven, Detroit, Kansas City, Atlanta, Milwaukee and Nashville, they wanted to "let well enough alone." If any legal censorship was truly inevitable, they preferred it to be federal, and there was a bill before Congress for a Federal Board of Censors.

The National Board of Censorship tried to strengthen its position by tightening its rules. To clarify the Board's position on films dealing with vice and crime, Dr. Orrin G. Cocks explained that there should be no glorification of the evildoer or attempt to affect public opinion on a matter before the courts; no portrayal of insanity where it appeals to "the morbid, harrowing or gruesome"; no drug-traffic scenes except when "dramatically necessary to point the moral." Producers should not show easy methods of obtaining drugs. The Board wanted to discourage scenes that weakened religious faith or committed sacrilege, portrayed drinking and drunkenness, or showed scantily dressed persons or women almost wholly dressed but displaying a lavish amount of lingerie. Women's smoking was to be discouraged. The Board condemned the showing of opium dens, gambling, dance halls, vulgar flirtations, and underworld scenes, if produced merely for entertainment. "Unwritten law" themes and "frontier justice" were frowned on, as were train-wrecking, arson, and suicide scenes, since these were thought to be a bad influence on young people. (As it happens, these themes were also very popular means of resolving plot lines, and they did not disappear.) The Board was also forward-looking about the evils of prejudice: "It declares against films which feature sectional, national and race prejudice."[30]

The National Board of Censorship began as an intelligent body of broad-minded citizens, able to look at each film as a whole, who aimed to purify films and thereby actually avoid official censorship. Instead, they were ending up with the literal-minded strictures of the real censor. Powerless to halt the movement toward legal censorship, they finally changed the emphasis of their mission to an effort to encourage the best in film quality, becoming, in 1915, the National Board of Review.

4

The Films:
Alternate Scenes

They [the films] are handed out over the counter like so many feet of sausage.

—*Moving Picture World*, 31 July 1909, p. 151

American films began to undergo a series of changes in 1908–1909 that would be as radical as those at any time in film history, marking as they did a major shift in the perception of the nature and function of the motion picture. Rather striking evidence of this shift is provided by Edwin S. Porter's THE LIFE OF AN AMERICAN FIREMAN (Edison, 1903), which was actually reconstructed sometime after its initial release, either to modernize the film or because the original order was thought to be a "mistake." But as modern researchers have now discovered, it is the reconstructed prints that are in error: in them, the fire rescue scenes inside the room and outside the house have been intercut to show their simultaneity, while in the 1903 version, the action of the woman and baby being rescued through the window was shown twice, in consecutive shots, once from the interior and again from the exterior, in the same way that such scenes were shown in slide shows. It is not known when the reconstruction took place, but the same kind of "correction" can be found in several other films made before 1908.[1]

As suggested in previous chapters, one important reason for such changing perceptions was the new audience for the motion picture. To be sure, the pre-1908 films were the ones that had attracted that audience to the nickelodeons in the first place. As Charles Musser has demonstrated in a study of the Edison sales records, it was the emergence of the story film, in 1904–1906, that drew people to the nickelodeons. Even though greater numbers of actuality films were still being produced at that time, many more copies of story films were sold. The attraction of the story film for the new audience was finally understood by the producers and sharply reflected in film production after 1907. The movie fan, the one who attended every day or went from show to show, existed before there was a star system or a fully integrated narrative system. It was this audience that presented at the same time a demand for stars, for a more complex narrative, and for more clarity in narrative techniques.[2]

By 1908 it was evident that the popularity of the story film was presenting new problems for the filmmakers. The most common criticism of specific films concerned the need for clarity. The *Moving Picture World* reviewer noted, " 'The Devil,' 'Dr. Jekyll and Mr. Hyde', etc., are clever plays but they have been presented in motion pictures in a way that the public do not understand them. The spectators cannot follow the plot and therefore they lose interest." Said a commentator on the task of the filmmaker in 1908, "His plot must be simple, the difficulties into which the characters are led as obvious as the sun, and the solution of them intelligent to the lowest understanding." Another, praising Edison's SAVED BY LOVE, remarked, "As the spectators could follow the plot, without the help of a lecturer, they were deeply interested." The help of the lecturer was available only in certain theaters, not in others, or was called upon only for special films. Films that could be understood without the lecturer to explain them could be shown everywhere.[3]

A greatly expanded audience from diverse cultures no longer had the same frame of reference. This explains some of the complaints about lack of clarity that were heard with great frequency in 1907–1908. Filmmakers could no longer expect the majority of the spectators to recognize the narrative events of a classic tale, a work of literature, a popular play, a familiar myth, unless they were in some way explained. Stereotypes of character and gesture would have to be reestablished for the new audience.

The second reason for change, and the one that the filmmakers all understood, was the uplift movement. Producers were being urged to make films that would be morally improving and educational for the mass audience. How was this to be done? Not the only but perhaps the most effective way would be to enlist the emotions of the spectator in a story. The film would have to carry a lesson or preach a sermon, and to do that it would have to learn to be expressive. The advantage of this method of educating was that it also would attract the audience, and that made good business sense. One could make moral and educational films and still lose the audience if they were dull or if the audience could not understand them.

A third cause of change was the need to standardize film production, to bring out films of the same length and within established genres. The film as standardized product would be one that was clearly understood without the help of the lecturer; one that would be reliably available on a regular schedule, that the exchange and the exhibitor could count on; one that would draw the consumer to brand names, that would be familiar; and one that would be under the control of its producer. The standardized film would make it possible to rationalize production methods and would be more profitable for the producer.

Another contribution to change was the fact that most of the new directors were entering the expanded motion-picture field with backgrounds in the legitimate the-ater and the road-show melodrama. The previous generation had been chiefly busi-nessmen, technicians, and cameramen, with some variety-show people, including magicians. The new producers and directors, without previous film experience, were much more apt to draw their models from the theater than from the variety shows, lantern-slide shows, comic strips, cycloramas, and all those varied pre-film sources that had inspired earlier filmmakers. It will be noted that changes in the style of filmmaking tended to come from the new generation, a D. W. Griffith, a Ralph or Thomas Ince, a Herbert Brenon, or a Sidney Olcott. Those who had begun in the early days, such as Edwin S. Porter or Alice Guy Blaché, were much likelier to hold onto the earlier styles.[4]

Throughout the period from 1907 to 1915, there were many who believed that the mission of film was to bring theater to the new audiences. They thought it signaled a great cultural advance for the masses. In 1913, Frank Dyer, a man involved in the administrative end of the industry for many years, could only describe the art of the film as photographing great stage plays. But even in 1908, a few people were able to articulate some of the differences between theater and film as they were then understood. One of them was Rollin Summers, writing in the *Moving Picture World*. In his view, several important characteristics were unique to the motion picture: (1) the silent film cannot explain action that happened before it begins or that happened elsewhere—it must be shown; (2) film cannot show precise mental states, but it can better show elemental emotion; (3) film, using real scenery, gains in atmosphere and heightens illusion; (4) where emotion is to be expressed, the film can be taken at close range: "The moving picture may present figures greater than life size without loss of illusion"; (5) film can have as many scene changes as wanted: "The principal characters, having once been well identified, may be separated and the scene may shift from one to the other and back again. If the sequence of the scene is well contrived there is a decided gain in the quality of the action and a perfected illusion of reality in the method." These were all prescient comments concerning the way in which film was going to develop, but it is the last that I would like to examine in this chapter.[5]

From this time onward, most people assumed that movies aspire to reality, for reasons having to do with the new emphasis on the story film. In earlier days, moving pictures were accepted as a spectacle, a magic show, an amusing entertainment. Verisimilitude was one of film's entertaining characteristics. The first audiences could marvel at how "lifelike" the motion picture was when it documented the world around them. When filmmakers began to relate more complex stories, however, there was a shift in attitude. Reality began to be demanded for the staged fiction film. The screen is not reality, of course, and every spectator knows that very well. What the fiction film came to represent was a dream world, founded on an illusion of the real world. No other medium could give such concrete "evidence" of reality. From this point in history, anything that dragged the spectator out of that dream was subject to criticism on the grounds of breaking the illusion of reality. When the French firm Pathé Frères attempted the popular American genre of the Western with A WESTERN HERO (1909), it was severely criticized by a reviewer because "[The audience] like to believe that the pictures are real photographs of the real scenes, and the public mind seems to resent any jolt which awakens them out of the pleasant dream." The details of the dream are concrete and must be consistent: dream logic must be observed, lest illusion break.[6]

Those who gave away the secrets of how movies were produced were criticized by others, who thought this to be unfair to the audience. Such an idea reminds one of the earlier concept of the cinema as magic act: the magician does not give away the secrets of his profession. In fact, audiences were fascinated with the details of how movies were made, as long as this information came from outside the film. But for the duration of the film, the spectator wanted to be able to suspend disbelief. In the fall of 1909 a spectator at the Bijou Dream on Fourteenth Street in New York described the rapt audience around him: "A tense, well-knit, immobile mass of human faces, with eyes alertly fixed on the screen." The audiences were caught up by the new narrative systems, held in a way they never had been before.[7]

To understand what the fundamental changes taking place in this period were, it may help to begin by examining more closely the films of 1907 and 1908 as the existing models on which the new films would be based.

All films in 1907 were one reel or less in length, from only two or three hundred feet to just over one thousand feet, with the rare exception of passion plays (Biograph's last release of a foreign-made film was Gaumont's two-reel LA VIE DU CHRIST in 1907) and the occasional prizefight film. There was room for variation within these lengths, but during 1909 and 1910, the lengths would become standardized. The time came when film after film directed by Griffith at Biograph would measure precisely 990 to 998 feet, or else a reel of just the same length would contain two films known as "split reels." This kind of regularity marked the films made for the Biograph Company, where standardization was perhaps more rigorous than at other companies. Nevertheless the tendency existed with all the producers, and as we shall see in chapter 12, exhibitors would complain if there was too much variance.

The comedies, chases, and actualities of the previous period were still the basic material of the films produced, but as Tom Gunning has suggested, the vein was becoming exhausted. The limits of these forms may have been reached and audiences may have tired of them.[8]

To be sure, many variations enriched the chase formula. For an example, there is Edison's charming JACK THE KISSER (1907), in which an overenthusiastic masher snatches kisses from unsuspecting ladies on the street and in the park, in one episode after another, until the actions culminate in the chase sequence typical of the genre. Here too there are fresh variations in the unusual locations, such as the stacked sewer pipes in a factory yard, through which the pursuit continues. The film exemplifies the expansion of narrative in this period by the adding on of episodes with a common motif—in this case, the kiss thief. Since the episodes are variations on a repetitive theme, the film may be lengthened or shortened according to the number of episodes the filmmaker chooses, without altering the narrative conception. Whenever the film is long enough, a final climax may be added to give closure to the narrative.

John Fell has called this kind of structure "the motivated link," while Tom Gunning prefers the term "linked vignettes."[9] The same loose structure may be found in many comedies of the period. Biograph's TRIAL MARRIAGES (1907) shows the comic effect of the inspiration a man gets from reading a newspaper article by a woman of advanced ideas recommending trial marriages. He then gives a tryout to a series of potential wives, all of whom have various faults. Repetition of the motif provides a relationship from shot to shot, one that is easily broken. It would not make much difference in which order the various "tryout wives" were shown, or if one were dropped or another added.

The chase comedy of 1907, however, maintained a formal relationship from one shot to the next that was not felt to be necessary for the other types of linked-episode comedy. The shots of the early chase films were linked by the direction of the pursuit in relation to the camera position. More often than not, shots show the participants in the chase, both pursued and pursuer, approaching from the distance and exiting in the foreground, to one side or the other of the camera, with the action and its direction repeated in the next shot but in another location. The shots are linked by this movement through space. Variations included reversing the direction of the chase or entering near the camera and running into the distance, as well as crossing numerous obstacles. This construction, familiar to audiences through endless repetitions, suggests a model for new narrative films. It connotes continuous space-time unrolling from one shot to the next.[10]

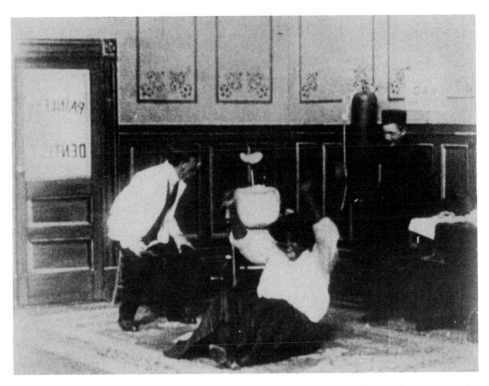

A linked-episode film: LAUGHING GAS *(Edison, 1907). The effects of a visit to the dentist.*

The type of story that can be told with the motivated link or by the movements in space of a chase comedy is limited, even with imaginative variations. In 1907 comedies were the most common fictional form. However, a handful of melodramas were also made that year, and producers of this genre found it necessary to explore other options. As they attempted to narrate more complex stories, viewers were beginning to notice a lack of connection. Alfred Capus, a French playwright involved in the Film d'Art movement, was quoted as saying, "If we wish to retain the attention of the public we have to maintain unbroken connection with each preceding scene." By February 1909 a writer in the *Moving Picture World* could say that "In the past few months there have been put out very many really beautiful, dramatic, tragic and serio-comic films. Films with real acting in them, which tell a beautiful and connected story." Yet the following month, with some fundamental elements of the new construction already in place but used with unequal skill by various filmmakers, another *World* commentator complained that "many film pieces that are produced fail because of some obvious disconnectedness in action." Even at the end of the year the *World* carried an editorial on the poor construction of many films, the lack of clarity, the lack of relation to printed synopses, quoting a spectator as remarking at the finish of a film, "Bit disconnected, isn't it?"[11]

The development of new ways to connect shots, or editing, was probably the most important change in film form to take place during the 1907–1909 period. Creating a spatiotemporal world, a kind of geography made of separate shots related to one

another, was crucial in the construction of a complex narrative. The development of
new editing methods would also greatly increase the potential for enlisting the spectator's emotions in the film. The new forms would integrate the spectator more
deeply into the film experience. Louis Reeves Harrison's articles on the fine art of
films were usually incoherent, but he was uncharacteristically acute when he noticed, in late 1910, that when the vaudeville act was over, the lights dimmed, and the
pictures went on, the audience became quiet and all attention. "There can no longer
be perception without attention," he said; "the loss of one scene means a chapter torn
from the story."[12]

In attempting to analyze the emerging forms of editing, David Bordwell, in *The
Classical Hollywood Cinema* (1985), has proposed a distinction between what he calls
crosscutting and parallel editing. He defines crosscutting as "the intercalation of two
or more different series of images. If temporal simultaneity is not pertinent to the
series, the cutting may be called *parallel* editing; if the series are to be taken as
temporally simultaneous, then we have *crosscutting*." In another part of the same
book, Kristin Thompson recapitulates this formulation a bit more simply: "Part One
has defined 'crosscutting' as editing which moves between simultaneous events in
widely separated locales. 'Parallel editing' differs in that the two events intercut are
not simultaneous."[13] (I would suggest that "widely" should be dropped from this
definition. "Separated," yes, but the distance of separation might be only inches:
imagine a sequence alternating on the two sides of a wall, for example.)

These definitions have a certain kind of logic that clarifies two functions of alternating shots. It should be noted, though, that since the thirties at least, the term
"parallel editing" has been used for both functions and especially for the kind of
cutting Bordwell and Thompson have called "crosscutting." To change the definition
at this point in time may be too arbitrary and confusing; perhaps it would be more
useful to differentiate the types of editing with some new terminology.

In any case, during the period under discussion, when all kinds of editing were
new and not yet established as conventions, the distinctions were not always articulated clearly in the films or in the language. Yet it might be suggestive to look at the
terminology of the time, for what it reveals of the intentions of those who used it. The
terms "parallel editing" and "crosscutting" do not appear at all. In 1908, when such
editing was quite new, it was referred to as "alternate scenes." That was the term first
used to describe the sequence designed to increase suspense, showing two or more
simultaneous streams of action that will come together in the resolution.[14]

In 1910 a New York journalist explaining the advantages that moving pictures had
over vaudeville and melodrama wrote, "The divided stage, with its broken partition
end on to the spectator, may also be sent to the lumber room. [He refers to the
divided screen found in many early films.] The motion picture has it in its power by
alternating scenes to show us what is going on simultaneously in two different places,
inside and outside a house, for example, or in adjoining rooms."[15]

The same term is very often found in the advice of the *World* to musicians who
accompanied the films: "Some pictures are shown in which the scenes alternate so
rapidly as to make it impractical to change music with every change of scene." Or,
suggesting music for A DIXIE MOTHER (Vitagraph): "The next scenes alternate
quickly. . . . This journey is shown in a number of scenes, and after each one the
mother is shown." In 1911, commenting on "a really good picture," Selig's THE
MISSION WORKER, the music columnist described how "the scenes alternate be-

tween Chinese scenes, a sick-room, and a parlor—many of them rather short." (The advice given to the musician in the case of rapid alternation of scenes was to select the dominant mood and stick with it.) In any case, the term "alternate scenes" was clearly understood by everyone.[16]

As for the kind of cutting that Bordwell and Thompson would call "parallel," the interweaving of events that are not specifically related in time, the terms often used at the time were "inserts" or "flashes," reflecting the usual brevity of the shots thus edited. At first, "insert" was applied to extreme close-ups of letters or newspaper articles used to forward the narrative, and also to extreme close-ups of objects, such as photographs, when it was necessary to identify them. As the concept of editing developed, the term was used for any shot that was "inserted" into the chronological sequence of events to show another time or place. In the beginning of this period, inserts were considered to be interruptive of the narrative flow. Although they were seen as a more "realistic" way of giving narrative facts than intertitles, it was nevertheless thought desirable to minimize their use and to keep them short when they were used, so as to interrupt as little as possible. (The terms "alternate" and "insert" will also be familiar to readers of Christian Metz.)

The famous 1913 advertisement in which public-relations men claimed for D. W. Griffith the invention of practically everything in use at the time refers to " 'the switchback,' sustained suspense." The "switchback," here, refers not to the flashback as we know it, but to a cut to the scene, in another location, that immediately preceded it.[17]

An English writer in a 1916 manual for scenario writers actually uses the term "flashback" for "the keeping of two apparently distinct stories running at the same time and not allowing them to converge until the time is ripe for them being dovetailed." This technique, the manual indicates, "will allow the writer to switch away from the scene when he wishes, either to show a lapse of time, or . . . the end of . . . action." (At the time, what we know as flashbacks were more apt to be called "memory flashes," indicating how they were usually understood, as the memory of a specific character.)[18]

The term "cut back," meanwhile, is clearly explained from a 1915 vantage point in Louella O. Parsons' *How To Write for the "Movies,"* although she may have the chronology of its function a little wrong:

> In the beginning, the cut back was used . . . to avoid showing the actual
> theft or murder or to close up a break in the action. Later, the cut back
> was used to give added surprise and intensity to the plot. The cut back
> refers to some particular scene that has gone before. The interest and
> suspense of the audience is intensified by using the cut back. . . . Griffith
> changed [the practice of direct continuity] by flashing from one scene to
> another, by a series of short scenes . . . keeping each character before the
> audience. . . . It is not used as much as it was formerly. The new school
> of motion picture acting seems to favor longer scenes and more deliberate
> action. The flashes or cut backs are still used when necessary, but not to
> the entire exclusion of longer scenes (*How to Write for the "Movies"*
> [Chicago: A. C. McClurg & Co., 1915], pp. 48–49).

In her explanation, Louella Parsons gives an additional motive for using alternate scenes: to avoid images that would be censored. Epes Winthrop Sargent had already suggested this idea in his advice to photoplay authors in 1911. He noted that a fight or struggle with a burglar might not pass the censors, but there would be no objection if it were broken "by contrasting scenes showing the police hurrying to the aid of the victim."[19]

The term "simultaneity" in Bordwell and Thompson's definition of crosscutting is not quite accurate because there is nearly always some time dropped out between shots. (In alternate editing, time may be expanded as well, in order to increase suspense.) The character racing to the rescue in an automobile is usually a greater distance farther on when we return to the scene than would be possible in continuous time. The ellipsis of time between the alternate shots permitted a compression of narrative events that was very useful for the one-reel film. As Parsons said, the use of alternation lessened in the early days of the feature film, but not only for the reasons she gave—there was also less need for such compression.

THE MILL GIRL (Vitagraph, 1907) is a useful reference film because, while it is not typical of the other surviving films of its year, it illustrates the point reached by film narrative on the verge of its great expansion. At a time when most of the films produced were comedies or actualities, this one is a melodrama. Over the next few years, it was the melodrama, particularly the psychological melodrama as articulated by D. W. Griffith, that would become the most popular medium for moral uplift. THE MILL GIRL has a young working-class man and woman for its hero and heroine. A girl in a textile mill is subjected to the unwanted advances of her employer. The young man she loves, a worker in the mill, comes to her rescue by knocking down the boss. The boss hires two ruffians to beat up the worker, who defeats them on two occasions by his superior strength and wit but is then dismissed by the boss. Free of interference, the boss again forces his attentions on the girl but is interrupted by a fire in the mill, which brings about his death. The heroine is rescued from the fire by the young worker.[20]

The film has one intertitle and thirty-one shots, a very high number for 1907. It is filmed at a kind of "stage distance," as almost all films were at this time: space appears at the bottom showing the floor in front of the actors' feet, and there is inactive space above their heads at the top of the frame. The distance between camera and actors is narrowed a bit more in the climactic scenes. When the actors enter and exit the frame, however, they often move on the diagonal to the axial plane, thus appearing much closer to the camera, in nearly a "three-quarters shot." At this point, the actors' knees are near the bottom of the frame and their heads near the top. For 1907 audiences, this composition would be familiar from the structure of the chase-film comedy. However, the significant action of the scene takes place only when the actors reach the center of the frame. Many films of the pre-1907 period presented a screen full of action, with no key, other than the lecturer who might have accompanied the film, as to what the spectator should be seeing. The movement into the center frame in THE MILL GIRL has the effect of leading the spectator's eye to the significant action.

The diagonal entry and exit contributes more than a directional arrow, however: it also serves as a system for linking the shots and outlining a geography for the action. The first two shots of THE MILL GIRL may be used to illustrate this. The film opens with a shot of a gate set in a hedge, representing the home of the heroine, where the hero joins her in the morning to accompany her to the mill. The hero enters from the right, stops at center to meet the girl at the gate, and they continue together toward the left, approaching the three-quarters shot as they exit. The following shot, in front of the mill, shows groups of workers entering from the same three-quarters position at left, going into mid-distance, and entering the factory gate in the center. Among them are the young couple. By following this direction principle with a fair degree of consistency, the filmmakers keep the action flowing continuously in a kind of synthetic space. The principle was taken over so thoroughly by other filmmakers that by 1911, spectators and critics alike called attention to any inconsistent direction of action from one shot to the next: "Any one who has watched pictures knows how often his sense of reality has been shocked by this very thing . . . as if [the actor] has gone half way around a building during the change of scene and was entering it from the opposite side."[21]

THE MILL GIRL contains a sequence that exemplifies alternate editing in its basic original form, inside and outside a building. This occurs when the thugs hired by the boss come to the worker's home during the night:

1. Exterior: hero enters scene from left and goes through gate to his home.
2. Interior: bedroom, the hero enters from right foreground, goes around bed, yawns, gets ready for bed, closes window, sits on chair to remove his shoes.
3. Exterior: another view of house, the employer leads his thugs into the scene, then sends them back out while he stands and waits.
4. Interior: A slightly closer view of bedroom, hero is now in bed. Hearing a noise, he puts hand to ear, goes to window, and looks out.
5. Exterior: the thugs come back with a ladder and place it against the house so that the top disappears from sight, while the boss gestures a command of silence.
6. Interior: the hero at the window, he turns and makes up a dummy shape in his bed, gets a stick and crouches below foot of bed, foreground.
7. Exterior: the thugs climb the ladder while the boss holds it.
8. Interior: the hero cups his ear, listening, the thugs raise the window, enter, attack dummy. The hero jumps up, knocks one man down while the other flees, then throws the first one out the window.
9. Exterior: the man who is thrown out falls down on the man at the bottom, the other already having fled the scene.

There are many sequences in pre-1907 cinema showing people jumping or being thrown out of doors and windows. Sometimes there is an overlap in time, or repeated action, from interior to exterior shots, as in the frequently cited THE LIFE OF AN AMERICAN FIREMAN (Edison, 1903) by Edwin S. Porter, in the sequence of the rescue of the woman and child from the burning building. In this film, the same action is shown twice, once from inside and the second time from outside the building. In the interior/exterior editing of THE MILL GIRL, there is simultaneity and/or an ellipsis of time between shots. In 1907 few films other than Porter's could supply any examples of repetition like that of THE LIFE OF AN AMERICAN FIREMAN, and a few years later, as we have seen, such editing would simply look like a "mistake."

In contrast to the model of alternate editing using adjacent spaces found in THE MILL GIRL, the use of the insert to link distant spaces turns up in a March 1908 film, OLD ISAACS THE PAWNBROKER (Biograph). Based on a script by D. W. Griffith and directed by Wallace McCutcheon, Sr., OLD ISAACS THE PAWNBROKER is an edifying melodrama about the life of the people who were considered to be the most significant audience for the movies: the new immigrants and urban poor. The slum-dwellers depicted in this film included some of high moral character, and they are shown to be more sensitive than their upper-class counterparts. The old Jewish pawnbroker wears a putty nose, but he is stereotypical only in appearance, not in character. In the course of the film he is shown to be very brave and to have a kind and understanding heart.

It should not be concluded from the two examples of melodrama provided here that most films in 1907–1908 supplied working-class heroes for a working-class audience. Only a small number did so, but it does appear that such films were particularly popular, judging from contemporary comments as well as the number of copies sold.[22]

By 1907 standards OLD ISAACS is for the most part conventionally made. The camera is always at stage distance, the diagonal entrances and exits of the Vitagraph film are lacking, the characters are stereotyped ethnic types without much individuality, and the acting is stylized to ensure the clarity of the action. A small girl goes to a charity institution to seek help for her invalid mother who is about to be evicted, but no action is taken pending investigation. In desperation, the girl goes to a pawnshop and tries to hock her mother's old shoes. They are rejected, and she brings her doll instead, drawing the attention of the kindly pawnbroker to her plight. The pawnbroker arrives with food and help for the little family just in time to stop the eviction. Continuity is achieved by using the little girl as the motivated link, followed from shot to shot. While the girl is at the charity offices, she is sent from one room to another. When she reaches the final office, an image is cut in, showing her mother at home (a "switchback" to a scene we have seen earlier), rising from her bed coughing and falling back down. The next shot returns to the charity office, where the child is refused the immediate help she needs. (The heartless charitable organization is a frequent theme of the era, occurring several times in the work of Griffith.) The shot in the office has been cut to "insert" the scene of the mother.

Elsewhere I have attempted to trace the origins of this shot to the "vision scene" common to stage melodrama.[23] Such scenes are also frequent in earlier films, but in those films the visions would be shown in the same scene with the person or persons having them, as a double exposure, as a superimposition, or with stop motion, as in trick films. The vision scene by double exposure would continue to be widely used for many years to come. However, quite another way of thinking is needed to imagine the vision scene as a separate shot in 1907. The insert represents a leap across space to link two people distant from each other. One doesn't know whether this shot represents the girl's thoughts, since she shows no reaction at all. She simply stands and waits. It may well be that the spectator of the film is the only participant in this drama who is witness to the mother's suffering.

The shot could be considered as the invisible narrator of the story who provides comments on it, a narrator who is neither a character in the story nor a real person standing outside the film, but a role that exists in some sense in the structure of the film. This "narrator" plays an essential role in the system of narration that Tom Gunning believes to have been developed in the work of David Wark Griffith during the next few years.[24]

About a month after Griffith began to direct, he took up the idea of alternate shots in THE FATAL HOUR (directed in July 1908). In that film, the purpose of the alternation was to increase suspense. A more direct link with OLD ISAACS THE PAWN-BROKER can be found in BEHIND THE SCENES, directed by Griffith in August 1908.

Mental images visualized in the flames: FIRESIDE REMINISCENCES *(Edison, 1908), directed by Edwin S. Porter.*

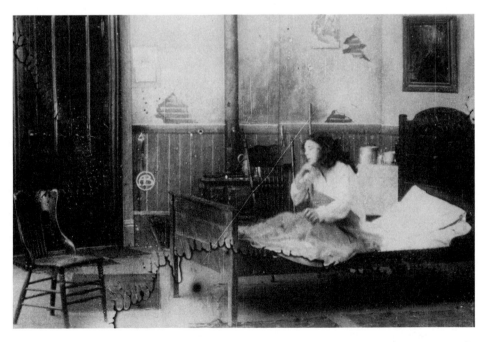

The inserted shot of the sick mother in OLD ISAACS THE PAWNBROKER *(Biograph, 1907), directed by Wallace McCutcheon. (The wiggly line on the photograph is due to deterioration in the original nitrate negative.)*

Once again it concerns a mother-daughter relationship, but this time the daughter is at home, seriously ill, while the mother is out earning her living as a cabaret dancer. She knows that her daughter is quite sick, and she is in haste to finish her work and hurry home. During her dance, she trembles a moment, and at this point there is inserted an image of her child, dying. Again, one cannot tell from the film itself whether it is the mother or only the spectator who sees the child. As the mother discovers when she hurries home, the child has died. According to the Biograph *Bulletin* issued with this film, "A mother's intuition assets itself and in her mind's eye she sees her little one—but only for the moment."[25] These words, we assume, express the intentions of the inserted shot, even though the film itself does not quite articulate it.

A couple of weeks later, Griffith used another mental image in AFTER MANY YEARS (released November 1908), the first of his films inspired by *Enoch Arden*. The faithful wife thinks of her husband lost at sea while he, in another shot, thinks of her. Their positions within their respective shots reflect the emotional relationship, each gazing at the space that the other would occupy if they were in the same scene. Nevertheless, the spectator knows for a fact what the wife does not: that her husband is still alive. Here is a clear example of Gunning's "narrator-system," at the same time able to show us the thoughts of the character and a fact that is not known to her.

Each change in film structure at this period seems to result from the new viewpoint of employing several shots where, earlier, one shot would have done. The idea of the "mental image" was not unusual at this time in films, but it would traditionally be shown in one shot. In Edison's FIRESIDE REMINISCENCES (January 1908) and Biograph's THE MUSIC MASTER (May 1908), the characters' mental images are implanted in the fireplace or on the wall, in the same scene with them. The Biograph *Bulletin* describes the latter as "a phantasmagorial portrayal of his thoughts, which bring him back to days of yore." In 1912, Theodore Wharton took advantage of the ease of the Bell & Howell camera's new frame counter to photograph the story a man is confessing to a priest in dissolving views placed within the *same* scene as that of his confession and in the same size. This was in an Essanay film called SUNSHINE, which was much admired at the time. Not everyone wanted to follow Griffith's way. Examples of the mental image shown in the same scene are very common in this period, more so, perhaps, than Griffith's editing system. In the *World* of 6 May 1911, it was said that keeping the characters on the screen while the story is told is "a much more realistic way of telling such a tale, than to tell it with the story teller hidden." On the basis of so few surviving films, however, it is difficult to decide what was a dominant mode, if any. In a film by a decidedly less talented filmmaker than D. W. Griffith, THE PUGILIST'S CHILD, made at the Powers studio in September 1910, insert editing is used very much as it was in OLD ISAACS THE PAWNBROKER. Here a professional fighter is winning in the ring while his child is dying at home, and editing cuts back and forth several times between the distant scenes.[26]

Some reluctance to adopt the new editing may be seen in the way scenes showing a telephone call were filmed. Here was a real link between distant spaces, newly familiar to everyone, since the telephone system was spreading across the land nearly simultaneously with the movies. In the 1901 film ARE YOU THERE?, made in England by James Williamson, a young man telephones his girl, but unknown to him, her disapproving father takes the receiver from her hands and listens. In the next and final shot, the angry father visits the young man and beats him. The participants in the phone conversation are shown in the same image, separated by a divided screen, which is signified only by the hanging of a curtain between the two telephones. In 1904, the Biograph Company's THE STORY THE BIOGRAPH TOLD showed a man at his office talking on the phone to his wife at the same time that he is embracing his secretary. In this case, to show simultaneity, the wife at home on the telephone is inserted as a superimposition on a part of the office scene. When Edwin S. Porter made COLLEGE CHUMS for Edison in 1907, he wanted to show both participants in a phone conversation and at the same time indicate the great distance separating them. The distance between is shown by a cityscape of rooftops; the woman telephoning is seen in a circle in the upper corner, the man at the left, and the two sides of the conversation in animated letters float across the screen, first to the left, then to the right. The space and the simultaneous event are shown graphically.[27]

The idea of showing two telephones with a landscape or city streets between by means of a triple screen became quite popular, especially when used for comic effect. A Max Linder comedy, MAX AND HIS DOG DICK, imported to the United States in 1912, used it so that Max's dog could telephone him across Paris to tell Max that his wife was receiving a visit from another man. In the same year, CANNED HARMONY (Solax), a little comedy directed or supervised by Alice Guy Blaché, contained another triple-screen version of a telephone call, this time with the central panel showing a quiet country road and a small animal wandering in the distance. SUS-

The telephone call in COLLEGE CHUMS *(Edison, 1907), directed by Edwin S. Porter.*

The telephone call in THE MEDICINE BOTTLE *(Biograph, 1909), directed by D. W. Griffith. Florence Lawrence is the mother at the telephone, Adele De Garde is her little daughter.*

PENSE (Rex, 1913), directed by Lois Weber and Phillips Smalley, offers a new variation: the screen is divided into three triangles, with a woman speaking on the telephone at the top right, a tramp at the top left who is outside the woman's house and trying to break in, and the husband at his office, at the other end of the phone, in the center. (Many years later the space separating two phones was made subject of gags in such films as PILLOW TALK [1959], where Doris Day and Rock Hudson sit in their baths, talking on the phone, with their naked feet touching the wall that separates the split screen.)

Another approach to the telephone call was the alternate scene, which had been used in this way since 1908 at least. The Pathé film THE NARROW ESCAPE, released in the United States in March of that year (although probably made in 1907), employs alternate editing for a sequence in which a family is being attacked by intruders, while the father, a doctor who has been called away from home, talks to his wife by telephone. The telephone call is alternated in three shots: the doctor phoning his wife, the wife speaking to him from the phone in his study at home, the doctor speaking to her; then, in another shot, the doctor hangs up and starts to the rescue.[28]

This kind of thriller based on alternate editing became one of the most successful genres of the time, with D. W. Griffith as one of its leading practitioners. In THE MEDICINE BOTTLE (1909), for example, Griffith used the alternating method to build suspense around the story of an innocent child about to give a spoonful of poison to her grandmother instead of medicine. The absent mother discovers she has carried off the wrong bottle and tries desperately to reach her little daughter in time by means of the telephone but is thwarted again and again by switchboard operators gossiping among themselves and neglecting their duty. The film alternates between the mother, the switchboard operators, and the little girl four times, until in the twelfth shot of the sequence the call goes through. The child answers, the mother talks, the child listens, and the position then shifts to a more distant view as the girl hangs up and goes to the bedside of her grandmother.[29]

In the same year, Griffith expanded on the interrupted telephone call in his famous thriller THE LONELY VILLA. In this variation on the theme of Pathé's THE NARROW ESCAPE (which is one of its possible sources), the phone is seen prominently on the wall at right in the second shot. When the doctor called away from home experiences trouble with his car, he enters an inn to telephone his wife and warn her of the expected delay in his return. At the very moment that he calls, his wife and children are besieged by burglars trying to break into the house. The sequence of the telephone call contains seventeen alternating shots, including various elements of interruption, until the wire is cut and the frustrated couple talking on the telephone find themselves to be "a bit disconnected." "The entire audience was in a state of intense excitement," reported the *World*'s critic after a showing of THE LONELY VILLA at the Fourteenth Street Theater in New York, noting that at the end, the woman seated behind him had exclaimed, "Thank God, they're saved!" Indeed, the form of this kind of thriller is so effective with audiences that it remains in use even today.[30]

The Vitagraph producers, already having used the rudiments of alternate editing for suspense in 1906 with THE ONE HUNDRED TO ONE SHOT and in 1907 with THE MILL GIRL, easily took up the new style. Their telephone thriller of 1910, THE TELEPHONE, shows the same kind of editing as THE LONELY VILLA. In this version, a woman and her child are at home alone and the husband at his club, when she

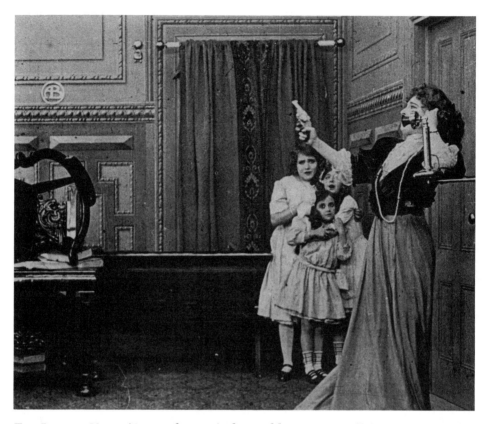

THE LONELY VILLA (Biograph, 1909), directed by D. W. Griffith. Marion Leonard (on phone), Mary Pickford, Gladys Egan, Adele De Garde.

discovers that the house is on fire. In a twelve-shot sequence, the film alternates between home, switchboard, firemen, and club. Several years later Griffith made another quite outstanding telephone thriller called DEATH'S MARATHON (1913), with Blanche Sweet at one end of the telephone listening to her husband, Henry Walthall, threatening suicide on the other end. In this case the conventions of the well-established genre are broken and the husband shoots himself before help arrives.[31]

But by this time Griffith and many others were also using alternate editing as the normal way to show any telephone conversation. In the light comedy TEACHING DAD TO LIKE HER (March 1911), Griffith directed a fifteen-shot sequence showing the lively conversation of a young man and his sweetheart, cutting from one to the other alternately, until the boy's disapproving father overhears and puts a stop to it. In this fluidly edited sequence, the overall average length of a shot is about five seconds. The sequence does nothing much to forward the story; it is there only to enrich the characterization. Vitagraph's PLAYING AT DIVORCE (December 1910), Reliance's JEALOUSY (March 1912), and Nestor's MUM'S THE WORD (March 1913), among surviving films, all use alternate editing to show telephone conversations, even if in some of the cases the filmmakers did not think of using it in other sequences. Yet, as we have seen, the older method of showing a phone call in one scene by dividing the screen did not disappear.

Two shots from THE TRAINER'S DAUGHTER; OR, A RACE FOR LOVE *(Edison, 1907), directed by Edwin S. Porter. The shot showing the bugler signaling the start of the race is inserted (cut into) the scene in the stables, where we see the reaction of those who hear the call.*

THE LONEDALE OPERATOR (Biograph, 1911), directed by D. W. Griffith. Blanche Sweet (telegrapher); Dell Henderson, and Joseph Graybill (tramps looking in a window).

For some filmmakers, the literal "links between spaces" of the sounds of a telephone call may have been needed to stimulate this kind of alternate editing. In other cases, a sound heard by a character appears to motivate a cut to another scene, although the sound was not in the silent film but was probably provided in many of the nickelodeons by external means. One has only to think of the sequence of alternate scenes in THE MILL GIRL, for example, in which the hero hears the attackers outside his window. Another example may be found in Edwin S. Porter's THE TRAINER'S DAUGHTER; OR, A RACE FOR LOVE (Edison, November 1907), in which a shot that shows a man blowing the horn to start the race, enclosed in a round matte, is cut into the middle of the shot in the stables where the characters react to hearing the horn. A Vitagraph production of May 1910, CONVICT NO. 796, directed by Van Dyke Brooke, uses the sound of a pure young woman's singing to motivate alternate cutting. An escaped convict in the adjacent room holds a knife ready to murder the judge, her father, who had sent him away; through alternate editing we see the convict's hand stayed by her voice.

The kind of alternate editing that compared images in order to contrast them came into use at the same time. According to Kristin Thompson, it was much more frequent in this early period than it would be when the classical cinema systems were established.[32] This is logical because, as we can see from the films themselves, it is a particularly apt narrative system for making moral statements, and the years from 1907 to 1915 were precisely the time when moral uplift was in demand. (Subsequently, it was not classical cinema that would take up this kind of editing, but Soviet cinema of the twenties, where it would be found useful for expressing another ideology.) A CORNER IN WHEAT (December 1909), for example, Griffith's most famous film of social comment, uses alternate scenes to contrast the harsh life of the farmers and the poor, who depend on the price of bread, with the exotic luxury indulged in by the wheat speculator. The characters never meet, although a direct cause-and-effect relationship exists among them. Kalem's A LAD FROM OLD IRELAND (November 1910), directed by Sidney Olcott, similarly contrasts the successful life of the Irish boy in America with the poverty of the loved ones he has almost forgotten back in Ireland. Here the use is mixed, as the characters are more directly related, and eventually they do meet, but the moral lesson of the contrast remains the dominant element.

Aside from these special uses of editing, which I would call "ideological editing," alternate scenes became a standard way of narrating a story, of ending a scene, of eliding time between events, and so forth. Audiences must have been accustomed to the technique by the time of Bison's THE EMPTY WATER KEG (February 1912), directed by Thomas Ince. Here, two threads of a story are told in alternate scenes with no link between them until very late in the film: one thread follows a discouraged prospector as he searches the desert for gold as a last resort, only to find it too late and die of thirst, while the other presents a romance between a cowboy and his sweetheart. It is only in the last quarter or so of the film that the lovers, who are out riding, look through their binoculars to see, in a circle matted shot, the dying prospector. The two threads are brought together in time for the man to give the lovers the location of his discovery, and they become rich. No particular moral lesson is evident in this use of alternate scenes. By 1912, the construction had become an ordinary way to tell a story.

Ideological editing: the rich life of the Wheat King is contrasted to the lot of the poor who cannot afford bread. A CORNER IN WHEAT (Biograph, 1909), directed by D. W. Griffith.

5

General Flimco
and the Pushcart Peddlers

> The unsteadiness of the pictures sent out by an American independent
> manufacturer who makes a specialty of depicting Western scenes in the
> wild woods of New Jersey prompted us to ask him what camera he was
> using. He replied that it was a 'Billiken.' American independent manufac-
> turers are no doubt handicapped in choice of apparatus, but we certainly
> can recommend the 'Billiken' for reproducing unsteady pictures.
>
> —*Moving Picture World,* 19 March 1910, p. 421[1]

*T*he Motion Picture Patents Company had everything sewn up at the beginning
of 1909. It took the best part of the year for the independents to get organized
and gain strength, but the movement was in existence from that day in early January
when William Swanson, president of the Film Service Association, found himself
without power to negotiate anything with the united producers. He was the first of
the exchange men to leave and declare himself independent. By 20 February there
was already an exchange named the Anti-Trust Film Company of Chicago. That city
was to be the hotbed of the independent movement. R. G. Bachman of the 20th
Century Optiscope Company in Kansas City announced his defection on the 3rd of
April with the advertisement "Bust the Trust—Go Independent."[2]

Great Northern, founded in January 1908 as the U.S. representative of Nordisk in
Denmark and the one manufacturer of any strength on the American market outside
the Patents Company group, immediately protected its position by instituting suit
against Biograph and promising its own customers protection against lawsuits insti-
gated by the Motion Picture Patents Company. The *Moving Picture World* defined
the independents at the time of the founding of the Patents Company (the end of
1908) as Great Northern, Film Import and Trading Company, Cameraphone, "and
others." In fact, the "others" were then all but nonexistent. Cameraphone, one of the
early attempts at a synchronized sound system, would not last a year. Import and
Trading, an importer of foreign films, held on for about a year, trying to dominate the
independent market. Also left out of consideration when the Patents Company agreements were signed at the end of the year were foreign producers or agents who had
been in the American market as recently as July 1908: Cines; Williamson; Williams,
Brown and Earle as agents for Cricks & Martin, Hepworth, Paul and Graphic; Lux;
Raleigh & Roberts; Aquila; Walturdaw; and Carlo Rosi. The last five had all been
represented by Kleine, and most of the others had been Biograph licensees.[3]

There was keen competition among independent importers to sign up the foreign producers who had been left out in the cold. John J. Murdock, a vaudeville magnate who wanted to ensure a continued source of supply for his chain of vaudeville theaters, quickly organized the International Projecting and Producing Company and got to the foreign producers just ahead of I. W. Ullman of Film Import and Trading. Murdock announced big plans for motion-picture production and manufacture of cameras as well.[4]

Meanwhile, the U.S. exchanges had to decide to sign up with the Patents Company and be licensed or risk going out of business altogether because they could not count on a steady source of supply, even if they escaped legal action. Carl Laemmle, owner of a big chain of exchanges and the future leader of the independents, actually joined the licensed exchanges at the beginning, only to desert them by 17 April of the same year. However, there were already some exchanges ready to battle it out, and on 11 January, they banded together in the Independent Film Protective Renters Association. With almost no ammunition, they promptly declared war on the Motion Picture Patents Company.[5]

At a meeting in Chicago on 26 January, members of the new group decided that they would sell prints instead of leasing them, that they would challenge the Trust in court, and that they would begin to manufacture the Bianchi camera. The Bianchi was the invention of Joseph T. Bianchi, former head of recording at the Columbia Phonograph Company, the old Edison Company rival. One of several cameras designed to get around the Edison patents, it featured continuous rather than intermittent movement. As such, it permitted the Columbia Phonograph Company to issue "licenses" to use it, in imitation of the Patents Company.[6]

Although the Bianchi camera could not give a reliable and steady picture, it served as an excellent smokescreen while illegal cameras continued to be employed. In April 1910, "rumor having alleged that the Bianchi camera in use at the Powers works is not satisfactory," Joseph Bianchi and studio executives were able to mislead "experts" from the *Moving Picture World*, who went to inspect its qualifications on the premises of the Powers Company, and again at the Thanhouser Company. Thomas Bedding of the *World*, who fancied himself knowledgeable about photography on the basis of his previous experience in England (he had come to America around 1906 or 1907), was allowed to examine the camera and put it to use. At both studios, test films were made, developed, and projected during the visit, and the verdict was that the camera worked just fine. "It didn't infringe," the cameraman Arthur Miller said much later on, "but neither did it produce a satisfactory picture. Like the rest of the experimental cameras, the picture it produced jumped all over the screen."[7]

Even if the independents had had a satisfactory camera, until raw stock could be obtained and regular production started, their exchanges were going to be entirely dependent on foreign imports. Eastman Kodak stock was supposed to be the exclusive property of the licensed producers. By buying "under the counter" and highjacking Eastman's shipments abroad, a token supply of stock could be obtained, but this was expensive and unreliable. The problem was resolved by September 1909, when a steady source of supply of raw stock was assured by Jules Brulatour, agent for the French manufacturer Lumière Frères, who signed up the independent producers for Lumière's stock.[8]

The Trust had yet another weapon up its sleeve. In the spring of 1909 Eastman Kodak came up with a noninflammable film stock, known in the trade as "N.I." stock.

Nitrate film stock, in use until the early fifties, is highly inflammable and was the cause of a number of disastrous or near-disastrous fires in the early days. Indeed, the Patents Company had made fire safety an issue in its campaign to overcome opposition to the nickelodeons (and to film exchanges, where the large quantities of nitrate film were a particular hazard). Since the independents were not allowed to purchase Eastman stock, whether N.I. or nitrate—or at least not to purchase it openly—their films would not be as safe as those of the licensed companies. Newark, New Jersey, ruled that only N.I. film could be shown there after 11 January 1910. The Patents Company, whose hand was very possibly behind that regulation, announced that all their films were being issued on N.I. stock. Even the independent producer Great Northern promised the same, since as a European manufacturer, they could buy Eastman stock at home.

Then the complaints started to come in from the exchanges and the exhibitors. First, the N.I. stock required a special cement. Second, the early releases of this stock were thicker than nitrate, and the film rolls would not fit on the normal-size reel and go into the magazine on the projector. Third, and much more important, it didn't last: it quickly became dry and brittle; splices parted, and perforations broke easily. The problem lay in the plasticizers used to make the film pliable, which evaporated too rapidly. Eastman's research department worked on this problem for many years, but it was not to be solved in our period. Lumière Frères retaliated in October 1909 by announcing its own N.I. stock but presumably encountered the same problems; little more was heard about it. The Patents Company, meanwhile, had made such an issue of safety that when they were forced to give up the N.I. stock after all, they had to try to notify everyone concerned that they were once again dealing with a highly inflammable product but at the same time avoid publicity that would alarm fire officials and the general public.[9]

It was essential to the independents that the supply of raw stock as well as the processed films could be imported at reasonable cost. The licensed companies, with the possible exception of Pathé and Kleine, wanted to see the duty on foreign imports raised, while the independents wanted it abolished or at least left as is. John J. Murdock of the International Producing and Projecting Company had spent the summer of 1909 in Washington, D.C., fighting the Aldrich tariff bill, and the victory he won there also gained him temporary leadership of the independent group. At the same time it made him a hero to the European manufacturers, who wanted to release films in the lucrative American market. In 1910 Pathé and Kleine managed to get processed films classified as photographs by the customs court in Washington, so that they could be imported at a lesser duty than raw stock. This decision was later reversed and motion pictures were declared to be dramatic works; on 24 August 1912, an amendment to the copyright law referred to them for the first time as motion pictures distinct in themselves.[10]

The Film Renters Protective Association emerged from a meeting held on 11 September 1909 in William Swanson's Chicago office as the National Independent Moving Picture Alliance, with John J. Murdock as president, Adam Kessel of the Empire Exchange as treasurer, William Swanson as secretary, and Ingvald Oes of Great Northern as part of the executive committee. At this juncture thirty-nine exchanges were represented in the Alliance, along with ten producers and importers, and five manufacturers of cameras and projectors.[11]

Murdock's good work in Washington may have made him president of the Alliance, but it also meant neglect of his own business. While he spent the summer in the nation's capitol, I. W. Ullman of Film Import and Trading (FITC) went to Europe and stole away Murdock's best suppliers. Within hours of the founding of the Alliance, Murdock left for Europe to mend his relations with foreign producers, but his company never recovered. Ullman had signed up Raleigh & Roberts of Paris, who were agents for a large number of European producers. Film Import and Trading announced that there would be simultaneous release dates on both sides of the Atlantic; films were to be shipped on standing order to the exchanges, and all prints would have FITC's imprint along the edge. It may not have made Murdock feel any better, but FITC did not hold on long either. By the end of 1909, other independents had managed to sign up directly with individual producers, such as Ambrosio and Itala in Italy, bypassing the Roberts & Raleigh agreements.[12]

Before we leave J. J. Murdock, however, it is interesting to note his adherence to the most modern of American efficiency systems for inventory control, orders and shipping. He was quite proud of having hired an expert from Sears and Roebuck, the best in mail-order business, to establish the system used by the International Producing and Projecting Company.[13]

By autumn 1909, the beginnings of independent American film production were well in place. Many a production company was founded and promptly failed, but the following survived long enough to make their mark:

- David Horsley had been making films in Bayonne, New Jersey, since 1907, but his was one of those companies so insignificant that the Trust decided not to take it in. Horsley survived despite being a constant target of the Trust lawyers. He changed the company name from Horsley Manufacturing Company to the Centaur Film Manufacturing Company in 1908, and issued the first release under this name, A COWBOY ESCAPADE, on 19 September 1908. A little more than a year later, Horsley also founded the Nestor Company; the first Nestor release was THE NEMESIS, on 6 January 1910.[14]

- Fred Balshofer, after an apprenticeship with the Lubin Company in Philadelphia, started the short-lived Crescent Film Company in New York in 1908. By the end of the year it was out of business—driven out by the Edison lawyers, according to Balshofer's memoirs. Balshofer then joined with Adam Kessel and Charles Baumann of the Empire Film Exchange to form the New York Motion Picture Company, trademark "Bison," in early 1909. The New York Motion Picture Company's first release, in May 1909, was called DISINHERITED SON'S LOYALTY. This company was an important one in the independents' war against the Trust and against each other. Its most famous director was Thomas Ince, who went there at the end of 1911.[15]

- Pat Powers' production company, the Powers Company of Mount Vernon, New York, completed its first film, A CHANGE OF COMPLEXION, in October 1909.

- The same week, Carl Laemmle's production company, the IMP, released its first production, HIAWATHA, directed by William Ranous. Initiating a practice that other independents would follow, the IMP lured Ranous away from Vitagraph, a licensed company. The initials IMP stood for Independent Moving Picture Company—which was the forerunner of Universal—but the full name was seldom used.[16]

David Horsley began making movies at 900 Broadway, Bayonne, New Jersey, in 1907.

Other new companies announced that year included Powhattan, the Carson Company, Columbia Film Company, the Western Multiscope Company of Salt Lake City, the United States Film Manufacturing Company of Cincinnati, Actophone (run by Mark Dintenfass, who had been associated with the now-defunct Cameraphone), Cinephone (another unsuccessful sound system using the Victor talking machine, marketed by FITC), Phoenix, Pantograph, Travergraph, Brinkmeier, Exclusive American Film Company, and World Film Manufacturing Company of Portland, Oregon. Probably this is not a complete list, but in any case they did not stay around all that long. Begun by independent exchange men or get-rich-quick schemers and dreamers, and harassed by the Patents Company, they soon folded. The individuals involved in them, however, often reappeared, associated with yet another company. By November 1909, independent exchanges could get an American-made reel a week from the Carson Company, Columbia Film Company, IMP, New York Motion Picture Company, Phoenix, the Powers Company, and World. Since seven new reels a week was not enough for most exhibitors, the rest of the program had to be made up from foreign imports.[17]

By the end of the year, the New York Motion Picture Company had contracted directly with two Italian producers, Ambrosio and Itala (ignoring Film Import and Trading's claim to exclusive contract through Raleigh & Roberts), and on 10 January 1910 began a regular release schedule of four reels a week—two of them their own production (under the Bison trademark), one from Itala, and one from Ambrosio. That gave the New York Motion Picture Company as solid an output as any of the licensed companies.[18]

At the meetings of the Alliance that November and December, the independents began to formulate distribution systems similar to those of the licensed group. They regulated release days, set a uniform selling price of eleven cents a foot, with discounts for return of old reels, and ruled that no film was to be sold at a lower price for thirty days. Throughout the period when they were trying to get established, the independents followed the practices of the licensed group rather than break new ground. An organized industry was just as essential to the independents, if they were to expand and grow.

The major business of those meetings of independents, however, was the never-ending legal battle. The feisty Carl Laemmle now began to take a lead in the fight, with the help of Robert Cochrane, a former advertising man whom he had hired to do publicity for his production firm, IMP. Laemmle advised the trade with some glee that one of the licensed manufacturers was selling to three independent exchanges at cut-rate prices. He may have been responsible as well for the stories about how easy it was for unlicensed exhibitors to show licensed films. It was said that the rules of the Patents Company were just a joke: an exhibitor would send his operator to the exchange for his daily supply of, say, three reels, and the operator then continued on to the independent exchange, trading one licensed for one unlicensed and reversing the trade the following morning.[19]

Many new production companies began in 1910. Early in the year, the Thanhouser Company established a high-class independent firm in New Rochelle. The first release, titled THE ACTOR'S CHILDREN, was ready on 15 March. Edwin Thanhouser had been a theater owner, manager, and director of his own stock company. He had applied for a license to the Patents Company but was refused. Deciding to go ahead anyway, he ordered his Bianchi camera, though he undoubtedly had another camera for daily use, and set out to make quality films with professional stage actors. The achievements of this company were more rapid than those thrown together by the frustrated exchange men to get around the Patents Company restrictions. Thanhouser's production of THE WINTER'S TALE was hailed as "The Thanhouser Triumph," and "after only two months in business." Edwin Thanhouser committed himself to the same degree of uplift and high quality as any member of the Trust, and they may well have regretted later that they did not take him in.[20]

In June 1910 there was a barrage of first films from new firms, though of little lasting importance. Nearly all of them were founded by independent exchange men: Electragraff in Philadelphia, founded by George B. Graff, released A MESSAGE FROM THE EAST; Motograph in Baltimore, founded by Harry Raver, released A CHILD OF THE REGIMENT. Atlas' first release was THE OUTLAW'S REDEMPTION on 8 June. The Yankee Film Company of New York, founded by William Steiner, first released some films showing Jack Jeffries on his ranch, in anticipation of the great 4 July fight. These were followed by Capitol Films of Washington, D.C., on 18 June with THE TURN OF THE TIDE, and Dandy Films, which on 15 June announced the release of the very same film as that listed by Electragraff, A MESSAGE FROM THE EAST. Both Capitol and Dandy were represented by A. G. Whyte of the Electragraff Company of New York and Chicago, who also organized Whyte Films about this time. In other words, all these new companies were not necessarily separate organizations, but it was to the advantage of film exchanges to appear to have a large source of supply. Owl Films announced its beginnings the same month; this was one of Adam Kessel's companies, with its studio on West Twenty-third Street in New York. The Defender Film

Company released its first film, called RUSSIA, THE LAND OF OPPRESSION, on 10 June. Defender was founded by William Swanson (the first exchange man to walk out on the Patents Company), Joseph Engel, and Edwin S. Porter, who had left the Edison Company. At Edison, Frank Dyer had brought in his friend Horace Plimpton as an efficiency expert, to head Edison production.[21]

In July, Mark Dintenfass, who had taken over the remains of Cameraphone and turned it into Actophone in the previous year, pursued by the Patents Company lawyers and keeping just one step ahead of a jail sentence, started the Champion Film Company and released its first film, THE ABERNATHY KIDS TO THE RESCUE. The Dramagraph Company of Fort Lee began with BEYOND ENDURANCE, released on 4 August.[22] In September the Columbia Film Company reintroduced itself after "our period of silence" with RIP VAN WINKLE, slated to appear on 1 October. The Revier Motion Picture Company set up in Salt Lake City, with a glass studio, a laboratory, and artists "brought over from France."[23]

In the autumn of 1910, the independents really began to swing into action, raiding enemy territory for their top talent. IMP had shown the way by stealing Florence Lawrence from Biograph in 1909 and Mary Pickford in 1910. Reliance Pictures, founded by the exchange men Charles Baumann and Adam Kessel, was the lead-off in the fall of 1910 with a mass of actors stolen from Biograph's list: Marion Leonard, James Kirkwood, Arthur Johnson, Henry B. Walthall, Anthony O'Sullivan, and Gertrude Robinson, together with Biograph scenarist Stanner E. V. Taylor. The first Reliance release, ready on 22 October, was THE GRAY OF THE DAWN, directed by Eugene Sanger and filmed by Max Schneider. This was the birth of the studio that would capture the great David Wark Griffith himself when he finally left Biograph three years later.[24]

The American Film Company, founded by exchange men John Freuler and Samuel Hutchinson, stole more than actors from Essanay in Chicago: they came close to stealing the whole studio. They took Thomas Ricketts as director of dramas, Sam Morris as director of comedies, and Frank Beal as director of Westerns. The as yet little-known Allan Dewan was taken as the scenarist; before long, he was Allan Dwan, the star director of the company. Seven actors went along, including the star J. Warren Kerrigan. Numerous technicians were also hired away. Just about all that American left for Essanay was Broncho Billy Anderson and his company way out West. George K. Spoor of Essanay had to ask "the *World* to deny the canard that the sudden departure of several Essanay employees and the summary dismissal of others had in any way crippled the factory resources." Spoor said it was only "a pruning of dead wood." But he had to hire an entirely new stock company and put Essanay production in the hands of Harry McCrea Webster, a former stage director. American's first release was ROMANTIC REDSKINS, on 14 November 1910.[25]

The third company to begin business that fall was Solax, with A CHILD'S SACRIFICE, as its first release. Solax announced that the new company was made up of Gaumont brains but had no Gaumont association. The Gaumont plant, a laboratory for printing in Flushing, was brought by its former manager, Herbert Blaché, together with American and Canadian rights to the sound system, Gaumont's Chronophone. Herbert Blaché was to be the presiding spirit, George A. Magie the business manager, "but chiefest and most valuable of all assets of the new company is the artistic personality of Mme. Blaché," the former Alice Guy, who had been responsible for much of the Gaumont production back in its early days in France.

Alice Guy Blaché, Herbert Blaché, and their daughter Simone, supervising the construction of the Solax studio in Fort Lee, New Jersey, in 1910.

Gaumont of Paris continued to be distributed by George Kleine of the licensed side, but Gaumont of New York was turned into Solax, an independent firm. By the end of 1911, Gaumont of Paris had gone independent on the American market, and Herbert Blaché became president of the American branch, while Alice Guy assumed the presidency of Solax in addition to her production duties.[26]

But let us return to April 1910, to examine the organization of the Motion Picture Distributing and Sales Company. The Sales Company, as it was soon known, began as the attempt of Carl Laemmle, Adam Kessel, and Charles Baumann, representing IMP and the New York Motion Picture Company, to take over the marketing of all the independent production. Unlike the Alliance, to which most of the independent exchanges belonged, which was only a trade organization, the Sales Company was a commercial firm that would contract with the production companies for their product and service the exchanges. The other independent producers, fighting for power with Laemmle and his friends, resisted joining the Sales Company at first, and aligned themselves instead with a short-lived organization called the Independent Manufacturers and Importers Association. But this maneuver succeeded only in splitting the field; neither side commanded a sufficient supply to be able to service the larger exchanges on its own. Then the Sales Company was reorganized as a cooperative venture that would serve all the producers equally, and it took over most of the independent field.[27]

In May 1910 a *World* editorial speculated whether the Sales Company was a legal combine or was contravening the Sherman Anti-Trust Act, but there was no way the independents were going to be able to organize themselves into one powerful unit as the licensed producers had done. Their competitive drive was too great. Yet another alignment, called the National Film Manufacturing and Leasing, Inc., organized in October 1910, gave some opposition to the Sales Company, taking in, by the following April, some ten very small companies in the United States and abroad: Revier, Royal, Columbia, Cines, United, Film de Art [sic], Colonial, Arrowhead, Capital, and Cameo. "Is the independent market controlled by a trust too? . . . Don't be bamboozled by the cry of independence and business freedom," cautioned a Revier Film advertisement.[28]

Nevertheless, the Sales Company gathered together an uneasy combination of all the production firms of importance on the independent market for a couple of years. In June 1910, the independents were distributing twenty-one reels a week, compared to the licensed companies' thirty. Twenty-one reels a week was the need of the average exhibitor, who used three reels for a show and changed it daily. It was estimated that the independents now served about three thousand theaters, while the licensed companies served about seven thousand. By January 1911, the Sales Company claimed that "in the year 1910 we succeeded in splitting the business of the country between the trust and ourselves on a 50 percent basis." This is undoubtedly an exaggeration, but the combined strength of the independents now provided solid competition for the Patents Company group. The Sales Company held together until the spring of 1912, when new alignments began to shape the future.[29]

Meanwhile, the real contravener of the Sherman Act, Jeremiah J. Kennedy, was quietly arranging to buy up all the licensed exchanges under the umbrella of the General Film Company. General Film was founded at the same time as the Sales Company, although it had been in the organizational stages (and in the rumor mill) for six months or more. Officially, it began operations on 18 April 1910 with a slate of officers that included Jeremiah J. Kennedy as president, George Kleine as vice-president, Jacques A. Berst of Pathé as treasurer, and William Pelzer as secretary. In a policy statement released in June, the General Film Company, or "General Flimco," as Cochrane immediately started calling it in the great Laemmle anti-Trust advertisements, announced that it was "organized to conduct a film renting business and has obtained exchange licenses from the Motion Picture Patents Company." By its charter, it was not to be permitted to own theaters or be an exhibitor. It had already acquired four exchanges from the Kleine enterprises, one from Lubin, and the Frank Howard exchange in Boston. The position of the federal government, when it brought suit on 16 August 1912, was that at this time the defendants "set out to monopolize the business of all the rental exchanges in the United States."[30]

Where did they get the money to buy up all the licensed exchanges? In fact, it did not cost them an enormous amount. Frank Howard, the first to sell, got a better price than many who came after. He sold for $80,000 plus $30,000 in preferred stock, at a time when he said that his annual profits were about $25,000. But the $80,000 was to be paid off over a five-year period, so it was not much cash up front. Of course, the Patents Company producers who owned their own exchanges were obliged to sell them to General Film. The American Vitagraph Exchange, managed by "Pop" Rock, was one of the pioneers of the business, established well before the nickelodeon era; it was now combined with a Kleine exchange and became a General Film exchange. Rock had to find another occupation, but just then he had the filming of the Johnson–Jeffries Fourth of July fight to arrange on behalf of the Trust companies, so he was able to keep busy.

The outside exchanges licensed by the Patents Company had little choice in deciding whether to sell, because their licenses could be easily canceled—immediately for breaking any of the Patents Company rules, or on fourteen days' notice for no cause at all. (The fourteen-day clause was the one that William Fox fought bitterly, and lost, back when the Patents Company first presented itself to the FSA exchanges.) The executives of the Patents Company and General Film later testified under oath that there was no collusion between the two companies, but as the executives were generally the same individuals, this is rather difficult to believe. When the owner of a licensed exchange proved cooperative, he could stay on as a hired employee of General Film.[31]

As one licensed exhibitor described what was going on that summer:

> I went to my exchange the other day and found quite a change. The routine was going on as usual, but the man who had owned the place was only the manager. It seemed to me that the change was made as quickly and quietly as the turning of a pancake on a griddle. Those people certainly have the dope (*Moving Picture World*, 27 August 1910, p. 459).

By the end of 1911, General Film owned every licensed exchange in the country with the sole exception of the Greater New York Film Exchange, owned by none other than William Fox, the fighter. If Kennedy had left him alone, Fox would not have ended up challenging him in court and the government might not have gone to court against the Motion Picture Patents Company. But General Film could not raise prices in the New York area as long as Fox was there providing competition in the licensed market. In September 1911, Kennedy set out to buy the Greater New York Film Exchange, but he and Fox did not agree on a price. Fox's license was canceled, and he agreed to sell, but sly Fox that he was, he asked for the license to be reinstated so that it would be a going film exchange when sold. He then refused to sell and got another cancellation, together with a refusal from Biograph to supply a contracted film shipment. At that point Fox sent for his lawyers. The litigation took years and was still unresolved when Fox was testifying on behalf of the government's suit against the Patents Company. Meanwhile the Greater New York Film Exchange was free to carry on business as usual, distributing licensed films.[32]

All the Motion Picture Patents Company manufacturers withdrew their advertisements from the *Moving Picture World* in October 1910. Just how the editors of this important trade periodical managed to offend the Trust, or more likely, I think, its president, Jeremiah J. Kennedy, is not clear, but the companies did not return their advertising to the *World* until the summer of 1911. Biograph was among the last to come back and a few months later withdrew its advertising again for another year or more. The specific cause may never be known, but the events illustrated Kennedy's irascible nature. His testimony during the trial of the government versus the Patents Company gives evidence of a hasty temper. One of the exchange men who negotiated a sale of his exchange to General Film talked to the press afterward expressing some dissatisfaction with the price, and Kennedy's story was that he immediately called off the deal, not even waiting to find out if the man had been quoted correctly. His reason for telling the story was to show that no one was forced to sell to General Film, but it also reveals something of an unreasonable disposition. As for the withdrawal of Trust advertising in October 1910, this might have been due to the *World*'s having published in the previous issue a brief article about the great trustbuster himself, Theodore Roosevelt, describing his interest in film and ending up with the declaration that "the owner of a motion picture theater in this land of freedom is not free to buy in an open market; is not free to show what pictures he likes."[33]

However the defection came about, after it happened, the trade periodical, which had always tried to represent all viewpoints of the field and had given support to the Trust, began open opposition to it in the editorial columns of Thomas Bedding.

The *World* also published some letters of complaint from exhibitors. In Athens, Georgia, far from the exchanges, an exhibitor wrote, "Am now powerless to secure a desirable service that will please . . . my patrons." He complained he did not even know what film he would be getting until the train arrived twenty-five minutes before his theater opened. If he were to turn independent, he said, he would "receive a service of stories without plots, and generally unintelligible to the average patron."[34]

Thomas Bedding, "Lux Graphicus" of the *Moving Picture World*, suffered an attack of acute depression at the end of 1910. He thought the business was going down, the country was going crazy about vaudeville, and picture quality was poor. With a careless disregard for the only advertisers the *World* had left at that moment, Bedding complained that the independents did not have the brains to make good pictures: "How can an ex-huckster, ex-bellboy, ex-tailor, ex-advertising man, ex-bookmaker know anything about picture quality? Hands that would be more properly employed with a push cart on the lower East Side are responsible for directing stage plays and making pictures of them."[35]

On 14 February 1911, Eastman Kodak's agreement with the Patents Company was amended to permit Eastman to sell to independent producers, and the independents rushed to get their hands on Eastman stock. Mark Dintenfass of Champion Film announced the signing of a contract to use Eastman stock exclusively. A reviewer of IMP's AT SWORD'S POINT noted, "The change in the film used by the firm is shown in the sharpness of the pictures and the stereoscopic relief which characterizes their appearance on the screen."[36]

The tide of never-ending lawsuits began to turn a bit in favor of the independents in this year. In June, the preliminary injunctions against various independent companies for using infringing cameras were dissolved, and the beater-type camera was declared noninfringing. These were not really significant decisions, in the sense that the beater-type camera had not proved successful anyway, but they enabled the independents to gain courage and perhaps to see that it was only a matter of time. When the Patents Company began a new round of suits on the Pross Shutter and Latham Loop patents in August, the Sales Company offered to defend any exhibitor in such suits, which it dismissed as just a bluff. The end to persecution came on 24 August 1912 when Judge Learned Hand, ruling in the case of the Motion Picture Patents Company versus IMP in the U.S. Circuit Court, overthrew the Latham loop patent. This was a very important victory for the independents. Free to use openly the best cameras they could buy and guaranteed the same reliable supply of raw stock as the licensed companies, they could now compete on an equal basis. Like the licensed companies when the Patents Company was formed in 1909, the independent producers now had confidence enough to expand their facilities and enlarge their production. Although the U.S. government filed against the Patents Company at the end of 1912, it was too late for the lawsuit to have much impact on the

independents because the Trust had already reached the end of its power to monopolize the trade.[37]

The Patents Company and General Film's policies of trying to control, regulate,
and uplift industry practices contributed to the eventual demise of the Trust. The
same system that enabled the licensed companies to bring stability into a chaotic
business eventually proved a stranglehold to growth and change. By eliminating and
combining licensed exchanges and by arranging that time should not be wasted
shipping prints to faraway theaters, copies of films were used efficiently and fewer
were needed to serve the exhibitors. The problem with this efficiency method was
that the only way for the licensed producers to increase their profits was to be able
to sell more copies to the exchanges, since they were limited in the number of
subjects and reels they could produce and the price they could charge. Now, fewer
copies were needed, and producers found it more difficult to increase profits.

In Boston, late in 1910, General Film tried to rationalize exhibition practices by
ruling that exhibitors could have only biweekly changes of films and could choose
only two kinds of service, all new films or all old films. Competition heated up. The
Olympic Theater on Bowdoin Square, owned by the Lasky Brothers, reduced its
admission price to five cents at the same time that it began to offer four reels of film,
all first-run, plus one vaudeville act and one illustrated song.[38]

By attempting to control exhibitor practices in various cities, General Film sought
to protect exhibitors against the spiraling competition of more and more films for the
same low admission price. In Los Angeles in the spring of 1911, licensed exhibitors
had to confine their programs to three reels for the five-cent houses and four reels for
the ten-cent houses. But when the licensed exhibitors tried to get the independents
to go along with this policy, they refused, and pressing their advantage, they made
inroads into the licensed business. The general practice was to increase the length of
the program, thereby preparing the way for audience acceptance of the feature-
length film, which arrived a couple of years later. Five, six, or seven reels for a nickel
became a common practice in many cities.[39]

General Film exchanges scheduled everything in advance, buying their film supply on standing order from the licensed producers. On Mondays they bought a set
number of copies of releases from Pathé, Selig, Biograph, Gaumont, and Vitagraph.
On Wednesdays, it was the turn of Kalem, Edison, and so on. An exhibitor with a
regular service who read a trade periodical would know what films to expect in
sufficient time to advertise them, although there was little or no choice, especially if
the exhibitor lived far from the large cities. There was a daily change of program in
most places, and as a rule no film that was especially popular could be held over,
because it was due somewhere else. General Film did not usually allow for extraordinarily popular films by buying extra copies. Since an expensive production sold for
the same price as the cheapest, the incentive was lacking, for both exhibitor and
producer, to improve. It was difficult to prevent first-class houses in the same part of
town, all wanting first-day release service, from showing the same film on the same
day, after which it would disappear from that neighborhood. The exchange could, of
course, protect a theater by declining to serve others in that area with first-day
release, but that would mean turning away its own most profitable business.[40]

By March 1911 it was noticed that exhibitors in Boston had stopped bothering to
renew the license when it expired, although they continued to show the films. More
and more, exhibitors ignored the rules and combined licensed and unlicensed films

on their programs. The competition of the independents was making it difficult for General Film's exchanges to enforce the regulations, since they risked losing a customer. If the rules of General Film were onerous, an exhibitor could now easily turn to an independent exchange. Nonetheless, that did not stop the Patents Company from trying to tighten up the rules in order to control the situation. At first the rules about the return of used films simply specified the footage that must be returned, allowing 10 percent or later 20 percent, for footage lost or destroyed in use. In 1911 the rules were changed so that films had to be returned to their own producers; that is, worn Biograph films were to be returned to Biograph. In 1912, another rule stipulated that exchanges must return the precise film title that was purchased and on a specific schedule. The tightening up of these requirements signals the fact that films were slipping out to independent exhibitors, and the Trust could not stop it.[41]

In August 1911, W. Stephen Bush noted in the *Moving Picture World* that control of the industry had passed from the hands of the exhibitors to the manufacturers. At this point, far too late to recapture their former position of dominance, the exhibitors managed to get together for the first time in a national organization, the Moving Picture League of America, formed in Cleveland on 1–3 August 1911, with M. Neff of the Ohio Exhibitors' League as president. The policy of the new national league was "self-protection, to raise the standard of moving picture films, to secure recognition of the National Censor Board, the regulation of prices for film service, to prevent breaches of contract, . . . regulate insurance rates, . . . protection against adverse legislation." By uniting, they might still be able to affect the practices of film exchanges, but they did not even mention any effort to negotiate with producers.[42]

At the end of this year, it was remarked that American films were beginning to dominate the world market. "It was said" that 80 percent were now furnished by American manufacturers. The basis of this statistic was not given, and the figure seems high for 1911. However, American films did far outnumber foreign films on the domestic market by this time. By the end of 1912, national production accounted for well over 80 percent of the American market, at least according to the number of film titles released (not copies sold). On the same basis, independent films now accounted for more than half of the domestic production, and the licensed films kept a slight edge only with the addition of their foreign-made product.[43]

6

Acting: The Camera's Closer View

Why, you can see them thinking."
—A spectator's comment on Biograph's THE WAY OF MAN,
in *Moving Picture World*, 3 July 1909, p. 11

*I*n 1908, the most important quality for film acting was clarity. The actors in demand were those who could tell the story with gestures, clearly visible at stage distance. It was then still fashionable to admire French filmmaking, and as Rollin Summers explained, the French were considered better film actors because

> [They] seem natural adepts at pantomime. An arch of the eyebrow, a shrug of the shoulders, a gesture of the hands, all these are aids in expression to them. The American relies in his daily life, more entirely, upon his words (*Moving Picture World*, 19 September 1908, p. 211).

In another issue, the *Moving Picture World* asked rhetorically:

> What is it in the films of some foreign manufacturers that makes them in such demand in this country? . . . The faculty of bringing out in pantomime the salient points of a story (17 October 1908, p. 295).

The Edison Company hired the celebrated pantomimist Mlle. Pilar Moran to make some films for them, but soon discovered that this was not what was wanted for the moving picture. Stage pantomime, with its stylized gestures and artistic traditions, was not going to be clearly understandable to the new audience, and in addition, it conflicted with the precepts of realism.[1]

The traditional gestures of the melodramatic stage lingered longer. Most of the actors and actresses, and their directors, were drawn to the film industry from the road shows, the barn-storming melodramas. Melodrama style was what they knew, and audiences across the country were familiar with it too. Given the distance of the actors from the camera in 1907 and 1908, stereotyped and familiar gestures made the simple stories clear. Gene Gauntier, leading woman for Kalem, remembered that in 1907:

> All points to be made, even in the foreground, must be given plenty of time; a stare must be held, a start must be violent. If the director wished certain words to register they were enunciated slowly and distinctly leaving no doubt of what they were, in the spectator's mind. . . . But one must remember that then the figures were very small ("Blazing the Trail").

Two reviewers of Biograph's AFTER MANY YEARS, writing in the same trade journal a week apart, disagreed on the quality of its acting. The first thought it poor, while the second insisted, "Anyone who sees this film cannot say that the American actor is not equal to the foreigner in pantomime." By the end of 1908 Biograph films were being praised for acting in almost every review, partly, perhaps, because critics didn't know how to identify the other components of Griffith's style that were making these films not only clear but expressive. Then the commentators began to note the change from melodramatic gesture. In THE WELCOME BURGLAR, it was pointed out, "characters act naturally, as real people."[2]

By 1910 the melodramatic style was under attack from the public as well as the critics. Such exaggeration was too disturbing to the illusion of reality; it wasn't "natural." "A Reader" wrote to the *World* to complain about excessive pantomime acting: it was better to explain in titles, if needed, and let the actors be "more natural."[3]

The replacement for the exaggerated pantomimic gestures was "facial expression." According to one reviewer:

> The most striking feature in [Pathé's MEMENTO OF THE PAST] is the facial expressions. . . . It can all be read in the two faces and is as graphic as it would be if the spoken words could be heard. . . . The action here is unusual and the control of the facial expressions is remarkable (*Moving Picture World*, 10 September 1910, p. 574).

When THE NEW MAGDALEN (Powers) arrived in late 1910, it was observed that Joseph Golden, the director, was an exponent of the facial-expression school—the Saxon (restrained/facial) as opposed to the Latin (whole body/exaggerated) acting style. The restrained style was exemplified in the acting of Pearl White: "Though she stands rigid and motionless, it is easy to read in the face of Mary Merrick that she is torn with internal emotion."[4] This positioning of Saxon versus Latin gives another clue to the reasons for the changes in style in the course of the Progressive uplift movement. Controlled emotions are approved behavior in Victorian society, the "excess" of the foreign-born immigrants from Latin countries and the films coming from such countries are to be feared, or at least found ridiculous. Naturalness is equated with restraint.

Pearl White standing "rigid and motionless" exemplifies another element of the new acting style. In 1907 producers considered it necessary to have "action, and more action." If they were called moving pictures, they must move. Now it was found that repose could be a more subtle and effective way of portraying feelings. A critic noted that it was "a peculiarity of the Biograph style" that when two women from opposite sides of the economic system meet in the "editorial-like" GOLD IS NOT ALL (March 1910), they gaze at each other "overlong"—"a trick that the Biograph players sometimes carry to an extreme," he thought. These actresses were employing the "pause," the better to emphasize the moment, the contrast that the two represented. If not well done, to be sure, it could resemble the over-obvious "stare" of an earlier time that Gene Gauntier described.[5]

The actors with D. W. Griffith led the way in this more restrained style, despite the fact that even in 1911 he was criticized for allowing his young actresses the excessive jumping that for him signified youthful exuberance. Thus, according to the *World*, the acting in Biograph's IN THE DAYS OF FORTY-NINE was "first-class all the way," but "this leading lady, capable as she is, has still the absurd habit of jumping up and down to express delight as a child of ten might jump."[6] ("This leading lady" was Dorothy West.)

Frank Woods, the *New York Dramatic Mirror*'s "Spectator," also gave credit to Biograph for the new style:

> Probably the most marked change that has taken place in the style of picture acting in the last year or two has been in the matter of tempo. . . . Generally speaking, it has given place to more deliberation. . . . One producing company, the Biograph, was a pioneer among the American producers in this reform, and its films have long been distinguished by deliberation and respose (*New York Dramatic Mirror*, 4 June 1910, p. 16).

Reviews of Biographs through the early months of 1911 continue to praise the naturalness of the acting. Louis Reeves Harrison noted the expressive qualities of eyes and lips:

> I have seen an accomplished young actress portray the vanishing of human reason so vividly that its light seemed to die out as we watched her. In another, more difficult role, she conveyed clearly the fact that she was exhibiting concealment and caution by her wistful scrutiny of a suspected husband (*Moving Picture World*, 11 February 1911, pp. 348–349).

A reviewer of IMP's THE SCARLET LETTER called the acting superb: "a play that draws as much upon facial expression and emotional work as it does upon action." The young comedienne in Pathé's THE LATEST FASHION IN SKIRTS was praised because "she is content to stand still without wringing her hands and feet, and to let the humor of the situation speak for itself. That is the very essence of successful acting before the camera."[7]

With the change of film styles, it became a rule that actors should never acknowledge the presence of the camera. The pretense of reality demanded that the spectator be hidden, a voyeur at the feast. To acknowledge his presence would be to destroy the illusion, even to embarrass him. The *Mirror*'s Frank Woods began a campaign on this subject midway through 1909:

> There is one important fault in the average pantomime acting that is being too much overlooked, viz., the tendency of nearly all players to appear

conscious of the camera. Doubtless the best players and the best directors
believe that they have overcome this fault. The good director is constant
and persistent in his instructions to his players to keep their eyes away
from the camera, and the good players try to obey the injunction. Many
of them succeed, but is the mere act of keeping the eyes off of the camera
enough? Should there not be absolute unconsciousness that the camera is
there—or rather should there not appear to be this unconsciousness ? . . .
All action must take place in such a manner that the camera takes the best
possible view of the picture, but is it not true that the nearer the players
can come to making it appear that they are unaware of the camera, the
nearer to absolute realism they will attain? . . . There are a number of
ways in which the best producers in some of their star pictures betray
what may be termed camera consciousness. A player will turn his face
toward the front in a way that he would not do were he participating in an
actual event. He does this perhaps to show his facial expression, but it is
often at the sacrifice of a natural attitude. . . . Again, the director may
display camera consciousness by the manner in which he disposes his
characters, as, for instance, when a company of soldiers is marched up and
halted, facing the camera as if to have their pictures taken (*New York
Dramatic Mirror*, 10 July 1910, pp. 15–16).

Woods was expressing a widely felt need to preserve the illusion of being present
at a real event, but it was not easy to get rid of camera consciousness. Some months
later, an anonymous correspondent in Washington, D.C., delivered a diatribe against
overdone pantomime and added that the same was true "for the actor or actress who
frankly gestures to the camera!"[8] At the same time an exhibitor wrote:

Wish you would suggest to the manufacturer that it is time to eliminate
the pointing habit. Why, oh! why is it necessary for the actor, every time
he goes forth, to stick out his arm and point the index finger in the
direction he is going? . . . It stamps the production at once as amateurish
if not ridiculous (*Moving Picture World*, 17 September 1910, p. 621).

Marion Leonard, meanwhile, having left Biograph and the direction of D. W.
Griffith, earned this complaint in 1911:

Thus we have Miss Leonard, of Reliance, compelled or allowed . . . to do
a lot of talking to the audience—looking directly at the camera and taking
the audience into her confidence. I imagine a Vitagraph girl who did it
would be fined! (C. H. Claudy, *Moving Picture World*, 10 June 1911, pp.
1300–1301).

In the beginning of 1912, reviewing the progress of the previous year, Frank
Woods suggested that the great advance in the art of acting had taken place prior to
1911:

Who can look back on the methods of picture playing three and four
years ago, without a shudder? In those days the actors were told to "step

high" in walking or running. Each player called by gesture on high heaven to witness each assertion. Talking, gesticulating, and grimacing at the camera was the constant habit (*New York Dramatic Mirror*, 31 January 1912, p. 51).

In the Famous Players version of THE COUNT OF MONTE CRISTO, directed by Edwin S. Porter late in 1913, the renowned stage actor James O'Neill looks directly at the audience and points at the wall of his cell to show how he plans to escape, as obviously as in any film of 1907. O'Neill's prestige was great, but this archaic style was definitely no longer acceptable to the film audiences. It broke the illusion that spectators were in his world. The audience couldn't feel themselves inside the film if the actors acknowledged their presence "out front."

Tom Gunning perceptively observes that toward the end of this period the avoidance of camera consciousness is pointed up in Griffith's films by the observance of a kind of reverse acknowledgment of the lens, the hiding of the most private emotions from the camera's steady gaze.[9] When Lillian Gish in THE MOTHERING HEART (Biograph, June 1913) watches from behind a tree as her young husband drives off with another woman, Gish's stricken face disappears from sight, and only her fragile little hand is seen to slide on the rough tree bark as she turns to flee back to her house. The most well-known example of these "hidden" scenes of private emotion is

Lillian Gish in THE MOTHERING HEART (Biograph, 1913), watching her husband go off with the other woman.

The "hidden emotion" shot: Henry Walthall as the soldier returning to his mother's arms in THE BIRTH OF A NATION *(Epoch, 1914) directed by D. W. Griffith.*

the return of the soldier in THE BIRTH OF A NATION (1915), where he is drawn back into the house by the arms of his unseen mother.

The call for naturalistic acting cannot be attributed entirely to differences between the stage and the film medium. There was a dichotomy in acting on the stage as well. When Sarah Bernhardt's QUEEN ELIZABETH was brought to America in 1912 by Adolph Zukor and Edwin S. Porter, it was a *succès d'estime*, a draw for the "better classes," but the common viewpoint was more in accord with the report of the following exhibitor:

> And by the way, if you run Queen Elizabeth, stop with the scene before the last, cutting out that absurd death flop into the pile of cushions placed before the throne for no other reason than to save the Bernhardt bones. It gives a comedy finish that is hurtful (*Moving Picture World*, 19 October 1912, p. 239).

If the divine Sarah's appearances in film seemed ludicrous to film audiences, it wasn't only that she didn't understand what was appropriate to the new medium. Her stage style was of the old school, larger than life, grandly eloquent, deliberately artificial and stylized.[10] Older audiences familiar with the legitimate theater were accustomed to this conception of high-style acting, but a new audience, knowing only modern film acting, didn't understand it. The Italian diva Eleanora Duse and the American star Minnie Maddern Fiske belonged to a newer school of naturalistic acting, which demanded a repose and a subdued intensity and was in keeping with the requirements of a naturalistic theatrical production style. This style was characterized in the following terms by Madame Simone, the French stage actress:

> No grand entrances because there are none in real life. No stagey exits, because they do not occur in real life. When two people talk they do not indulge in elocution, they just say the words that come to them without thinking of their stage value. When a lot of people are being entertained in a room they do not all stand about silently listening to the conversation of two people. They talk among themselves, and the buzz of subdued conversation pervades (*New York Dramatic Mirror*, 7 February 1912, p. 29).

And, added the journalist who reported Madame Simone's observations, "Persons who have studied motion picture productions realize that the principle here avowed by Madame Simone is a matter of common practice in the better examples of motion picture playing."

In 1913 Louis Reeves Harrison invented the term "intense drama" to describe a drama with depth of characterization, where, he said pointedly, the characters are not puppets.[11] The intensity Harrison was trying to identify was not entirely the result of the actors' ability to convey emotions by facial expression. Thus, Richard Griffith observed that the 1915 film THE COWARD "makes conspicuous dramatic use of pause, even of immobility, to draw the spectator close to the emotional core of the action." With regard to the acting of Charles Ray and Frank Keenan in the film, he wrote:

> The players seem to project with great intensity, but the rhythm of their performance is actually established by camera angle and by cutting, and it is these that really create the dramatic tension. The resulting seemingly involuntary revelation of unconscious passions is a form of acting unique to the film medium. "Soul-fights" was the period's phrase to describe this (*Film Notes*, ed. Eileen Bowser [New York: Museum of Modern Art, 1969], pp. 19–20).

The emphasis on facial expression led naturally to the need for a closer view of the actor, because the stage distance of nearly all filmmaking in 1907 and 1908 made it difficult to see such detail. Indeed one of the more startling experiences in looking at films from 1907 together with those from about 1912 onward is the difference in relative closeness of the camera to the actors. If one spends some time looking at the early films and then goes to a later one, it is as though the film has sprung to life, become dynamic. There are many other factors that contribute to this feeling, but the closeness, and the intimacy it creates, is one of the strongest. As a spectator in 1907 would not have had the same experience, it is necessary to struggle a bit to see such changes as they might have been seen at the time. What is to us a very small change in camera position may have seemed striking to that audience. In fact, the contemporary comments on these changes, or the memories of those who experienced them at the time, when filtered through a modern conception of a close camera position, have led to distortions or actual mistakes in the history of use of the close-up.

Although the giant close-ups of faces to which we later became accustomed are the most impressive manifestation of this intimacy, they were actually rather rare throughout this period, with the exception of just a few films. When writers in the period 1907–1912 speak of close views, this should be thought of as relative to the other shots. They are not usually speaking of close-ups, or "bust shots" as they called them when they first began to be used.[12] In 1907, for scenes of significant action, the actors were almost always placed at least as much as twelve feet away from the camera, in compositions that showed part of the floor or ground in front of their feet and the top third of the frame above their heads—what I have sometimes referred to as "stage distance." There were certain exceptions in 1907, of which I will speak in a moment.

When commentators first began to mention close views, they were probably speaking of the so-called "nine-foot" line, which came into use in 1909–1910. When this distance is combined with the camera placed at right angles to the chest level of the actor, rather than at eye level, the "empty" space over the actor's head disappears, and the actor's feet or ankles are at the frame line. Barry Salt believes that this practice began with some Vitagraph films in 1909 and was gradually adopted by most of the other companies the following year. It is really not possible, of course, to be certain about such matters, since so few films survive, but there is some evidence to suggest that other companies also introduced the practice in 1909. None of the companies used the new composition consistently, even in 1910. In any event, the closer camera position was apparent to editor Thomas Bedding of the *World* when he discussed the acting in Biograph's THE WAY OF MAN at the beginning of July 1909. He noted that the photographer "puts his camera near the subjects . . . and you see what is passing in the minds of the actors and actresses."[13]

Later in the same month, in an article entitled "The Factor of Uniformity," the closer camera position brought a complaint:

> These figures were so large that they occupied the entire perpendicular dimension of the sheet, that is, the figures that were nearest to the camera. The consequence was that the people in the theater had the idea that the film showed a story that was being enacted . . . by a race of giants and giantesses (*Moving Picture World*, 24 July 1909, p. 115).

Unfortunately we do not know what film was being complained about, but I think the reaction does show that the closer position was already being used in July 1909. The twelve-foot distance (stage distance) became known to cameramen as the "French foreground" because European filmmakers kept to it long after the closer position, known as the "American foreground," became widely accepted in the United States.

In May 1910 the *World* claimed that Thanhouser was the company with the reputation for closer views, while the *New York Dramatic Mirror* at the beginning of 1912 described Biograph as "the first company—at least in America—to introduce heroic figures in its pictures."[14] But while it is always interesting to speculate, it is of little use to look for "firsts" with so many films of the period other than Biograph unavailable for viewing.

Barry Salt suggests that the influential LA MORT DU DUC DE GUISE might have introduced the lower camera angle in America. There the camera was placed sufficiently low to give the impression of looking slightly up at the actors, as on the stage, which gave them a heroic look even though the distance remained at twelve feet. If this is indeed the source of the idea in the United States, the timing was right, because the French Film d'Art was a big event in America early in 1909. Tom Gunning thinks the *succès d'estime* of the film may have impressed itself on D. W. Griffith for this and other reasons, including its restrained acting style.[15]

In September 1909, the use of the low camera angle came in for criticism from the *World*, in the review of Biograph's THE MILLS OF THE GODS:

> The photography of this film is quite up to the standard of the Biograph studio in definition and tone values, but apparently the photographer has been sitting at the feet of Dunkoop. Some of his figures tower almost up to the ceiling in their heroic size (*Moving Picture World*, 11 September 1909, p. 345).[16]

This is an extraordinary exaggeration to our eyes, but confirms my theory that what seem to us slight changes were much more noticeable to people of that time. When Bedding of the *World* delivered a diatribe against closer views as late as 1911, it is startling to realize at the end that he is speaking not of close-ups, but only of the "nine-foot line":

> There is nothing more absurd on the part of the manufacturer, nothing which destroys the art and beauty of the scene more than showing us greatly enlarged faces of the leading actors. The manufacturer does not care if he shows us the leading lady wearing the same dress for five years. No, such details do not concern him; all that he wants is to show us how she can twist her mouth and roll her eyes. In too many cases these enlarged pictures show all the defects of the makeup; but the manufacturer does not worry at such small details. . . . Many beautiful scenes are marred by showing these enlarged figures, with the head touching the very upper part of the frame, and the feet missing (*Moving Picture World*, 11 March 1911, p. 527).

Vitagraph's AULD ROBIN GRAY, released in October 1910, used a cut from stage distance to a shot of the actors at their waist level, which left the top third of the frame "empty" above their heads. In most of the surviving films from the period, this kind of shot seems to me to be quite as frequent as those in which the heads brush the top of the frame. But once again, there was so much inconsistency of styles within films and within groups of films at this time of great changes that, combined with the fact of so many lost films, statements about who may have led a change in style are still very inconclusive—and that includes D. W. Griffith, who was to be credited in 1913 with having invented just about everything. These changes of distance and angle are slight and may occur in only one or two scenes in a film. The precise angle of the camera is difficult if not impossible to determine when the distance between camera and subject is great. Modern-day audiences are unlikely to notice them, but they were probably more striking then. In any case, they were not universal in 1910 or even 1911. Further research and the restoration of other films for viewing may make these matters more clear.

For a long time to come, the *World* continued to complain of closer shots, finding an unacceptable distortion in them. The critic chiefly responsible was editor Thomas Bedding, who, it will be remembered, considered himself something of an expert on photography.

Extreme close-ups were used on occasion, but only to show an object, a letter, or a newspaper insert, to help clarify a plot. The actor's face was not considered a proper subject for such a close-up until about 1912. In the period before 1908, real close-ups, while not common, are not unusual either. They appeared, first of all, in the single-shot subjects called "facial expression" films, in which the entire subject matter consisted of grimaces, sneezing, laughter, and so forth. It is of interest that this very term used in early cinema was revived in connection with the new style of acting.

In addition, close-ups or semi-close-ups of faces were used as introductory or ending shots in the early story films, shots that are "about" the story but not integral to it. The "optional" shot of THE GREAT TRAIN ROBBERY in 1903—showing the man shooting the gun at the spectator, which could be placed at the beginning or end of the film as the showman chose—is very well known. Such shots, while no longer optional with regard to placement, can still be found with some frequency in the period 1907–1908, and even later, positioned at the beginning or end of the film. Today's film theorists describe them as nondiegetic or emblematic shots: they are related to the film and comment on it, but are definitely not part of the events of the narrative.

Edison's LAUGHING GAS (December 1907), a linked-episode comedy about the contagious effect of a laughing spell, begins with a close-up of a big black woman's face, looking at the camera, her jaw tied up to indicate a toothache. Following a visit to her dentist and the administration of gas, she enters a subway car in a state of uncontrollable laughter, and every passenger catches it from her; then she passes it on to a milkman, a policeman, and a judge, and finally she disrupts a church service. It is a typical antiestablishment joke of the pre-reform era. The last shot is a close-up of her face, again looking into the camera lens, laughing.

A later example is the final shot of THE ABORIGINE'S DEVOTION (1909, World), in which the camera is placed much closer to the actors than anywhere in the rest of the film. An Indian who has been left with the care of the trapper's child after the white man's death defends the child when a fur thief appears. In the last shot, the noble Indian directly faces the camera, holding the white child he has protected. The composition is reminiscent of a Raphael *Madonna and Child*, all curves and drapery. Vitagraph's PLAYING AT DIVORCE (December 1910) has a similar emblematic shot at the end. When the parents have given up their plans to separate after seeing their children making a game of divorce, there is a cut to a closer view, in which the couple are seen head-on, hugging the children as a kind of summation. This might be thought of as a little more integrated than earlier examples, although the act of facing the camera effectively removes it from the narrative context at the time when this film was made, because it was no longer acceptable to break the illusion by acknowledging the presence of the camera. The spirit of the emblematic shot lingers on in many kinds of narrative structures; it becomes more integrated but still retains the final position, making a kind of statement about the film after the actual narrative events have ended and the film has "closed."

More rarely, in films before this period, closer views of the same scene can be found in the midst of the narrative, if not exactly integral to it. One of the latest of such pre-1907 examples, and the one most resembling the modern use, is found in Biograph's THE SILVER WEDDING of 1906. Here, in the course of a robbery of the wedding gifts, there is a cut on action, quite well matched to the previous shot, to give us a closer view of the work of the thieves.

We do not usually find these closer views integrated into the narrative structure of 1907–1909 films, I think, because filmmakers at the time were struggling with the problem of continuity of the scenes. For them, given the models available to them, closer views would have interrupted the smooth flow of the narrative.

This attitude is reflected in the conservative views of those critics who, from 1909 on, rejected the newer methods and condemned the "inconsistency" of varying camera distances. The *World* took this position in July 1909 in "The Factor of Uniformity," from which I have already quoted the part about "giants and giantesses." From that point, the writer continues:

> A little later on in the course of the picture the figures had been photographed at a greater distance from the camera and so were less monstrous to the eye; while, in even a third part of the picture, the figures were so far away from the camera that they appeared of their natural size. . . . Now, here there was a total lack of uniformity, due entirely to a want of intelligence on the part of the producer and the photographer, and the effect on the minds of the people who saw this picture was extreme dissatisfaction (*Moving Picture World*, 24 July 1909, p. 116).

At the beginning of 1910, an exhibitor made a similar complaint about Vitagraph's THE LIFE OF MOSES, where the inconsistency was particularly noticeable because of painted backdrops that lacked perspective. In his view, the fad of facial expressions was being overdone, the camera had to be too close, and the actors were packed in like sardines. When you can see the feet, the exhibitor wrote, you can scarcely see the heads, and when the heads are shown you can't see the lower part of the bodies. What he wanted, by contrast, was spectacle: "the stage should be large and deep" in order that the Egyptian chariots can be seen in full, not in parts. The *World* editor who reprinted this letter, however, did not agree with him.[17]

A similarly conservative attitude was maintained by one or two writers on the *World* for several years, until almost no American was keeping to the earlier stage-distance style except for Edwin S. Porter, who retreated to an even more conservative stance than usual when he first began to direct feature films based on stage plays for Famous Players. When Porter was still at the Rex Company in 1911 the *World*'s editorial position was:

> The Rex releases are examples, to our mind, of the proper thing to do. Here Mr. Porter works on a large stage, and places his camera at a considerable distance from his actors. The result is that he avoids abnormality of size, and when you see the pictures on the screen, they express the proper sensuous impression of size (*Moving Picture World*, 15 April 1911, p. 815).

These opinions seem rather ludicrous to us now, but at the time they may have represented the typical reluctance of some people to abandon the familiar art for new directions. Given the popularity of the films directed by Griffith for Biograph, however, it is probable that audiences in general found films more exciting as camera positions were varied.

During this period, a closer camera position was often taken for a practical reason, or what was at that time a practical reason. The characters are standing and then sit down, for example, and the producer wants to keep them at the center of the screen. In such cases, sometimes the producer cuts to a more distant view of the same scene because (1) the characters are about to stand up, or (2) another character is about to enter and space must be made for him. (A slight tilting or panning movement of the camera would serve the same purpose, but we still discuss the use of camera movement in a later chapter.) Whenever small children are part of the scene, the cameraman places his lens closer to their faces. In 1911 Epes Winthrop Sargent explained some of the practical uses of a close-up:

> Bust pictures . . . are useful in determining action that might be obscure in the large scene. It not only magnifies the objects but it draws particular attention to them. . . . Many points may be cleared in a five-foot bust picture which would require twenty to thirty feet of leader to explain, and the bust picture always interests. Sometimes in a newspaper illustration a circle surrounds some point of interest. . . . The bust picture serves the same purpose (*Moving Picture World*, 5 August 1911, pp. 281–282).

It is when such changes in viewpoint are used for emphasis or expressiveness, however, that they become important to the narrative system being developed in this period.

Where the closer views are integrated in the narrative structure, the opportunity arises for more subtle and detailed facial expression, as well as for a more restrained and natural acting style, which the *World* commentators wanted to encourage. In Rollin Summers' prescient article of September 1908, he noted that where shades of emotion are to be expressed, the picture as a rule should be at close range: "The moving picture may present figures greater than life size without loss of illusion."[18] This aspect of film form is closely related to the changes in acting style: as long as the actors remained at stage distance, broad and stylized gestures were needed to make the spectator understand what was going on.

The 1910 editorial in the *New York Independent* referred to in chapter 4 speaks knowledgeably of the ability of the director to

> vary at will the distance of the stage, giving us a close view at critical moments. When we would see more clearly what emotions the features of the heroine express or what is in the locket she takes from her bosom we have no need to pick up our opera glasses. The artist has foreseen our desire and suddenly the detail is enlarged for us until it fills the canvas (quoted in *Moving Picture World*, 15 October 1910, p. 865).

The intimacy of the closer view permits the spectator to gaze on the faces of the actors as an unseen voyeur. Thus, a commentator on Griffith's BRUTALITY remarked:

> The Biograph producer plays upon his characters as though they were musical instruments, and we are full of admiration for the impressions he

Mabel Normand best known for her comedy roles, played dramatic roles as well when she was still with the Biograph Company. Here, she rocks an imaginary baby in her arms, in THE ETERNAL MOTHER *(Biograph, 1912), directed by D. W. Griffith.*

Lillian and Dorothy Gish in the Biograph thriller AN UNSEEN ENEMY *(1912), directed by D. W. Griffith*

Blanche Sweet in JUDITH OF BETHULIA *(Biograph, 1913–1914), directed by D. W. Griffith.*

Lillian Gish grieves for her dead baby in THE MOTHERING HEART *(Biograph, 1913), directed by D. W. Griffith.*

is able to make just by facial expression. In his beautiful photographs his characters appear as through fine opera glasses. Every change of expression is more clearly pictured than if they were truly before us, and one isn't embarrassed drinking the effect in. Is it not truly soul-music? Can such impressions be created in any other way than on the screen? (*Moving Picture World*, 14 December 1912, pp. 1081–1082).

The significant term here is "one isn't embarrassed." The appeal of this new closer view of the actors is to the fantasy life of the voyeur in all of us. We can share in the intimate life of another human being without the person's being aware of it and without any obligation on our part. The closer view is an essential part of the new style that was to become the classical Hollywood cinema. It is only as it becomes part of a complex of varied camera positions that break up the spaces of a scene, or our viewpoint of a scene, that it joins this new narrative system.

Earlier, we saw how the chase films of 1907 and before used closer views at the point when the actors entered or left the frame. The same movement was used in more complex narratives, such as THE MILL GIRL of 1907, to link shots in space and time. The significant action was always reserved for the moment when the actors reached the center of the composition and were at stage distance. The composition was symmetrical and centered. The new use of closer views of actors' faces took advantage of this same movement toward the camera, but now the important action or emotion sometimes could be portrayed off-center, without losing the attention of the spectator. Such occasional asymmetry added to the dramatic moment, throwing the composition off-balance, giving more vitality to the image. Moreover, having the actors move into a close-up instead of cutting to it alleviated the producers' feelings that a close-up would interrupt the narrative flow or the emotion or mood. As a result, the movement into close-up (rather than cutting to it) characterized the use of the closer view of the human face for quite a long time, while "inserts" of inanimate objects or parts of a body, such as hands, appeared as direct cuts. The reluctance to cut to the close view of the human face seems to me to show that such images were not thought of in the same way as "inserts."

Griffith made a film at the very end of 1909 using this kind of close-up as the dramatic climax of his narrative structure. This was THE LAST DEAL, released on 27 January 1910. The sequence in question shows the progress of a poker game, with some players in midshot or semi-close-up, their backs to the camera. The hero is an inveterate gambler, and the scene is intercut with shots of his wife at home, praying for his salvation. When the gambler leaves the game, ruined, he comes into midshot, and then into semi-close-up. The spectator is shown his realization of where his compulsion has led him, while the other actors in the film may not see it. After this, the gambler returns home, determined to reform, and the film closes with the scene of domestic happiness and tranquillity that occurs at the end of so many Griffith films.

The most dramatic use of this kind of "actor moving into close-up" can be found in THE MUSKETEERS OF PIG ALLEY (1912), when rival gangs stalk each other through city slums and back alleys in a sequence of movements as carefully choreographed as a ballet. Elmer Booth as a gang leader brings his men around corners, pauses, and slowly, slowly, edges up to the lens of the camera. Booth's face fills the lower right side of the screen in extremely tight close-up and is held there some seconds with deliberate intention. This is another of those archetypal images from the films of D. W. Griffith, an image of threatened violence and terror. He repeats it in the second episode of HOME, SWEET HOME (1914) when a man contemplates the murder of his brother and again with the face of Gus, the would-be rapist in THE BIRTH OF A NATION (1915), but surely never again with as strong an effect as in THE MUSKETEERS OF PIG ALLEY, where he holds the shot for some seconds, a pause before the violence that follows.

Mae Marsh, in *Screen Acting*, speaks of the craft of acting for the camera, a craft she learned as an inexperienced young girl working for Griffith in this period. In her opinion, "The effectiveness of the closeup seems to be in inverse proportion to the amount of facial action in it."[19] Restraint, the least possible movement, the smallest of gestures: these were the characteristics of an acting style for the intimacy of the close-up lens.

Lillian Gish, in THE MOTHERING HEART (1913), in the boldest of close-ups, on a direct cut, challenges the rule that an actor does not look into the camera lens. She plays a woman in shock at the death of her baby: she seems to stare directly into the camera, absolutely unmoving, almost expressionless. As she sees nothing, in fact, she does not make that fatal eye contact with the spectator, but in coming close to it, the image more daringly conveys raw emotion.

Within this period, the close-ups of actors' faces are usually saved for such dramatic moments, keeping their full impact. Mae Marsh recalled that actors longed for the opportunity the close-up gave them, until directors accused them of wanting a film made up of only close-ups. The close-up would play a part in the intimacy demanded by the star-worshipping fan. Up to 1915, however, it was used sparingly.

7

Brand Names and Stars

"Whose make is it?"

—Two ladies in front of the Herald Square Theater,
quoted in the *Moving Picture World*, 1 November 1913, p. 486

*B*efore the rise of the star system, films were perceived and sold by brand name. The motion-picture industry in 1909, like any manufacturer in twentieth-century America, advertised and distributed its products by the brand. Under the system of the release day and the standing order, exhibitors, exchanges, and the public were expected to request films by company names, not by specific titles or stars. The price to the distributor was the same for any brand and any film. Competition among producers consisted of selling a greater number of prints to the exchanges; that number, which ran from seventy-five to several hundred copies in 1909, was determined by the popularity of their brand names.[1]

Such a system depended on the uniformity of the product manufactured. As Frank Woods explained:

> The popularity of any one brand of pictures will be found on analysis to depend almost altogether on the one point . . . how nearly the average output approaches dependable uniformity of excellence. Nearly every manufacturer has at some time or other produced a notable film—one that can compare favorably with the world's best—but not every manufacturer makes a practice of getting out films of this class, or anything like it. In the case of some makers the great films are few and far between, in other cases they come with uncertain frequency, but it is only in a very few instances that they can be said to approach dependable uniformity of excellence. Any manufacturer who desires to establish his trademark at the top can better afford to throw a film, that he knows is not up to the mark, into the scrap heap, than to issue it and thus injure his reputation with the public (*New York Dramatic Mirror*, 9 April 1910, 17).

Some exchange men discussed the demand for brand names during the trial of the U.S. government versus the Motion Picture Patents Company in 1913. Charles F. Haring, an exhibitor in Jersey City, recalled that when he entered the motion-picture business "some five or six years ago":

> There were fourteen releases [a week]. Two that we could not use or
> would not use, and they were Lubin's and they were so nasty, and so bad,
> that we would not use them. Well, our exchange merely bought twelve
> reels. In other words twelve releases, and a three-reel program a day
> would mean the repeating on yourself of one reel every day, and two on
> your nearest competitor (*US* v. *MPPC* 4:2042 December 1913).

J. A. Schuchert, manager of the Buffalo office of the General Film Company, trying
to explain why one combined exchange would be better than two serving the same
territory, testified:

> They would probably all be buying, for an example, Biograph, and
> certain makes that were most in demand, where, with a man with the
> eighteen reels [a week], he could buy an assortment and divide them up
> between the customers, which would be to their better advantage (*ibid.*,
> 4:1021).

Robert Etris, formerly with the Lubin Film Service and now manager of a branch of
General Film, was asked whether the exhibitor was at full liberty to select his own
program. He replied:

> Not absolutely, because they would naturally select nothing but the
> so-called better makes, there are certain films which every exhibitor
> seems to want: Biographs, Vitagraphs and some others (*ibid.*, 4:2149).

Albert Goff, manager of the Cleveland office, agreed:

> I don't just get your idea when you say "select"; you understand we are
> dealing with a limited commodity, and there ain't much selecting. For
> instance, an exhibitor is running 35 reels [a week], and your output is 50.
> There is only 15 left. He don't want certain reels, a Méliès, or something
> like that (*ibid.*, 4:2346).

Indeed, Edward Augur, manager of the St. Louis branch, confirmed that he no
longer, in 1913, bought any of the Méliès films:

> The exhibitors were complaining of the fact that these particular films
> were highly educational, and were describing methods of acting in the
> South Seas, and also scenics, and educational films, generally (*ibid.*,
> 4:2434).

Samuel Shirley, manager of the Wilkes Barre branch, also said that he had not
ordered any Méliès films for about a year and a half.

The discredited Méliès films mentioned in this testimony were the product of
Gaston Méliès' long voyage to the South Seas, the Far East, and the Southern
Hemisphere, from August 1912 through the spring of 1913. They were mostly travel
and educational films, recording native life and customs of anthropological interest.

Gaston Méliès' reputation, while never at the top, had not been that low during the year or so that the company had spent in Texas making Westerns in 1910–1911. Gaston retired at the end of this apparently unsuccessful trip to the Far East and died within a couple of years, leaving his son Paul in charge of a practically defunct company. In 1914 a studio was established in Flushing to produce the Méliès "G" brand comedies for General Film, and a little later, Vitagraph bought out what was left of the American Méliès Company.[2]

The Lubin brand, meanwhile, so despised by Mr. Haring of Jersey City in 1908, improved as the years went by. In November 1910 an exhibitor, speaking of what he perceived as a decline in some much-admired brands such as Biograph, Selig, Pathé European, and Edison, contended that "the only licensed manufacturer steadily improving is Lubin."[3]

There is no doubt that the Biograph brand stood for the best. Vitagraph was second in reputation, even though it was the better-known brand in Europe at the time, thanks to the establishment of overseas distribution offices and a more effective system for European distribution. Before the advent of D. W. Griffith at Biograph, Vitagraph had also probably enjoyed the best reputation in America, but after Griffith had been directing for six months, it would be difficult to dispute, at least in America, the Biograph lead. This was the company "whose productions have so steadily and surely forged ahead that they are being eagerly sought for by the exhibitor and the public." A review of THE RESURRECTION similarly observed, "Step by step the Biograph Company is making for itself a unique position among American manufacturers. Within the last few months its reputation among exhibitors and the general public has increased by leaps and bounds." Griffith was never mentioned in these contexts, as directors' names were not advertised or generally known at this time. An exhibitor who owned four nickelodeons in Chicago advised, "Copy after the Biograph, they deliver the goods and all exhibitors are fighting for them." And the Casino in Easton, Pennsylvania, calling itself "The Home of the Biographs," advertised in the local paper, "Every Day a Biograph Feature." Ben Morris, manager of the Olympic in Bellaire, Ohio, reported that "any Biograph, advertised, will draw," while an exhibitor in Independence, Missouri, reported, "This town felt that there was only one firm in the business that could make a motion picture. Anything that carried the Biograph title was good and every other make was rotten." Then he switched to the independent side and discovered Thanhouser, and in fact, his letter was printed in a Thanhouser advertisement, but the statement about Biograph in such a context has a certain ring of truth.[4]

"Henry," the *World*'s New England correspondent, reported on a visit to the Orpheum in Boston, "As usual, we noted the subdued exclamations of 'Oh, here's a Biograph,' when the leader was flashed on the curtain."[5] To which Thomas Bedding, also of the *World*, soon added his own opinion:

> I do not know their staff, their producers, actors or anybody associated with the Company, yet mere mention of a Biograph picture seems to awaken in me a desire to see that picture. I have always felt I could get into the skin of their subjects, and think as their producers and actors and photographers thought (*Moving Picture World*, 12 November 1910, p. 1100).

The Star System

The most popular actors may not be the most skillful. The popular actors seem to have the indefinable quality of taking a good photograph, and making appeals by reason of their inherent magnetism (Frank L. Dyer, 11 November 1913 [*US* v. *MPPC* 3:1538]).

In the first decade of the century, the theater, opera, and vaudeville all operated to a large extent on the basis of a star system, in which the personal magnetism of a particular performer often outweighed other considerations of artistic talent, or the value of the drama or music.

Yet the industrialists who organized the film business did not take the star system into account. As we have seen, they were manufacturing a product, trying their best to standardize it, and expecting the consumer to ask for it by brand name. The producing and distributing systems set up in 1908–1909 were resistant to change. When the public insisted on their interest in star players, the industry at first declined to exploit it. The producers did not seem to recognize the presence of the actor in the movie theater. The films were only photographs, after all.

In any case, there could scarcely be stars before 1908 or even 1909 because there were few regularly employed actors and actresses and no regular production schedule. Gilbert M. "Broncho Billy" Anderson and Ben Turpin of Essanay were regularly employed from 1907 on, but they were exceptional. In the sense that they were known and recognized, they could be called the first movie stars, but there is no indication that they inspired that kind of devotion in filmgoers at this early stage. Ben Turpin signed his name to a short article in a trade journal in April 1909, and he was mentioned in a review or two of his films. A story on Anderson's Essanay company out West appeared in the *Denver Post* in December 1909, and there all his cast and crew were mentioned by name, but Anderson did not become known as "Broncho Billy" until July 1910.[6]

Most actors were hired by the day. Many of them were from the lower ranks of the theatrical profession, glad to get a few days' work in between engagements, or in the summertime, when they were waiting for a new season to begin. This is the way that D. W. Griffith, his wife, Linda Arvidson, and many others got into moving pictures at the end of 1907. Only when the industry could offer a guaranteed weekly wage and a future did some of them give up the struggle for a theatrical career in exchange for a steady job and a chance to stay at home instead of living in hotels and boardinghouses.

During the nickelodeon years up to about 1912, many actors and actresses of the "real" theater did not want it known that they were working in the pictures and hoped no one would notice. The *Dramatic Mirror* in July 1909 noted that "there is still a reluctance among the greater part of the prominent players to consider offers from the film manufacturers."[7] This reluctance was mainly felt by those insecure players who were in the middle ranks of the profession; the unknowns were glad for a source of income, and the exposure could not hurt those at the top. Now and then really well known stage stars could be hired and advertised, when they were specially engaged for a particular film. After all, there was the example of Bernhardt, Réjane, and the celebrated French actors of the Comédie-Française who appeared with great fanfare in the Film d'Art. Many of America's own stage stars were not prepared to

make their screen debuts for a few years yet. Yet Vitagraph's OLIVER TWIST, released in May 1909, bore a credit title, years before they were commonly used, to
announce "Miss Elita Proctor Otis as 'Nancy Sykes' "—a title that appeared at the
point where the actress enters the narrative. Edison advertised the appearance of
Miss Cecil Spooner in the dual role of THE PRINCE AND THE PAUPER in the first issue
of the Edison *Kinetogram* in the summer of 1909. Champion swimmer Annette
Kellerman was the subject of a publicity release when she posed for Vitagraph that
summer. Although Otis and Spooner may not be remembered today, they were
celebrities on the American stage at that time.[8]

But lesser mortals had to fear the effect of such publicity on the theatrical managers. In November 1909 the producers Klaw and Erlanger, stung by the competition of the picture houses, publicly forbade actors under contract with them to appear
in films. Other actors said they feared less money would be offered them if it were
known they had worked in the movie studios. The disastrous effect of nickelodeon
madness on the vaudeville circuit of the country was quite enough to make enemies
of the impresarios.[9]

However, this phase passed rather quickly, as the industry became more respectable. The steady and ever higher wages began to make it very attractive. It was
possible for an actor to have a real home life and more security than most of them had
ever known. Ordinarily, they no longer had to work nights, and they could end the
weary travel from town to town all over the country. The idea that the theater was
somehow better and more intellectual never quite died, but the stars that movies
made were mostly content with fame, fortune, influence, and a cozy fireside, in
addition to an extraordinary outpouring of love from the millions. Billy Garwood,
who left Thanhouser to go on the road but came back to the moving pictures,
purchased a car in 1912, still a sign of success at that time. He said he missed the
footlight applause, but actors in "stock" didn't buy autos. When Miss Carey Hastings
of Thanhouser was called back to the stage at about the same time, she remarked how
things had changed: it no longer mattered to theatrical interests that she had become
a picture actress.[10]

A ground swell of public interest in the movie actors began to appear in letters to
the moving-picture studios and trade periodicals and in the daily conversations a
good theater manager had with his customers. Even though the star system in other
media was a familiar phenomenom, the strength of feeling that moving-picture spectators developed for the actors and actresses was more than the manufacturers could
have expected. After all, this was the first real mass audience in history—the number
of fans an actor could have was multiplied to astronomical proportions. Beyond that,
a more intimate, if imaginary, relationship to the star was possible. The actual person
was not present in the movie house; he or she was an enlarged image in the private
dream world of the spectator. When the eighteen-year-old Blanche Sweet signed
with Jesse L. Lasky at the end of 1914, a writer struggling to describe "screen
magnetism" insisted that "the man doesn't live who could watch a good Sweet picture
without feeling a sense of her actual presence—without almost believing that he
could touch flesh if only his hand could come in contact with the figure on the
screen."[11]

The player, in absence, belonged to the spectator in a closer way than would ever
be possible in reality, but that didn't stop some of the more avid fans from confusing
the image with reality. It was the public who harangued the theater managers with

questions about their favorites, who wrote to studios, who asked for photographs, who sent in proposals of marriage and less proper invitations. It was this special private relationship of spectator and star that led to the familiarity of first names and the dropping of honorific titles. In theatrical tradition, players were usually addressed as "Mr.," "Miss," and "Madame." There was proper distance and respect for one's stage idols. While in the beginning, in print, it was similarly "Miss Pickford," the fans persisted in saying "Little Mary," and "Doug" Fairbanks, and "Charlie" Chaplin. In time, this familiarity spread to other public personalities as well, but it began with the movies.

The often-repeated assertion that the licensed companies refused to allow actors to be named, while the independent companies exploited the star system is not, when one looks into the record, entirely accurate. Both sides resisted it at first, and both began, to a small extent, to draw upon star attraction as an advertising ploy at about the same time in early 1910. Edison and Vitagraph did exploit the names of Otis and Spooner and Kellerman in 1909, but the advertising of names famous outside of the movies was a different case. The value of these names was preexisting. The true movie star is the one whose fame derives from his or her movie appearances.

The only exception to the beginning of the star system in 1910 is to be found in the practice of the Biograph Company, which persistently refused to supply the names of their actors, actresses, or other staff until the spring of 1913.[12] It is this example that stands out in the public mind as a refusal of the star system, however, because the Biograph stars were the most popular of all. They were also the players other companies tried to lure away. Why Biograph resisted the tidal wave of audience love for the players three years longer than the other producers remains difficult to understand, but the original refusal may have been perpetuated because so many of the company's best actors and actresses left. Why advertise actors who will leave? The company brand name remains; people go. As a woman in the Berkshires wrote in November 1910, "I attribute the success of a good many films to the popularity of the players, the Biograph artists formerly leading in public favor, but now their ranks are sadly depleted, and we have to go to the theater showing independent films to see the old favorites."[13]

The director D. W. Griffith may have been responsible for the company's stern policy, but if so, he never explained. Perhaps Griffith's views are reflected in the comments of his friend Frank Woods, who wrote in 1912:

> Discussion of the apparent tendency toward a policy of exploiting stars in motion pictures continues to command attention of producers, many of whom look upon the drift as to a rock ahead that may mean great danger to the art. Those who see trouble in the undue featuring of star players have in mind the experience of the theatrical stage, where the exploitation of stars had admittedly proved a handicap and a great deal of a nuisance. The craze for stage stars has caused the artificial making of regiments of near stars, whose only claim to special distinction may have been good looks, a scandal or a "pull." . . . It does not, however, seem reasonable to suppose that the star craze will or can work out in the same way in pictures, because conditions are so vastly different. In pictures, the star is called on to appear in . . . hundreds of roles—literally hundreds. She or he must prove absolute ability and versatility, and even then it goes for nothing if the supporting company and the plays do not

prove equally good. The situation, therefore, becomes more analogous to the old stock company conditions where every player had to be of equal ability. . . . A well-balanced company, strong in every part, is the logical answer to the question of best policy in the organization of picture stock companies (*New York Dramatic Mirror*, 24 January 1912, p. 32).

In 1908–1909, Griffith's actors were expected to play leads and bit parts interchangeably, as in a stock company, but this was a general policy in other companies too. Then he began to depend more on a star system within the company, selecting the same actors, and especially actresses—Mary Pickford, Blanche Sweet, Mae Marsh, Lillian Gish—to play the leads in one picture after another. But the company still continued to refuse to name them. Nor was Griffith's own name used on the films or in advertisements. Griffith could take pride in regularly being able to find unknown players who crept into the hearts of the fans. His players were always stolen away from him by other companies, and yet he could replace them. He was the "teacher," and his students could then go out into the world and do well. Still, it is hard to understand how he would not resent the continual suppression of his own name in favor of that of the company, when his was the chief hand responsible for its great reputation.

In August 1911 the name of a Biograph actor, Verner Clarges, was mentioned in a review of the Civil War film SWORDS AND HEARTS, but by then Clarges was dead, and it couldn't do him much good professionally. An exhibitor in Riverside, California, insisted that "it would be well if all producers included the cast of characters in their bulletins." Agreeing that a cast list should be supplied with every film, F. H. Richardson declared, "It is hardly up to them [the producers] to dismiss the matter with the curt announcement 'We don't wish to.' It would seem that the exhibitor ought, of right, to have some say in a matter of that kind."[14]

But perhaps the perpetuation of Biograph's refusal to name players, in the face of great public pressure and long after all the other companies had begun to do it, is to be attributed to the hot-tempered Jeremiah J. Kennedy. Biograph advertising was withdrawn from the *Moving Picture World* once again in 1912, when the *World's* inquiry columns began to leak out the names of Biograph's actors and actresses to an eager public. I don't know whether the two events are specifically connected; however, the *Dramatic Mirror* also had an inquiry column, and indeed claimed to be the first to have started one, but they steadily refused to supply the desired information about Biograph films, and they kept Biograph advertising.

Another reason given for not naming players was that a moving-picture star would demand more money. This argument falls down to some extent, however, because the star players got recognition and fan mail whether they were named or not. The writers just addressed their letters to "The Biograph Girl" and "The Vitagraph Girl" and "Dimples" (Florence Lawrence, Florence Turner, and Maurice Costello, respectively.) Charles Inslee of the New York Motion Picture Company was getting mail addressed to "The Indian" in 1909, because of his naked Indian roles in films made in the Catskills that summer.[15] "The Biograph Girl" would be as able to ask for a raise on the basis of fan mail as Florence Lawrence. Still, there was such a perception. Griffith's friend Frank Woods reported:

A certain motion picture director, one of the best, by the way, declares that the letters written to The Spectator regarding identities of players and the replies thereto are causing the very deuce to pay with some of the actors and actresses to whom publicity is thus given. According to this complaining director the players immediately swell up and want fabulous salaries. *Mirror* in hand, one of them will assail the powers that be and, pointing to his or her name in agate type, will declare: "See what a great player I am. Why, here's a person out in Punxsutawney, Pa., who wants to know my name. Gimme more pay or I quit" (*New York Dramatic Mirror*, 8 March 1911, p. 39).

And by 1913 Frank Dyer would testify:

> When I was President of the Edison Company in 1908, $50 or $75 a week was considered a very good price to pay for an actor, because he was given employment all year round, and was able to live with his family, and did not have to work nights, the way they have to do on the regular stage, whereas at the present time, there are actors who receive from $500 to $1,000 a week for their services (*US* v. *MPPC* 3:1574 [12 November 1913]).

In 1907 and early 1908, before permanent stock companies were established by some of the manufacturers, actors would get five dollars a day, if they worked in the movies. If they didn't find work, they got nothing.[16]

As Tom Gunning has pointed out, before there could be movie stars, they had to be close enough to the camera to be recognized from one picture to the next. The previous chapter discussed the relationship between the changes in acting style and the closer view of the actor, and the fact that the slightly closer view began to be used in 1909. The same factor also applies to the rise of the star system. There is evidence that the public was already following movie stars by the spring of 1909, when a review of LADY HELEN'S ESCAPADE declared: "The chief honors of the picture are borne by the now famous Biograph girl, who must be gratified by the silent celebrity she has achieved. This lady combines with very great personal attractions very fine dramatic ability indeed." Florence Lawrence was noticed again in the following month in a review of Biograph's THE RESURRECTION: "We do not know the lady's name, but certainly she seems to us to have a very fine command of her emotions."[17]

An amusing and charming letter from P. C. Levar of the *Daily Coast Mail* in Coos Bay, Oregon, argued with considerable intensity about which of the actresses was the real "Biograph Girl." The real one, he insisted, was the one who played Mrs. Jones and had appeared lately with the IMP Company. Although he could not name her, that was Florence Lawrence. The "other one," still at Biograph, was Marion Leonard.[18]

Kalem, a licensed company, seems to have been the first to offer photographs of their stock company for display in theater lobbies. According to the *Moving Picture World*, this kind of advertising was slow in coming, despite public demand. After one year of a stabilized production system, the trade paper was already predicting the coming of a star system for the moving picture, doubtless because the waves of public enthusiasm were reaching the *World*'s shores with increasing force. Then the New York Motion Picture Company, an independent firm, announced in a press release

The Kalem Stock Company in 1909. Amelia Barleon, Kenean Buel, Louise Melford, Sidney Olcott, Gene Gauntier, James Vincent, Jane Wolfe, Robert Vignola, George Melford, Tom Santley. Gene Gauntier's notes on the back of this photograph describe it as the "first published photo of a stock company." It appeared in the 15 January 1910 issue of the Moving Picture World.

the names of all the actors in the Bison stock company, out in the Northwest, including the name of the director, Fred J. Balshofer.[19]

In March 1910 Carl Laemmle and Robert Cochrane of the independent IMP Company published the famous "We Nail a Lie" advertisement that declared:

> The blackest and at the same time the silliest lie yet circulated by enemies of the "Imp" was the story foisted on the public of St. Louis last week to the effect that Miss Laurence (the "Imp" girl, formerly known as the "Biograph" girl) had been killed by a street car . . . (*Moving Picture World*, 12 March 1910, p. 365).

While the ad was obviously a publicity coup, the story told by film historian Terry Ramsaye in the twenties that Carl Laemmle and Robert Cochrane were pulling the first movie publicity stunt to announce the acquisition of Florence Lawrence has some weaknesses. In the first place, she had been working for their company for about six months before she was even named in their advertisements or releases. Her departure from Biograph was noted by the *World* some time before the IMP advertising man thought of claiming her. The exchange in correspondence about the identity of the Biograph Girl in the *World*'s columns at the end of 1909 may have been the inspiration for Robert Cochrane's press releases at last naming Miss Lawrence ("Laurence," in these early advertisements). And in fact, the first mention of her name in an advertisement was not the one Ramsaye reported, based on fake death reports that had been printed in the St. Louis papers. Her portrait but not her name appeared in an advertisement of 18 December 1909, with the caption "She's an Imp!"; another advertisement on 29 January 1910 mentioned her name, and the advertisement for IMP's MOTHER LOVE, released on 7 March 1910, read: "Miss Laurence, known to thousands as 'Mrs. Jones,' does the most excellent of her remarkable career. . . . Talk about your films d'art! This is a film d'peach, a film d'great, a film d'magnifique!!!"[20] ("Mrs. Jones" had earned this title from her performance in the Biograph MR. AND MRS. JONES comedy series.) This advertisement appeared later than the stories that had appeared in the St. Louis papers about her death and before the "We Nail a Lie" advertisement.

The same issue of the *World* that carried "We Nail a Lie" featured an editorial stating that the public was now known to be "unmistakably interested in the personalities of the chief performers. This interest is growing." This comment came in response to the suggestion that authors ought to get credit for their scenarios, which the *World* thought was probably not worth doing because the public was not interested in who wrote the film. Actually, Edison had been making a practice of hiring and naming the famous authors of their screenplays, such as Rex Beach, beating by quite a few years the Samuel Goldwyn "Famous Authors" idea. But most authors of the films were unknown and likely to remain so.[21]

At the same time, one of the Trust companies, Vitagraph, was reacting to public demand for more information about the players. A Vitagraph spokesman said the company received many requests from people wanting to know the names and get to meet the players. Yet it was "incomprehensible," to the spokesman for anyone to "fall in love" with actors seen on the screen.[22]

Florence Lawrence and Florence Turner were really tied for the honor of being the first big movie stars. In the same month that Florence Lawrence and King

Baggott were making personal appearances in St. Louis (to "prove she was not dead"), Florence Turner, the Vitagraph Girl, was making personal appearances in Brooklyn. She went out to the movie houses to introduce a new song called "The Vitagraph Girl." In June 1910 the *New York Dramatic Mirror* printed her photograph and captioned a full-column story about her "A Motion Picture Star," which might be the first time that title was awarded in print. In an interview in the *North American*, Florence Turner said that she had received thousands of letters proposing marriage. She began to give out photos of herself that summer and continued the public appearances. An exhibitor gave his customers photographs of "the Vitagraph girl, who, by the way, is quite a favorite with our people." Another exhibitor asked if the producers could supply slides of their leading players. The patrons were always asking who the actors were, he explained, and he couldn't tell them. If they knew in advance that Maurice Costello and Florence Turner were going to be in the coming attractions, he could assure a full house. When F. H. Richardson attended one of Turner's appearances, in Jersey City, at the Academy at 342 Central Avenue, he found a small-scale riot of people who were not able to get in. Expressing surprise, he remarked that "it was an enlightening illustration, or demonstration, of the hold the moving picture itself has on the people." Maurice Costello joined the personal-appearance tour circuit in November 1910, first at the Fulton Auditorium, later at the Park Row Theater, and proved to be as popular in person as Florence Turner.[23]

If Florence Lawrence got the first big publicity for a movie star who was not already a celebrity in another field, it could only have been by a few days. Nor did IMP benefit very long from the buildup of the star, because she left the company before the end of 1910. She went next to Lubin, where she played again opposite Arthur Johnson, the former Biograph star. The IMP Company then returned to Biograph and this time acquired Mary Pickford. She was going to be just about the biggest star of all, but she didn't stay long enough either for them to get the full benefit of her growing fame. A year later, after working in some of Thomas H. Ince's first films at IMP, she and Owen Moore, her husband, signed with Majestic, a new independent company. After about only three months there, she returned to Biograph in March 1912. Her face and name had been advertised widely, and she had achieved the enormous distinction of a cover photograph on the 5 December 1911 issue of the *New York Dramatic Mirror*, which was ordinarily devoted to a theatrical star. At Biograph, she had to return to a nameless status, but everyone knew her now, and she got a chance to play more leading roles than before, in decidedly better films than those she had appeared in while away from Biograph.[24]

The independent Thanhouser Company adopted a policy of naming its players from its beginning in 1910, the same time that IMP and Vitagraph were first advertising Florence Lawrence and Florence Turner. Although its players were drawn from theatrical stock, Thanhouser began on a determined note of high-class production and would not be the company to admit that any stage actors risked their reputations by appearing in their films. In the spring of 1911, Frank Crane of Thanhouser was claimed to be the first of the independents to make personal appearances. Of course that claim properly belonged to Florence Lawrence a year before, but it is an interesting perception. The Vitagraph stars, representing the licensed companies, must have been much more on public view than she was during the intervening year.[25]

The advertising value of players was very clear to all exhibitors by the end of 1911.

Mr. M. B. Golden, manager of the Princess Theater in London, Ohio, declared: "Having studied my audience, I know their favorite actors and advertise the pictures and their favorites' names on a banner in front of the theater. I find the actor or actress to be the drawing card, regardless of what they are in." Mr. Golden found Harry Myers of the Lubin players to be one of the best drawing cards he could announce, except Florence Lawrence.[26]

The industry first began to incorporate the star system into its practice by providing photographs of the favorites for display. By 1910 most of the companies were issuing group photos of their stock companies for display in the lobbies of movie theaters, sometimes with special easels so they could be brought out when the producer's films were playing. Vitagraph was already offering the photographs in color in March of that year. In the autumn, the Powers Company had the foresight to issue a calendar for 1911 with a portrait of Pearl White on it; theaters could obtain it in quantity at cost, with the name of the theater printed on it, for giving away to the fans.[27]

The shift from brands to stars in the public mind is indicated by a suggestion of "Our Man About Town" in the *Moving Picture World* during the fall of 1910. Noting that new exhibitor publicity schemes included a voting contest to determine which manufacturer made the best pictures (brand names), he thought that a contest to name the most popular player (star system) would be good—once the manufacturers finally acceded to the demand for display of the players' photos in the lobbies. The *World* noted that: "There is an extraordinary demand throughout the country by exhibitors for photographs of the actors and actresses. . . . Managers say they are asked daily by regular patrons. . . . The patrons say they want to *get a closer view* of the people" (emphasis added).[28]

The fan magazines appeared next. The trade periodicals, intended to serve the profession and not the general public, began to get inquiries from fans who found their way to them, and the periodicals created regular departments to try to answer the questions. The *Moving Picture World* started a special "Inquiries" column in the fall of 1911. The *New York Dramatic Mirror*, a theatrical paper that was therefore accustomed to the personal popularity of stage stars, claimed to be the first to respond to public demand:

> In devoting to portraits of players so much of the extra space allotted to motion pictures in this annual number, The Mirror is merely responding to the desires of the picture public. The extent to which requests for portraits and inquiries regarding the identity of players have developed since this paper, the first of all publications, commenced replying to questions of this character, has been one of the most striking developments of the past year. . . . The same pressure that the Mirror felt was experienced by the manufacturers, and the most of them responded by preparing sets of portraits of their players for distribution and display, until now it is one of the recognized features of the business (*New York Dramatic Mirror*, 31 January 1912, p. 51).

Motion Picture Story Magazine was begun by J. Stuart Blackton of the Vitagraph Company at the beginning of 1911, with the cooperation of the other licensed companies. It printed stories (illustrated by frame enlargements) of the Trust's films and

Exhibitors depended on the star system to draw audiences to their theaters and used "giveaway" items to get repeat business.

FLORENCE E. TURNER
OF THE
VITAGRAPH PLAYERS

MAURICE COSTELLO.

Norma Talmadge,
of the VITAGRAPH PLAYERS.

JOHN BUNNY
OF THE
VITAGRAPH PLAYERS

Postcard photographs of movie stars promoted the star system and were collected by the fans.

sections with full-page portraits of the players, omitting only the Biograph players until 1913. An enormously popular section was added to supply answers to questions from the fans and publicity stories, and material from the independents was later included as well. George Pratt points out that their expansive "Answers to Inquiries" department sometimes provides the only source for certain film credits. It could be argued, of course, that the *Motion Picture Story Magazine* was begun as promotion for the films themselves, and therefore it didn't start as a fan magazine. But under pressure from its readers, it quickly became one, and it was only the beginning of a flood of such publications.

In April 1911 K. A. Williams of Fox Street, New York City, was offering postcards of stars' photos, which exhibitors could sell to their patrons for five cents each—as much as the admission price in most places. His selection included Mr. Johnson, Mr. Costello, Mr. August, Miss Lawrence, Miss Turner, Miss Leonard, and Miss Robinson. Lois Weber, leading lady of the Rex stock company, got her picture in the *World* at that time. American hired a new leading lady, Pauline Bush, and sent her photo and a story to the trades. Sending pictures of beautiful women to the press was a time-honored way for the newer production companies to get some publicity.[29]

The second annual Sales Company Employers' Ball, held in New York on 14 October 1911, was the signal of a more deliberate building of the star system. It was announced that "attendance of all film actors will be compulsory." The public could buy tickets to these balls, and it had been discovered that they were extremely eager for the opportunity to see their idols in the flesh. Soon motion-picture balls were being held in several major cities by exhibitors' associations and every segment of the industry that could command a group of stars. By the time of the December 1914 Motion Picture Exhibitors' Association Ball, held in New York on the main floor and mezzanine of the Grand Central Palace, all the companies, licensed or independent, took boxes along the sides of the dance floor. That year, Mary Pickford and Francis X. Bushman, Anita Stewart and Earle Williams, Clara Kimball Young and Paul Panzer led the grand march. In Boston, the New England Exhibitors' Association ball had Mary Pickford, Francis X. Bushman, Edwin August, Paul Panzer, Pearl White, Marguerite Snow, Orrin Johnson, Hughie Mack, and Gladys Hulette, while out in San Francisco the Screen Club succeeded in luring up from Los Angeles Charlie Chaplin, Mabel Normand, and Roscoe "Fatty" Arbuckle. Such balls provided the inspiration for the delightful song recorded by Bobby Short, "At the Moving Picture Ball," about dancing on the feet of Miss Blanche Sweet.[30]

The star system was in process of being integrated into industry practice. This integration was as much or more the work of the licensed companies as it was that of the independents. Still, during 1910, 1911, and 1912, most films were released without any naming of the players on the film itself or even in advertisements. The *World* asked for these names to be supplied in a November 1910 editorial. It was difficult, the editorial said, to offer criticism when you didn't know the names:

> We suggest [that] each picture or reel be preceded by the full cast of the characters in the play, with the names of the actors and actresses playing the parts. . . . The veil of anonymity has been gradually turned aside and the public is getting to know these moving picture players (*Moving Picture World*, 12 November 1910, p. 1099).

In 1911 the Edison Company was the only one to give full cast lists in the advertisements for every film. This company also listed directors and authors. I think they did so more in the spirit of their intention to make high-class pictures and give proper credit, as one did in playbills in the legitimate theaters, than to build star publicity. The Edison Company was rather short of real stars at this time anyway. Although almost all of the companies were quite ready to publicize the names of the members of their stock companies, they were just that, members of a company. Few of them were stars or potential stars.

It is difficult to find the beginnings of credit titles by looking at surviving films, not only because most films of the period are lost, but also because few prints survive with original beginning titles intact, and sometimes credit titles were added later when a film was reissued. Among surviving films, one of the earliest to show original credits is Kalem's WHEN THE SUN WENT OUT (September 1911). The cast credits appear on a title that also gives the time and place, as a playbill might do. When Edison credited all the cast members in their production of AIDA (May 1911), including Mary Fuller in the title role, it was said that "the fact that the names of the actors are given is notable." The requests for the practice continued. A fan letter of May 1911 repeated the constant refrain: "I would like a cast shown with film, as it is interesting to compare the different parts played by one person." By the end of July 1911 Edison, Pathé, Gaumont, Selig, Vitagraph (all licensed brands), and Great Northern and Eclair (independent) were said to be introducing the leading characters at the beginning of "important reels." The practice was still uncommon enough in the spring of 1913 to be subject for comment in a review of a film released by the Vitagraph Company: "Another thing about Playing with Fire is worth noting. The names of the players are flashed upon the screen immediately before the scenes in which they appear," or, in the case of a film released by the American Company: "The names of the players are flashed in consecutive order at the start of the picture, each name occupying the screen for a moment."[31]

Stars were great drawing cards for the exhibitor. They didn't do so much for the producer at a time when his best possibility of increasing profits was to either (1) reduce production costs, or (2) get an exchange to order more copies of all of his films on a regular basis. As a *World* editorial pointed out in 1911, "The present system limits the money he [the producer] can make," even if he spent more on the production, except for the very rare special. No wonder the producer worried about the demand for higher salaries that a star system would create.[32]

Until about 1913, under the established industry system, it was still the brand name that was to be advertised and to be sold. As the system changed, the power of stars expanded. The coming of the feature film influenced the building of a star system (see chapter 12), and so did the establishment of Hollywood as a production center, because news about actors began to be supplied by sources other than the faraway studio executives. A Los Angeles correspondent for the *World* innocently gave some brief biographies of "local" players, including Dorothy Bernard and Florence Barker of the Biograph, seemingly unaware these names were supposed to be secret.[33]

When Marion Leonard and her husband, S. E. V. Taylor, formed the Monopol Company to exploit Leonard's talent in feature films early in 1913, they publicized her salary of $1,000 a week on a forty-two-week contract as "probably" the "largest salary of any actress in motion pictures." Her former bosses at the Biograph Company must have shuddered. Since those days, she had appeared with Vitagraph, Reliance, Rex, and Gem. I don't know if she was really getting the largest salary in the business, but the advertisement of it marked a new stage in the exploitation of stars.[34]

In November 1913 the *Ladies' World* ran a Great Moving Picture Hero Contest. This was the same popular periodical that had tied up a promotion with the Edison Company previously, publishing the stories in the series "What Happened to Mary" while Edison produced films based on them. Now exhibitors could get free ballots and an advertising slide for a one-day performance of the contest. The candidates for Moving Picture Hero were: Carlyle Blackwell, Arthur Johnson, Crane Wilbur, Maurice Costello, Warren Kerrigan, Francis X. Bushman, and King Baggott. Following in the path of Francis X. Bushman of Essanay in 1913, Paul Panzer made a personal appearance tour, with a show of film clips of his performances. James Waldo Fawcett, editor of the *Pittsburgh Mirror,* announced ominously, "Hero worship is something tangible in the moving picture business. . . . The future of the moving picture lies with the player. The manufacturer who fails to appreciate talent is doomed."[35]

Actually, I think everyone appreciated talent by then, even Biograph, now that they had no more star attractions left. The era of star exploitation was only just beginning: Theda Bara had yet to be invented.

8

Movie Palaces

Is the two-dollar-a-seat picture theater in sight?

One might believe from the trade periodicals serving the motion-picture industry that nickelodeons began to disappear about 1909–1910 in favor of movie palaces and that blue-collar crowds were being replaced by refined upper-class bejeweled audiences arriving at the theater in automobiles, while the films to be seen were all educational, high-class, and respectable. It was the task of the trade periodicals to promote this concept of improvement. But if one reads the small type and between the lines, it appears that changes were not achieved as easily as the industry hoped. In defending the industry against attack, the trade periodicals revealed the continued opposition in the press and in politics to the conditions of the nickelodeons, making it clear that not all theaters had become safe and clean, much less respectable.

Nickelodeons were no longer such great producers of golden eggs as they once were: "If you look for nickelodeons with 175 seating capacity yielding $200 and $300 per week . . ." you won't find them anymore, advised the *World* at the beginning of 1910. "The days when the boom was at its height, when one reel and a song won nickels galore, are past never to return." In San Francisco, out of a dozen or more houses on "Nickelodeon Row" on Fillmore Street, only two were left in the fall of 1911, and their time was thought to be limited.[1]

While this chapter examines some of the newer "palatial" theaters, it should be remembered that the old-style nickelodeons continued to exist in large numbers, particularly in the urban ghettos, and some of them far past 1915. In the spring of 1911 in New York City, sanitation measures were being recommended for Lower East Side five-cent theaters like these:

> Some of these places are perfectly filthy, with an air so foul and thick that you can almost cut it with a knife. The floor is generally covered with peanut shells, and as there is no stove to spit on everybody spits on the floor. Imagine this in the summer time, and epidemics of various kinds raging in the crowded districts. No wonder the societies and health authorities try to bar children from the moving picture shows! (*Moving Picture World*, 11 March 1911, p. 539).

Even the lonely traveling motion-picture showman, that relic of the pre-nickelodeon days, could still be found somewhere, carrying his own projection equipment to

isolated places. In April 1911, Mr. H. H. Greenfield wrote from Esterhazy, Saskatch-
ewan, enclosing his subscription to the *Moving Picture World:*

> My brother and I are on the road. We have a new Motiograph, pur-
> chased last year, and some very good films, including "The Huguenot,"
> "Italy's Marvelous Cavalry," the "Burning of Rome" and a good assort-
> ment of really funny half-reel comedies. We give them five reels and six
> assorted songs, the music being supplied by a large Victor gramaphone.
> The show goes well and we have received many compliments, but we
> don't find there is much in it, as the expenses are high (*Moving Picture
> World*, 17 April 1911, p. 838).

In rural southern Missouri, Arkansas, and Texas, in 1911, a "touring car" gave one-
and two-night stands showing moving pictures. This show was under the direction of
Mrs. Chris Taylor, traveling with her son Walter, William Wind, and William Avery,
all of Kewanee.[2]

The unique quality of the motion-picture audience, people kept saying as the
middle classes were seen to enter the improved theaters, was its democratic mixing
of the classes. This could be true in small towns, but in the large cities, as J. M.
Blanchard of Sunbury, Pennsylvania, pointed out,

> the picture shows "cater to an entirely different class of people" from the
> picture show patrons in smaller cities—"the thirty thousand population
> class," as he put it. "We cater to our best people," he said, the reason
> being that in towns of that size the picture show "must have them all."
> They need the money. From this standpoint and from watching his pa-
> trons he argued that it is a mistake to suppose that picture spectators
> cannot see through intricate plots. Intelligent people, he found, wanted
> films that stimulate thought ("The 'Spectator's' Comments," *New York
> Dramatic Mirror*, 21 December 1910).

In the large cities one did not find "an entirely different class of people," but it is true
that the type of audience depended a lot on where the theater was. The very poor
living in the crowded tenement districts were probably attending the fetid nickelodeon described above. In Chicago, a visitor to the Orchard Theater, capacity five
hundred, found that "the audiences, though of almost every nationality, are most
well behaved and thoroughly enjoy the entertainments."[3]

In New York, the "better classes" were reported to be attending in the evening at
one theater where children were seldom seen; another theater drew almost all children of the better classes, and at another, businessmen and women attended all day
and night. It was also said that there were different audiences for different brands,
such as the Biograph audience, and the Pathé audience, although nobody explained
how they were to be distinguished. The Audubon Theater in Washington Heights,
New York City, had a family atmosphere and an audience composed of young people
"of the better class" plus a sprinkling of older people. A reporter visiting the new
Parkway Theatre in New York at 110th Street and Central Park West, "one of the
best parts of the city, inhabited by people of wealth and social position" (in 1910),

wrote, "We . . . were agreeably surprised at the high-class character of the patrons; . . . quite a family aspect."[4]

The uplifters promoted the movie theater as a place for family entertainment. It was important to preserve the family unit in a time when industrialization, urbanization, and immigration had created new patterns threatening to the old stability. "Family" was the name of one of Philadelphia's movie houses, indicating the atmosphere the owner hoped to create.[5] The National Board of Censorship declared:

> Moving pictures are now the most important form of cheap amusement in the country. They reach the young immigrants, family groups, the formative and impressionable section of our cities, as no other form of amusement. . . . They are the only theaters which it is possible for the entire family of the wageworker to attend (*Moving Picture World*, 22 April 1911, p. 879).

An editorial in the *Kansas City Star* urged the whole family to patronize the nickel theater, from baby to grandpa, and even the dog would be welcome. It was intended for everybody. "Broaden your horizons," suggested the *Star*, and help keep it a clean and decent place.[6]

In the small mill town of Butler, New Jersey, there was Goldie's on Main Street, one of the two picture houses in town, seating 450 and running independent films and "fairly good vaudeville for a country theater." There was one illustrated song with each show, "a young lady of the town alternating with the projectionist," who left the booth while an usher projected the slides for him. Goldie's had a family patronage, where everyone knew everyone else.[7]

At that Boston Bijou theater managed by Mrs. Edward H. Clement, "the character of which is such that its good name has gone out into all the surrounding towns, . . . the refined touch of an educated woman is evident in every detail," commented another woman, Louise Chadwick, who added:

> The ticket-taker is a quiet refined girl—not the giggling, gum chewing kind; . . . the man at the ticket receiving box is most gentlemanly; the woman in charge of the coat room is a lady who might well grace a drawing-room; the ushers, all women, are courteous and thoughtful, and the show itself beyond possible criticism. There is no comedian, with his disgusting and stale bowery jokes; the illustrated song is not twanged out to a rag-time tune, accompanied by pictures so crudely colored that one wonders where, in these days of color-photography, such crudeness could have been found. And as to the pictures themselves, not one is presented that has not some strong lesson to teach ("The Current Problem and Opportunity of the Moving Picture Show," *Moving Picture News*, 11 January 1913, p. 20).

In 1912 Mrs. Clement gave a paper on "Standardizing the Moving Picture Theater," which she read at a meeting of the Massachusetts State Conference of Charities. Among the celebrated managerial methods she discussed was the inclusion of classical music. "I have found my audience at the Bijou listening with unmistakable

enjoyment to the music of Florina, to solos from La Boheme, Tosca, Madame But-
terfly and many other operas, and I do not believe that my audience is the only one
which is capable of enjoying just such music," declared Mrs. Clement. A woman of
sound business sense as well as refinement, she obtained her musical performances
from student musicians, which cost her "only a nominal amount."[8] Earlier that year,
"resenting the treatment accorded them at some of the moving picture houses" in
Denver, Colorado, a group of blacks opened their own theater under the management of Mrs. Laura Hill, "a social leader among the negroes."[9]

In 1914, Mrs. A. C. M. Sturgis took over the Lafayette Theater, in Washington,
D.C., and according to press reports, "from the attendance and the aspect of the
theatre outside and in, the observer is aware that the Layfayette has changed hands,
and this to advantage." Mrs. Sturgis then explained her policy:

> I mean to keep the Lafayette clean, comfortable and well ventilated. By
> the frequent use of the big exhaust fans, the air in the theatre is changed
> in four minutes, and by the hourly spraying with a perfumed deodorizer
> the atmosphere is kept healthful and pleasant. It is attention of this nature
> that is a strong point in a woman's management of a picture house.
> Already I have been able to increase the attendance of women and the
> young folks. My program will include the best that can be afforded by a
> five-cent house. I am making arrangements to show the suffrage play,
> "Your Girl and Mine," and I mean to do all that I can to interest the
> women in the Lafayette, and I am inviting suggestions from my patrons
> as to what they want. That is the best way to create good fellowship
> between manager and patrons and an effective manner of studying your
> attendance (*Motion Picture News*, 19 December 1914, p. 37).

An exhibitor in Goodell, Oklahoma, with a four-hundred-seat theater, reported
that he had

Overcoming the odor of humanity in the nickelodeons.

three classes to cater to: first the cowboy spirited ones; the "will-be-married-some-day" class, and the old, old ones [who] like the rest, [love] that good old comic. But, alas, we get all cowboy, or all love stories or all comic. Why? Because the exchange has not got the time to fool with us "little folks" as they call us in small country towns, although the advance agent will give all kinds of promises (*Moving Picture World*, 5 August 1911, p. 301).

Not all the exchange men were so uncaring. One day in the summer of 1911, when the morning train arrived in Laramie, Wyoming, with no film on it, an exchange manager named Buckwalter drove hundreds of miles from Denver overnight in a pouring rain on unmarked roads, in a big Packard, to deliver the program in time. Bets were placed on his making it. He did.[10]

Throughout this period, programs continued to grow longer, until, as already noted, by the time of the feature-length film, many audiences were already in the habit of attending an evening's entertainment instead of going from one theater to the next or just dropping in for half an hour. It would prove more difficult to get them to adjust to the idea of attending at the start of the performance, accustomed as they were to a variety show. In the "Family Theater" of Philadelphia mentioned above, the program consisted of two reels and a song. The Philadelphia theaters were not engaging in the long-program competition then going on in New York, where it was said that "the duration of the average entertainment ranges between forty minutes and an hour and a half. That is our experience at moving picture theaters in New York City. Probably the rule generally applies." The Open Air Theater Park at 138th Street, operating in the hot summer months of 1909, had a program lasting three hours. This undoubtedly included a lot of vaudeville and illustrated songs. They supplied a place for checking baby carriages and all kinds of refreshments at five cents a portion. By 1913, programs commonly contained from five to eight reels: I am speaking about short films, still usually shown for a five-cent admission, not the ten-cent houses, where feature films were shown.[11]

When new theaters were built, replacing the store show houses, conditions of moviegoing improved tremendously. Lary May's research has shown that many of the new theaters built from 1908 to about 1916 borrowed a lot from the classical styles, associated, May suggests, with classicism and reason. The "balance, clarity and angularity of these styles" were equated with order. Later, as this period came to a close, exoticism and romantic rounded arches and curves began to be employed, but the first condition, in 1908, was to bring a sense of control and order and safety to the movie houses. Whether the architectural styles selected were only related to the architectural fashions of the whole society or were more specifically tied to the needs of the motion-picture industry, I am not really sure. However that may be, builders of film theaters had a lot of help from the trade periodicals, which published whole sections of their journals dedicated to theater design and decoration.[12] The introduction to a surviving Decorators Supply Company catalog of the period illustrates perfectly the concern for high-toned surroundings:

> The Motion Picture Show Places have become a fixed institution in this country, they have found a permanent place as American Enterprises, and are here to stay. Recognizing this fact, we have assembled in this catalog

a few illustrations showing the beautiful effects obtained by using our ornamentation for the enrichment of exteriors and interiors of said theaters. Of the many hundreds of places we have furnished the ornamental work for in different cities, we have reproduced here a few characteristic ones. We want to interest you, prospective Theatre Builder, in the fact that only through the medium of our class of ornamentation can you hope to have your place rank in beauty and attraction with the best in the country. The time is past when a cheaply fixed up place will pay. You must make a strong effort to get a fine Show Place to make money. The few prices we have inserted in this catalog will convince you that you can well afford a nice, ornamental front for a reasonable price. Pick out the illustration you desire to have, write to us, give us the measurements and conditions existing at present at your place, and we will make you a correct design showing what can be done with your theatre with our ornaments. We will also make the working drawings for the carpenter, plasterer and electrician, in conjunction with showing our ornaments, so that you can make all changes at the building from drawings furnished by us.

Among the first improvements suggested for the nickelodeons, it was recommended that theater seats should have a wire hat holder beneath the seat and on the back of each seat a small ring through which ladies might thrust a hatpin to hold their headgear instead of being obliged to keep them in their laps. Furthermore, it was noted: "All theaters should have a sloped floor. The day of the flat floor is past." That might be, but more theaters still had flat floors than sloped ones.[13]

All kinds of amenities were brought in to make the new theaters comfortable, elegant, and refined. The unwashed might be made to feel a little out-of-place, and the better classes more assured. Marble, beveled glass, polished oak and walnut, dazzling electric lights, lavish carpeting, and huge mirrors began to appear in newly redecorated theaters. Restrooms became a necessity rather than a luxury with longer programs, and these were finer facilities than many customers had at home. Exhibitors were told that the "well-conducted motion picture houses have uniformed attendants." These gave an appearance of order and encouraged good conduct.[14]

Automobiles, not yet in the possession of every family in America, were a sure sign of "the better classes." Ownership of automobiles signaled good wages for actors and success for the exchanges and exhibitors. Bill Steiner of the Imperial Film Exchange in New York claimed to be the first to use an automobile to institute a film delivery and pickup service. His idea was taken up by C. Calehuff of Philadelphia, who sent a specially built car on the rounds. Automobiles were also a mark of high-class customers if they parked in front of your theater. "Around the Bijou, you see no crowds of dirty urchins hanging about, but there are plenty of automobiles," they said of the newly built theater in Springfield, Massachusetts, when it opened in April 1910. Furthermore, the press reported, "the house is lighted up during the running of the pictures—a great gain with the best people." When the new T.N.F. Theater opened in "aristocratic Flatbush," it had to overcome neighborhood resistance in the exclusive Midwood residential section. Here, the owners offered claim-check parking for the automobiles, and it was a great success. In St. Louis, meanwhile, the Gem Theater was said to be "coining money and at night you can see a string of automobiles in front of the house, showing that the best society of St. Louis is not averse to motion pictures." And when Kinemacolor pictures played at the Herald Square

The Decorators Supply Company Catalogue offered prefabricated ornamentation to transform the nickelodeons into movie palaces. Boston Theatre, 116 East Madison St., Chicago.

Theater in New York City, the automobiles outside convinced Robert Grau that the patronage was not of a transient character. "The audiences come . . . in automobiles, carriages, and they arrive . . . at the exact hour," he noted, while the headline on his story asked, "Is the two-dollar-a-seat picture theater in sight?"[15]

Thomas Saxe's new Princess Theater in Milwaukee "opened a new era in elegance" in 1910. Seating nine hundred, it boasted a pipe organ and a seven-piece orchestra, electric fountains in the lobby, retiring rooms, and beveled plate-glass and mahogany doors. At this time in Milwaukee, the majority of the theaters regularly employed a lecturer for all the films and for giving out the announcements. The exhibitors followed a pattern of changing the film program three times a week instead of daily, and they employed uniformed women ushers. The reporter of this "fad" thought it should not be a job for a young girl, and perhaps with reason, because Milwaukee appears to have had a difficult problem in controlling the male patrons. In June 1911 it was decided to make lighted theaters mandatory. Not only that, but theater owners agreed to station mature married men at their doors, to lessen the danger of "mashing." In Chicago in 1910, it was also "the policy of the first class theaters . . . [to employ] lady ushers."[16]

Classical music in a movie theater, as in Mrs. Clement's Bijou in Boston, was a sign of uplift. A visitor to a large Chicago theater where Biograph's A FOOL'S REVENGE (based on Rigoletto) was playing noted with pleasure that "a pleasant variation from the eternal ragtime was a refined deliverance of classical music corresponding to the character of the picture, including Schumann's 'Traumerei' and Beethoven's 'Moonlight Sonata.' The first time, indeed, we ever heard Beethoven in a five-cent theater." A visitor to the Empress in Washington, D.C., was "somewhat astonished to hear 'The Barcarole' from 'Love Tales of Hoffmann' being played in a truly artistic style. This strain continued during the love passage . . . but as soon as the theme of the story changed, so did the music."[17]

ELEKTRA, Vitagraph's film version of "the powerfully tragic story of ancient Greece that forms the basis for the famous Richard Strauss opera," appeared the same season that the opera was performed. One might think the subject was chosen mostly for its timely news value: the dissonance of Strauss's score had made the opera quite a sensation. However, the film was accepted as another example of high culture by its audiences, even though Vitagraph advertisements advised exhibitors to "bill it like a circus—it will draw bigger crowds than any film you have ever had." The film was reported to be roundly applauded, which motion-picture audiences "of the better kind" rarely did. It was shown at Keith and Proctor's Bijou Dream on Twenty-third Street, where the pianist chose to accompany it with popular modern music, which seemed ridiculous to the reviewer. There were letters praising the film from exhibitors who showed it to "refined and intelligent" audiences in Lima, Ohio, and New Orleans, Louisiana. The manager of the 1,700-seat Shubert Theater in New Orleans, who used four reels for a program and normally changed the program three times a week, held over ELEKTRA for four days. "The class of patrons we have are made up of the best people in the city," boasted the manager.[18]

The World editors kept track of the motion-picture theaters advancing on Broadway and pointed out as a sign of progress the Savoy Theater on Thirty-fourth Street, which became a movie house in 1910. This street was "the center of things in respect of fashion." Two years earlier, they wrote, there was not one good theater in New York specializing in moving pictures; now there must be a dozen. "Small country towns can boast of moving picture palaces that put to shame any New York show. . . . The farther West we go, the more the picture is in evidence as the amusement of the classes."[19]

In San Francisco the first nickelodeon to be erected in the heart of the aristocratic residential district was built in the fall of 1910 at Presidio Avenue and Sacramento Streets. That same fall, Charles Keeler, a writer and a prominent member of the literary colony of Carmel-by-the-Sea, opened a movie theater where he promised to show films that would stimulate an interest in art and industry, for an audience that would include the Board of Education of Berkeley and the faculty of the University of California.[20]

Clune's Theater in Los Angeles opened on 10 November 1910. It seated nine hundred and had three projectors plus two stereopticons (at a time when having two projectors was already the sign of a high-class house). For an admission price of ten and twenty cents (for loge seats at the back), one got five full reels of licensed films on the first run, two illustrated songs, and one "song specialty," adding up to a program of an hour and a half. If those were really full reels, that means the projectionist at Clune's speeded them up at a tremendous rate. An eight-piece orchestra and two singing booths, one on each side of the screen, were available for the music.[21]

About this time Keith and Proctor's six houses in New York and New Jersey gave up having any illustrated songs, although they still used illustrated lectures and vaudeville with the movies. The manager of the Bijou in Catlettsburg, Kentucky, announced soon after, "I have discontinued using illustrated songs, as they are all trashy." He had a "high-class patronage" and wanted no more Westerns or melodramas or the silly comedies from Europe. But if he avoided these categories, there was not much left to fill his program.[22]

When Bedding visited the theaters of Cincinnati, Ohio, that month, he found:

> Today things have changed, the dirty little dumps, with small seating capacity and poor ventilation are fast passing away to make room for large, palatial houses, and the moment that the exhibitors called the attention of the public to a much better class of houses, a new class of spectators appeared and are now eager for motion pictures (*Moving Picture World*, 14 January 1911, p. 1069).

Still, efforts to upgrade the movie theater could misfire. In Lowell, Massachusetts, a mill town with poorly paid workers, the brand-new Colonial Theater closed after two months in 1911. It had 350 seats, waiting rooms, lavatories, and a well-equipped projection booth and used an expensive licensed service in addition to vaudeville— but the admission price was ten cents. There was not a large enough public in Lowell able to pay that on a regular basis.[23]

With special films and a knowledge of showmanship, great things could be achieved even in poor neighborhoods. In Providence, considered a poor factory town, DANTE'S INFERNO played the Opera House at fifty cents admission to crowds who came out in the pouring rain. W. Stephen Bush from the *Moving Picture World* was appearing there and lecturing with the film. The Joliette Theater, Boston, gave its annual presentation of THE PASSION PLAY throughout Holy Week every year from 1906 and reported in the fifth year, 1911, that these weeks had given the theater its biggest attendance. The manager had printed fliers, more than half of them in Italian, giving the synopses of the thirty-nine scenes in the picture—an indication of the ethnic neighborhood from which the Joliette drew its customers. The manager of the Virginian in Washington, D.C., got the schools to take up the subject of "The Fall of Troy" in their history courses and then ran the film for four days during the Easter holidays, filling the house with students. The same energetic showman-manager showed slides of the terrible Triangle shirtwaist factory fire in New York, accompanied by a funeral dirge.[24]

In 1914 New York City began to catch up with the development elsewhere of the "palatial" movie theater. Two big movie theaters opened up on Broadway, the Vitagraph and the Strand. The forward-looking Vitagraph Company leased the Criterion, which was at Forty-fourth Street, renamed it the Vitagraph Theatre, and opened it on 7 February, while the Strand, at Forty-seventh Street, opened 11 April.

To The MANAGERS and PROPRIETORS
of MOVING PICTURE THEATRES

Gentlemen:

It is a recognized fact that the public is becoming tired of ILLUSTRATED SONGS. It is true there are always new songs and new slides on the market, but they all have the same SING SONG SWING to them with their tales of LOVESICK MAIDS etc., and it becomes MONOTONOUS.

In introducing our LECTURETTES to you, we believe we are on the right track, as people NEVER TIRE OF LECTURES as long as they are well read and properly IL-LUSTRATED.

They are INSTRUCTIVE as well as ENTERTAIN-ING, and it gives your patrons a chance to see THE WORLD AS IT IS without going out of their own sphere, and they DRAW THE BETTER CLASS OF PEOPLE to your thea-tre.

Our LECTURES are well written and anyone employed in the theatre can deliver as good a lecture as a professional. THEY ARE BRIGHT AND SNAPPY and just long enough, so that they will not become monotonous, or CRACK THE SLIDES which is an ITEM IN ITSELF.

The Keith & Proctor houses in New York have introd-uced these lecturettes, between the moving pictures, and this feature has met with unqualified success and their houses are crowded nightly

These lecturettes will prove a valuable attraction for your house, and the cost is so small that you can well afford same. New sets are being added, and we guarantee you NO REPEATERS.

On the next two pages you will find a list of the sub-jects issued by us to date; on the last page of this folder you will find OUR NEW PROPOSITION.

Look into it carefully and see if it is not THE BEST SLIDE OFFER EVER MADE TO YOU.

The illustrated songs began to fade away, but the illustrated lecture continued to give an atmosphere of refinement to the moving-picture theater.

Oil paintings of the Vitagraph players were hung around the foyer of the former Criterion, and it was all newly decorated for the occasion. The program for the opening night included a live pantomime performance by John Bunny and the other Vitagraph players called "The Honeymooners," and a two-reel film comedy, a bril-liant parody of the melodrama, called GOODNESS GRACIOUS; OR, MOVIES AS THEY SHOULDN'T BE, followed by a four-reel feature film, A MILLION BID, directed by Ralph Ince. The dramatic critic of the *New York American* attended the formal opening and reviewed the performance. A week or so later, the Vitagraph Theater installed a Hope-Jones symphonic orchestra, a $30,000 instrument manufactured by the Rudolph Wurlitzer Company. This was no ordinary movie theater, changing its films every day or twice a week: as in the legitimate theater, the film program was to be played there as long as there was sufficient public to see it. The seats were sold on a reserved basis, for twenty-five cents up to a dollar. It was not a "poor man's entertainment."[25]

It was Roxy Rothapfel, managing the new Strand at Forty-seventh Street, who really understood what attracted the middle-class audience. Samuel L. "Roxy" Rothapfel started out as an exhibitor in the small town of Forest City, Pennsylvania, population 4,279. In the beginning of 1910 his special qualities as a showman must have come to the attention of somebody at the *Moving Picture World*, because he was invited to contribute a column on topics of interest to the exhibitor. (In the same issue in which his articles began, F. H. Richardson initiated his long series of technical columns for projectionists, and exhibitors in general, commenting on all aspects of exhibition.) Rothapfel's first columns were on the importance of the order in which the films were shown, and the question of whether music should be continuous throughout the performance.[26]

The great showman's name was already marketable in 1911.

What "The Belasco"
of Motion Pictures has to say of the
MOTIOGRAPH.

DE LUXE PICTURE ENTERPRISES
DE LUXE PICTURE COMPANY (Incorporated)
Direction of S. L. ROTHAPFEL

LYRIC THEATRE

THE FINEST AND MOST ARTISTIC
PRESENTATION OF ANIMATED
PHOTOGRAPHY IN AMERICA

EXCLUSIVELY USING THE CELEBRATED
DAYLIGHT PICTURES INVENTED
BY MR. S. L. ROTHAPFEL

Minneapolis, Minn.___ Dec. 5, 1911 ___191__

The Enterprise Optical Mfg. Co.,
    564 West Randolph St.,
        Chicago, Ills.

Gentlemen:

    Replying to yours of recent date asking me to give my opinion upon the machine that I am using in my De Luxe presentations, I respectfully submit the following:

    I selected your Machine, the "Motiograph", in preference to the others, because I found the principle therein envolved answered my purpose better than any other machine on the market and I have never regretted for one instant my choice. I am not in the habit of giving any testimonials to anyone, but if this will do you any good, you may use same.

    It may interest you to know, that during the recent agitation against Motion Picture Theatres of Minneapolis, I made every conceivable fire test in the presence of the officials with the most satisfactory results. It was impossilbe to burn more of the film than that which covered the aperture plate. I then took a piece of the film and protruded same from upper magazine; I lighted it with a match; it burned to first roller and there withered and died not injuring or effecting the film beyond that point. The same test was conducted with the lower magazine and several other tests of an equally satisfactory nature were all made with the result that the officials of the Fire Dept. in the city, were very high in their praise of the instruments which I use.

                                Respectfully yours,
                                Rothapfel

But his future was not as a columnist. A year later, the great showman was found at the Lyric in Minneapolis at the Christmas season of 1911, staging "The Passion Play." This theater had a capacity of seventeen hundred seats, and "The Passion Play" was shown there for four days in early December, returning the entire week of 18 December. There was a prelude of two silent films with no music and no sound effects: WILD BIRDS IN THEIR HAUNTS and THE HOLY LAND, both from Pathé. When the audience was settled in, the doors closed, the house darkened, the stage curtain lowered. There was a distant pealing of chimes. "The Holy City" was played by the pipe organ. The curtain was raised and perfume of lilies wafted over the house. Twenty choirboys in white vestments were onstage. The baritone sang "Holy City," the choirboys joined in, a pale blue light was gradually diffused, fountains played with pale blue lights beneath, and several dozen roses were carefully strewn on the steps and stage. Then, with the showing of the feature, there was a performance of "Holy Night," "Adeste Fideles," "Christmas Carol," "Praise Ye the Father," "The Palms," and "Calvary." All this before Rothapfel even made it to New York City.[27]

In November 1913 Rothapfel was in New York, managing the Regent on 116th Street, a high-class place charging ten, fifteen, and twenty-five cents. "Few of the old-fashioned 'illustrated singers' survive to this day," it was said, but Rothapfel hired "real artists." When the Strand Theatre opened in the spring of 1914 a few blocks up Broadway from the Vitagraph, it was also under Rothapfel's management. This movie palace seated 3,500 people. Roxy's opening program included a concert by the orchestra, conducted by Carl Edouarde, a song short, orchestral music, the Strand Quartet, a comedy film, and for the feature film, THE SPOILERS. Roxy insisted on conducting rehearsals with the orchestra and the film in advance of the first showing of every program. Films in his theater would be accompanied by a full orchestra that was prepared to interpret the film, not just play along with it or against it. The careful pacing of the whole performance from opening concert through the short subject and the feature was an ingredient in his success.[28]

Even small-town managers were capable of the Rothapfel type of showmanship, as Ropthafel himself had demonstrated back in Forest City in 1910. A little town in Indiana in 1911, population twelve hundred, had three picture shows, and the competition must have been rather intense. The manager of one of them, which seated 275 people, reported this success:

> On last Saturday we had the great Reliance picture, "The Vows," and during the last scene where the young man is brought back to the church by his sweetheart, Miss Worth sang "The Rosary" (Nevin) behind the screen, accompanied by Miss Kolmorgan on the organ, and Mr. Karl Kurtz (an efficient drummer) on the chimes, and the effect was very beautiful and very much appreciated. We are very particular about trying to put on the effects at our place and we spare no trouble or expense to prepare for them. . . . On last Saturday we showed to over one-sixth of the entire population of the town, and that in the face of the fact that there are three other picture shows here, and the church people with a special production of "Esther" were playing at the opera house (*Moving Picture World*, 11 March 1911, p. 538).

The appeal to religion and church people was important, because they were the respectable society in most small towns, and often in the cities as well. On the other hand, films on religious subjects often fell afoul of interdenominational sensibilities. The National Board of Censorship explained after some complaints that it did pass a film called THE NUN, because their task was to decide whether or not a film was immoral, not whether it was in poor taste.[29]

When Kalem previewed its five-reel feature FROM THE MANGER TO THE CROSS for church people in the fall of 1912, it was highly praised, but it ran into some trouble with hostile clergymen. After years of the film industry's using religion as uplift, it was now asked whether religious films were suitable for showing in a theater for entertainment purposes, reviving the troubles that passion plays had encountered at the end of the previous century. The clergymen wondered if FROM THE MANGER TO THE CROSS could be treated with proper reverence in a theater. It might be sacrilegious to charge admission to see a religious film. FROM THE MANGER TO THE CROSS was made "on the original locations" in the Middle East, and the backgrounds appeared to be much more real than the old painted flats of earlier passion plays, which were more like the illustrations in a Sunday School picture book. It was almost as though the old Sunday School book were now illustrated with photographs of movie stars. FROM THE MANGER TO THE CROSS shared with those earlier films the tableau style of production, but the camera was a little closer and the people and the surroundings had a tangible solidity that may have contributed to that feeling of sacrilege. The critic W. Stephen Bush concluded that its chief claim to greatness was its realism (in a statement that implied the film did not have other claims). Perhaps the film was also considered rather dull, after all, like many of the uplifting films, in the context of the numerous other films in 1912 that employed dynamic editing systems to bring excitement, suspense, and thrills to their audiences. Such pretentious films as FROM THE MANGER TO THE CROSS were no longer as much in demand. The film PILGRIM'S PROGRESS, an hour and a half of religious biography and allegory, Louis Reeves Harrison decided, was "too rich an offering for . . . ordinary mortals." It would be suitable for churches and schools, he thought, but not for motion-picture theaters. In fact, by 1914, a number of churches were being turned into movie theaters.[30]

As one exhibitor frankly acknowledged:

> Fact of the matter is, folks in this town don't care for the big educationals and classics. They want short snappy stuff, a live Essanay or Edison comedy, a spirited Kalem railroad or adventure film, but let me advertise a religious piece or Shakespeare and it means an off day in the box office (*Moving Picture World*, 9 November 1912, p. 643).

At the end of 1912 W. Stephen Bush editorialized that cooperation among exhibitors had achieved the "checking of cheap vaudeville and the spread of the Sunday exhibition." The next most pressing problem, he thought, was the price of admission. The names "nickelodeon" and "nickolet" were badges of cheapness and were obsolete. The five-cent theaters should be reserved only for the old films. Feature films, showing in big theaters, were getting as much as two dollars, and were bringing in a higher class of people. There was also, he observed, a higher quality in films now.[31]

According to Louise Chadwick:

> The dimes of the higher grade people are as good as those of lower;
> moreover, one often hears people say that they would rather pay an extra
> nickel to see something worthwhile and be reasonably sure of not finding
> himself wedged in between uncleanly people—a feature of the moving
> picture show that militates no little against its patronage by decent people
> and will have some time to be reckoned with (Chadwick, "The Current
> Problem and Opportunity of the Motion Picture Show").

On 20 October 1913 Loew's Herald Square Theater in New York City began a
first-run program of five reels, with admission fifteen cents everywhere in the house
in the evening. Four days later, the new Nostrand Theater opened in Brooklyn, the
first of the New York City houses to be enlarged from 299 to 600 seats under the new
ordinance. It had a sloped floor, two projectors, restrooms, and music provided by a
violinist and pianist. The prices of admission were ten and twenty cents. There was
one afternoon show and two in the evening, and they used the General Film Exclusive Service (for which they paid top prices), changing the program every other day.
The Vitagraph matinee idol Maurice Costello, just back from a round-the-world trip,
made a personal appearance for the opening of the Nostrand.[32]

But then, over in East New York, a study conducted by the local exhibitors'
association showed that all the exhibitors were running four reels for a nickel and on
weekends, five reels for ten cents. In Pittsburgh, it was reported: "It seems to be the
policy here for the exhibitor to give as big a show as he can give for five cents. The
Lyric is the only one that sticks to the three reels." And Denver, as we know from
an earlier chapter, was still "Nickel City of the West."[33]

Buffalo, New York, was experiencing a theater building boom in mid 1914. It was
said that "Buffalo has become a permanent motion picture center and . . . the popularity of film drama here is constantly increasing." The Palace, a downtown theater
on Main Street, opposite Shelton Square, was expected to cost $150,000, and "ar-
chitecturally, will be a revelation." The interior decorations of Rothapfel's Strand in
New York City were to be used as a guide for the new Palace. This was only one of
several large new houses being built at that time: "In the larger houses capacity
audiences are the rule every evening. At the new Elmwood, Allendale, and Strand
hundreds are seen every evening waiting in the lobbies. It looks as though the
five-cent house was doomed, as the big houses are getting all the business."

According to Daniel Savage, manager of the local General Film office:

> There is not any possible way for the exhibitor to keep the admission at
> five cents, as the trend of the trade is for better and larger produc-
> tions. . . . Up until three years ago the manufacturer produced one-reel
> subjects and would spend from $300 to $700; at the present time the
> lowest they consider is $2,500 to an unlimited amount, to get a satisfac-
> tory picture. The only outcome that I can see is the larger houses charging
> accordingly (*The Motion Picture News*, 13 June 1914, pp. 47–48).

Here is a case history of how exhibitor Harry Nichols raised admission prices from
nickels to dimes with some of that Roxy-type showmanship: When Nichols took over

management of the Garden Theater in Waterbury, Connecticut (population 85,000) in January 1914, it was a nickel house with a thousand seats. It was on its last legs and barely surviving. Step by step, he got a better film program and used gimmicks to attract a larger public, giving away gold pieces, admitting children under twelve free at matinees when accompanied by an adult, and sending a weekly program schedule to all who requested it. Then he redecorated his theater. He bought new tapestries covered with roses and placed giant artificial rose bushes and vines onstage and all over the house, including the lobby. These were advertised as fireproof, tested by the fire commissioner. His stage he called "futurist," in honor of the modern-art movement. Futurism, although little understood by American popular culture, had become a fad word for anything rather *outré* or excessive. This "futurist" stage had an Oriental living room on the right, and on the left a den, with special lighting effects. In keeping with the search for suitable family theaters, then, he presented a kind of illusion that his stage was a home, albeit a rather more modish home than most in his audience had. The Oriental motif in interior decoration was becoming very fashionable. In back of the curtain there was a transparent screen through which various tableaux could be seen. Early in December 1914 this was a shipwreck scene. The spectators waited until the curtain rose, and the multicolored lights played on the scene, to eagerly applaud whatever special effects were presented for their delight and amazement. The Famous Players program was playing there until October, and Nichols booked his Sunday features on the open market. The daily program consisted of five-reel features with two or three single ones as "fillers." The Paramount program began after that, with such films as THE VIRGINIA with Dustin Farnum and THE LOST PARADISE with H. B. Warner. Nichols then reached the point where he dared to change the prices from a nickel to ten and fifteen cents. He admitted:

> Of course, it's going to drive away my five cent patrons, but it means that a better class is coming in. . . . I am going to put on a new three piece orchestra consisting of violin, piano and cello. Right now I am sending out 5,000 pamphlets to my clientele telling of the new change in program and increase in prices. I plan to run only one show an evening when I start the Paramount, although I may be obliged to run two of the reels a second time for the tardy ones. I propose to increase my force of girl ushers by two more, making four in all. Pretty good plan, don't you think so? (*Motion Picture News*, 19 December 1914, p. 116).

Paramount Pictures Corporation's Christmas greeting to the trade in 1914 was: "The Dawn of a New Era: Better Pictures, Finer Theatres, Higher Admission Prices." By that time the business had grown to the extent that lists were available naming 20,192 moving-picture theaters in the United States and Canada, and for the United States alone, 795 exchanges, 70 film producers, and 34 manufacturers and dealers in motion-picture equipment.[34]

Some commentators felt that the new middle-class audience might have special sensibilities. When the Champion Film Company released THE BLOOD OF THE POOR, a tragedy of a poor Jewish tailor and a rich landlord, in January 1912, a trade critic thought that it would be "hailed in certain quarters," but he added, "Subjects of this character are calculated to arouse class prejudice unless treated in the most delicate manner and it is open to question if good can result from accentuating the social differences of the people."[35]

Considering the number of films of the period that dwelled on similar subjects, it is unlikely that the audience was really that sensitive. Rather, such statements only reflect the uncertainty, the insecurity, of some segments of the industry *vis à vis* "the better classes," as they came into the theaters.

In 1910, "Spectator" Frank Woods was asked by a correspondent, "Which is the most correct, 'motion pictures' or 'moving pictures?' " Taking this inquiry quite seriously, Woods went over the history of use of the two terms and concluded that "motion pictures" had begun to replace "moving pictures" as films improved. The pictures were no longer in constant movement, acting had improved, and "motion pictures" was a better term for a period of uplift. Accordingly, he undertook to change the name of his weekly column from "Moving" to "Motion Picture Notes."[36]

Hay and Nicholas of the Haynic Theater in Fairmount, Minnesota, wrote to their local paper in 1913, asking them to avoid the use of the word "movies." "It is unpardonable slang, emanating from the gutter, and its use is deplored by everyone who wishes to see the photoplay occupy the dignified position which it deserves." This was a losing battle, though. When Louella O. Parsons published her manual for scenario writing in 1915, she called it *How to write for the "Movies."*[37]

Whatever the audiences now filling the moving-picture theaters were, they were in the process of being welded together, and not only by the conditions of the theaters. As the reviewer recalled the showing of THE LONELY VILLA in the Fourteenth Street nickelodeon where the woman exclaimed, "Thank God, they are saved!" he commented, "The entire audience was one person and the woman who spoke voiced a common feeling."[38]

9

Trademarks, Titles,
Introductions

The Down Express is on the wrong line. My God! It's bound to crash into
the local!

—An intertitle in "A Partner to Providence,"
number 8 in the series THE BELOVED ADVENTURER, September 1914

To prevent the piracy rampant in the early days of the industry, the production
companies began to place their trademark on the sets of nearly every scene, on
the walls of the set, or even on trees when the scene was shot outdoors. The practice
began in American films around 1907, as a way of avoiding the expense of copyright-
ing, since infringement of a trademark was a felony, and if someone made an illegal
duplicate copy of a film, it could be easily identified. Vitagraph had a winged "V,"
Lubin had a bell, Biograph used an "AB," Essanay had a circle with "S & A" inside
of it, Pathé a cock (or rooster, as it was called in refined American circles), Kalem a
sun (which, when used as an "end title," was an animated sun with rays that re-
volved). Thanhouser used a wreath enclosing comic and tragic masks as well as
intertwined company initials, and American had a winged "A." These trademarks
were sometimes made of wood or metal in order to be easily moved from scene to
scene. The design of the trademarks often changed slightly from one year to the next,
which has sometimes made it possible for film historians to arrive at an approximate
date for an unidentified film.[1]

The importance of showing a trademark in the film is underlined by the fact that
it was required by the licensing agreement that producers signed with the Motion
Picture Patents Company at the beginning of 1909. According to article seven, the
licensee agreed "to photographically print the licensee's trade-mark in each picture
of at least one scene of each subject." This rule was changed only in the renewed
agreements signed on 6 June 1912, which still required the trademark to be printed
on the film, but not on the image. The new regulation stipulated that the trademark
must be placed on the title of each positive, a practice that was already widely
followed by this time.[2]

During the struggle between the licensed and independent producers, many an
exchange man or exhibitor switched the main titles of films to cheat the rules,
pretending a film was licensed when it was not, or vice versa. This did not fool
viewers much because the trademark was still there on the wall of the set. The use

The trademarks of the productions distributed by General Film Company. Examples of the way in which trademarks were placed in the sets may be seen on pages 46, 66, 68, 237, and 247.

of trademarks in the scenes didn't prevent piracy, either, if one were really determined. Fred Balshofer has recounted how he began his career in the motion-picture business in the basement of Lubin's Philadelphia store, painstakingly brushing out the trademark from every frame before proceeding to duplicate films from such producers as Georges Méliès.[3]

Of more significance for the production of films after 1908 was the fact that the trademark appearing in the film was inconsistent with the illusion of reality. As long as the trademark was on the wall of an artificial set, it might not be very obtrusive, but nailed to a tree, it became ludicrous. Nevertheless, it lingered on in the films of most producers until mid 1911 or 1912. Probably it remained in use beyond the period when such inconsistencies were really acceptable because of the tensions of the distribution-exhibition systems of the license-holders versus the independents.

In February 1911 the *Moving Picture World* called the attention of producers to the anomaly. Ridiculing the practice because it destroyed the illusion, the author of this criticism blamed the continued use of the trademark on the advertising departments. I don't know whether this accusation betrayed ignorance of the original reason for using the trademark or whether indeed the trademark had come to be used to emphasize brand-name values as well.[4]

Nevertheless, some companies continued to use the trademark within their films during 1911. In THE PENNILESS PRINCE, one of the films the IMP Company produced in Cuba in early 1911, the heroine is walking with her lover through the grass. When she passes the large IMP trademark stuck into the ground, she is compelled to lift her skirts and to step around it. It would be impossible for a spectator of the film to ignore its presence. The scene is so awkward that it would probably have been retaken if it weren't that these films were being made as cheaply as possible. The producers were sending the negative back to New York for processing and would not have seen how obvious her move to avoid the trademark was until much too late. The IMP trademark can still be found in the other surviving Cuban productions of this year, including IN OLD MADRID and SWEET MEMORIES. (These films are among the first group of pictures directed by Thomas Ince, as is THE PENNILESS PRINCE.)

Kalem still used their trademark in TANGLED LIVES (filmed in Florida and released in May 1911). Thanhouser used it in THE PILLARS OF SOCIETY (May 1911), and it can be found in a Solax film, GREATER LOVE HATH NO MAN (July 1911). The Vitagraph Company, usually in the forefront of industry practice, was nonetheless criticized for the absurdity of their winged "V" plastered against a column in a temple of ancient times in FIRES OF FATE (June 1911).[5]

I have noticed the trademark rarely when viewing the surviving films later than mid 1911, despite the Motion Picture Patents Company agreement, but even at the beginning of 1913 a trade periodical commented that "some manufacturers have not as yet eliminated their trade-marks from the doors, walls, trees and other settings in the pictures. Some way should be devised to forego this custom, which so frequently spoils an otherwise artistic setting."[6] The trademark continued to be used to distinguish the film company even later than this, but producers began to place it on the intertitles instead of on the picture. Titles were not considered part of the illusion; therefore trademarks could be accepted on titles more easily than within the images.

Back in 1907 film narratives were becoming more complex, in spite of the limited narrative modes then in existence. As a result, more and longer intertitles soon began to be used to fill the gaps in the means of expression. In an earlier period, when every shot was to some extent self-sufficient, films often used a title to announce each change of shot. When the time came that the producers began to consider a group of shots more closely related, they found that one main title could be used to label the group. The term "leader" was frequently used for intertitles, the same word that is now in use for the blank film used to thread up the film in the projection machine before the picture starts. In its very name is the perception that it "led" the scene, that it announced what the scene was going to be before it started. In the variety show, a sign announcing the act was placed onstage before it began. The "leader" was this kind of sign. The first concern in putting "leaders" in film was that the type should be large enough and the title run long enough to be read, allowing for the projectionists' all-too-frequent tendency to speed up when there was a crowd waiting outside to get in.[7]

Some films made in 1907 and later still provided titles for every shot. Producers, in order to make a film that was a self-contained unit, to be sent where no lecturer would be provided, often increased and lengthened intertitles. In 1908 and 1909, one could "read" many a film. All the key events and facts were conveyed by the leader, and the image that followed merely illustrated the title. This was the way that Vitagraph, for example, managed to convey the complexities of Shakespeare's A MIDSUMMER NIGHT'S DREAM to its audiences in December 1909.

Intertitles were also found useful for covering great lapses of time, and for compressing time to suit the one-reel narrative. Vitagraph's AN ALPINE ECHO (September 1909) told its story of childhood sweethearts in the Alps meeting again in America as adults with no less than five such titles in one reel: "A year later," "Ten years later," "One month later," "Two years later," and "One month later." When multi-reel films arrived, they didn't eliminate the need for such titles, but fewer were necessary.

There were two compelling reasons to change or eliminate the intertitles when the new narrative system was introduced. First, with the technique of editing alternate scenes the suspense that could be created would be harmed by titles that told in advance what was going to happen. Second, intertitles could interfere with the illusion of reality by reminding the spectators that they were being told a story instead of actually seeing it happen.

By 1911 some producers were trying to tell stories with an absolute minimum of words, and this was thought of as the artistic ideal. Great Northern's Danish import THE SON OF THE EXECUTIONER was admired because it told its story successfully without "the aid of those funny sub-titles." It would be better, thought Robert Grau, to eliminate the need for subtitles, and also written inserts such as letters and newspapers, which interrupted the illusion and harmed the clarity of the recital. As an alternative, Grau proposed that the spectator lip-read the lines spoken by the actors. Some producers actually tried this expedient: Grau commended PYGMALION AND GALATIA (June 1911), directed by Francis Powers, because the cast literally mouthed all the lines.[8]

S. E. V. Taylor achieved an even greater feat by making a feature-length film without any titles. While I cannot be sure from the context whether the film was deliberately made without intertitles or whether it was being shown to critics before the titles had been put in, I think it was intentional. The film in question was Marion Leonard's effort for Monopol AS IN A LOOKING GLASS (February 1913), and the critics who saw it in preview were reported to be of the unanimous opinion "that the story told itself remarkably well." The impetus to make films with no intertitles has been ascribed to the aesthetic movements of the twenties, so it is interesting to find that the desire actually arose much earlier, although with slightly different motives. Where a later generation looked for unity and purity of form, the earlier filmmakers were most concerned with the illusion of reality.[9]

In July 1911 Everett McNeil advised aspiring scenarists, "Use sub-titles or leaders sparingly—only when necessary to the proper understanding of the play. Make the action in the pictures tell the story. . . . Never use a note or a letter, unless the action absolutely demands it." The trend to eliminate intertitles was pervasive enough that later in the year Epes Winthrop Sargent found it necessary to warn, "Don't be stingy with the leaders that clarify the plot." He urged that the titles be left long enough on the screen for everyone in the audience to read them. The letter

1- *handwritten* 1/26/12
5- *handwritten* 1/26/12

```
              -DRAMATIC-        (OFFICIAL)
              - ASSEMBLY -
                 # 558-

              Children Who Labor

               by Ethel Browning
```

Produced in Co-operation with National Child Labor Committee.

SUBTITLE:-The appeal of the child laborers.
SCENE 1- EX--FACTORY--CHILD RAISING HANDS TO UNCLE SAM ETC. THE WORD
                                  GREED APPEARS IN CLOUDS-----------
SUBTITLE:-Child labor against the working man.
SCENE 2- EX----FACTORY---FATHER APPLYS FOR POSITION--HE IS REFUSED----
SUBTITLE:-Mr.Hanscomb, a large employer of labor, asked by a child labor
                     representative to help abolish the evil.
SCENE 3- IN---ROOM--MEN CONVERSING--HANSCOMB REFUSES TO AID THE CAUSE----
              DISSOLVE INTO--------
              EX----FACTORY----FATHER SENDS DAUGHTER TO GET JOB------
SUBTITLE:-Mrs.Hanscomb and Mabel on a trip.
SCENE 4- IN------TRAIN---CHILD GOES OUT---------
SCENE 5- EX------TRAIN----CHILD DROPS HANDKERCHIEF---THEN MISSES TRAIN--
SCENE 6- IN----TRAIN------CONDUCTOR PASSES THROUGH----------
SCENE 7- EX----TRACK---LITTLE CHILD MEETS POOR CHILDREN--THEY TAKE HER
                                                     WITH THEM----
SCENE 8- IN--TRAIN---MOTHER AND MAID MISS CHILD---CONDUCTOR SENT TO LOOK
SUBTITLE:-Hunger is a universal language.   FOR HER--------- ---
SCENE 9- IN---POORHOUSE----FATHER ENTERS---ASKS RICH CHILD TO HAVE
SUBTITLE:-In New York.   SOMETHING TO EAT-----------
SCENE 10- IN--PARLOR-----FATHER READS TELEGRAM-------
SCENE 11- TELEGRAM---MABEL LOST,ETC.---------
SCENE 12- IN---ROOM---FATHER WORRIED---------
SUBTITLE:-Her pay their only income.
SCENE 13- IN---POOR HOME----GIRL BRINGS HOME PAY----------
SUBTITLE:-A detective employed.
SCENE 14- IN----PARLOR---DETECTIVE TAKES PHOTOGRAPH OF CHILD------
SUBTITLE:-Necessity knows no law.
SCENE 15- IN--POOR HOME---RICH CHILD SENT TO WORK------
SUBTITLE:-In a corner of the spinning room. Almost found.
SCENE 16- IN--FACTORY---DETECTIVE WITH PHOTO---LOOKS AT GIRL---
SUBTITLE:-Mr.Hanscomb is hardened by his loss.
SCENE 17- IN---PARLOR----MOTHER WORRIED--DETECTIVE ENTERS AND SAYS HE
                                  CANNOT FIND THE CHILD------
SCENE 18- IN--FACTORY--FELLOW KISSES GIRLS---HIDING FROM EMPLOYER------
SCENE 19- EXTERIOR--ROAD FROM FACTORY---CHILD TAKEN SICK ON ROAD---
                                  CARRIED HOME BY CHILDREN------
SUBTITLE:-By buying the mill Hanscomb unknowingly becomes the employer of
                     his own child.
SCENE 20- IN--PARLOR----MEN CONVERSING---MAN BUYS MILL----
SUBTITLE:-Inspecting his new purchase.
SCENE 21- EXTERIOR----FACTORY---PEOPLE GET OUT OF AUTOMOBILE----
SUBTITLE:-Again fate intervenes.
SCENE 22- IN--FACTORY----CHILD FALLS ON FLOOR---SICK--CARRIED OUT BY MEN--
SUBTITLE:-Mrs.Hanscomb pities the unknown child.
SCENE 23- EX------FACTORY-----CHILD CARRIED OUT----WOMAN TAKES NAME
                                  AND ADDRESS OF HER---------
SCENE 24- IN--POOR HOME--MOTHER ENTERS --RECOGNIZES HER-----
SUBTITLE:-Mr.Hanscomb learns his lesson.
SCENE 25- IN--ROOM-----FATHER ENTERS AND OFFERS POOR MAN MONEY------
SUBTITLE:-The better way.
SCENE 26- EX----FACTORY--CHILDREN GOING TO SCHOOL------
SUBTITLE:-Lest we forget.
SCENE 27- EX----CHILDREN RAISE HANDS TO UNCLE SAM FOR HELP-------------

                                        JAN.26,1912.
```

*The assembly sheet for Edison's* CHILDREN WHO LABOR *(1912), from the Edison Script Collection, The Museum of Modern Art.*
```

inserts should be written realistically in order to be retained as part of the illusion. However, the intertitle was more than just the narrative information it included: one use of "leaders," he explained, is to "break" scenes, like a sort of drop curtain, so you can get people on and off stage for the next scene or shift scenery. Nonetheless, he agreed that the fewer the better.[10] "Leaders," he said, interrupt the action:

> For this reason many directors hold the action slow for a moment following the leader, just as they refuse to let in a leader in the middle of a scene, even though a word or two at the moment would clear the plot and obviate a later and more lengthy leader. Sometimes the line is flashed before the scene opens, but this is objectionable in that it removes the element of suspense. Leader is also used to "break" scenes where required. It may happen that two scenes are to be played in the same setting with an interval between. Without the leader the two scenes would follow with nothing to show the lapse of time. The action would be continuous and the characters would either leave the stage to reappear immediately or another set of characters would fairly jump into the scene. . . . Leader . . . serves as a drop curtain to separate the scenes (*Moving Picture World*, 12 August 1911, p. 363).

Sargent also suggested using a cut to another scene to give a time lapse: while the lady changes her clothes, while the man digs a hole. "For some reason," he observed, inserts of letters are better accepted than leaders; they are part of the action. "When the erring wife confronts her wronged husband and he is seen to take her back, the vision of a dead child will explain his reasons."[11]

The intertitles, then, could be used to perform some of the same functions as alternate scenes and as inserts, described in chapter 4, but were less realistic. They could also be a great economy. A title reading "After the storm," in Selig's A TALE OF THE SEA (December 1910), could take the place of a very big, expensive, and difficult scene, or cover a failure in trying to film it.

One exception to the rule of employing as few titles as possible came when a film was based on a poem. In that case it was thought desirable to quote the lines of the poem before most of the scenes, as was done in the IMP Company's first film, HIAWATHA, based on Longfellow's poem *Hiawatha* (October 1909), directed by William Ranous. The use of Longfellow's lines here, like the use of Charles Kingsley's lines in Griffith's THE SANDS OF DEE (July 1912), adds greatly to the rhythmic pacing and the poetic mood. Lois Weber, an experienced screenwriter, was the one who called attention to these poetic exceptions to the rule. She believed that one should not throw out all the subtitles in any case, but should manage to write some better ones than those that commonly appeared.[12]

Charles Gaskill, director-manager of the Helen Gardner company, shared this belief:

> I have never seen a motion-picture drama in which it was not necessary to explain some part of the action by word. . . . It must be used not only to define the action; it must indicate the logic, the poetry, the sentiment, the philosophy and other abstract quantities found in the picture—it must illuminate. . . . It may be stated as a principle that the interscript should

be used to carry the action over a hiatus, when it will serve to intensify the power of the story, whenever its presence proves a grace in the story, whenever its use will grip the point intended by the action of the story. Too much attention has been paid to the scarecrow . . . that a word should never be used in a motion picture unless it is necessary to "help" the action ("Function of the Interscript," *New York Dramatic Mirror,* 8 January 1913, p. 31).

D. W. Griffith himself was not at all averse to using titles to comment on the story, point out a moral, or instruct the spectator. Although the intertitles in the Biograph films are not excessive compared to those of other producers, the narrator's voice that is such an important part of his editing structure is sometimes heard in the titles as well. The Biograph *Bulletin* subheadings often represent a title that appeared on the film itself and made an editorial comment on the story: A CHILD OF THE GHETTO is presented as "An Innocent Victim of Fate's Cunning"; THE WAY OF THE WORLD as "A Lesson in Christian Charity," and HER AWAKENING as "The Punishment of Pride." The introductory title to Biograph's RAMONA (May 1910) not only credits the author, but offers the additional information that "this production was taken at Camulos, Ventura County, California, the actual scenes where Mrs. Jackson placed her characters." By the time of THE BIRTH OF A NATION, Griffith's titles were supplying history lessons.

The Gaumont Company, releasing through the Film Supply Company late in 1912 and represented in America by Herbert Blaché, attempted to use good intertitles as an advertising point and proposed a contest for the best ones:

> To be able to tell an exhibitor that one's pictures have titles that really tell something and tell it well is a talking point. . . . Audiences are bound to get more pleasure from pictures whose text matter is congruous with the photography and the story, titles which strengthen the atmosphere and spirit of the delineation, adding point, verve and connection (*New York Dramatic Mirror,* 13 November 1912, p. 35).

By the beginning of 1912, Selig, Vitagraph, Biograph, and Kalem had begun the practice of adding the main title of the film in small type to the subtitles. At the time this practice was commended for the benefit of spectators who came into the theater in the middle of the film. It was fortunate as well for the subsequent identification of a film, because the first parts of a film to disappear are the main and end titles, through the wear of projection and careless rewinding and packing of the reel. Even then, there was a constant cry on the part of exhibitors: "Where are the titles?" As F. H. Richardson explained, "Under modern practice, since takeups have come into use," the main titles were being used to thread up the film. This was, of course, the wrong thing to do, and the professional projectionist was supposed to add a length of film for this purpose if the exchange did not supply it.[13]

The reluctance to break into the shot was initially very strong. Dialogue titles, with the spoken words enclosed in quotation marks, would as a rule precede the scene in which they were spoken, following the same practice as ordinary narrative titles. Therefore, one often finds lines of dialogue "spoken" long before the characters seem to say them. Since this time lag might leave the spectator in some suspense as to who was speaking, and consequently create confusion, many producers chose to avoid the use of dialogue as much as possible.

Another solution, however, was to add character names to the dialogue, outside the quotation marks, as in a play script. While the purpose in the beginning was to make clear who was saying the line, when the words appeared before the shot began, this practice was continued as late as 1914, when the dialogue titles were customarily intercut in the scenes, with little possibility of confusion. The intercut dialogue titles of THE SPOILERS (1914) carry the name of the character speaking the line: for example: "Glenister: 'You have taught me a lesson.' " The same procedure may be seen in DAMON AND PYTHIAS, the Universal feature released at the end of the same year. The use of the characters' names when they spoke dialogue titles at this late date, when it was no longer needed for clarity, was a reflection of the entry into films of producers from the legitimate theater who were following practices familiar to them in play scripts. This is yet another example of the influence of legitimate theater on film style in the early teens, when, as we shall see in chapter 12, the feature-length film began to be an important factor in the production system.

The *Mirror*'s Frank Woods felt strongly that dialogue should be cut into the image at the very point where it is spoken. He conducted a small campaign on this subject early in 1912. "The only right place for a speech to appear," he insisted, "is when it comes in naturally." As he admitted, "One very capable scenario editor argues with much reason that if the action in a picture at a vital moment be suspended for the insertion of a quoted speech the hold on the spectators will be lost." But while agreeing with this point, he noted that it was only an argument for trying to do away with dialogue titles. "There is this to be added to the claim—self evident as this writer believes—that quoted speeches should only appear in films where they rightly come in: The insertion if made at all should be brief, pointed, and distinctive, and should not be anything that would have been perfectly apparent to the spectators without the insertion." But since the "hold on the spectators" had become such a vital consideration by 1912 that nothing was to be permitted to interrupt it, many producers were not yet prepared to follow Frank Woods's advice.[14]

In the fall of 1911, Nestor Films briefly employed an alternate method in the MUTT AND JEFF comedies. Here dialogue was placed at the bottom of the image on a black background, where it would normally appear in the cartoon strips on which the series was based. Horsley was quite proud of this device and claimed to have entered a patent on it. He advertised the films as "talking pictures."[15]

It is quite difficult to make definitive statements about the use of intertitles in films of the period 1907 to 1915, not only because few films survive but also because the titles are frequently lost—or, if the print is a reissue or was preserved in another country, because the titles are often not the original ones. Judging from those surviving films which do have their original titles, however, dialogue titles cut into the shot in the place where the dialogue is taking place were quite rare as late as 1913. There are some intercut dialogue titles in A RANGE ROMANCE, produced by the New York Motion Picture Company in December 1911, in IMP's SHAMUS O'BRIEN in March 1912, in Kay-Bee's THE ARMY SURGEON in November 1912. Yet in January 1913 Powers released MAMMY'S CHILD with a dialogue title appearing in advance of the shot in which it is spoken, and Solax did the same with A HOUSE DIVIDED in April 1913. Even in a very modern-looking film such as Essanay's THE LOAFER in December 1911, which uses a kind of scene dissection in a crosscut conversation sequence, the dialogue titles still appear in advance of the shot.

The surviving Edison and Biograph scripts and assembly sheets confirm these findings for at least two important companies of the period. In the case of Biograph, it is possible to pin down the change rather precisely. It was as late as December 1914 before dialogue titles were regularly cut into the middle of a scene. The title assembly lists before this month indicated where dialogue titles were to be placed at the beginning of which scene. The first film-title assembly sheet of December 1914 to clearly indicate that dialogue titles should be cut in the middle of a specific scene was for HIS OLD PAL'S SACRIFICE, production no. 4452. This was the procedure followed on all subsequent productions. In fact, the intercutting is likely to have been in practice sometime before the written instructions began to indicate it systematically. Accordingly, the title lists of the films released in December 1914 immediately before HIS OLD PAL'S SACRIFICE—THE ROMANCE OF A POOR YOUNG MAN and THE WAY BACK—are ambiguous: they list both a narrative title and a dialogue title to be placed at the beginning of the same shot, which is a most unlikely procedure. I think this may mean that they had begun to place the dialogue titles in the middle of the shot but had not yet altered the format of the assembly sheets to reflect the change.[16]

Of course it was possible to avoid the use of dialogue altogether, and many film-makers did, during the period of short one-reel narratives. It was considerably more difficult in the multireel feature film, however, and here the problem had to be faced. Most filmmakers accepted the solution of intercutting the dialogue titles.

In 1911, as indicated in chapter 7, some producers began to use credit titles at the beginning of the film, or at least at the beginning of some of their special releases, to name the actors and sometimes the author or the director. The use of introductory sequences to show the actors as well as name them began in the same year. Pathé American appears to be the company that initiated the practice of showing the actor at the beginning of the film, bowing before a stage curtain, as though at a stage performance, and giving the name of the player and the role. The company may have brought the practice over from France. In any event, it was commented on in a review of A CLOSE CALL, released in May 1911; the film apparently showed one actor alone bowing before a curtain before the story began, prompting the writer to remark, "It is hard to understand why he was chosen for this honor among the others." George Pratt has discovered an earlier use of what he describes as "prior curtain calls" in a Vitagraph film of February 1909, SAUL AND DAVID, which apparently introduced the principal characters before the beginning of the story but did not identify the actors.[17]

When Pathé American used the device again at the beginning of THE STEP-SISTER (July 1911), it was again worth mentioning in a review, but this time it was asked, whether they shouldn't do their bowing after the film, not before. This point was discussed for some time to come in the trade periodicals, because, of course, if theatrical tradition were followed, actors would only be acknowledged after the play was over.[18]

In the fall of 1911 the "present method," it was said, was "to flash upon the screen a full-size portrait of the actor in character and costume." This return to the nondiegetic, or emblematic, introductory shot, used before 1907 and mostly abandoned, may be attributed to the incorporation of the star system into industry practice. Gaston Méliès claimed to have applied for a patent in October 1911 on an "invention" that elaborated on the method of introducing characters. This consisted of showing the leading player in his everyday clothes, then dissolving into a shot showing the actor fully costumed for the role. Méliès first used it in RIGHT OR WRONG (2 November 1911) to introduce William Clifford and Francis Ford undergoing the metamorphosis from actor into character. Méliès' MEXICAN AS IT IS SPOKEN, distributed with RIGHT OR WRONG, employed a precise reversal of the process. After the film was completed, Henry Stanley posed in costume, then dissolved into Stanley in conventional clothes, thus satisfying the notion that the actor should be acknowledged after the play is over, as in the theater.[19]

Another variation in 1912 led from the nondiegetic opening into the narrative itself with a dissolve, employed in HIS LIFE (October 1912), Edwin August's debut film for the Lubin Company. According to a reviewer, it began with

> an initial curtain which, being parted, reveals the title of the play and an announcement of the stars; these, in turn, fade into an animated photograph, introducing Miss Hawley and Mr. August, which is all very prettily done, the two shaking hands and bowing and smiling; the photograph dissolves into the opening scene of the play—Mr. August caressing the hand of his crippled mother (*Moving Picture World*, 26 October 1912, p. 349).

This sort of thing was considered to be one of "the refinements of the screen," which continued to be in vogue throughout the period. According to a commentator of the time, in the first issue of RUNAWAY JUNE (Reliance, January 1915), the film begins with the authors sitting down to discuss what stories they will write. Two little statuettes on the table, a man and a woman in miniature scale, come to life while the writers talk. The miniature man holds up a bunch of grapes and asks the woman to beg for them.[20]

By 1913, with the influx of theatrical impresarios and stars to the screen, the use of introductory credit titles spread. "Daniel Frohman presents James O'Neill in his own version of THE COUNT OF MONTE CRISTO" (November 1913) was the title that began that film, and "Daniel Frohman presents America's Foremost Film Actress Mary Pickford in the famous tale of a woman's heroism, TESS OF THE STORM COUNTRY" (April 1914) was the first title of another.

The introduction also began to grow in length. In TESS OF THE STORM COUNTRY, an introductory shot of "Miss Mary Pickford as Tessibel Skinner" shows Mary coming out on a stage in a beautiful and simple white gown against a dark background, in three-quarter shot. She bends to take a graceful sniff of flowers in a huge vase almost as tall as herself. This shot is completely nondiegetic: she is not in costume or character for the film that follows. The producer was getting full star value for his money.

"Jesse L. Lasky presents Max Figman in Harold MacGrath's THE MAN ON THE BOX" (July 1914) was Lasky's introductory title, but in presenting the cast he went much further than Frohman. We are shown a coachman sitting on his box, and a herald standing beside the carriage blows a horn out of which come the credits in animated letters, such as "Lolita Robertson as Betty Annesly." The actress in costume for her role then steps out of the carriage, bowing to left and right at an unseen audience behind the camera. The same pattern introduces five other actors emerging from the same carriage in turn. The herald seems done with his task when the coachman gets down from the box, pushes him out of the scene, and introduces himself, "Max Figman as Bob Warburton." Fadeout, and finally the film begins. This sort of introduction must have cost more to produce than an entire film in the days of the one-reeler, three or four years earlier.

In THE WRATH OF THE GODS (June 1914) and again in THE TYPHOON (October 1914), the New York Motion Picture Company used the device of drawing the stage curtain to introduce each actor as himself or herself, and, in the manner of the Gaston Méliès "invention," continued with a dissolve into a shot of the actor in costume for the film. THE BARGAIN (December 1914) similarly introduced "Mr. William S. Hart as Jim Stokes, the Two-Gun Man." When the curtain is drawn, Hart is revealed in full-dress white tie, wearing gloves, in "hip to head" shot. He gazes left, right, then bows. There is a dissolve on his bowed head, and when he raises it he is wearing Western costume, his hand on his gun. Four more characters are introduced in similar but varied ways, concluding with James Rowling, playing a minister. When his introductory shot emerges from the dissolve he is in costume, riding a donkey, carrying an unfurled umbrella.

Universal's ambitious production DAMON AND PYTHIAS (December 1914) used up the best part of a reel introducing its cast. Each actor has a separate introductory title, such as "Mr. William Worthington, who portrays the character of Damon the Senator and friend of Pythias," and each has a separate bit of business. They don't wear the costumes designed for their roles or step into the character. Mr. Worthington, for example, dressed in a business suit, stands in an arbor in full shot and walks forward. Herbert Rawlinson walks down steps from the arbor into three-quarter shot. Ann Little gets out of a limousine and hands flowers to her maid with a gesture to take them into the house while she walks forward. In these nondiegetic star-worshiping shots, there is no acknowledgement of the audience, and there is much solemnity and pretentiousness.

By 1915, the *Moving Picture World* would write: "It has for some time been customary . . . to introduce the characters upon the screen one at a time prior to the beginning of the action. When this was first done it was generally in one routine manner—the character appeared before a curtain, bowed and disappeared." The *World* praised the imaginative innovations showing the characters in some typical pose or action. They thought it "artistic" when the Lasky Feature Play Company introduced THE GHOST BREAKER with H. B. Warner, the hero, conducting the movie audience through the gallery of family portraits in an ancient castle of Spain. Before each portrait, the painting changed to show the subject's modern descendant. The *World* also approved when the same company introduced the characters in CAMEO KIRBY by having Dustin Farnum sit at the gaming table, showing the cards one by one, and from each card one of the characters emerged. Clever introductions amused and entertained the audience in the spirit of the pre-1907 cinema. They could provide an elaborate frame for the production. However, this kind of special trick work could not be permitted to break the spell once the spectator had been drawn into the drama, or until it reached its end.[21]

10

Detours on the Way to Hollywood

Oh! the spaciousness of this great picture. The limitless plains, the wild
scurry of the horses, the freedom.

—Review of Selig's RANCH LIFE IN THE GREAT SOUTHWEST,
in *Moving Picture World*, 9 July 1910, p. 78

*I*n 1909 the great film centers were New York and Chicago and their suburbs.
Chicago came close to rivaling New York in the importance of its production. Two
big Patents Company producers, Selig and Essanay, operated out of Chicago, and the
important importer-distributor George Kleine had his headquarters there. At the
same time, the city was the center of the independent movement, the place where
the exchange men rebelled against the Trust and began new, independent production companies. Outside of these two cities, Philadelphia was home to the Lubin
Company, and there was some minor production in many other places, as is evident
if one notes the location of independent companies founded in 1909 and 1910.

Under the conditions of an organized distribution system, a producer had to be
able to depend on steady production, week in, week out. The long winter months of
New York and Chicago presented problems for that kind of production, however,
especially among those producers who did not yet have a well-equipped studio and
adequate artificial light. The hours of daylight grew too short, the sun too uncertain,
and the weather too severe to stay outdoors making movies. As a result, the film
producers of Chicago led the way westward in search of landscape and sunshine,
while the New Yorkers were more apt to head south when they wanted a place to
make films in the wintertime. Nobody, it seemed, stayed put in one place all the
time.

By 1910, to keep up with increased production demands, major producers had
several stock companies filming in various locations in different parts of the country
at the same time. The rapid growth of the industry by that year is reflected in the fact
that film companies could afford to rent private railroad cars to transport large groups
of players, directors, and cameramen across the continent, or to send stock companies overseas by ship. A lot of players had to give up some of their newly acquired
home life after all, as production companies traveled all over the country and outside
of it searching for the ideal backgrounds, sunny weather, and exotic atmosphere. But
the idea of trooping around the United States to make moving pictures probably
seemed natural to those who once spent all their days with touring stock companies.

In a single sentence Fred J. Balshofer of the New York Motion Picture Company supplied the two reasons generally given for the shift to Hollywood as a production center: "Los Angeles with its mild climate and sunshine beckoned as an escape both from the winter months of the East as well as the ever-present Patents Company detectives." Thus, he went on, "late in November, 1909, found our little company of players . . . departing for the West Coast."[1] Of the two reasons, the mild climate and sunshine must have been the stronger one, because the New York Motion Picture Company had already managed to escape the Patents Company's pursuit just by going to Neversink in the Catskills that summer. Furthermore, by Balshofer's own account, they were easily found by Patents Company spies in California a short time after they got there. At the same time, the Trust companies, which had nothing to hide, were also discovering the great California winter sunshine. Nonetheless it could be said that the move was a delaying factor for the independents because lawsuits had to be carried on in different court systems far from Patents Company headquarters.

The witnesses for the defense in the case of the U.S. government versus the Motion Picture Patents Company swore that there were never any detectives or hired spies to go after the independent producers who violated their patents. Files now open for research at the Edison National Historic Site supply ample evidence that these witnesses were not telling the truth. In any case, there was already a network of exchanges and exhibitors all over the country, a substantial part of whom would be loyal to the Patents Company. It was an existing "spy network," which became a tighter web in 1910 with the setting up of the General Film Company exchanges. One now-obscure Los Angeles "spying" case of 1911 was reported openly at the time because the spy gave evidence in court. A cameraman named Harry A. Kelly was an employee of the Patents Company who "inveigled himself into home and family" of Fred Siegert for the purposes of detection. He testified that Siegert was using a Pathé camera, and a California federal court decision put Siegert out of business.[2]

When Mark Dintenfass enlarged the Champion studio in Fort Lee, New Jersey, in the fall of 1911, he explained to a reporter that the existing buildings

> are not pretentious, [but] it must be remembered that they were built at a time when it was extra hazardous for anyone not working under a license from the Edison Company to own anything tangible. . . . Such structures were called upon to serve not only the purposes of the manufacturer, but to preserve secrecy and afford defense as well against the prying eyes of a score of detectives and United States marshals looking for violations of the patent laws (*Moving Picture World*, 18 November 1911, p. 542).[3]

As Champion was little more than a year old at this time, and as Dintenfass mentions an Edison license, one can't be sure whether he was referring to mid 1910 or some earlier period when the studio was constructed for another company. It might be concluded that there was no longer any reason to worry about prying eyes in the fall of 1911, but that was not yet the case. The independent movement had become quite strong and confident in the past year; however, the Patents Company was still looking for evidence of illegal use of their camera patents until the court decisions of 1912 made such evidence useless.

As for the landscape, which offered a far less ambiguous motive for the establishment of Southern California as the center of the industry, it was not only spectacular but extraordinarily varied. Summer greenery and winter snow, sunny beaches, barren deserts and rocky mountains were all within a short distance of each other. Florida and Texas could supply the climate for year-round outdoor filming, but they did not have quite the range of scenic choices within a day's trip from the studios. Even the light of California was different, gently diffused by morning mists rolling in from the Pacific or by dust clouds blowing off the sandy hills. The rugged western landscape and the wide-open spaces were felt as enormous attractions in the rest of the world. The lasting popularity of the Western genre owed a lot to these spacious lands.

Gilbert M. Anderson, who left a job with Selig in 1907 to establish the Essanay Company in partnership with the exhibitor and exchange man George K. Spoor, led a small expedition in the summer of 1908 to make Westerns in rugged landscapes around Golden, Colorado, and that trip was so successful that it was repeated in September 1909. On the 1909 trip Anderson traveled with his cameraman, Jesse Robbins, Jack O'Brien (who played the villains), and five other members of the party. Anderson himself played the leading roles as well as directing and writing most of the stories. He picked up leading ladies and the rest of the cast from stock companies he encountered along the way. In the West he recruited genuine cowboys who could rope and ride, which was more than he could do himself. Declared Anderson, "Colorado is the finest place in the country for Wild West stuff. Some of the Eastern companies try to use the Adirondacks, but they don't get the effect that the Rockies give."[4]

Anderson was already looking for a place to set up a permanent western studio. Otherwise he had to return to Chicago to shoot the interiors for his films, and in order not to delay production on a long location trip to the Rockies, would also have had to restrict himself to exterior shooting. He had to send his negatives to Chicago for printing. In November 1909 he set off from Denver for El Paso, Texas, and went on to Mexico in his determined search for rugged locations for his Westerns. Perhaps he also wanted to avoid the windy city in the winter months. At any rate, "Broncho Billy," as Anderson was to become known, didn't stop traveling until he reached Niles, California, where he set up Essanay's western studio early in 1910. Essanay advertisements in 1910 emphasized films "made in the West, in the very heart of the Rockies, amidst scenes of beauty which are alone well worth viewing. The Essanay Western pictures are genuine, and that's the reason they are so successful."[5]

Francis Boggs, a stage actor like Anderson, came to the Selig studio in Chicago in 1907. As adventurous a traveler as "Broncho Billy," he also went through the Southwest, and is said by some historians to have been in Los Angeles on a location trip in the fall of 1907. He was definitely there no later than the beginning of 1908, because he did the exterior shooting for THE COUNT OF MONTE CRISTO in Los Angeles. A surviving Selig film, THE CATTLE RUSTLERS, released in September 1908, shows genuine western backgrounds and was probably made by Boggs on his summer trip through the Southwest. He was far from the first to actually make films in California, because there had been films shot there in the previous decade, but he may have been the first representative of a major company to come there on location and then return to establish a studio. Boggs came back again on another trip in 1909 and set up what have been called "permanent facilities" by renting the back lot of a Chinese laundry on Olive Street. The Selig studio was established by Colonel Selig in Edendale the following year, and the more famous Selig studio and zoo were constructed in 1913 in the Lincoln Park area. Boggs may have been a real pioneer, but he didn't live long enough to enjoy that status. In October 1911 he was murdered by a man identified as "a crazed Japanese gardener," who also shot but didn't kill Colonel Selig.[6]

The independent New York Motion Picture Company arrived in Los Angeles in November 1909. Balshofer said it was intended to be temporary, and the facilities were rented, but they never went back East. That fact should give to Fred J. Balshofer nearly as much claim to be the first pioneer as Boggs. In the first six months of 1910, many more companies arrived, although when they came for the first time, nobody thought they were going to stay permanently.

The third big company to set up temporary quarters in Los Angeles was Biograph. Griffith brought out a group of about fifty people by train at the end of January 1910. They stayed until April, when they returned to New York by way of San Francisco, resolved to return the following winter. Many of the eastern producers who stayed in New York must have felt a racing pulse when they viewed the dramatically beautiful films the Biograph Company had produced in California: the breathtaking mountain vistas in RAMONA, the memorable seascapes in THE UNCHANGING SEA, the gripping desert scenes of GOLD IS NOT ALL. Nothing made in Biograph's little enclosed studio on Fourteenth Street in New York could compete with such films.[7]

Before there was a Hollywood film industry, the production companies were traveling everywhere. The Kalem Company had no studio in the fall of 1908 and depended on exterior shooting for everything. Frank Marion decided to take the Kalem

The Kalem players in Jacksonville. Max Schneider (cameraman), Kenean Buel, James Vincent (leading man), Quincy "the High Diver," Gene Gauntier, Mrs. Schneider, Ben Owen, Tom Santley, Minerva Florence, Sidney Olcott (director). (Identifications by Gene Gauntier.)

The Kalem players crossing the Atlantic. Allen Farnham, Mrs. Clark, J. P. McGowan, Robert Vignola, Gene Gauntier, Alice Hollister, Jack Clark (on lifeboat), Arthur Donaldson, Agnes Mapes, Sidney Olcott, and George Hollister (photographer). (Identifications by Gene Gauntier.)

players to Florida for the winter of 1908–1909. The adventurous Kalems were the first to start production in Jacksonville, Florida. This sleepy southern town had a population of sixty thousand in the fall of 1908, and two store shows for movies, one for whites and one for blacks. There the Kalems set up production and a home base for several years, specializing in Civil War films. Gene Gauntier wrote and starred in the GIRL SPY series there, and a permanent studio was established for other Kalem companies to work in while the company led by Olcott traveled elsewhere around the world.[8]

Early in November 1910 the *Mirror* remarked on the peripatetic motion-picture companies: "How far will a modern motion picture company go to get 'atmosphere' for a film drama? This question has been answered a good many times . . . during the last year or two." In the summer of 1910, Kalem, with a company under the direction of Sidney Olcott, and Gene Gauntier as leading lady and scriptwriter, had set off on a filmmaking trip to Ireland and Germany. It was, said the *Mirror*, "merely to get the local color for two or three motion picture stories." Reviewing A LAD FROM OLD IRELAND, one of the first pictures that came back from the O'Kalems, as they were soon to be known, the *Mirror* concluded, "The picture is genuine Irish and needs no labeling to prove it. It carries its authenticity on its face."[9]

THE COLLEEN BAWN (1911), filmed by the "O'Kalems" in Ireland. Directed by Sidney Olcott from a script by Gene Gauntier. From left: *Mrs. Clark, Gene Gauntier, Jack Clark, Arthur Donaldson.*

A LAD FROM OLD IRELAND showed its authenticity by beginning with picturesque scenes of peat diggers, the men doing the digging while a woman with a basket on her back picks up the clods with a practiced hand and throws them back over her shoulder into the basket. Scenes were also made on the ocean liner on which the Kalem party traveled, and real immigrants were seen arriving in America. Like most of Kalem's Irish pictures, the story was about the Irish coming to America and fulfilling the fantasies of many in the audience by becoming rich in the golden streets of the new land. In danger of forgetting those he left behind, the "Lad from Old Ireland" returns to get his sweetheart just as the family is about to be evicted from the old home.

The O'Kalems' Irish venture was repeated the following summer. Fifteen people sailed on the White Star Line's *Baltic* on 3 June 1911 and took up residence near Dublin. The group didn't return until the end of September, but by 6 November they were back at work at the Jacksonville studio. However, Sidney Olcott was not ready to stay in one place. By 2 December he headed a company sailing for the Middle East. By Christmas the company was in Rome on their way to the Holy Land, and they didn't return until late in 1912, bringing with them the feature production FROM THE MANGER TO THE CROSS (at first known under the title THE LIFE OF CHRIST). During the absence of the world travelers, a new Kalem company headed by Kenean Buel was sent to work in Jacksonville. By this time, Kalem also had two companies working in California, the newest one under the direction of P. C. Hartigan with Ruth Roland as leading lady.[10]

While southern California was being settled, Jacksonville was becoming quite an active production center too. For a few years Florida's warm climate was competitive with California's. Florida labor costs were low, as was the price of land, and the Kalem players were only the first to set up a studio there. The Selig Company established its Jacksonville studio for the winter of 1910–1911 and built there one of the menageries for which Selig was famous. Arthur Hotaling, Lubin's director of comedies, had taken his company to Florida and the West Indies in 1909 and to Los Angeles in the 1910–1911 season; in September 1912 he was sent back to Florida to select a permanent location for the Lubin comedy company. Under his direction, Jacksonville became the permanent home of this division. Oliver "Babe" Hardy got his start in moving pictures with Lubin's Jacksonville comedy company in 1913. When Gene Gauntier and Sidney Olcott left Kalem to produce features under the name of the Gene Gauntier Feature Players at the end of 1912, they too chose Jacksonville for the winter home of their company. Majestic had two companies at work in Jacksonville early in 1913, and its PEDRO'S REVENGE (April 1913) used the local color of an orange ranch to enliven its worn-out tale of two dismissed workers who kidnap the heroine. The sign of the Bank of South Jacksonville appears in one of its street scenes. Thanhouser also maintained a studio in Jacksonville at some point, and Metro was to come to the city after the close of our period.[11]

For a time Jacksonville used the slogan "World's Winter Film Capitol." According to a study by Richard Alan Nelson, this claim died rather abruptly in 1917, owing to a combination of factors, including the defeat of a movie-promoting mayor in a primary election, the failure of the Trust companies, price gouging, and a decline in banking support. All the studios closed up at about the same time, although intermittent filming continued in later years.[12]

Back in 1910, meanwhile, the fields and woods about Fort Lee, New Jersey, were crowded as usual with moviemaking that spring. But unfortunately for those filmmakers, all the great new locations beginning to appear in films made it quite impossible to go on shooting cowboy-and-Indian pictures there. One exhibitor complained about "an Indian picture in which they use toy bows and arrows, a western with scenes in Philadelphia suburbs labeled 'out west,' . . . and painted backgrounds with salt all over the place for snow." The *New York Dramatic Mirror*'s "Spectator," meanwhile, began to use "Jersey scenery" as a symbol of all that was mediocre in filmmaking. This tack brought down on his head the wrath of civic-minded New Jerseyites, and new searches were made to find some picturesque and not overused locations in that state.[13]

In March 1910 Colonel Selig not only had a company in Los Angeles, but had other touring companies in New Orleans and Mexico and was just preparing to send companies to Japan and the Orient. The following month he sent a special train to the Southwest under the direction of Otis Turner, loaded with "Indians, cowboys, cowgirls, rough riders, bucking broncos and steers, cavalry horses and paraphernalia, work stock and equipment, commissary and hospital department," according to the press story. If true, the train would seem to have been carrying coals to Newcastle, which gave a good laugh to the folks in New York who had been wounded by Chicago's remarks about "Bowery cowboys." It was during this trip that Turner picked up future cowboy star Tom Mix, a rodeo expert, to help with the horses and the cattle in the production of RANCH LIFE OF THE GREAT SOUTHWEST. Mix's name was used in advertising this production, but not as a movie actor; rather, his skill in western crafts was advertised to demonstrate the authenticity of the film. July 1910 found Mix helping out with a Sahara picture that Turner was trying to produce out at Dune Park, east of Gary, Indiana. Turner had brought a group of blacks from the city streets of Chicago and put them in loincloths. Perhaps Turner imagined that people dressed that way under the merciless sun of the Sahara, or that his audiences wouldn't know the difference. The city-bred fellows lost control of the camels and trusty Tom Mix rounded them up.[14] A 1913 publicity story reported:

> Tom Mix, last week, unloaded at Prescott, Arizona, a choice carload assortment of scenery, properties and small arms. . . . After the picturesque Mix had unlimbered his hard work, he opened a second car of trained horses. . . . Tom Mix has a silver plate on his saddle, stating that he is the champion roper, steer, bull, dodger and broncho buster. His association with the company, under the direction of producer William Duncan, means a very efficient factor in that hard-working organization (*New York Dramatic Mirror*, 8 January 1913, p. 31).

The Méliès Company in the first months of 1910 transferred its operations from Brooklyn to San Antonio, Texas, and concentrated on making Westerns. Méliès acquired William Haddock as the chief director, William Paley as cameraman, and Francis Ford and Edith Storey as actors, as well as a group of experienced cowboys to provide the roping and riding stunts. The most ambitious of the Méliès projects in Texas was the filming of the Battle of the Alamo, called THE IMMORTAL ALAMO (released 25 May 1911). In the spring of 1911 the company moved again, to Santa Paula, California, and a little more than a year later what was left of it began the prolonged voyage to the Far East, the South Seas, and the Southern Hemisphere. Gaston Méliès said he had had his fill of the frontier drama and decided that the public would like to see something else. Unfortunately, as we saw in chapter 7, the films he made on this journey did not fit the bill.[15]

As early as November 1909 it was announced that Vitagraph was building a studio in Paris, and J. Stuart Blackton was taking over a group of the Vitagraph actors to instruct French artists in the Vitagraph style. Pathé Frères soon returned the courtesy by opening a studio in 1910 in Bound Brook, New Jersey, under the charge of Ferdinand Zecca's experienced assistant, Louis J. Gasnier. The first release was a Western, THE GIRL FROM ARIZONA, on 16 May 1910. Pathé came to America to be able to make the authentic-looking Indian and Western pictures that were so overwhelmingly popular on both sides of the Atlantic, but New Jersey wasn't much better than Europe for that purpose, and the American branch of Pathé followed the American producers to Los Angeles that winter. The Eclair Company, after deciding to make its way into the lucrative American market by setting up its own distribution office in February 1910, and joining the independents in the Alliance, also decided to begin production, but it experienced many delays. Eclair's first American production, a two-reel film called HANDS ACROSS THE SEA, was not released until November 1911.[16]

Vitagraph players moved around nearly as much as the Kalems. At the beginning of 1910 Vitagraph sent a company to Jamaica in the West Indies, and in the summer a company directed by Lawrence Trimble was at work on the coast of Maine, with Florence Turner, Charles Kent, and the dog Jean. At the end of 1910, Vitagraph sent a company to San Diego, California, for winter filming.[17]

A section of the Lubin company sent to Florida for the winter of 1910 moved on to Nassau, and after returning to home base in Philadelphia, director Arthur D. Hotaling took his company out West to set up a Lubin studio near Hollywood. In 1910 Edison sent a stock company to Cuba, where they filmed THE PRINCESS AND THE PEASANT, SISTERS, and A CENTRAL AMERICAN ROMANCE. That same year, Essanay filmed exteriors in the Isthmus of Panama and in Mexico for THE HAND OF UNCLE SAM: troubles in Nicaragua inspired this film in which the U.S. Marines were sent to the rescue of an American engineer.[18]

The Columbia Film Company, a new independent producer still struggling for existence, announced that after 15 October 1910, "we will make our productions at Miller Brothers 101 Ranch in Oklahoma." This Wild West show and rodeo, where the old western traditions and crafts were carefully preserved, provided the action for many movie companies that came to Oklahoma for location shooting. The Miller Brothers then decided to set up their own film production unit, but while Oklahoma could supply the materials for an authentic Old West, it could not supply a warm climate for year-round filming or the spectacular scenery of the California Westerns. Consequently, a large contingent of Miller Brothers "101" Ranch cowboys, Indians, and livestock wound up wintering in California in the season 1911–1912. The New York Motion Picture Company, brand name Bison, hired the entire outfit and set them up in the Santa Ynez canyon. With Thomas H. Ince in charge, the Bison "101" films became the most spectacular and beautiful re-creations of the Old West yet seen, giving new life to the genre.[19]

IMP, one of those companies working in the woods around Fort Lee in the summer of 1910, went off to Cuba at the end of the year, taking along Mary Pickford and Owen Moore, who were, as it happens, on their honeymoon. Nearly all of the IMP company staff went along, and the *World* headlined the news about the company's trip, "The 'IMP' Company Invades Cuba." There was talk about moving other plants to Canada or Bermuda. "Whatever other construction may be put upon this move of the Imp, it at any rate evinces great enterprise on the part of Carl Laemmle," hinted the reporter. While it may be that IMP was fleeing the wrath of the Trust, the move was no secret. Probably the more overpowering motive was the lack of a well-equipped studio and the need to find a warm place to make films in the winter. Soon there were two IMP stock companies at work in Cuba. As one reporter remarked, "Local color is the order of the day in moving picture making."[20]

Thomas H. Ince began directing for IMP in Cuba, and some of his first films made there still survive. His talent is not particularly visible in these early films, which were cheaply and hastily made and look old-fashioned for their time. Neither Ince nor the staff could see the results of the work, because the negatives went back to New York to be printed, the usual practice for touring companies at that time. Ince, a man of the theater recently come to the movies, probably hadn't yet enough experience to know how the films would look without seeing the daily "takes." THE PENNILESS PRINCE did get some local color into its fanciful story of a down-on-his-luck European aristocrat who finds manual labor and true love in the tobacco fields. The opening shots showing the ships in the harbor may well be stock footage from some other film, but the scenes showing the tobacco plantations were made with the actors for this film.

In the early part of 1911, Bill Steiner and his Yankee Film Company spent several months in Bermuda, where, with two directors and a company of forty-six people, they turned out four reels a week. One of Yankee's surviving productions, HER MOTHER'S FIANCEE (released 25 March 1911), was probably filmed there, but nothing in the film shows the "local color." Like the IMP films in Cuba, it was cheaply made. It features a garden party and an escapade in a rowboat on a lake or inlet, but one doesn't see the sea, and it might have been made almost anywhere.[21]

The outbreak of revolution in Mexico drew film producers to the scene of the combat like flies to honey. I. W. Ullman spent a month early in 1911 as a guest of President Porfirio Díaz, whose lengthy rule was being challenged, while Ullman's partner in Columbia Film, Revier, was at the front as the guest of the rebel general Pasqual Orozco. They announced that Columbia Film had been under contract with the Mexican government for the past six months, but that contract soon came to an end with the downfall of Díaz's regime. The United States government clamped down on Mexican war films, or that was the rumor, since any such directives, if given, were secret.[22]

"Mexican Subjects Delicate Ones" was the headline on the trade-paper story that followed the deployment of U.S. troops on the Mexican border, and as the article explained:

> It is to be expected that the enterprising film companies now operating in Texas and Southern California will make full use of the opportunities afforded by the concentration of an American army division along the Mexican border. It is not likely, however, that any reputable film company will so far forget its patriotic obligations as to produce any pictures that may embarrass this country in a critical situation (*New York Dramatic Mirror*, 15 March 1911, p. 16).

Kalem's THE MEXICAN FILIBUSTERERS was announced to be the first of a series on the subject of the Mexican revolution, but objections were reported to have come through the office of the Los Angeles district attorney. There was no need to be alarmed by the outbreak of Mexican-war films. As the reviewer of Kalem's THE INSURRECTO commented, "If this represents the Mexican imbroglio accurately, there is little inducement for soldiers of fortune to follow the insurrectos further into the Mexican domain."[23]

The Ammex Film Company, which had a studio in San Diego, rented Lower California from the Mexican government for exclusive filming rights in the beginning of 1913. This would probably have been an agreement with the government of Francisco Madero, which was also of short-term value.[24]

In 1914 Harry Aitken of Mutual signed up General Pancho Villa and sent Raoul Walsh to Mexico to make a film with him. According to Walsh's story, Villa staged battles with some of his own soldiers in federal uniforms for the benefit of the motion-picture cameras. The film, completed in California with W. Christy Cabanne as the director and Walsh playing Villa as a boy, was called THE LIFE OF GENERAL VILLA.[25]

Despite all the wanderings of the motion-picture companies, by 1911 it had become evident that Los Angeles and its surroundings would be an important permanent film center. Location companies belonging to Essanay, Lubin, Kalem, and Nestor (the new company founded by Horsley, owner of Centaur) all showed up there during 1910. As early as November of that year, the *Los Angeles Times* was reporting, "It is predicted by theatrical men that Los Angeles will be the moving picture center of America next year."[26] Nearly all the major companies arrived in California during the winter season of 1910–1911, although the majority of them still did not have the intention of staying on indefinitely. In 1911, however, Los Angeles began to have a more established film community.

With the issue of 7 January 1911, the *Moving Picture World* got its first regular West Coast correspondent, screenplay writer Richard V. Spencer. He became Bison's scenario editor in August of that year. Spencer's second report covered the story of the 1 January arrival of Biograph on their second annual trip, with a company that had somehow grown from the fifty people with whom it reportedly left New York to seventy-five by the time it arrived in Los Angeles. Biograph's production in Los Angeles was now a serious matter. The previous winter's trip had been an experiment, but now the company had permanent quarters for a studio, a laboratory, and developing rooms. The negatives would be completed, ready for printing, when sent to New York. They planned to remain at least until spring and to return in all future winters.[27]

Los Angeles at this time had a permanent population of 319,198 (according to the 1910 census), plus 150,000 tourists in winter, for Southern California had become a great tourist attraction. The suburban towns within a thirty-mile radius added another 150,000 to the population. There was a large percentage of wealthy and middle-class residents, according to trade-paper reports, and all kinds of entertainments were said to be heavily attended in Los Angeles, where the theaters were clean and respectable because the major portion of the population was "well educated and refined." There were two dramatic stock companies in residence, the Belasco and the Burbank, which could supply theater professionals for the movie industry. The "wine halls" had been closed a few years before, leaving the young people without amusement, it was said, and they took to going to the movies. There were ninety-five motion-picture houses, ranging from hole-in-the-wall nickelodeons to modern picture palaces such as the Clune Broadway, the Hyman, and the Liberty. Of the ninety-five houses, sixty-five were in the suburban districts, and the other thirty were in the downtown business districts. Los Angeles was a contender with Chicago for the title of "most moving picture houses per capita."[28]

At the same time that the Biograph Company was descending on Los Angeles for its second visit, Kenean Buel arrived with his stock company and headed for the Kalem studio in the foothills to specialize in Indian films. James Young Deer, Western producer for American Pathé, was ordering more studios to be built at Edendale, and Joseph De Grasse, former Belasco director, was added to the directing staff. Essanay had a company working at San Jose this year under the direction of John O'Brien, and it traveled to the Redlands for the summer months. In Los Angeles local papers reported in February that Art Acord, local broncobuster, had managed to subdue Bison's famed "Cyclone" for the benefit of the cameras. Selig was filming the Tournament of Roses at Pasadena, and Francis Boggs took a company off to Santa Barbara. The Los Angeles park commissioners threatened to revoke permits to film in Griffith Park because there were so many complaints about the filmmakers' bad behavior and annoyances to the public and officials. In this "largest city park in the world . . . the incessant firing of blank cartridges scares the deer and elk that roam the park." Griffith Park was so large that production companies sometimes erected temporary sets there and left them over several nights without being discovered. Biograph and Pathé had trouble with a three-week rainy season in February, but Bison and Selig were reported to have a good backlog of films to carry them through it. It was, of course, quite necessary to keep up the steady flow of releases to serve the system. Large producers had several companies at work in different parts of the country, but Biograph, dominated by a single-producer system, was all in Los Angeles at the same time and the New York Fourteenth Street Studio was unused. Since the previous year, there had been reports of work going on to build a large Biograph studio in the Bronx, but in fact no studio was ready for use there until the summer of 1913.[29]

In an April 1911 article on "Los Angeles as a Producing Center," Richard V. Spencer reported that "within the short period of two years [Los Angeles] has reached a position in the moving picture manufacturing field where it is second only to New York." According to Spencer, this remarkable growth was attributable first of all to the climate, which "provides 320 days for good photography, out of the 365." But the diversity of locations was also a factor:

> Twenty miles to the west lie the pleasure beaches with a score of high class beach resorts within a forty minutes' trolley ride to the city. . . . There may be taken resort comedies with an Atlantic City or Coney Island background. Within the same radius on the same beach were taken the marine dramas made famous by the Selig and Biograph companies. Here were taken such pictures as: "The Unchanging Sea" (Biograph); "A Tale of the Sea" (Selig); "Fisher-Folks" (Biograph); "The Buccaneers" (Selig); "A Message of the Sea" (Bison); the sea scenes from "The Padre," a recent Selig release, and others. . . . Various street scenes and scenes in the city parks have been pictured by the Selig, Biograph and Essanay companies.
>
> Within the same twenty-mile radius may be found some of the most beautiful country homes and gardens in the world. Several of these have been photographed by the Selig and Biograph companies, among which were the famous sunken gardens of the Busch estate in Pasadena, and the residence of Rudolph Schiffman of the same city. A scenic mountain railway offers the weary tourist an allurement in the shape of a trip from roses to the snow line in forty minutes. Within the same radius and near Pasadena are two historic missions, San Gabriel and San Fernando. Here were photographed "The Two Brothers" (Biograph) and "The Padre" (Selig).
>
> Los Angeles and vicinity have acquired their reputation in the production of Western and Indian pictures. Here, of all places, is the ideal location for the production of such films. Here is found the necessary rolling country cut up by foothills, treacherous canyons and lofty mountain ranges in the background. . . .

Each of the companies working in Los Angeles, he noted, had found its own kind of location:

> The Selig Company chose Edendale, a city suburb, and have here erected a $75,000 plant. Within a block of them is the Pathe West Coast Studio, which, when completed, will probably represent a similar investment. A block below the Pathé Studio on the same side of the street is the Bison Studio. It is shortly to be enlarged and improved with new buildings. The Biograph Company last year occupied temporary quarters in Pasadena, but this year finds them at home in their new studio at Pico and Georgia streets in the heart of the city. The studio is to be permanent and will be occupied every winter by the company. Nine miles away, near Glendale, the Kalem Company have erected a studio in the foothills for the production of their Western and Indian films. Some sixty miles away, near Redlands, the Essanay Western Company are hard at work. At Long Beach, a local beach resort, a new Independent producing company is rushing operations to get into the market with their film (*Moving Picture World*, 8 April 1911, p. 768).

In the following winter season of 1911–1912, the Nestor Company bought property at Gower and Sunset, in Hollywood, where they had been working temporarily. On that corner, they built the first Hollywood studio, that is, the first Hollywood studio in name. All of Southern California was in the process of becoming "Hollywood," but that symbol was not yet born. As Spencer indicated, the wonderful California climate and 320 days of sunshine, before there was any smog, made it something like paradise for motion-picture people. California was also a very forward-looking place. The state had already given women the right to vote, and the first women were serving on juries there. By May 1911 there were ten motion-picture companies reported operating in Southern California, and it was said that three new independent producing companies were forming. The studios were beginning to have to fend off curiosity seekers. Southern California was reportedly going "picture mad," and every

The Nestor studio at the northwest corner of Gower and Sunset, said to be the first studio actually located in Hollywood.

day a new producer was announced. By the spring of 1915 the Los Angeles Chamber
of Commerce claimed in an advertisement that 80 percent of the country's motion
pictures were produced there.[30]

The migration of movie companies everywhere around the country, and even the
wide world beyond the borders, and the settlement in California, influenced films in
several ways beyond the local color they picked up. During the early stages of these
trips, the filmmakers were removed from the enclosed studios of home and without
facilities. The films made on distant locations were mostly filmed out-of-doors and
reflect the freer positioning of cameras and the movement of actors and horses and
all living creatures deep in space. Because the action spread over a wider range than
in a studio, it was more difficult to keep in the center of the frame, and the cameraman had to pan to follow it. The hazards of exterior filmmaking encouraged the
use of more and shorter shots. Of course some filmmakers could travel three thousand miles and still set up a rigid, stagelike picture area to which men on horseback
rode up and posed stiffly facing the camera, but the more talented ones found that
filming on location loosened up some of the methods they had learned and gave them
new ideas. Also, far from head offices, there was less opportunity for conservative
executives to say, "You can't do that." By the time the negatives were shipped back
by train to the office, it was too late.

Equally important was the emergence of spectacle as a more significant quality in
picture making. It was to be of special importance to the growth of the feature film.
While spectacle could be provided with enormous and costly sets, as the Italians did
it, in California the landscape itself was ready to perform this function. The extreme
long shot became an important element of the spectacle: there was no other way to
do justice to the wide open spaces. The scenes filmed from the top of a California hill
looking down into a California canyon, a nearby figure or bush on the hill giving scale

*The Selig Company on the West Coast in 1914. The muslin sheets hanging overhead
served to diffuse the California sunlight.*

The New York Motion Picture Company studio at Santa Monica, California.

THE LAST DROP OF WATER (Biograph, 1911), directed by D. W. Griffith; filmed at San Fernando and Lookout Mountain, California.

FISHER FOLKS (Biograph, 1911), directed by D. W. Griffith. Filmed at Santa Monica, with Linda Arvidson.

THE GIRL OF THE GOLDEN WEST (Jesse L. Lasky Feature Play Company, 1915), directed by Cecil B. DeMille. House Peters.

to the distant action—where good guys chased bad guys on horseback, the Indians encircled the covered wagons, the cavalry rode to the rescue, and the battles of war were fought with explosions and smoke: these are scenes engraved on the collective memory of moviegoers and fans of the Western. The Kalem pictures made in the green hills of Ireland contained some of these high-angle deep landscape shots as well, looking down from steep hillsides onto the seashore. By contrast, the films made in the flat lands of Jacksonville and San Antonio lacked this kind of visual excitement.

In Biograph's RAMONA, filmed on the first California trip, the mountainside settings provided startling high-angle and extreme long-distance shots. The final scene shows a distant mountain at such a dramatic angle that it fills the frame, and no sky can be seen. Composition had to be affected by such rugged settings. Similarly, the extreme nobility of behavior of the characters in the films Thomas Ince was making for the New York Motion Picture Company seemed to conform to the mountain grandeur and the open spread of the plains. The opening title in THE BARGAIN (New York Motion Picture Company, 1914) announces: "The West! The Land of Vast Golden Silences Where God Sits Enthroned on the Purple Peaks and Man Stands Face to Face with His Soul." The scene fades in on a magnificent landscape that fully meets these grandiloquent words with an extreme long shot of rocks and canyons, on which the camera plays a long, slow pan. Nature itself gave a vitality and a spontaneity to the films of this period that diminished once producers began to work more consistently in enclosed studios under artificial light, where there was the possibility of more control over the process of making films.

11

The Genre Film

The Lubin directors are priding themselves upon the fact that they have brought out a story in which two sisters from the country come to the city and neither goes wrong.

—*Moving Picture World*, 2 April 1910, p. 511

Genre may be considered as standardization of the film product. The audience has some idea what to expect from a comedy or a Western, just as consumers know what to expect when they order a specific kind of sausage. Genre films certainly existed before this period, but with the organization of the industry they were incorporated into the system of production, distribution, and exhibition.

The peculiarity of this period of genre-film history is that as long as the program consisted of several films, there was a demand for a balance among them. Exhibitors wanted dramas, comedies, and Westerns represented in equal numbers in the day's program and resented it when they were served too much of one kind. They complained of the split reels with two comedies back-to-back on one reel because they thought it better to intersperse them with drama. As production increased and stabilized, each of the major producers tried to offer a balanced program of its own films. By mid 1911 an exhibitor who subscribed to the whole output of General Film might expect a regular diet consisting of a Western, a drama, and a comedy released on alternate days from each producer. Put together, these provided the nutritionally balanced program thought to be good for the audience. In June 1911 Vitagraph announced an increase to four reels a week and promised that one of the weekly releases would be a Western. Beginning on 1 July, Lubin increased its output from two to three reels a week, one a drama, one a comedy, and one a Western. By the first of August, Vitagraph was up to five reels each week: a military film, a drama, a Western, and a comedy, in addition to a special feature every month. Smaller companies began to concentrate on Westerns or comedies only, but when their product was contributed to a combined program such as that offered by the Sales Company, a balanced program of independent films could also be provided to the exhibitor. This kind of specialization by genre was a forecast of what would happen to the single reel when the coming of the feature film changed the system.[1]

In the early days of uplift, audiences got perhaps more than they wanted of classical dramas and of sentimental melodramas preaching sermons at them. In December 1908 Burton Allbee visited a number of nickelodeons to find out what the public was looking for. He concluded that it was plenty of action, pathos, crime detection, comedies (if good), religious films (in some cities), patriotic films only if there were battles, uniforms, and fighting, and love stories with happy endings. In February 1909 a critic reported, "Over and over again these last few weeks I have heard people say they are sick and tired of gloomily ending film subjects; of subjects which depress; of subjects which deal with the seamy side of life." An exchange man explained what was wanted out West: dramatic films were chiefly in demand; "blood and thunder" subjects were not popular in the Midwest, but they went well in Oregon. In the South and Midwest, they preferred comedy. In Mexico, he said, OTHELLO would draw only 30 to 40 percent capacity, but murder and bullfight subjects would bring in 100 percent. A letter from Irving Wallace Landgraf, a Chicago exhibitor with a "family" audience, said that his clients preferred sensational pictures, war pictures, Indian and cowboy films; "some of us would starve," he said, on scenics, industrials, and educationals. In February 1911, aspiring scriptwriters were advised that the scenarios most in demand were original comedies of modern life, high-class Western comedies and dramas, and "refined dramas depicting modern American middle class life."[2]

In July 1910 the *Mirror* conducted a study of the entire American production for the month, consisting of 242 subjects. The purpose of the analysis was in fact to demonstrate that there was no need for censorship, but it is useful for us because it gives some statistics about genre midway through the second year of the industry's production after the organization of the Motion Picture Patents Company. The results are based on actual film viewing, a condition impossible for us today, and the perceptions of those films are probably somewhat different than ours would be if we had the films in front of us. The report on 242 films counted 52 "more or less thrilling melodramas," 23 of which were Westerns. According to the *Mirror*'s analysis, 35 percent of the films were "humorous," 34 percent of them were "dramatic," 19 percent were "melodramatic," 3 percent were trick and novelty films, and 9 percent were "educational" (including scenic and industrial films). Those films they considered to be of "special literary and artistic merit, independent of educational and novelty pictures," represented 15 percent of the total. At the time, there was a distinction made between "dramatic" and "melodramatic" that is not entirely clear to today's viewers, but we know at least that dramatic films were perceived to be closer to the events of everyday life as experienced by the spectators. However, among those "everyday" happenings there frequently occurred such events as the loss of memory caused and restored by a blow on the head; the loss of sanity caused by grief or shock and restored by the innocent face of a child; selfishness, crime, and immorality reformed by the purity of a child; suicide as a noble act to avoid standing in the way of true love, or to prevent incest or bigamy; the extraordinary coincidences of meetings of lost family members or lost loves after years; blinding by explosions and restoration of sight by miraculous operations; and so forth. The *Mirror* also demonstrated by their survey that the licensed companies were producing a much higher proportion than the independents of the films they considered to be of "artistic and literary superiority."[3]

In October 1912 would-be scenarists were asked by the *World*'s columnist Louis Reeves Harrison to avoid the following plots, now considered to be clichés: Mother recovers her sanity after she loses a baby when another is brought in; the nightgowned child in prayer reforms a crook; the lady and burglar, telephone and police station; the girl reporter gets a scoop; the railroad operator saves the train or the heroine from destruction; the kidnapped child; the fuse-sputtering bomb. It does not appear that scenarists took this advice. After all, it probably was not possible to come up with original plots day after day, week after week. However, a shift in emphasis was noted by Harrison late in 1913: he found a trend toward sociological stories, detective stories, and stories of abnormal mental states, and more use of symbolism. By abnormal mental states, I think he was referring to the many films using hypnotism as a plot device at about that time. Harrison thought that directors were displaying more intelligence toward their audiences, and he credited this in part to the open market. When motion pictures were "no longer a mere means of cheap amusement," he wrote, "[they] may soar." At the same time, however, critic W. Stephen Bush hoped for an end to the emphasis on thrills and sensation. These two writers signal some of the changes in film genres and subjects that were taking place in the midst of the shift from short film production to the feature.[4]

Westerns

The extraordinary life of the Western genre in this period is demonstrated by the fact that balance demanded having one on every program. The predominance of the Western gave the uplifters some problems. When Kalem tried to introduce a series of films especially made for children, for example, they gave up after a few weeks because the exchanges told them, "The demand is all for Wild West drama." Mr. Quimby of Zanesville, Ohio, who spent his summers running a showboat on the rivers, reported that what the people wanted were Wild West pictures. He covered a lot of territory, he said, and this was what they asked for all over. Reformers claimed that the demand came only from small boys and the European market, but it is evident that a large number of American adults were eager to see them as well.[5]

"Broncho Billy" Anderson in an unidentified Essanay Western.

A "necktie party" in A ROMANCE OF THE OZARKS *(Lubin, 1913).*

Selig and Essanay led the field in Westerns in 1908 and 1909. Based in Chicago, they were the first to send companies out West. The films, made far from home base, were full of action and usually did not have any interior scenes. Much of the time the actors were on horseback. The producers found it easier to use shorter shots and more dynamic camera positions outdoors and to avoid the staged compositions that seemed appropriate inside small studios. It was possible to find experienced horsemen in the western states, cowboys who could rope cattle and break wild horses as it had been done in the Old West. Producers found fast action, rugged landscape, and authenticity.

The Western film genre was a rediscovery of the wide open spaces, of the days of freedom and adventure, not very long before the time of these films, when the American people opened up a wilderness. If that were all, of course, the Western would have concerned itself with the tales of the explorers and the settlers, which actually made up only a small part of the subject matter. Instead, in this time period, many producers simply took the elements of stock melodrama and comedy and transplanted them to a western setting, which might be the Old West but also could be in the present day. There already existed a considerable body of western literature and dime novels to draw on for elements of the mythology of the West. The Wild West had been in show business for years, in the form of appearances, demonstrations, and entertainments by legendary frontiersmen and Indian fighters like Buffalo Bill Cody, with their troupes of Indians and cowboys, and exhibitions of the old western skills of riding, shooting, branding, and roping.

Selig's THE CATTLE RUSTLERS (September 1908) is an example of a film that uses some of the traditional western elements found in dime novels. It has cattle rustling, branding, a chase on horseback, a shooting with lots of gunsmoke, a man-to-man struggle, a shoot-out at the cabin where the outlaw has gone to recover from his wounds, and a "necktie party" that avoids the hanging scene itself because of the self-censorship of the time. The film was shot rather far from the camera in authentic western landscapes. Someone accidentally moved into range beside the camera for a second when they were shooting this film, but in those days of rapid production, the producers did not bother to cut out the mistake. Reshooting would have been out of the question because the error would not have been seen until they got back to Chicago and developed the film.

Essanay's A RANCHMAN'S RIVAL (December 1909), on the other hand, used a well-tried formula from the melodrama in a modern western setting with western characters. A city man drives up to a western post office in a car, courts and wins the ranchman's girl, and pays another man to fake a marriage ceremony. The heartbroken ranchman, ready to leave town on the train, meets a woman at the station who is looking for her husband. When the ranchman sees the photo in her locket, he recognizes the bigamist from the city and rides to the rescue of his sweetheart. Every shot of this film is in the actual setting, the real houses and the real train station of Golden, Colorado, showing the extensive vistas and mountains around it.

"Broncho Billy" Anderson, who played the hero in A RANCHMAN'S RIVAL some six months before he earned his nickname in BRONCHO BILLY'S REDEMPTION (July 1910), made hundreds of Westerns, more than any other Western star. Only a handful of his films survive, and one must depend on the synopses in the trade periodicals for an idea of what they were like. These sources indicate that in the course of the years he spent making one-reel Westerns, from 1907 to 1914, he ended up writing, directing, and enacting just about all the Western plots that ever were invented, drawing as he did on dime novels, pulp magazines, and stage melodramas. In keeping with the period, there was usually a moral and very often a tragic ending. "Broncho Billy" was a noble character, every now and then playing the Good-Bad Man type that William S. Hart was to personify so well, an outlaw who reforms through the influence of a beautiful woman or an innocent child. Noble and self-sacrificing behavior was a key ingredient in Westerns in this period, together with fast action, rugged landscape, and swift riding.

In 1908 Griffith used the scenery of the Palisades cliffs in New Jersey, the lovely wooded surroundings of Cuddebackville, New York, and the Delaware Water Gap to make such Westerns as THE FIGHT FOR FREEDOM, "a story of the arid Southwest," THE GREASER'S GAUNTLET, set in the Sierra Madre, and THE GIRL AND THE OUTLAW and THE RED GIRL, both taking place "on the frontier." In 1909, he made fewer western subjects, although he still kept on making an occasional Indian picture, at that time a special genre of its own. This may have been because Biograph represented the forefront of uplift and specialized in the moralistic melodrama, or because the authentic western scenery appearing in Selig and Essanay films was making eastern landscape less acceptable, or for both reasons. In any case, the first Biograph expedition to California at the beginning of 1910 had a dramatic effect on the landscape and atmosphere of his films. The barren desert, for example, was the scene of the somber OVER SILENT PATHS (May 1910), set in the gold-mining days. Without knowing his identity, a girl falls in love with the man who murdered her father; when she discovers the truth, she turns him over to justice. The openness of the setting seems to have liberated Griffith to greater fluidity, to cutting on action, to avoiding some of the entrances and exits of earlier films, to permitting the actors to move on diagonals and to approach the camera. From 1911 through 1913, the use of extreme long shots emphasized the spectacular in Biograph's epic Westerns such as THE BATTLE, THE MASSACRE, and THE BATTLE AT ELDERBUSH GULCH.

The Selig Company's acquisition of Tom Mix greatly increased the thrills to be found in their Westerns. Charles Silver undoubtedly expresses the attitude of many spectators of an earlier day when he writes, in recent times, that "when you come right down to it, it was surely more fun to watch Tom Mix dangle from a cliff than it was to see Hart struggling with his damn conscience again."[6] Some of the reasons for Mix's later popularity may be seen long before he had reached stardom, in Selig's SAVED BY THE PONY EXPRESS (July 1911). The film shows a novel square dance on horseback, which might be an invention of the Wild West shows from which Mix entered pictures. The plot concerns a false accusation of murder: the note that will clear the accused of the crime has to be carried by the pony express rider in a race against time. The film is perhaps not very well made and does not even make any important use of landscape—in fact, in an interior set probably made back in the studio in Chicago, a painted backdrop can be seen through the doorway. Nevertheless, it is fascinating to see the ease of the players in the saddle, especially the pony express rider, played by Mix, who jumps off his horse and onto the waiting horses with show-off skill. Mix never pretended to be a great actor, and even at the peak of his stardom chose to be filmed at a long distance from the camera most of the time.

The demand for Westerns was so great that in April 1911 the American Film Manufacturing Company undertook a policy of specializing in that genre alone. Beginning on 24 April two reels of Westerns were to be released every week. A new trademark was designed for these films, showing a cowboy on horseback throwing a lariat.[7] Allan Dwan was the chief director. One of American's Westerns that survives today is THE RANCHMAN'S NERVE (July 1911). In it a pony express rider is held up by the bad man of the mountains, and the sheriff leads a posse, but when the sheriff is wounded, the other men lose their nerve. The sheriff has to find a replacement, and, in a test, J. Warren Kerrigan proves his "nerve" for the job. He undertakes to bring in the outlaw single-handed and without a gun, which he does by outfacing him and grabbing the gun from his hand. "For sake of the women," he tells the outlaw, "I'll give you one hour to get across the border." But the bad man's sister has to shoot him to save the life of Kerrigan. The scenery is grand, the westerners look authentic, and there are plenty of thrills.

By 1912 the epic Western was being expanded by Thomas H. Ince with the help of the Miller "101" Ranch company, contracted to the New York Motion Picture Company for mass scenes of Indians, cowboys, and horses. Old stagecoaches and props of all kinds were bought up by the studios for use in the epics of frontier days. The clouds of dry California dust that settled on props, costumes, and the faces of actors, and the way the light fell on them, as well as the worn clothes of cowboy extras and stuntmen and the experienced way they sat in a cowman's saddle, probably contributed more to this illusion of reality than any strict observance of historical fact. The ideal of recapturing the real West inspired the former stage tragedian William S. Hart, who began to make films for Thomas Ince in 1914. He was not a westerner, but his childhood memories of traveling the American West deeply influenced him. The strong element in his films was not his adherence to historical details (which were not always correct), but the conviction he could convey by his stern and noble face.

THE DESERTER (March 1912) is among the few surviving films directed by Ince. Unlike the handful of films from his IMP period that may be seen today, the New York Motion Picture productions show Ince to have become a skilled practitioner of the modern style in which Griffith worked. THE DESERTER is the often-told story of the deserting soldier who encounters a wagon train of settlers and, when the Indians attack, goes to the army post for help, risking court martial and redeeming himself in death. The central sequence illustrates the classic Western composition: an extreme long shot of a wagon train, with Indians in the foreground looking down at it in a canyon; a medium shot of one of the covered wagons where the deserter tells the heroine his story, in a flashback; a return to the present; a return to the extreme long shot to show the Indians riding down on the wagons, now drawn up in a protective circle; a medium shot of the settlers interrupted at their meal by the attack; a long shot showing the confusion of the battle, the Indians riding around the circle, a horse falling and struggling. Later, when the deserter is riding to the rescue, alternate editing between the scenes of action adds to the suspense. All these scenes have been played in Westerns hundreds of times, and yet they still have the capacity to thrill an audience.

Indian Films

Indian films might be considered a branch of Westerns, but in the early years they constituted a separate genre. They could be made in the eastern or southern part of the United States, as well as in the Far West, without departing from authenticity. The attractions of Indian films included the beautiful landscapes and free movements of Westerns films plus elements of exoticism, nobility, and romance. There was also the allure of nudity (of men only), which had the same respectability as the nakedness of indigenes in travel films from distant lands. Fred Balshofer's testimony confirms this: "Inslee made a striking appearance on the screen, and the ladies simply went gaga over him. Oh's and ah's came from them whenever he appeared on the screen in one of his naked Indian hero roles, so naturally most of his pictures were on that order."[8]

When Pathé American first made Indian films, they could boast that "all the actors . . . are real Indians or sufficiently well made up to pass as such." Pathé's "real" Indians were very naked-looking Indians, as some were quite fat. They can be seen in the *World*'s illustration for A CHEYENNE BRAVE, and also in the surviving Pathé American film THE RED GIRL AND THE CHILD. The New York Motion Picture Company boasted about their two genuine Indians, Young Deer and Miss Redwing, both of the Winnebago tribe. James Young Deer, born in Dakota City, Nebraska, was with traveling circuses until he was hired for the movies by Kalem. Young Deer also worked for Lubin, where he wrote, directed, and starred. Biograph hired him to appear in THE MENDED LUTE, and Vitagraph for RED WING'S GRATITUDE; he became a director-actor for Pathé American from its beginnings in the east (A

CHILDREN OF THE FOREST (Essanay, 1913).

IN THE DAYS OF THE THUNDERING HERD (Selig, 1914).

THE BATTLE AT ELDERBUSH GULCH (Biograph, 1913–1914), directed by D. W. Griffith.

CHEYENNE BRAVE, THE RED GIRL AND THE CHILD) and, as noted in the previous chapter, established Pathé's West Coast studio. Authenticity was an important advertising point for Indian films and was used with even more emphasis here than for the Westerns of the period. When the *World* did its 1911 survey of exhibitors to find out what the public wanted, they reported that the highest praise for Biograph's THE MENDED LUTE came from the Dakotas, which, they said, spoke well for its authenticity.[9]

But the genre's strongest attraction in the heyday of the sentimental melodrama was the history of the native American. No longer simply the stoic, the stock type of the stage, he was the noble and tragic hero. In the words of Mrs. Austin, author of the play *The Arrow Maker:* "Indians love as romantically, as poetically, as the most sentimental white man. Every Indian is a born poet." And according to the *Moving Picture World*, a book that appeared in July 1911, *The Soul of an Indian*, said to have been written by a native American, showed "that the red race was intensely spiritual and had a child-like, but sublime conception of God and of man's duty to man."[10] In this same spirit, THE REDMAN AND THE CHILD, one of Griffith's first films for Biograph in 1908, featured

> a Sioux Indian, who besides being a magnificent type of aboriginal American, is a most noble creature, as kind-hearted as a woman and as brave

as a lion. . . . What a magnificent picture he strikes as he stands there, his tawny skin silhouetted against the sky, with muscles turgid and jaws set in grim determination (Biograph *Bulletin* No. 156, 28 July 1908, in Bowser, ed., *Biograph Bulletins 1908–1912*, p. 5).

In fact this actor was not an authentic Sioux but the same magnificent Charles Inslee who was hired the following summer by the New York Motion Picture Company to make Indian films in New Jersey.

In the mythological view of the first Americans, Indians behave more nobly than the white man. In Biograph's THE REDMAN'S VIEW, the members of the Kiowa tribe, of the Shoshone family, are driven from their ancestral lands farther and farther west. The chief's son, whose sweetheart is kept as a slave by the white intruders, leaves her to follow his duty, to stay with his dying father and take over the leadership of his tribe when the end comes. Only after the burial (an opportunity to show quaint Indian rituals) is he free to go back for his true love. In THE ABORIGINE'S DEVOTION (World, 1909), the Indian takes care of the trapper's child, left to him when his friend died, and kills to protect him, saying, in a title, "I have done my duty."

Indians were mistreated by the white man, forced off the land, enslaved and slaughtered, and yet, should a white man, woman, or child be kind to an Indian, the time would come when the Indian would sacrifice his or her life for the white. In Biograph's THE BROKEN DOLL (1910) the little Indian girl runs to tell the white settlers who had given her a doll that the tribe is on the warpath. She is wounded and dies in the conflict. In RED GIRL AND THE CHILD (Pathé American, 1910) an Indian girl heroically rides after the kidnappers of a white child whose father had protected her from the rudeness of drunken cowboys. In AN APACHE FATHER'S VENGEANCE (1913, "101" Bison), when the Apaches attack the fort, the chief's daughter rides for help to save the white officer who has protected her. The loss of family honor causes her Indian father to shoot her. The whites, to honor her, drape an American flag over her body and kneel in front of her in homage.

Nonetheless, contact with white civilization was dangerous for the Indian. Many an Indian educated by the white man's college at Carlisle found himself rejected by both Indian and white society, as in Selig's CURSE OF THE REDMAN (1911). While it was usual for love affairs between Indians and whites to end in tragedy, to avoid miscegenation, the moral values of the time could override even this prohibition on occasion. In Pathé American's FOR THE SQUAW (1911), the white man is compelled by his duty to remain with his Indian squaw and his child instead of marrying his white sweetheart.[11]

Eventually, owing to the enormous numbers of Westerns produced, and perhaps also to a poverty of ideas, it became common to use Indian treachery and warfare as a plot motive in action Westerns, with scriptwriters feeling no need to explain Indian actions on the basis of the white man's mistreatment. Indians changed from the tragic central figures to convenient villain stereotypes. Every once in a while, someone would remember their nobility and suffering at the hands of the white man and return to the subject, but by 1913 the amateur scriptwriting public was informed that Indian scenarios were not wanted by the studios. They were considered to be an exhausted vein, while the Westerns continued to be as strong as ever. The market for Indian plots was diminishing at the same time that the peak years of the uplift movement were coming to an end. People were interested in action, thrills, mystery, and happy endings, not tragic heroes.[12]

Civil War Films

The Civil War film was nearly as popular as the Western and Indian film in this period. Its numbers swelled in 1911, in direct relation to the beginnings of the fiftieth anniversary memorial activities, and the culmination came in 1915 with THE BIRTH OF A NATION, half a century after the end of the war that split the nation. The Civil War was a topical subject in all the media at this time. Copyright records for the period show at least a dozen Civil War films in 1908, twenty-three of them in 1909, thirty-two in 1910, with a leap to seventy-four in 1911, only fifty-eight in 1912, another leap to ninety-eight in 1913, and just twenty-nine in 1914. (These figures do not account for all such films because not all films were copyrighted, and others may not have been identified as belonging to this genre.) The two biggest years, 1911 and 1913, were marked by major anniversary celebrations, which included enormous encampments of the Grand Army of the Republic on the sites of Civil War battles, dedication of monuments, and other ceremonies.[13]

In November 1908 Griffith brought out the first of his several films on the subject that would lead him seven years later to THE BIRTH OF A NATION. This was THE GUERRILLA, in which a Union soldier rides to the rescue of his sweetheart, whose home and virtue are threatened by a drunken guerrilla disguised as a Confederate colonel. The plot is similar to the other melodramatic thrillers that he was beginning to make at that time, containing the essential elements of home and family threatened by intruders and using the war only for a setting. However, THE HONOR OF HIS FAMILY (Biograph, January 1910) and THE HOUSE WITH CLOSED SHUTTERS (Biograph, August 1910) were different. These were chillingly grim civil War tales of Southern chivalric ideals. In the first, a father shoots his own son and lays his body in a gray, bare, twisted-briar corner of the battlefield rather than let the family name be stained by his cowardice. In the second, a mother locks up her cowardly son in mystery and gloom for the rest of his life to hide the fact that his sister died in his place to save the family honor.

Many of the Civil War films were stark tragedies of split families, loss and death, high nobility, and cowardice hidden by murder and suicide. Others were filled with thrilling battles and heroic deeds and spectacle. In these films producers tried out the ways to film and edit two sides of a battle scene in order to make clear to the spectator which side was which. If it were not for the uniforms, in many cases, they would not have succeeded. Such is the case in the Kay-Bee film THE FAVORITE SON (February 1913), directed by Francis Ford. The battle scenes are edited with shots alternating between the Yankees and the Confederates, but both armies fire their weapons in the same screen direction. When battle scenes are shown in alternate shots with each army firing consistently from opposite sides of the screen, a principle Griffith already followed in his Biograph Civil War films, it is much easier for a spectator to understand which side is being shown. According to a contemporary observer, "Northern officers invariably have black whiskers, while the Confederate officers wear gray whiskers."[14]

Love crossed the battle lines in most of the films, with heroines torn between loyalty to the flag and to their hearts. Sometimes they chose one, sometimes the other; sometimes they died, sometimes they were reunited with their lovers after the war. Spies of both sexes and escaping soldiers were hidden in wells with great frequency. Abraham Lincoln was shown granting pardon to all the spies, deserters, and sentinels who fell asleep at their posts during the entire war, on the plea of pretty sisters and wives or aged mothers. Once or twice General Lee did the same. Kalem's THE RAILROAD RAIDERS OF '62 (June 1911) reenacted a historical incident without any single hero or fictional story, for the sheer spectacle of a chase by railroad, and launched another popular genre, the railroad thriller.

The *World* first noted in the spring of 1909, when reviewing Selig's BROTHER AGAINST BROTHER, that "war dramas are becoming popular." Initially, the sympathies of the majority of the films seemed to be with the Northern side, resulting in some protests from the Deep South that came to a head after Kalem released ESCAPE FROM ANDERSONVILLE, about the horrors of the Confederate prisoner-of-war camp. The next year, an exhibitor in Charleston, West Virginia, wrote to the *World* to ask, "Why do all civil war pictures have the Northern army come out ahead? . . . Everyone knows the South won some battles . . . and a picture [like that] would simply set 'em up down here." The *World* explained that the reason was not a lingering prejudice against the defeated South, but that there were no manufacturers in the South and even the exchanges were fewer and more distant from the theaters. It was a question of the market.[15]

Even before the notorious ESCAPE FROM ANDERSONVILLE, Kalem had begun a series in their Florida studio that was to compensate in some degree for this oversight. The first venture was THE GIRL SPY, featuring scriptwriter-star Gene Gauntier as the heroic female spy working for the Southern side. She ought not to be overlooked when one reviews the beginnings of the motion-picture serials with their plucky heroines. Even at the time, a reviewer pointed out that the Civil War film "as a rule has emphasized the heroism of the North. . . . Kalem ['s film made] . . . during their sojourn in Florida . . . should be especially dear to Southern audiences."[16]

Producers soon discovered that the more romantic, noble, and heroic ideals to be found in the defeated South were attractive to both North and South. The emphasis of the Civil War genre shifted to give the edge to the Southern side. From 1911 on, the films that seem to reflect a Southern point of view, based on the published synopses, are more than twice as numerous as the opposite. This does not mean that such films claimed the South to have been correct politically, of course, but only that the film's heroes and heroines are the Confederates. In such films, former slaves often loyally risked or gave up their lives for their former masters: in UNCLE PETE'S RUSE (IMP, October 1911), Uncle Pete is a faithful black who pretends his master has died of smallpox to help him escape the enemy and persuades the Yankees to bury the coffin.

There was also the essential conflict of a dramatic scenario inherent in the tale of families split by the war, a theme that did not belong more to one side than the other. Many Civil War films took place in border-state communities where such tragedies were common. The Lubin film THE BATTLE OF SHILOH (November 1913) demonstrates the fairness doctrine in practice. Two soldiers on opposing sides respect each other and behave nobly when one is falsely accused of being a spy. They become prisoners of war when each soldier's sister betrays the other soldier, and they are exchanged at the war's end.[17]

Slapstick Comedy

The favored fictional genre before 1908 was slapstick comedy. But slapstick was vulgar, amoral, and anti-establishment, and reformers in the post-1908 period wanted it suppressed.

When Biograph's THE CURTAIN POLE was reviewed early in 1909, a critic admitted that the audience loved it but lamented the use of "the wornout scheme of foreign producers." This was Griffith's one attempt at a French chase comedy of the old style, and a delicious example it is: an inebriated Frenchman, played by none other than Mack Sennett, future champion of slapstick, tries to carry a long curtain pole through the streets, with disastrous results, including the traditional comic pursuit. Nonetheless, Biograph quickly discarded this outmoded genre.[18]

About this same time, the *Moving Picture World* observed "a noticeable increase in long subjects of real, legitimate comedy, as distinguished from the absurd 'breaking-up-a-houseful-of-furniture-and-chase-through-the-street' type."[19] For his part, Ben Turpin, a former vaudevillian who had started out making comedies at Essanay in 1907, recalled with a note of nostalgia:

> I had many a good fall and many a good bump, and I think I have broken about twenty barrels of dishes, upset stoves, and also broken up many sets of beautiful furniture, had my eyes blackened, both ankles strained and many bruises, and I am still on the go. This is a great business (*Moving Picture World*, 3 April 1909, p. 405).

In fact, the little cross-eyed comic had many years to go when he wrote this in 1909, but one might guess that his article marked a slowing of the slapstick vein at Essanay, in response to the demands of uplift. It is difficult to know, however, because most of the Essanay films are lost. In any case, by the end of the year, an exhibitor was to complain, "There is too much high class drama, which cannot be understood by the average working man. . . . A very large proportion seems to thoroughly enjoy the old Essanay slap-stick variety."[20]

Many comedies were still made at this time, but not compared to the days before 1908, when they constituted 70 percent and more of the fiction films. The ratio of drama to comedy completely reversed itself from 1907 to 1908, and comedy grew even more rare in 1909. The producers struggled to find a more polite form. Griffith's MR. AND MRS. JONES series at Biograph was typical of the move to less vulgar comedy, and indeed, it enjoyed great popularity. The role of Mrs. Jones gave a name that her admirers could attach to the anonymous Florence Lawrence besides just "the Biograph Girl." The Biograph production figures for 1910–1911, typical of these years, reflect the renewed interest in comedy: the ratio in 1910, for Biograph, was 29 percent comedies to 71 percent dramas, while in 1911 it became 46 percent comedies to 54 percent dramas.[21]

The genial and monumental John Bunny, previously a stage actor who had worked with Maude Adams, held sway at the Vitagraph studio from 1910 until his death in

MRS. JONES ENTERTAINS *(Biograph, 1909), directed by D. W. Griffith. Florence Lawrence and John R. Cumpson as Mrs. and Mr. Jones.*

1915. His gentle comedies were based on such simple situations as the henpecked but flirtatious husband, the homely wife (usually played by Flora Finch), and the beautiful young "typewriter." Bunny was among the first movie stars to be known all over the world, "rapidly becoming the most famous comedian the world has ever known," it was reported in 1911. When Sidney Drew, "the famed legit comedian," signed with Kalem to act and direct in his "well-known farce, 'When Two Hearts Are Won,' " it was called a great step for high-class comedy. When Drew later went to Vitagraph as director and star comic of a series, he produced the type of polite comedy based on real-life incidents that uplifters were calling for.[22]

By June 1910 the *World* reported that "the percentage of comedy releases is about one in five." The problem was that exhibitors, and, we suppose, the public, considered comedies to be an essential part of the program. The public could tolerate the uplift and the heavier stuff if there was a laugh in between. One exhibitor asking for more comedies wrote, "Just think, we have twelve short comedies out of fifty-seven subjects put on this market this week." A *World* editorial in mid 1911 claimed that tragedies outnumbered comedies at a ratio something like sixteen to one. It is not clear whether these figures included the slapstick comedies that continued to be imported from Europe, where comics such as Max Linder and André Deed were flourishing, but in any case they appear to be an enormous exaggeration compared to release charts. Nevertheless, the editorial demonstrates the growing demand for comedy.[23]

In 1910 "the comic policeman, . . . the chase, the mother-in-law joke, the mischievous boy, comedies with displays of lingerie or deformities, the cheap melodrama," were discussed by W. H. Buckwalter as clichés to be avoided. Except for the melodrama, these belonged to the period before 1908 and were already mostly suppressed in American cinema. But they were all to return unredeemed in the golden age of the slapstick comedy, which began to germinate after 1910 and exploded about 1915.[24] Indeed, an insightful critic was to write in 1912:

> G. M. Anderson and Thomas H. Ince, both in their respective individual ways, have appeared to show us the true vitality of the Western drama. They have proven that the offense is not in the kind, but in the quality—the manner of presentation. It now remains for some wise producer to push through the field of darkness and show the field the correct handling of so-called slapstick in pictures. . . . Who is to prove . . . that since burlesque is a legitimate form of amusement, there is a successful means of expression, devoid of crudity, before the camera? He shall wear a cap of discretion, see further than the greatest artist and walk hand in hand with human understanding—but he will appear (*New York Dramatic Mirror*, 2 October 1912, p. 24).

This grand prophecy was promptly fulfilled, in his own way, by Mack Sennett, bursting forth from the Biograph Company, home of the moralistic melodrama. No doubt the prophet would have considered him replete with crudity, but nevertheless, he represented in his comic talents a heartfelt reaction to the repressed period that began in 1908–1909. With the backing of Adam Kessel and Charles Baumann of the New York Motion Picture Company, Sennett founded an independent production company, Keystone, which would prove to be a veritable fountain of slapstick comedy. It is entirely fitting that the home of the moral melodrama provided the gestation of the greatest slapstick comedy (and the comedies Sennett made while still at Biograph should not be overlooked), but his talents only began to expand extravagantly after he left Biograph that September. The first Keystone releases included THE WATER NYMPH and COHEN COLLECTS A DEBT (23 September 1912). Sennett's films burlesqued the old Biograph thriller and turned traditional melodrama upside down. In FOR LIZZIE'S SAKE (January 1913), for example, a young woman is kidnapped by a villain who tries to force her to agree to marriage by tying her to a rock at sea during low tide and waiting for nature to take its course. Reformers were satirized in THE DEACON'S TROUBLES (November 1912), in which the head of the "Purity League" is caught flirting with a dancing girl in the show he wants to suppress. Civil War films were parodied in THE BATTLE OF WHO RUN (February 1913), and Westerns in FORCED BRAVERY (February 1913).[25]

The Canadian-born Sennett brought the new Keystone Company (including Biograph's comics Mabel Normand and Fred Mace) to California in late 1912. Charlie Chaplin, English music-hall comic, came to the Keystone comedy factory in December 1913; his first film, MAKING A LIVING, was released on 2 February 1914. At the end of that year he went from Keystone to Essanay, and on to world fame.[26] It took some time to find the unique rhythm of the Keystone slapstick comedies. Many of them, no doubt hastily made, consist of meaningless running about and falling down. The best of them, however, have been savored for generations for their surrealistic delirium and manic pace. The Sennett-Keystone films burlesqued everything that Americans took seriously, from melodrama, uplift, progressivism, patriotism, and mother love to the Ford car.

Chaplin's first film, MAKING A LIVING, *2 February 1914, produced by Mack Sennett and directed by Henry Lehrman. Chaplin is wearing the costume of his stage act.*

MABEL AT THE WHEEL, *18 April 1914, produced by Mack Sennett. Directed by Sennett and Mabel Normand. Mabel Normand and Charlie Chaplin.*

The slapstick films challenged new narrative systems by returning to some of the forms of pre-1909 cinema. In slapstick comedy, actors could play directly to the camera, the whole figure of the actor would more commonly be kept full in the frame, and the gags would often be based on the camera magic of the early trick films. A lot of the fun resulted from the playing with those sacred illusions of reality that in other films must never be broken. Jay Leyda has called this new American version of an old genre "California slapstick." It drew on the cheerfully amoral traditions of pre-1909 American film and vaudeville as well as the French and Italian slapstick comedies, and it mocked the excesses of the melodrama.[27]

The idea that slapstick comedies were to be deplored as vulgar, tasteless, and not for refined audiences persisted as a legacy of the reform period, but the spirit of joy in pre-1909 slapstick cinema was too strong to be held down for long. Audiences loved it. The idea that slapstick comedies might represent a new art form, however, was unlikely to have occurred to anyone (other than those closely involved in modern art movements) in the period covered by this volume. It would certainly have come as a surprise to Mack Sennett and his merry crew.

Of course, Sennett did not create the revival of slapstick entirely on his own. Other companies were also rising to the demand even before he started out. The Hank and Lank comedies coming out of Essanay in 1911 and featuring comics Augustus Carney and Victor Potel were full of slapstick. Al Christie, although less a slapstick specialist, was already making films for Nestor, and, like Sennett, training a coming generation of comics. Among the hundreds of comedies he created for Nestor and later for Universal, there was the Mutt and Jeff series in 1911. Arthur Hotaling was directing a comedy company for Lubin in 1912 in Jacksonville, where Oliver Hardy began his

THE CANNON BALL (Keystone, 1915). Chester Conklin.

MERRY MODELS (Essanay, 1915). Ben Turpin and Wallace Beery in the background.

film career, and the Punch Comedy series was being produced in the same town. Lloyd Hamilton and Bud Duncan created the witty Ham and Bud series for Kalem beginning in 1914. Hal Roach, Sennett's greatest rival as a comedy producer, was just starting to make his mark in 1915 with the films of Harold Lloyd.[28]

The comedy reel played a distinctive part in the revision of the distribution system to accommodate the feature film. In 1914, many exhibitors were still tied to the system of standing orders for a regular service of short films and thus compelled to pay an extra sum to get the feature from outside the system. But an alternative was in sight, as A. Trinz of the Rainbow Theatre in Milwaukee, Wisconsin, suggested at the end of that year:

> Let the feature concerns supply a reel of comedy with each of their feature productions and they will have a lot easier time getting bookings. . . . Many of the houses are in a position to play exclusive feature programs, but cannot afford to play features all the week around and pay for the regular service which is not used with the exception of the comedy reel. If all four and five-reel features had a reel of comedy with them, it would be possible for the exhibitor to get away from his film exchange if he was in a position to play features right through the week. As it is, he has to pay as much for the occasional reel of comedy as he would for an entire program (*Motion Picture News*, 19 December 1914, p. 102).

Newsreels

Newsreels, according to Raymond Fielding in *The American Newsreel*, were popular in Europe before they appeared in the United States. Topical films had always been enormously successful in America, but it was difficult to build a regular release pattern based on sporadic events, and under the pressure of the organized production and distribution system, the number of such films had fallen off. Some producers thought that the newsreel would be best undertaken as a cooperative venture. Pathé Frères was producing a weekly newsreel in Europe that did not appear in America, probably because of the constraints on Pathé's releases in the Trust agreements. In 1911 Pathé proposed to produce an American edition of their newsreel to which all the licensed companies would contribute, but, says Fielding, Vitagraph was opposed, and that scheme fell through. Instead, Pathé launched its own American edition of the Pathé Newsreel in August 1911. It was to become the longest-running American newsreel. Two weeks later Vitagraph started its Vitagraph monthly, "Current Events," but this lasted only five issues.[29]

The independents, to meet the newsreel competition, contracted with another French company, Gaumont, whose Animated Weekly introduced an American edition, distributed through the Sales Company, in 1912. Although the American edition lasted only ninety-two issues, from 22 February 1912 through 10 December 1913, the Gaumont International Newsreel was distributed in America for many years. Selig teamed up with the Hearst newspapers to produce a newsreel in 1914, the beginning of another lengthy run. Once the feature film was firmly established in the exhibition system, the newsreel, together with the comedy, took a permanent place in the program.

Mutual released the Mutual Weekly beginning on 1 January 1913 and continuing for the next five years; in January 1914 it began a series called OUR MUTUAL GIRL, which ran for a year. OUR MUTUAL GIRL was not a newsreel, but a curious mixture of fiction and reality somewhere between a newsreel and a serial. Our Mutual Girl, played by Norma Philips, was a fictional character, a young woman from the country on a visit to her aunt in New York City. In the course of her modest adventures she visited all the fashionable places, the Plaza, the Ritz, Central Park, and Fifth Avenue, saw all the latest fashions of the top New York dressmakers, and met every celebrity of the day, whether in society, politics, theater, or opera. In one of the early issues, the producers persuaded Andrew Carnegie, Billie Burke, Mayor Mitchel, and District Attorney Whitman to appear before the cameras. Through the films, small-town audiences could participate in the life of big-city sophisticates.[30]

Detective Films, Serials, and Feminism

The independent firm Yankee began a detective series in October 1910 with THE MONOGRAMMED CIGARETTE, in which "the fearless daughter of a famous detective" solves her first case after the father is killed. Another film in this series, THE WOMAN WHO DARED, was described at the time as "an excellent detective story, showing the famous girl detective in one of her most fascinating unraveling acts." According to the

Moving Picture World, "It is mysterious up to the last scenes, when the solution is given. . . . There is an interest which never flags from the time the picture begins until the last scene has disappeared." These films reflect the current fascination with scientific apparatus for detection, such as the "dictograph," which enabled girl detectives to overhear the crooks' conversation, as the heroine does when tracking down the white slave traffickers in TRAFFIC IN SOULS (1913). Detective mysteries were also becoming an increasingly popular literary genre at the same time. By late 1911 a disgruntled exhibitor who had resigned himself to receiving one Indian picture for every show remarked that he was dismayed to note an influx of detective stories.[31]

Like the girl spy of the Kalem company, Yankee's girl detective anticipated the serial queen. THE EXPLOITS OF ELAINE, succeeding THE PERILS OF PAULINE from the Pathé Company, had as "an added value" the "use of genuine scientific methods in the detection of crime." This included the use of the "detectaphone" which the real-life Burns Detective Agency was said to have adopted for its work. In the new serial, *Motion Picture News* reported: "The general scheme . . . will be to present a series of high class scientific detective stories. Instead of thrills created by smashing property, there will be those caused by tense situations and marvelous achievements of science."[32]

The serial with its brave heroine signaled the emergence of the New Woman. She wore less restrictive clothes, she was active, she went everywhere she wanted, and she was capable of resolving mysteries, solving problems, and escaping from danger. In the movie industry the New Woman was not only adored as a star, but also pioneered a new profession known as "script girl" (keeping track of every detail during the shooting of a script), and she formed teams to assemble the separate shots and titles of each film positive. She also managed movie theaters in respectable numbers, wrote a large proportion of the film scripts, and found it easier to get into directing than she would in later periods of film history. Prominent female writer-directors included the pioneer Alice Guy, wife of Herbert Blaché and the chief executive of her own company, Solax; Gene Gauntier (working with Sidney Olcott); and Lois Weber (with Phillips Smalley). When a writer for the *World* mentioned Miss Jeanette A. Cohen, a poster sales*woman,* he added, "Why not?" Sometimes patronized, sometimes feared, the New Woman was nevertheless welcomed by reformers for the refinement and culture she could bring to the industry.[33]

The Progressive cause of women's rights was echoed most directly in a lot of comedies in which the humor comes at the expense of those funny suffragettes, but also frequently mocks their opponents. However, there were also quite a few serious films on the subject. Vitagraph made a film called DAISIES (August 1910), in which the heroine insists on an education over the objections of her fiancé and nearly at the sacrifice of her engagement. By the end of this feminist film, the fiancé is compelled to admit that the young woman was right. The film was shot in part at Vassar College. The intertitles were wreathed in flowers, and the critic Louis Reeves Harrison, noting the graceful movement rather than the feminist message of the film, speculated that a woman had something to do with it. Undoubtedly some woman did, but, unfortunately, her name is not known. The film itself is lost.[34]

The subject of women's rights was hot in 1912, an election year. Teddy Roosevelt, leader of the Progressive party, was advertised in a campaign film as "the first American statesman to recognize the right of American womanhood to help rule the country." In bold type, the advertisement proclaimed, "Women want to see him."

But Wilson won the presidential election that fall. Universal suffrage was postponed until after the war.[35]

The Congregational Church of Appleton, Wisconsin, showed Reliance's two-reel drama VOTES FOR WOMEN on the program with a talk by Harriet Grim, a "well-known Wisconsin suffragette." Other nights, this progressive church had shown the tuberculosis films with educational lectures. The Edison Company, trying to launch its newest talking-picture device, the Kinetophone, with the characteristic Edison message of reform, offered Mrs. O. H. P. Belmont, "one of the most prominent leaders of the Suffrage movement," the opportunity to deliver a six-minute speech by means of the newest invention. The great English militant Mrs. Emmeline Pankhurst and the American leader of the Women's Political Union, Mrs. Harriet Stanton Blatch, appeared personally in WHAT EIGHTY MILLION WOMEN WANT—? (November 1913), a fiction film exposing corrupt politics in New York City.[36]

Edison's HOW THEY GOT THE VOTE (1 January 1913), directed by Ashley Miller, was a fantasy in which time is stopped, probably a direct inspiration from Jean Durand's ONESIME HORLOGER (1912), a French film in which time was speeded up in order that a man could collect his inheritance sooner. In the Edison film, a young man wants to win the daughter of a suffragette, and to win favor, he must do something for the cause:

> He visits a magician who gives him the images of the god of progress and the goddess of sleep, and he tries their power on the crowded thoroughfares of London. He finds to his delight that they give him the ability to bring traffic to a standstill. All London is mystified by the strange happenings and the prime minister is in a quandary. The young man declines to better matters unless the prime minister favors "votes for women" (*New York Dramatic Mirror*, 8 January 1913, p. 28).

A direct link between feminism and serials is illustrated by episode 13 of THE HAZARDS OF HELEN (Kalem, February 1915), where Helen Holmes loses her job as the railroad telegrapher after she is robbed by two tramps. A man is sent to replace her, but the intrepid Helen sees the tramps fleeing on a freight train and captures them herself, dropping off a bridge onto the moving train, engaging them in hand-to-hand combat, and falling from the train into water with one of the crooks. She gets her job back.

The opposite side of the coin, the fear that the New Woman engendered, may well have given rise to a new type of female villain, the vamp, exemplified by Theda Bara in Fox's A FOOL THERE WAS (January 1915). Theda Bara was far from the first of these. In 1910, Selig produced THE VAMPIRE, described as "the sensation of the age—from the most talked-of poem ever written and suggested by Sir Ed. Burne-Jones' Famous Painting." A year earlier, the poem and the painting had provided the sources of a popular stage play, *A Fool There Was*, which was also the basis of the Theda Bara film. By 1912–1913, the vamp type was frequently found in films. Rosemary Theby's portrayal in Vitagraph's THE REINCARNATION OF KARMA (December 1912) is only one of many. The character may be seen fully developed and perhaps better motivated in Vitagraph's RED AND WHITE ROSES (March 1913), in which "the Woman" is found reclining chin down on a tiger-head rug, smoking, in the extreme lower-left corner. She boldly propositions a married man, a reform candidate for governor, contrasting her charms to those of his wife: "She is a white rose, pale and colorless—I am a red rose—glowing and made for love."[37]

Prohibition Films

The cause of prohibition gave rise to many lurid melodramas. It was a subject very well suited to the uplift movement and yet could exploit violence and dramatic thrills. Drink led to the breakup of the home, a major social concern of this era. Biograph's contributions to the cause of prohibition included A DRUNKARD'S REF-ORMATION (March 1909) and WHAT DRINK DID (June 1909). In the former, scenes from the play *Drink* are reenacted, effecting reform in the drunkard who attends the performance. *Drink* was Charles Reade's dramatization of Zola's *L'Assommoir* (*The Drunkard*), in which Charles Warner made his New York debut at the Academy of Music on 14 September 1903. In October 1909, there were "awestruck crowds" at the showing of Pathé's two-reel film version, DRINK, at Keith and Proctor's Bijou Dream in New York. As we know from the later results, prohibition was not favored by the majority of the American people, and DRINK did not play so well in the provinces. Some of the anti-prohibition exhibitors complained of the influx of films on the subject. A review of a film with a temperance lesson included the gentle aside "but one doesn't always care to be sermonized in a moving picture theater." An exhibitor was more outspoken about "the gory and ridiculous anti-drink pictures" that the Anti-Saloon League of Indiana was asking exhibitors to play, even paying them to do so. The *St. Louis Times* reported that an exhibitor was nearly ruined by rumors that he was a prohibitionist: his customers went from three hundred a night to forty, until he made a sworn oath to the contrary and displayed it behind glass outside his show.[38]

Labor Films

The subject of organized labor and labor unrest, a very big issue in the period before the war, loomed up in many films. When Vitagraph's CAPITAL VERSUS LABOR was filmed in the streets of Flatbush, the mounted police were called. They charged into the crowd of actors playing the strikers. Whether a bystander or a Vitagraph publicity person called the police is unclear, but the results were reported to be almost disastrous. The *World* took a management position on this genre, declaring that CAPITAL VERSUS LABOR "is much too realistic to be comfortable. . . . Perhaps the picture will have a salutary influence during this season when strikes pervade the air and from almost every section of the country comes talk of industrial complaint." In another issue, a writer complained that "it is not the story of an American strike, but an anarchist revolution, with no moral lesson to it."[39]

Most of the labor films portrayed a greedy capitalist with a progressive son or daughter or foreman who could negotiate and reason with the strikers and bring about reform. The formulas of the moralistic melodrama were readily applied to this subject too. Films were made by capitalists, after all, even if they were progressives. Improvement in labor relations, they felt, was to be brought about by education and reform, and certainly not by a change in the system. Reliance's LOCKED OUT (1911), however, according to the description of its plot, was extremely pro-labor. It showed starvation in the homes of the strikers, police shooting strikers, and the ghosts of these martyrs confronting the owner of the factory, who dies from the shock. The *World* complained that the National Board of Censorship should have rejected this film. In its view, exhibitors should not "excite the masses by showing them innocent women killed in the act of earning their daily bread."[40]

In Essanay's THE LONG STRIKE (8 December 1911) the boss's arrogant son takes over on the eve of a strike, but the daughter of a striker saves him from the violence of the workers and appeals to the owner to settle the strike. As one reviewer noted:

> In this labor melodrama the workingman is treated more as a normal man than in most film stories dealing with this delicate subject . . . yet . . . while the workingman is not represented as a child and the employer as a patronizing snob, there is a plain tendency to assume that a strike must necessarily have its crimes and violence. Recent events show that there is a distinct element in labor's ranks ready to resort to crime, but it is not pretended that this element is in majority. The masses of Union Labor know nothing about dynamite plots. . . . The matter-of-course way in which the strike leaders in this picture are made to plot arson will not therefore commend the picture to working people. As The Mirror stated some time ago, picture producers will show wise discretion by letting labor subjects severely alone (*New York Dramatic Mirror*, 13 December 1911, p. 33).

BY MAN'S LAW, a Biograph film of November 1913 directed by William Christy Cabanne, took quite an extraordinary point of view for a capitalist producer and stout member of a trust then under attack by the federal government. An oil magnate ruthlessly buys up independent rivals until he controls the industry, then cuts wages and closes factories, causing much suffering among the working classes. As a result of the evil capitalist's greed, a young working girl becomes a member of the unemployed and nearly falls into the hands of the white slavers.

The development of film genres standardized the manufacture and distribution of the product for a newly organized industry. For audiences, the genre film made it possible to achieve satisfaction in the fulfillment of expectations, and at the same time to be entertained by variations of the form. The genre film facilitated the lulling of the spectator into the cinematic dreamworld.

12

The Feature Film

Part two of this picture will be shown in one minute.
—THE BARGAIN (1914)

What is a feature film? The term "feature" was an inheritance of the vaudeville program. When the "feature film" was first marketed, it meant a special film, a film with something that could be featured in advertising as something out of the ordinary run. It was not just another sausage.

A feature was a film that cost more to make, more to buy, more to rent, and sometimes, though not always, it cost more to see. That usually meant longer films, and after 1909 "feature" was the term generally used for any multireel film. In 1909 a feature film was 1,000 feet long or a little less, running from fifteen to twenty minutes at its slowest speed. A short film, called a "split reel," was 500 feet or less. In May 1910, when the Motion Picture Distributing and Sales Company established its rules to determine prices and to identify the minimum of six reels a week that cooperating exchanges were obligated to buy, a reel was defined as not less than 700 feet and not more than 1,050 feet, which could only be billed as 1,000 feet. However, over the next five years, the term "feature" could be applied to a film of two to eight reels, and only very rarely to a single reel. The longer ones were often distinguished by such terms as "special features" or "big features." Adding to the confusion, up to the beginning of 1915, the two-reel film might be reviewed in the trade papers either in the feature section together with the longer films or in the regular program section. In short, there was no real precision in the use of the term in this period.[1]

As we have demonstrated in earlier chapters, the motion-picture theaters were running variety shows. Despite the difficulties the manager might be experiencing in obtaining the specific films or kinds of films wanted, he or she still exercised the power of the showman to decide in what order the films would be shown and to combine them with the vaudeville acts and illustrated songs of his or her choice, as well as the musical accompaniment. The move to the long feature film, then, could be construed as another way for producers to have more control, a stronger voice in the consumption of their product. The longer the film, the less opportunity there was for the showman to intervene, and the less time available for nonfilmic elements. The exhibitor, perhaps unconscious of this loss of control, nevertheless strongly resisted it. As many of the exhibitors pointed out, one unsuccessful short film in the program could be offset by a good one, but if the feature was poor, the show could not be saved.

Any factor that brought higher prices to the exchange, which had fixed contracts with the exhibitors, was naturally resisted as well. "We wish to complain," wrote three Los Angeles exchange men to the Motion Picture Patents Company in November 1909, "against the extra charges levied by the Pathé Company for coloring and acting, which they attach to about every third reel, and upon which extra charges we are allowed no rebates. It seems to us that there is an established price per foot, and therefore, the question arises, why this extra charge should be exacted?" The mention of "acting" as a reason for a higher price is an interesting example of the "extra" qualities, in addition to length, that defined a feature in 1909.[2]

The producers belonging to the Motion Picture Patents Company are usually said to have been too conservative in clinging to the single-reel film and thus to have caused their own downfall. The fact is, however, that it was the rental exchange and the exhibitors, both licensed and independent, who were most reluctant to change. The whole system tended to keep films at the same length; in other words, the system that gave stability to the industry was also the system that resisted change.

At first, the exhibition format itself was the strongest barrier to increasing length. The nickelodeon was a gold mine only if there was a quick turnover of the audiences. But competition to offer the most reels for a nickel had worn away this concept in many areas of the country, thus contributing to the eventual acceptance of multireel productions. When the number of theaters with a large seating capacity increased, it was less necessary to have rapid turnover to make a profit. The public continued to cling to the habit of entering at whatever point in the program they wished, which did not matter much when, in the short film program, each new reel was a new beginning.

The multireel feature films began to be distributed after 1910 outside the established system and in the process created a new one. Feature films could be road-shown, as plays were, with stock companies playing the provinces. This was the method used to distribute Helen Gardner's big feature film CLEOPATRA in late 1912. Numerous companies were sent out on the road with a print of the film, an advance man, a lecturer-projectionist, and a manager. Features were shown as special attractions in the local opera houses and town halls and legitimate theaters at advanced prices and stayed for as long as there was enough business to support them.[3]

The separate distribution of features in large theaters marked the beginning of cracks in the existing system. The price of renting such a show was, of course, much higher than for the one-reel films from the exchanges. If the film was not being road-shown, or if that tour was completed, it could be sold by "states rights." The "states rights" system meant that an individual or a small company could buy the rights for a specific territory and then go out and get whatever the market would bear from the special exhibition places or from an ordinary movie house. Pliny P. Craft gave himself credit for originating the system when he was working with the Buffalo Bill Wild West Show: inspired by the success of the Johnson–Jeffries fight film, Craft convinced Buffalo Bill to let the Wild West Show be recorded on film and then found backing for a three-reel feature. He claimed that "the states rights idea came into vogue with this picture as a necessary after-consideration. Film exchanges could not be induced to buy the Buffalo Bill Show film because it was thought to be too long." After this experience, Craft went to Europe looking for another feature that he could exploit in a similar fashion and came back with DANTE'S INFERNO in 1911.[4]

When a road show had milked the cities of all the money to be gotten for high-priced tickets, the worn and scratched print, without the extra costs of the special

Contract for Pictures of the
Buffalo Bill Wild West & Pawnee Bill Far East Show

THIS AGREEMENT made and entered into this....*8th*....day of....*March*....A. D. 19..*11*, by and between Collins and Collins of Utica, N. Y., Party of the First Part, and .... of ....*Oxford*.................................... State of ....*New York*.......... Party of the Second Part, WITNESSETH:

Whereas, The Party of the First Part owns and controls the New York State Rights of the Original Authorized Motion Pictures of the Buffalo Bill Wild West and Pawnee Bill Far East Show.

~~And, Whereas, The Party of the Second Part wishes to exhibit the above Motion Pictures of said Buffalo Bill Wild West and Pawnee Bill Far East Show.~~

~~Now, Therefore, The Party of the Second Part, in consideration of the agreement hereinafter mentioned, agrees to rent said Original Authorized Motion Pictures of said Buffalo Bill Wild West and Pawnee Bill Far East Show from the Party of the First~~ Part for a period of....*one day*...............from the........*16*........day of....*March*...., 19..*11*, to the...............day of....................., 19...., ~~both dates inclusive~~, to be used only in the....*Opera House*....Theatre, in the City of........*Oxford*........ and State of New York, on the following terms:

The Party of the Second Part further agrees to pay to the Party of the First Part..*70% Gross Receipts*. ~~for rental of the above-mentioned Motion Pictures of the Buffalo Bill Wild West and Pawnee Bill Far East Show for the time above specified.~~

It is mutually agreed that the prices of admission be...*15¢ 25¢ 35¢ Few list 50*......

The Party of the Second Part further agrees to return the above mentioned pictures to the Party of the First Part in the same condition as when rented, necessary wear alone excepted, immediately upon the expiration of the time and date above specified and agreed upon, and in the event of said Motion Pictures of the Buffalo Bill Wild West and Pawnee Bill Far East Show being damaged or injured in any way, the Party of the Second Part agrees and undertakes to pay as liquidated damages fifteen cents (15c) for each and every lineal foot of said Motion Pictures of the Buffalo Bill Wild West and Pawnee Bill Far East Show so damaged or injured, within five (5) days after receipt of bill from the Party of the First Part.

The Party of the Second Part further agrees to return said Motion Pictures of the Buffalo Bill Wild West and Pawnee Bill Far East Show to the Party of the First Part same day this contract and agreement expires, and if this is impossible, then by the first express the morning of the day thereafter, and upon failing to do so, the Party of the Second Part agrees and contracts to pay to the Party of the First Part the sum of one hundred dollars ($100.00) per day for each and every day said pictures are retained beyond the time mentioned above.

The Party of the First Part, in consideration of the agreement herein set forth, hereby agrees to rent and deliver to Party of the Second Part (unless delayed by causes beyond its control, such as strikes, failure of express companies to make prompt deliveries, railroad accidents, destruction of films, etc.), the above mentioned Original and Authorized Motion Pictures of the Buffalo Bill Wild West and Pawnee Bill Far East Show, in accordance with the terms of this agreement and contract as above set forth and specified.

It is further agreed that the Party of the First Part reserves the right to cancel this contract at any time within 24 hours prior to the opening date as above written.

It is understood and agreed that when the above designated films of the Buffalo Bill Wild West and Pawnee Bill Far East Show are leased at a daily cash rental said Parties of the First Part are hereby authorized to ship said films by express, C. O. D., such daily rental to be collected on the delivery of such films to said Party of the Second Part, together with all carrying charges added thereto.

In Witness Whereof both parties hereto have set their hands and seals the date aforesaid.

Lectures will attend & describe every scene

Witness: COLLINS & COLLINS.

....   By..*J. P. Collins*..........(Seal)

"States Rights" contract for BUFFALO BILL'S WILD WEST AND PAWNEE BILL'S FAR EAST SHOW "in motion pictures," to play the Opera House, Oxford, New York, on 16 March 1911.

manager, advance man, projectionist, and the like, could then be billed as a special attraction at the nickel theater, which might or might not add on a higher ticket for that performance. In many parts of the country, Sunday was the day set aside for special "uplifting films," and therefore Sunday was often the day for the occasional showing of a feature in the smaller theaters that ran the regular short film program the rest of the week. Here, the prestige of the special showings, although now fading, could be counted on as an attraction. Such methods, used outside the normal distribution system, were adequate during the period when the number of feature films was still small compared to the regular one-reel releases.

Hobart Bosworth in the three-reel feature, MONTE CRISTO, later renamed THE COUNT OF MONTE CRISTO (Selig, 1912). Directed by Colin Campbell.

When Mabel Taliaferro, a celebrated theatrical star, agreed to appear in Selig's three-reel CINDERELLA (1911), the trade press noted:

> It may be that the only way stars can secure exceptional pay in motion pictures will be by appearing in some such way as was recently announced, regarding Sarah Bernhardt in Kinemacolor—a four-act play with Miss Bernhardt in the leading part. This picture could then be circulated much as the coronation films or as Dante's Inferno—as travelling attractions at higher prices than the five and ten cent picture shows (*New York Dramatic Mirror*, 13 December 1911, p. 28).

Similarly, when Mrs. Fiske, "the first really great American actress," agreed to preserve her act for eternity by signing a picture contract with Daniel Frohman to appear in her most famous role as Becky Sharp, the same trade journal reported that "the pictures will make up a complete evening's entertainment, and will not be presented in the regular moving picture theaters, but in the prominent theaters and under special conditions." (Mrs. Fiske's first film was TESS OF THE D'URBERVILLES, Famous Players, 1913; she did not make the film VANITY FAIR until 1915, for Edison.)[5]

With the increasing prestige of motion pictures, the situation began to change:

> Scarcely a film company of any prominence but has been approached repeatedly on behalf of stars of the first magnitude looking to their appearance in some sort of feature film production. The stars have been willing enough, but the manufacturers have not seen the way clear to carrying the projects forward with profit. . . . Single reel pictures marketed on the system that has been built up in this country could result in only moderate profit for each individual production. There is little or no fluctuation in output for any company from one release to another. Standing orders tend to bring all productions of each company to a dead level of circulation. It has been to the interest of each company, therefore, to improve and maintain its general standard of excellence, rather than to produce a big feature film once in a while (*New York Dramatic Mirror*, 13 December 1911, p. 28).

When it came to departing from this rule, it was one of the members of the Motion Picture Patents company, Vitagraph, that led the way. In 1909, the same year that standardization in length was achieved throughout the industry, Vitagraph began to experiment with some multireel releases. However, as was to be the practice throughout most of 1909 and 1910, the multiple-reel films were released sequentially in single reels, a week apart. This may seem strange now, but it was the result of the existing distribution system (and was probably less strange to a public accustomed to the issuance of novels in weekly parts in periodicals). Each producer associated with the Motion Picture Patents Company—and the independent producers in the Sales

TESS OF THE D'URBERVILLES (Famous Players, 1913), directed by J. Searle Dawley. The film debut of Minnie Maddern Fiske.

Company as well—had a specified release date during the week and a set number of reels, while the exchanges and the exhibitors had their standing orders. The highest price was for the first-day release, considered as one reel. To change this system meant changing everything. If you managed a high-class show house, you bought first run. If you had a second-class place and were unable to pay for first run, you had the option to run the separately released films together, as one film. Gradually, that did happen, but only when the films were no longer "new."

When Vitagraph's pretentious feature NAPOLEON, THE MAN OF DESTINY (1909) ran at a crowded Broadway house, the manager was asked if it could be held over for another day, whereupon, "he launched forth against full reel subjects and said that what he wanted was short comedies so that the house could be emptied and filled more frequently."[6] In fact, the film that the reluctant manager had shown was only one of the two reels of the feature known as THE LIFE OF NAPOLEON. The first part, NAPOLEON AND THE EMPRESS JOSEPHINE, had been released a week earlier. There was no imperative to run both reels together, because they were not treated as modern story films, with a continuous narrative. Rather, the first American "features" tended to revert to the pre-1908 forms. Thus the two Napoleon reels were tableau films, illustrating separately the events in Napoleon's life. In the case of NAPOLEON, THE MAN OF DESTINY, these episodes were linked by memory: the great man himself was seated, sunk in reveries of past glories, each of which appeared in turn, announced by the date and place appearing directly on the image. The tableau style, consisting of a series of carefully composed scenes often resembling famous paintings or book illustrations of well-known events, was also typical of the passion plays, the earliest of the special features. It was not a matter of asking audiences to come back next week and see how the story turned out.

ITALIAN CAVALRY RIDE, an Italian film in two reels, was released in the United States by an independent firm in the same month as the Napoleon films. Made by Ambrosio and released by the Chicago Film Exchange on 28 April, it began its run outside the regular distribution system. The Eden Musee in New York showed it to great acclaim, and subsequently it made its way into the unlicensed nickelodeons, glowing with the prestige of the earlier showings. However, it is quite possible and indeed very likely that most nickelodeons did not show the full version. An advertisement in a trade periodical reveals that it could be had in a length of 2,100 feet, but a version of 800 feet was also available. Rather than change the system, the product could be cut to fit.[7]

In July 1909, in time for the national holiday, Vitagraph released another two-reel film, THE LIFE OF GEORGE WASHINGTON, one reel at a time. This was followed in August by a truly ambitious work, LES MISÉRABLES, in four reels. All during the autumn months, the Vitagraph studio worked on the five-reel THE LIFE OF MOSES, which was also released, as all these films were, in separate reels. But in 1910 the same films began to be shown here and there as multireel features, with all the reels in the same program. THE LIFE OF MOSES was as good as a passion play, and all five reels were in the exchanges before Lent. "In large houses," reported the World, "the entire five reels may be run in one day, preferably Sundays, or they can be run on successive days."[8]

The Shubert Theater in New Orleans, among others, ran all the reels together. In April 1910 they held the show over for eight days, which could not ordinarily be done in the first runs because the prints were always due elsewhere to meet the prior commitments of the standing orders. The film was accompanied by piano and organ and a vocalist "to render 'Holy City' as Moses ascends the mountains to die." As already noted, this was the theater whose manager boasted of attracting the best people in the city.[9]

In addition to the Vitagraph multireel films, the 1909–1910 season saw the entry of longer foreign films into the American market. Other countries did not face the same limitations of an organized film industry in determining the length of their product, and when these foreign multireel films were imported, they would usually be shown outside the established distribution system, in their entirety instead of one reel at a time. It was Pathé Frères, a licensed producer, that first tried to change the practice of showing longer films in separate reels in the regular movie houses. Thus DRINK, the adaptation of Zola's *L'Assommoir* that, as we have already seen, opened to "awestruck crowds" in October 1909, was shown complete—"in a magnificent 2,000-foot presentation"—in its first screenings. Pathé was still a foreign producer at that time, not having opened its American production studio, and its multireel productions were made for the European market. To get back the cost of bigger productions, Pathé would certainly have wanted to show them on the American market, and a special arrangement with the Patents Company may have been necessary to make this possible.[10]

But DRINK faced other problems, as Jacques Berst of Pathé testified in 1913:

> I remember it because we had quite some trouble in placing that film in the market. The exchanges at that time had no use for multiple reels, and they would not stand for it, and in order to be able to make them accept it, we had to release one reel one week and the second reel, the following week. They would not take it as a whole in one week. The market at that time was not adapted to multiple reel subjects (*US* v. *MPPC* 4:1949 [December 1913]).

The resistance of exchanges and exhibitors is again demonstrated by the next part of the letter previously quoted, from three Los Angeles exhibitors who complained to the Motion Picture Patents Company in the autumn of 1909:

> The 'Pathe Drink Picture' of some 2,100 feet, and costing us in the neighborhood of $235.00, has proven to be almost a dead loss to us, inasmuch as the larger cities do not want it and the smaller ones cannot use it. However, we are obliged to take it and pay the extra charges on coloring and acting (Clune, Tally, and Krantz, *US* v. *MPPC* 3:1465).

At just the same time, an editorial in the *Moving Picture World* reflected some industry concern about the trend to longer films. It was noted that among the current licensed releases, there were no less than seven subjects of about 1,000 feet. Few producers, it was argued, could fill 1,000 feet with excitement, and the average 600-foot film did much better with the public.[11]

Part of the exchange men's objections came from the fact that the licensed producers were using the new noninflammable stock, which at first was thicker than ordinary stock. A full 1,000-foot film could not be wound on a 10⅜-inch reel and could not fit in the magazine of the projector. This meant cutting out part of the film, which, distributers complained, represented "an absolute loss to the exchange. Secondly, where the film is too long, the first 50 feet and the last 50 feet are ruined in about one week of friction. . . . Members said they would cut off standing orders to those manufacturers who insisted upon sending out 1,000-foot subjects." Over time, however, these problems were ameliorated by technological changes: the film stock, even the unsuccessful noninflammable type, was made thinner, and by August 1910 Edison was offering larger reels, up to eleven inches. In October of the same year, Motiograph advertisements for its new projector announced, "The fireproof film magazines have been made considerably larger . . . for films that may be considerably in excess of 1,000 feet." They also described longer reel arms to accommodate the larger magazines. And by October 1913 the *Moving Picture World* reported, "The two-thousand-foot magazines now in use and growing in popularity promise to revolutionize present methods of presentation. A four-reel feature presented in two parts will seem much more acceptable than the four-reel division with its incident delays."[12]

The same exchanges that complained about the 1,000-foot films also objected to the release of two reels separately: people who had seen the first, they contended, did not come back for the second because they thought they had already seen the film. Different posters were needed to advertise each reel. The Reverend H. F. Jackson, resident clergyman on the staff of the *World*, further complained of the difficulty of reviewing these multireel films one reel at a time: "This instalment [*sic*] plan of presenting any important work is decidedly detrimental to its best interest."[13]

Despite all these problems with longer films, the limitations of the 1,000-foot reel were beginning to be felt. Louis Reeves Harrison, reviewing Edison's THE STARS AND STRIPES in July 1910, asked rhetorically, "When are we going to have two-thousand-feet reels?" and added, "We miss the best part of the fight, the hand-to-hand conflict. . . . [There is] not enough room in a thousand-foot reel." In November the *World* editorialized, "If filmmakers would put the same amount of good work in one subject four times the duration of four subjects, they would be able to produce . . . some of the best subjects of the times." The same editorial called for an end to the daily change, noting the problems with Vitagraph's UNCLE TOM'S CABIN, first shown in "sections," and now being shown complete, but only for one day, so that the eager customer was unable to catch up with it. The daily change was yet another part of the distribution-exhibition system that the coming of the feature film altered. Feature films cost too much and took too long to make to show them for just one day.[14]

Another editorial at the beginning of 1911 found that many films came to an abrupt and unsatisfactory conclusion and that the fault lay in conforming to the standard length of a reel:

> It would seem that the time has come when the length of the film should in no way have anything to do with the subject matter; there is too much evidence of "cutting off" to the detriment of the continuity of the pictures and this slaughtering of the subject only increases the ambiguity of the whole. . . . Clear, well sustained plots, carried to a full and finished ending, leaving with the audience a feeling of satisfaction and completeness, are demanded (*Moving Picture World*, 7 January 1911, pp. 14–15).

When one of the Keith and Proctor houses in New York played the two reels of FAUST in July 1911 with two acts of vaudeville between them, the *World's* W. Stephen Bush was shocked at such ignorance or hostility. Attempting to make the best of the system, Edwin Thanhouser later released a 1,500-foot film with a short film added to make it two reels. "It was a matter of being artistic," he explained. "It seems too bad that a producer must sell a story in a given length." Meanwhile, independent producer Herbert Miles felt himself forced to give in to the single-reel distribution system and announced in November 1911 that his Republic Film Company, "bowing to the will of the majority of the exhibitors in this country, . . . will no longer release two-reel films on the same day, but a week later."[15]

Overall, in the view of the *World*, at least, the new feature films were part of an upward trend in quality. In a June 1911 editorial, the journal had top praise for the two-reel ENOCH ARDEN (Biograph) and admired as well Vitagraph's A TALE OF TWO CITIES:

> It is bound to come and, in two or three years it will be the rule rather than the exception. . . . We cannot do justice to the subjects especially worth while in a thousand feet of film. The play, even with the spoken word, takes from two to three hours. . . . It is, however, absolutely essential that two and three-reel subjects be shown together. To show one on Monday and the other on Thursday is ridiculous (*Moving Picture World*, 17 June 1911, p. 1355).

At this point, however, the *World's* gift for prophecy was undermined by the special interests of the editor, a professional film lecturer who now took the opportunity to state that such films needed to be accompanied by lectures. Otherwise, he declared, it is too much strain on the eye and the brain. In the same issue, a reviewer of ENOCH ARDEN pointed out:

> Just as the absorption of the audience is complete, the first reel comes to an end. It is to be greatly regretted that upon the first run the second reel cannot be seen by the audience until June 15th, three days after the run of the first reel, but this is a disadvantage which can, of course, be overcome later (*Moving Picture World*, 17 June 1911, pp. 1358–1359).

The lack of two projection machines was another factor that hampered the showing of multireel films. The first nickelodeons, running short films in a variety format, had no reason for more than one projector. Most newly built houses, acknowledging the growth in the length of the program, included a booth large enough for two projectors, but for a very long time to come, there were a lot of places where audiences had to wait while the reels were changed, even in high-priced theaters, if the projection facilities had not been modernized. In the days of single reels, the time needed to change reels had often been filled with an illustrated song or a vaudeville act, but that meant a loss in continuity for the multireel film.

When the three-reel TEMPTATIONS OF A GREAT CITY, a Danish import, was shown in 1911, a reviewer remarked: "The interest is so strong that one actually becomes impatient while the reels are being changed. We would advise exhibitors to use two machines, if possible, when showing this film."[16]

One other problem was, as far as I know, unique to Boston, where a city regulation of 1908 limited continuous showing time to twenty minutes, interspersed with another form of entertainment for at least five minutes. The original purpose of the law was said to have been to protect the eyesight of the spectators. It had never been consistently enforced, and in 1913, as feature films became common, there was a move to amend this outdated provision.[17]

The titles at the end of reels in this period, when they have survived the wear and tear of projection, show that the break was expected. Like many of the surviving prints, THE BARGAIN, released as late as the end of December 1914, has a title at the end of the first reel that reads, "Part two of this picture will be shown in one minute." When reel two begins, it is with a duplicate of the film's main title.

More significantly, filmmakers also planned for the break in the construction of the film. To achieve a sense of completion in itself, each reel would reach a kind of conclusion at the end. Similar motives were at work even when all the reels were released together, because they might be shown with a break for the changes. It was thought desirable to end each reel in a kind of climax that would carry over the break. The next reel would then begin more slowly, to build up the interest once again and draw the spectator into the mood of the film. The structure of the multireel film was formed in the early years, and the climax or completion of an episode at the end of a reel continued long after it was made necessary by these conditions, a clear example of how exhibition practice can have an effect on the formal structure of films.

When Vitagraph's three-reel A TALE OF TWO CITIES was announced for three release days in February 1911, F. H. Richardson admonished his readers:

> Now Mr. Manager for the love of Mike don't run these reels separately. Wait until all are released and run them together as a complete play. . . . In this I believe you are given a slight foretaste of what will be the future of the photoplay. I believe the time is not far off when complete plays of five, six or seven reels will be the regular thing, rather than the novelty (*Moving Picture World*, 25 February 1911, p. 427).

His recommendation was followed by the Olympia Theater in Boston (illegally, according to the city ordinance), and exhibitors in Washington, D.C., in Brooklyn, and in Portland, Oregon. From Washington came the report that the film showing at the Pickwick

> created quite a stampede before this house. For four days this film was eagerly sought by the public, who viewed the dramatization of the great novel with educational and entertaining interest. It is always Manager Brylawski's intention to uplift the masses, so the usual price of five cents was maintained during the display of this costly film (*Moving Picture World*, 25 March 1911, p. 639).

For the uplift movement, the feature film meant prestige. The biggest excitement of the spring 1911 season came from an Italian import, THE FALL OF TROY, though the version distributed was only two reels long. This was Giovanni Pastrone's historical epic of 1910, LA CADUTA DI TROIA, the beginning of a series of Italian spectacle films that gave great impetus to the feature film in America. It was not its length—by 1911 there were quite a lot of 2,000-foot films—but its lavish production values, sets, costumes, and crowds that impressed viewers. THE FALL OF TROY successfully revived (for American audiences) some of the earlier forms of narrative construction. It used a variety of spaces within the single shot for playing out its action without cutting, a practice not unknown in America but one that seemed fresh in 1911, which was a peak period for fast cutting of short shots, at least for those who worked at the forefront of modern American style. Similarly, THE FALL OF TROY reminded American filmmakers of the use of pans to follow action, another practice of the earlier days in America that had fallen off by 1911. Pastrone's employment of this system prepared the way for the complex camera movements of his CABIRIA in 1914.

THE FALL OF TROY was a great *succès d'estime* for the Sales Company, which released it in competition with Vitagraph's A TALE OF TWO CITIES. It ran for four days at the Virginian in Washington, D.C., thanks to an energetic manager who enlisted the participation of the local schools as part of their history courses, and when it was shown at the Janet Theater in Chicago, masses of people waited in the lobby and in the street to get in. At the Ideal Theater in Chicago, it broke all house records as people came back two and three times to see it again. The Exhibitors League of Ohio complained that the Sales Company did not buy enough copies of it to satisfy demand, in order to force exhibitors to take all the rest of their (very inferior) product. THE CRUSADERS; OR, JERUSALEM DELIVERED, in four reels, followed THE FALL OF TROY into the American market in July 1911 and was accordingly hailed as "the second great epic in films that has come to us from Italy."[18]

Meanwhile, American films were still being shown for the most part one reel at a time, and audiences were becoming impatient with the practice. When Thanhouser's three-reel DAVID COPPERFIELD played the Gem in St. Louis in November 1911, the first reel was run and then "much disappointment resulted from the fact that the other two reels were not forthcoming."[19]

The licensed companies began to distribute some special features for purposes of uplift as well as to offset foreign and independent competition. At first, they offered such features as a group: all the member companies joined together in the release in order that no one company would get the benefit of the larger profit. One of the cooperative releases was the two-reel ROOSEVELT IN AFRICA, filmed by Cherry Kearton traveling with Theodore Roosevelt on a well-publicized big-game safari. The prints were made by the Pathé Company at its laboratory in Bound Brook and distributed by the licensed exchanges (about to be combined into General Film), which had to pay nearly double, twenty cents a foot. It was expected that the theaters would pay special prices as well, and that an advance admission would be charged. Kearton retained the right to market the film in Europe, although the prints were to be made by Pathé in America.[20]

The Trust was not fortunate in these cooperative ventures, however. ROOSEVELT IN AFRICA, released on 18 April 1910, was a box-office failure (a "lemon," the exhibitors called it), despite a big publicity campaign and despite the magic of Teddy Roosevelt's name as an attraction. The next unlucky joint project was the filming of the 4 July 1910 prizefight in which Jack Johnson, a "person of color," knocked out the white ex-champion, Jim Jeffries, in Reno, Nevada, where the fight had been moved after the governor of California refused to permit it to take place in that state. Prizefights and passion plays, a peculiar combination, certainly, had comprised the first feature films made before 1907. Prizefights were not exactly high-class, and were illegal in most areas (but not the films of them). Nonetheless, society people sometimes attended the fights, and so did some of the moving-picture producers. Reformers' protests against the brutality of prizefight films did not get far, until race prejudice got mixed up in the uplift game. "Pop" Rock, recently freed of his duties as the manager of the Vitagraph rental division by the organization of General Film, together with George Kleine, negotiated rights to film the fight on behalf of the combined producers of the Patents Company. J. Stuart Blackton undertook to oversee the filming of the fight with nine cameras in relays of three at a time, and the cameramen of Essanay, Selig, and Vitagraph worked together on the project. Blackton and Rock hurried back to New York from Reno with the fight negatives, planning a film longer than two hours, which would not be shown in the regular distribution system, of course, but at big theaters as a special attraction.[21]

But national attention was now focused on the film. Had the aging white boxer won the fight over the young black upstart, the same uproar presumably would not have occurred. As it turned out, the film was banned in many cities, such as Washington, D.C., and Baltimore, Maryland, for the reason, said the officials, that the showing might cause a race riot. Why would it cause a race riot? Why, the blacks would take the occasion to gloat over the whites. Race riots did not erupt, but in every city there was a great deal of attention to the question of whether showings would be permitted, with racial feelings exacerbated in the process. The moving-picture trade papers called the "hue and cry . . . silly." What these reformers should have done, they said, was to prevent the fight, not the showings of the film, and they further argued that the pictures would be shown as a full program in themselves and would be advertised as such. Those who did not want to see them could stay away. The *World* noted with alarm that "There was never a time when the general interests of the moving picture business were more at stake than during the period following the Johnson-Jeffries fight at Reno, Nevada. For years and years fights have been reproduced in moving pictures . . . with no intimation of objection." This project really backfired on the Trust.[22]

After his victory, Jack Johnson went into vaudeville, in the form of a filmed monologue about the fight, which was recorded on records for the Cinephone. He traveled with (and later married) a white woman. According to fight historian Jim Jacobs, this action resulted in the enactment of the Mann Act, under which Johnson was subsequently imprisoned. In any event, his notoriety displeased the forces of uplift. Later, film historian Terry Ramsaye quoted George Kleine as saying in justification, "We were not so excited about making the fight picture, but we did not want some of the Independents to get them and do a lot of exploiting that would have been harmful to the business." In other words, Kleine claims that the "irresponsible" independents would have stirred up more notoriety than the Trust, in order to promote the film. But Kleine could hardly have anticipated prior to the fight the storm of scandal that would erupt. In fact, I think the Trust's only motive was trying to beat the Independents to the profit.[23]

Two years later, as a direct result of the scandal, Congress made interstate traffic in fight films against the law. Until this happened, the Patents Company sold the fight film on a states'-rights basis, which enabled them to distance themselves a little from the notoriety. The film's length, if nothing else, would have made it unsuitable for the regular distribution system. It was shown in the advanced-ticket theaters, that is, in cities where it was permitted, such as New York, and there it was "a gold-mine."[24]

Frank Dyer, trying to explain the system of distribution, while at the same time illustrating the Trust's efforts to try to upgrade the motion-picture business, testified in 1913 that "for a short period, a year or more ago [General Film] acquired certain multiple reel subjects by paying the negative costs of the manufacturers, and I know in one or two instances, extra payments to the manufacturers have been made over and above the footage price. The further exception is 'From the Manger to the Cross,' which we handled for the Kalem Company, and sold out the various State rights for most of the States." The negative cost of FROM THE MANGER TO THE CROSS, produced by the Kalem players when traveling in the Holy Land, was, he said, $25,000.[25]

In a year-end summary of the important trends of 1911, the *Mirror* singled out "the tendency toward longer subjects" and went on to observe:

> Films of more than one reel are no longer a curiosity, and, generally speaking, they have been received with favor. House managers who had found Vitagraph's Uncle Tom's Cabin in three reels a money maker for them became eager for other subjects of feature length, and again the manufacturers responded. Several films of two and three reels were issued during the year, and all found ready demand. Indeed, not a few met with phenomenal sale in Europe as well as America (*New York Dramatic Mirror*, 31 January 1912, p. 51).

The "phenomenal" European sale of features was a convincing reason to enter into regular feature production for those Patents Company members who depended on the European market for an important part of their business. In May 1912 the Trust brought the multireel film into the system of distribution for ordinary movie theaters in an organized way by offering a special feature service through General Film, which could be obtained, in addition to the regular service, at a higher price. The service began with Selig's three-reel THE COMING OF COLUMBUS, released on 6 May 1912.

The three reels of THE COMING OF COLUMBUS were meant to be released and shown together. However, the structure of the earlier multireel films carried over. Reel one ended with a big spectacle scene showing Columbus being named admiral by King Ferdinand, which, a reviewer noted, "forms a fitting close to the first reel." Reel two ended with Columbus' arrival in America and the planting of the Spanish flag. The final reel ended with Columbus being carried off in chains to Spain to stand trial, with an editorial comment in the last title, "Sic transit gloria virum." The Latin tag gave class but was probably too much for the ordinary viewer, because on the surviving print the title appears in English as "So goes the Glory of Man." Selig's motive in selecting this subject was the presence in Lake Michigan of replicas of the Santa María, Pinta, and Niña given by the Spanish government to Chicago's park commission after the Great Columbian Exposition. There was an additional advertising value in appealing to the Knights of Columbus, for whom special screenings were arranged. Later, a copy of the film was presented, through an emissary, to the pope, who responded with the gift of a special medal for Selig.[26]

Only the larger theaters or higher-priced ones would buy the General Film Special Feature Service, because it cost more than the regular one, and this was to contribute to the eventual forcing out of the nickelodeon. The little store show, with its limited seating capacity and five-cent admission, could not afford the feature service and lost out to the competition. For the producers and distributors, however, the Special Feature Service was the solution to the problem of the sporadic release of multireel films, which were really difficult to fit into a standing-order service. Now, it was agreed, two- and three-reel films would be made by all the licensed companies on a regular basis. By November 1912, production of multireel features had reached a steady two per week, released every Monday and Friday, in addition to the forty-two one-reel subjects per week. "They will not interfere with your releases regularly booked and are only an added attraction for your patrons," advised General Film.[27]

Not all the Patents Company producers were able to contribute at first, and Biograph contributed few if any multireel films to the special program until 1914. As in the case of some of the other Biograph policies, the reasons are not clear. Griffith was directing some two-reelers, none longer, with increasing frequency during 1912 and early 1913. In the summer of 1913 he made his first big four-reel spectacle, JUDITH OF BETHULIA, reportedly without the permission of the Biograph executives. The last multireel films he made for Biograph, including JUDITH OF BETHULIA, were put on the shelf and were not turned over to General Film for distribution until 1914, long after Griffith had left the company.

In a 1913 advertisement listing the two-reel releases produced by Kalem, Essanay, Vitagraph, Pathéplay, Selig, Lubin, and Cines-Kleine, General Film declared:

> Some so-called features are merely single-reel stories "padded" to fill more than a thousand feet of film. Not so, however, with General Film features. In every case the story must require more than a thousand feet to tell it clearly or it is not accepted in the form of a multiple-reel. A favorite trick with some producers of features[?] is to use certain big scenes, as for example, a battle in a war drama, in several different pictures (*New York Dramatic Mirror*, 4 June 1913, p. 31).

The longer the film grew, the more the producers had to struggle with the complexities of narrative. Feature films brought many of them back to the legitimate theater as a model. At the same time, feature films began to attract theatrical producers to the medium. In the fall of 1912 major theatrical interests began to get seriously involved in the motion picture, and there was an enormous amount of excitement about the future of the long film. One reason for the renewed interest of theatrical managers was clearly the tremendous publicity and prestige surrounding the importation of Sarah Bernhardt's QUEEN ELIZABETH that summer. Managers thought that with multireel films and the new talking-picture devices, it would soon be possible to produce "canned theater" and send it out on the road like so many stock companies. Robert Grau, himself a theatrical manager, predicted:

> The season of 1912–1913 will be a noteworthy one, in that the leading theatrical managers who were wont to decry the motion picture industry are nearly all interested heavily in what are called special releases, and it is a fair statement to proclaim that one-third of the nation's playhouses will revert to the silent drama, while a score of new and palatial theatres will be dedicated solely to its use. The Metropolitan

OLIVER TWIST (General Films, 1912), featuring Nat C. Goodwin. A five-reel film.

Opera House . . . will be the scene of A. H. Woods's film production of Max Rembrandt's [*sic*] The Miracle. . . . Nathaniel C. Goodwin and Blanche Walsh are emulating Bernhardt and Rejane in capitulating to the cameraman, and Madame Nazimova is to follow in their footsteps. . . . At least two of our greatest inventors have announced that all the problems for the perfect synchronization of the cinematograph and the phonograph have already been solved, and already in Europe the chronophone (the Gaumont invention) is a sensational success, in that . . . Il Trovatore, is to be heard. . . . In the Fall the Edison speaking pictures will make their advent . . . (*New York Dramatic Mirror*, 24 July 1912, p. 13).

In fact, the Edison "speaking pictures" were not ready until February 1913 and then not truly ready. When the Chicago press saw the demonstration at the Palace Theater, a report noted that while the registration was perfect, the sound quality was not, and the conditions of recording appeared to be quite limiting. But of course, he said, Edison would be able to perfect it, and then "we will hear and see Sothern and Marlowe, Nazimova, Mrs. Fiske and all the rest for the modest sum of fifty cents. Later we will hear and view them for a quarter, and then a dime." Other companies revived all the failed projects and inventions for sound films that littered this period, but the story was the same. Synchronization, amplification, and fidelity were not sufficiently satisfactory in practice to justify investments in new equipment for the theaters, nor for the producers to make drastic changes in their production methods. The "talkies" remained a novelty for traveling showmen to exploit in the big theaters on a temporary basis. Sound was still much desired, in the name of realism. "It is unnatural to see something happen that naturally produces a noise and hear nothing," declared an advertisement for the Excelsior Sound Effect Cabinet in November 1913.[28]

The feature-length film brought new interest in novels as well as plays as source materials for the motion picture. Short stories and episodes gleaned from newspapers, satisfactory as sources for one-reel films, were beginning to seem insufficient for multireel features. Nell Shipman, an experienced scenarist and movie agent for the top-selling novelists, signed up George Randolph Chester, Emerson Hough, Louis Edmund Vance, and Anna Katharine Green. "The growing demand for the book photodrama marks another milestone in the advance of the photoplay industry, and in keeping with this spirit of progress, it is unlikely that any more 500 or 1,000 feet scenarios will emanate from Nell Shipman's pen," announced the *Mirror*. Hobart Bosworth achieved a great publicity coup by signing a contract with Jack London for all his works to be filmed in multireel features. London himself appeared in introductory passages of these films as a kind of guarantee of authenticity. The first one filmed was THE SEA WOLF, in seven reels, released in December 1913 and distributed on a states-rights basis.[29]

The peculiarities of the system that caused multireel films to be issued one reel at a time on the first run also made the industry receptive to one of the genres mentioned in the last chapter, the serial. Series films, with separate stories but common leading characters, were made by Kalem in 1909 in their GIRL SPY series, by Biograph the same year in their MR. AND MRS. JONES series, and by Yankee in 1910 in their GIRL DETECTIVE series.

In 1912 the Edison Company teamed up with the *Ladies' World* to publish the stories of the WHAT HAPPENED TO MARY series in conjunction with the release of the film versions. The practice of linking films with serial publication in magazines and newspapers was the essential ingredient that now led to the great success of the serial. The scheme provided enormous publicity for the films from a source that had previously given scant attention to movies (except to attack their scandalous nature): the daily newspapers, which had discovered a potent device for increasing circulation. The MARY series, starring Mary Fuller, is usually not classed as a serial, since each story was supposed to be complete in itself, but in fact, there was some suspense introduced: at the end of episode 3, for example, audiences were left with the question: "Which way will she choose?" And they were expected to return to see the next episode. The standing-order system meant that a theater that got the first run of a specific company would show all the episodes of a series as soon as they appeared. The import of Feuillade's FANTOMAS late in 1913 gave impetus to the suspenseful ending that eventually defined serials: "The end of the feature leaves the spectator in profound suspense. It was the exact psychological moment for the 'Continued in Our Next' effect," remarked Stephen Bush. The long chapters characteristic of the European serials, however, did not catch on. Many American serials consisted of one-reel chapters; some were two reels and began the first chapter with three reels, but none were four or five reels. The restrictions of the distribution system were no doubt influential here as elsewhere.[30]

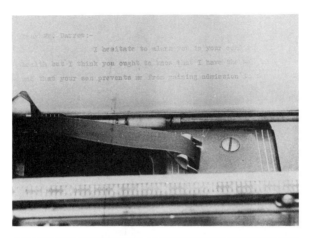

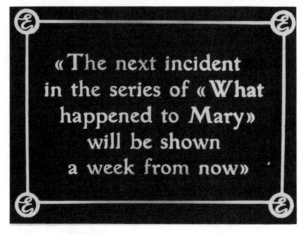

Frame enlargements from WHAT HAPPENED TO MARY, Episode #8, "A Will and a Way" (Edison, 28 February 1913). Directed by Charles J. Brabin and starring Mary Fuller. The "insert" of a text in the typewriter gives narrative information that otherwise would have required an intertitle. The fire-engine run is recycled footage from an earlier film.

In the Path *of the* Fast Express

THANHOUSER'S
THE MILLION DOLLAR MYSTERY

Episode No. 11

Story by　　　　　　*Scenario by*
HAROLD MᴬᶜGRATH - LLOYD LONERGAN

Read the story in the newspapers

SOLVE THE MYSTERY *and* WIN $10,000.00

See it in Moving Pictures here

Publicity stills for the Thanhouser serial, THE MILLION DOLLAR MYSTERY, *which began its run in June 1914. Directed by Howard Hansel, it featured Florence La-Badie, Sidney Bracy, Marguerite Snow, and James Cruze.*

The series of films usually defined as the first real serial was THE ADVENTURES OF KATHLYN, starring Kathlyn Williams. The first chapter, "The Unwelcome Guest," was released by the Selig Company on 29 December 1913, simultaneously with serial publication of the story in the *Chicago Tribune*. At the end of January 1914, Edison brought out DOLLIE OF THE DAILIES, starring Mary Fuller, which was syndicated to a group of newspapers. Pathé-Eclectic's THE PERILS OF PAULINE, directed by Louis J. Gasnier and starring Pearl White, began on 23 March 1914, and Thanhouser's MILLION DOLLAR MYSTERY in June. By the end of the year, Thanhouser had launched ZUDORA, and Pathé THE EXPLOITS OF ELAINE. The suspense ending that came to characterize the silent serial is perfectly illustrated by the ending of the twelfth episode of THE PERILS OF PAULINE: someone has sent Pauline a basket of flowers in which a large snake has been hidden, and she buries her nose in the flowers. "There the film ends, which is something like breaking off a story in the middle of a sentence," commented one bemused reviewer.[31]

Lubin neatly met the problem of exhibitors' differing needs with its first serial, "a series of single reel dramatic photoplays under the general title of THE BELOVED ADVENTURER." Begun on 14 September 1914, this series was based on stories by Emmett Campbell Hall that were to be published in book form at the same time and distributed by the film company at a special low price as a promotional item. Arthur

The longest-running serial, HAZARDS OF HELEN (Kalem), began in November 1914 and continued through February 1917, changing directors and leading women in the course of its run. This illustration is from Episode 58, "The Wrong Order," with Helen Gibson in the title role, directed by James Davis.

Pearl White in THE EXPLOITS OF ELAINE *(Pathe, 1915). Directed by Louis Gasnier and George B. Seitz, the fourteen chapters were issued beginning in January 1915.*

Johnson and Lottie Briscoe were the stars. The advertisement presented the serial as "a series of 15 single reel dramatic pictures, which might be run singly, as released or used in threes and fives as special features." Such flexibility toward changing distribution and exhibition practices was characteristic of the business brains of the Lubin Company. Unfortunately, there were other factors that prevented Lubin, like the other Trust companies, from surviving long after this period.[32]

By 1914, which might be called the year of the serials, some theaters were specializing in feature-length films, and the serial, like the single comedy reel and the newsreel, fit neatly into the program. All three genres were equally adaptable to the theaters still running single-reel programs.

On 21 April 1913 the Italian spectacle film QUO VADIS? premiered at the Astor Theater in New York, presented by the theatrical managers Cohan & Harris. The *New York Dramatic Mirror* headlined it as "A Masterpiece." The film was accompanied by the Wurlitzer Automatic Orchestra, and following stage conventions, the eight reels were shown in three acts, with intermissions. "The scenes have depth, and the massive furnishings appear so genuine," wrote the reporter, "that the spectator feels as if he might walk down the orchestra aisle and enter Nero's banquet hall." All the most thrilling scenes, including the eating of the Christians by the lions, won spontaneous applause.[33]

By June, while QUO VADIS? was running twice daily at the Astor, the film was also playing at McVicker's Theater in Chicago, the Garrick Theater in Philadelphia, the Academy of Music in Baltimore, and Teller's Broadway Theatre in Brooklyn, and was just beginning its run at the Cranby Theatre in Norfolk, Virginia. It was being booked as a theatrical attraction by Cohan & Harris, rather than through the moving-picture theater distribution system. The shrewd importer of this big success was George Kleine. It was bought through his contract with the Italian producer Cines, which had replaced Gaumont productions in his licensed imports when the Gaumont contract ended on 1 January 1912.[34]

George Kleine, a stalwart member of the Trust, had nonetheless reached outside the system the Trust had established to find a way to release the big Italian feature. The success of QUO VADIS? was so enormous that Kleine decided to invest in the production of more Italian spectacles and distribute them in road-show companies. He contracted with Ambrosio for OTHELLO and THE LAST DAYS OF POMPEII (GLI ULTIMI GIORNI DI POMPEII). The language of the contract describes some of the characteristics of the Italian spectacle film: "There is to be the most liberal use of performers, and one or more scenes are to be spectacular in the full extent of the word. The staging in all scenes is to be as elaborate as possible."[35]

For the release of THE LAST DAYS OF POMPEII, Kleine hired the Chicago composer Palmer Clark to write a fifty-page score, which was bound and sent in advance to the theater musicians. "This is probably the first case on record where a composer has been hired to write his score from the motion picture," announced the publicity story. (It was not.) When it was shown at the De Luxe Theater on Wilson Avenue in Chicago, "despite the fact that the evening was cold and rainy, a mob swarmed into the De Luxe, almost wrecking the box office, and requiring special police to keep order." Although they may have almost wrecked the box office, this was definitely

Ralph Ince directing Earle Williams and Anita Stewart in Vitagraph's serial THE GODDESS *(1915).*

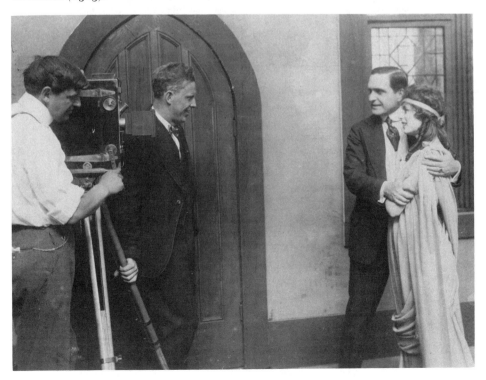

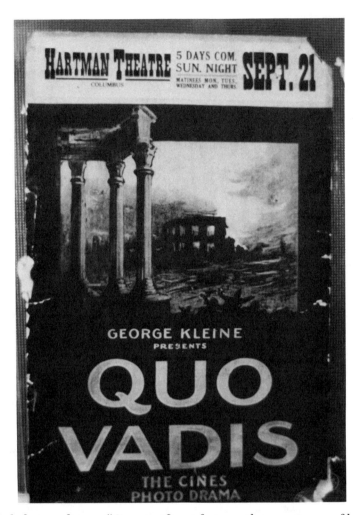

not a nickelodeon audience: "One significant fact was the appearance of hundreds of automobile parties, whose cars lined the streets for blocks on either side." Kleine was building a big studio outside Turin when the outbreak of war in 1914 brought an end to these expansive plans.[36]

Attending a movie theater where only short films were shown was an everyday affair, but attending a feature was a special event. In December 1913 Jacques Berst of Pathé testified that special features were the most important part of the program: "The public nowadays . . . think a special feature of two or three reels [is] like if they go to a theatre and see a big show, whereas in the single reels, of course, it seemed to get to be monotonous and an every-day affair." This impression was confirmed by Harry Marsey, an exhibitor in Buffalo, New York: "It seems it is the general sentiment of the people. They want to see features or productions produced in more than one reel. It is a case where everybody is doing it, and we had to do it too." But, he added, "I, personally, do not favor it."[37]

Matthew Hansen, an exhibitor with three theaters in Yonkers, New York, stated that he was exhibiting six reels of special features a week; twelve features each week (two new ones each day) at the Getty Square Theatre: "One each day I get from the

General Film Company and one from an outside source." At the other theaters, he was showing "licensed, with every now and then, to strengthen the show, an outside feature." Asked if special features were an important part of the program in his theaters, he replied: "I consider it so, for the simple reason that up to three weeks ago at Getty Square, we were playing for a five-cent admission to the General Film program of four reels, and I decided to put in an outside feature each day and advance the admission to ten cents, and my business has just doubled."[38]

Ike Van Ronkel, manager of a Chicago branch of General Film, gave the following details of the distribution situation at the end of 1913: "Famous Players can now supply a feature a week that is a full evening's entertainment, exhibitors are getting regular short film service from either General Film Company, Universal or Mutual for six days a week and taking Famous Players features on the seventh day. The top-rated features rent for $50. a night, while the short film service the rest of the week averages $45. Exhibitors are paying more for one night than for the rest of the week. If that isn't convincing evidence that features are the future, I don't know what is." And still farther to the West, G. P. Hamilton, president of the Albuquerque Film Manufacturing Company reported that in New Mexico and adjoining states, "Features are the thing right now. They're all using features, mostly the three-reelers. The exhibitors in the West will go to all sorts of trouble to book a feature, and then they play it up well in advance, especially the fellows in the remote and inaccessible towns where it is hard to get features because of shipping troubles. Features sure have a grip on them out there."[39]

But had the feature film replaced the short-film program by the beginning of 1915? Let us look at the release charts published in the *Moving Picture World* for the month of December 1914, as shown in the accompanying table.

FILM RELEASES BY DISTRIBUTOR

	Number of Reels				
Combination	*1*	*2*	*3*	*4*	*5*
General Film Program	122	33	1	2	—
Universal Program	57	28	5	1	—
Mutual Film Program	105	35	—	—	—
Paramount Pictures	1	2	2	10	20
United Film Service (Warner's Features)	20	3	8	7	9
Box Office Attraction (William Fox)	1	7	10	8	6
Continental Features	—	—	—	—	—
Alliance Films	—	—	—	—	13
Alco Film	—	—	—	1	4

Long features might well be getting all the attention, and some theaters were beginning to play features every day, but the figures make it clear that single or double reels were still shown on a regular basis. Many theaters used the formula of a regular service of short films, as in the past, but added a Sunday evening show with features booked separately from one of the companies specializing in them.

In a series of articles written in July 1914 on the passing of the single-reel film, Stephen Bush admitted that there were still many small-house exhibitors showing eight or nine reels for five cents, while the newer, bigger houses were showing features at ten to twenty cents. In fact, the length of the program had nothing much to do with the higher admission prices: it was the special qualities of the "features," even though these may have been only two- or three-reel films.[40]

In spite of the enthusiasm for features, exhibitors holding a convention in New York in June 1914 passed a resolution in which they "expressed their disapproval of the production of reels of 1,000 feet and upward." They proposed that manufacturers reduce the unit to 500 feet. At the end of the year, P. A. Powers, president of the United Film Service, called for a return to the five-cent admission (many theaters did still charge five cents at this time) and continued to maintain that film is "a form of variety," not comparable to the legitimate stage.[41]

The feature film was the future, certainly, but it was viewed with reluctance, even disbelief, by many distributers and exhibitors. As for producers, there were conservatives among both the licensed and the independent companies. "That the single

Advertising brochure for HYPOCRITES *(Bosworth, 1914), directed by Lois Weber.*

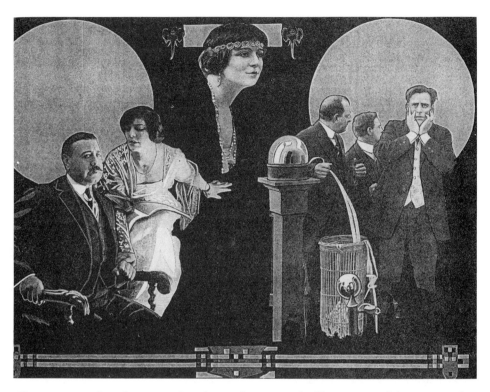

Illustration in the advertising brochure of THE PIT *(William A. Brady's Feature Play Company for World Film Corporation, 1914). "Wilton Lackaye's greatest stage triumph." Lackaye was supported by Gail Kane and Milton Sills.*

reel photo-drama is the keystone of the motion-picture industry becomes more apparent daily," Colonel Selig observed in July 1914, explaining, "Patrons of the film drama want their programs as diversified as possible." He acknowledged that feature films were valuable, but, he said, "These will be offered in another class of theaters." Horace G. Plimpton at Edison was more uncertain of the future. In his view, the 1913 craze was overdone, and now there was a reaction against the four- and five-reelers.[42]

The future belonged to other producers.

13

The Lid Comes Off

It is not uncommon to see licensed and independent films on the same
program these days.

—"The Answer Man," *Moving Picture World*, 25 October 1913, p. 375

*T*wo series of events in 1912 marked the beginning of a realignment of the film
industry comparable to that of 1909 in terms of the changes it brought to the way
motion pictures were made and seen. The first was the series of court decisions and
legal actions that signaled the beginning of the end of the Motion Picture Patents
Company. The second was the breakup of both licensed and independent combinations, owing in large part to the fact that new methods of distribution were required
if feature films were to be profitable.

The Latham loop patent was overthrown in *Patents Company* v. *IMP* in February
1912 when Judge Learned Hand held that the patents claim did not cover cameras;
this opinion was upheld by the U.S. Circuit Court in August of that year. Although
it had not been mentioned in the lawsuit, Judge Learned Hand volunteered his
opinion that the patent would be equally invalid if applied to the projection machine,
because it had been anticipated by Armat and Jenkins and others. Even then, the
Patents Company continued to bring suits against the independents on the basis of
the Edison reissue patents as late as mid 1914, but it was far too late to save the
power of the Trust. During 1912 William Fox's Greater New York Film Exchange
brought suit against the Patents Company, charging restraint of trade. The Fox
lawsuit was not the deciding one on this issue, inasmuch as the complaint lost, was
appealed, and was finally settled out of court. But it was the trigger for the United
States government's suit against the Patents Company under the Sherman Antitrust
Act, filed on 16 August 1912. The government's position in the petition was that "On
or about April 1910, defendants set out to monopolize the business of all the rental
exchanges in the United States, their purpose being to drive out of business all
persons so engaged and to absorb to themselves the profits theretofore made there-
in." The government went to trial in January 1913 and the lawsuit continued well into
1914. The lower court's decision against the Trust was handed down in October 1915,
and the Patents Company was ordered dissolved not long thereafter.[1]

General Film was already in difficulty in the marketplace. In August 1912 the
Motion Picture Exhibitors' League of America convention at the Hotel La Salle in
Chicago passed a resolution calling for legal action to end the "extortion" of the
two-dollar fee from licensed exhibitors and to prevent the Patents Company from
interfering with licensed exhibitors who used independent feature films. The court

The Lubin Company's glass studio in Philadelphia.

decisions of that year made these steps obvious. The exhibitors further resolved that General Film should be asked to explain why prices on the special feature releases varied from fifteen dollars in Detroit to seventy-five dollars in San Francisco.[2]

General Film held on through 1915 and presumably made the final payments that year on the exchanges that were bought in 1910. However, there were already signs of defection in 1913. In the struggle to find ways to distribute feature films, some frustrated licensed producers began to make separate agreements with other companies. General Film's Feature Film Service was not sufficient for them, not when they could see the big profits being made by independents who were producing and importing features, then selling or leasing them on the states rights plan. At the same time, the Patents Company producers did not cease producing the shorter films for the regular General Film program. The previous chapter has shown that the process of marketing big features was giving rise to a new distribution system, which would eventually swallow up the old film exchanges.

When Pathé ran into difficulty distributing its European features in the important American market because the General Film system limited the number of features it could issue and the profits it could make, the French producer set up the Eclectic Company as an independent importing firm. In April 1913, the newly founded Eclectic imported Pathé's gigantic twelve-reel LES MISÉRABLES, directed by Albert Capellani. Pathé's ownership of this company was not openly acknowledged in the American trade journals until the following year, when Eclectic began domestic production at the Pathé plant and with Pathé staff, for the celebrated serial THE PERILS OF PAULINE. By that time, Pathé-Eclectic had set up its own system of exchanges, as the newer feature production companies were doing.[3]

In the spring of 1913, General Film charged Kalem with violating their agreement on the exclusive rights to the William J. Burns film EXPOSING THE LAND SWINDLERS. According to the request for an injunction restraining both the Kalem and Kinetograph companies from handling this film, "after leasing the exclusive rights to the picture in question, the Kalem Company violated its contract by leasing a number of films to the Kinetograph Company." In other words, General Film found itself distributing the film in competition with a rival distributor, the Kinetograph Company. The strange aspect of this affair is that Kinetograph was a company established by General Film executives. It is not clear from the published records why they set up such a company, but Kinetograph may have been an attempt either to establish a new distribution system for features or, somewhat underhandedly, to avoid the charges of monopoly that were then being pressed by the government. Frank Dyer replaced Kennedy as president of General Film, and Kennedy, together with Percy Waters, general manager, resigned from General Film in December 1912 and formed the Kinetograph Company. Kinetograph then got a license from the Patents Company to conduct exchanges. On 9 February 1913, Kinetograph announced distribution of the full Patents Company program. The Kinetograph Company established several branch offices, but it could not compete, so it was said later, with the system already set up by General Film, which then absorbed it. In February 1914, Kennedy and Waters reassumed their positions at General Film. When Kennedy was questioned about Kinetograph during the government suit against the Patents Company, he refused to discuss it.[4]

The Biograph Company had contributed little or nothing to General Film's efforts to incorporate multireel films into the distribution system through the Special Service, although Kennedy was still at the head of Biograph while acting as organizer and president of General Film. In June 1913 Biograph announced a contract with theatrical magnates Klaw and Erlanger and with Al H. Woods, who had formed the Protective Amusement Company that spring to produce two big features a week from the play productions owned by these impresarios. The films were intended to be shown at advanced ticket prices in big theaters, including the chain owned by the producers, and Marcus Loew's fifty theaters were said to be already booked for the service. The contract was reported to be a big shock to director D. W. Griffith when he returned from the winter filming in California. He had not been consulted about the arrangement, and he found himself expected to supervise the production of the Klaw and Erlanger features, while his wish to make his own feature films had been rejected. That October he left the company.[5]

The release of the Klaw and Erlanger productions was delayed long beyond the announced date. The first one, THE FATAL WEDDING, was premiered at the Palace Theatre on Broadway in New York on 19 January 1914. (Klaw and Erlanger did release an imported film while they were waiting to get out the Biograph productions; this was the four-reel German film THE LIFE OF RICHARD WAGNER.) Actually, quite a number of the Klaw and Erlanger films were produced in 1913, but they were not released until well into 1914. The cast lists included the names of people who left Biograph with Griffith in October or at least before the year was out. Klaw and Erlanger's plans were not fulfilled and their agreement with Biograph came to an end in 1914, leaving Biograph with ownership of the features. According to Kemp Niver's account, Klaw and Erlanger persisted in believing that the prestige of their theatrical

D. W. Griffith directing Lillian Gish in THE BATTLE OF THE SEXES *(Mutual Film Corporation, 12 April 1914). This was Griffith's first feature after leaving Biograph. It is a lost film.*

productions would justify higher admission prices than for other features, but audiences were not ready to pay them.

It may have been the Klaw and Erlanger attempt to market the films at too high a price that delayed their general release. In any event, these films and the delayed release of Griffith's JUDITH OF BETHULIA in 1914 gave Biograph a belated entry into the feature-film market. JUDITH OF BETHULIA, a historical spectacle film, was very successful and remained in distribution for at least two years. In September 1914, Biograph began to issue a two-reel film on a regular basis, every Tuesday, in addition to their one-reel and split-reel productions. Including the delayed release of the Klaw and Erlanger films, 18 percent of their production was longer than one reel in 1914. The Biograph staff grew larger. The annual trip to California at the end of that year included 125 people, seven of them directors. Biograph continued to increase the production of features in the next couple of years, but they lagged much behind other companies in following the trend.[6]

The independents were breaking up over the same question of feature-film distribution. As in the case of the licensed companies, it was a matter of economics. In April 1912, for example, the New York Motion Picture Company explained a new policy whereby their two-reel "101" Bisons were being sold by the states-rights method. When features were distributed in the normal way, reported the producers of the Bisons, the Sales Company "found it impossible to obtain adequate returns.

. . . They were unable to obtain more than fourteen orders from the exchanges." Now that the New York Motion Picture Company gave exclusive territory to a list of exchanges and increased the price from ten to fifteen cents a foot, they could place fifty prints.[7]

A meeting of independent manufacturers and exhibitors was held in Chicago on 30 March 1912, precipitated in part, rumor said, by the organization of the Mutual Company by Harry Aitken. The minor rumblings inside the Patents Company were nothing compared to the explosions within the Sales Company. The purpose of Aitken's new company was announced as the buying up and consolidating of film exchanges, as General Film had done in the licensed field. "Another consideration that enters into the situation," the *World* reported, "is the experience of the Bison Company with its big and really high-class Western two-reel features."[8]

The beginning of trouble in the Sales Company group might be traced back to several raids on Carl Laemmle's IMP Company. In the fall of 1911 Harry Aitken founded Majestic, with Thomas Cochrane, formerly of IMP, as general manager, and Mary Pickford and Owen Moore as star players. Majestic's first release was THE COURTING OF MARY (November 1911). Actually, Cochrane had already left IMP to work briefly for Lubin in Philadelphia before going to Majestic. Harry E. Aitken, unlike many of the leading independent men who were forming the new segments of the industry, was an American-born Anglo-Saxon Protestant. Born in Wisconsin in 1877, he had been an insurance man before starting the Western Film Exchange in Milwaukee. In the fall of 1911 he purchased the Reliance Company and its studio on the former Clara Morris estate in Yonkers. Charles Baumann, former owner of Reliance, explained that he had sold the studio in order to concentrate on the "101" Bison Westerns. Baumann and his partner, Adam Kessel of the New York Motion Picture Company, had picked off IMP's best director, Thomas Ince (the one responsible for those "high-class two-reel Westerns" under the Bison trademark), and the players Ethel Grandin and Ray Smallwood.[9]

The Sales Company declared that it was entitled to more of a percentage for distributing Majestic's product on the grounds that Majestic was not one of its founding members. Similar rules probably would have been applied to the other companies launched in autumn 1911 and joined to the Sales Company: these included the American branch of the French company Eclair, which after many delays finally started production concurrently with Majestic, in November 1911; and the Crystal Film Company, organized by Ludwig G. B. Erb as president and Joseph A. Golden, formerly with Selig, as director. Aitken, who did not think the increased percentage fair, filed suit against the Sales Company and left the organization, taking with him Majestic, American, and Thanhouser (which had been purchased by Aitken's associate Charles J. Hite). They then founded a new combination, the Film Supply Company of America, which soon added Solax, Great Northern, and Lux.[10]

Seriously weakened, the Sales Company regrouped as the Universal Film Manufacturing Company in June 1912. Included in this combination were IMP, Crystal, Frontier, Mecca, Victor, Yankee, Champion (Mark Dintenfass), Nestor (David Horsley), Eclair, Powers, Rex, Ambrosio, Itala, and, briefly, the New York Motion Picture Company.[11]

By the end of 1912 Aitken's chain of Mutual exchanges had grown to about thirty, and he deserted the short-lived Film Supply Company. Mutual would now distribute Majestic, Reliance, Thanhouser, and American. This combination gained great strength by adding the New York Motion Picture Company, which was now out of Universal. In April 1913 Herbert Blaché, gathering together the remnants of the Film Supply, which had "gradually thinned out in the last few weeks," organized the Exclusive Supply Company, with himself as president, Ingvald C. Oes of Great Northern as vice-president, and Harry Raver as secretary and treasurer. It distributed the product of Great Northern, Solax (owned and managed by Blaché's wife, Alice Guy), and the Blaché Company.[12]

By 1914 Mutual had a total of fifty distributing offices in the United States and Canada as well as several in Europe. These offices handled the product of Thanhouser and Princess of New Rochelle; American of Chicago and Santa Barbara; Reliance of Yonkers, New York City, and Hollywood; Komic of Yonkers; Majestic, Kay-Bee, Broncho, Domino, and Apollo of Los Angeles, and Keystone of Edendale, California. Mutual established links with Continental Feature Film Corporation for distribution of its most important features, which were produced by D. W. Griffith Films, Reliance, and Majestic. This is a typical example of the two-pronged distribution system that developed during the beginnings of the feature film.[13]

With D. W. Griffith and Thomas Ince producing for Mutual, and the actors and staff they brought with them, Aitken had some of the best talents available to form a strong program. Griffith was supposed to be in charge of all production of Reliance and Majestic features as well as his own. In the days of one- and two-reel production at Biograph, he had shown himself to be a skillful and efficient producer as well as a brilliant director. (Here we speak of the specific role of "producer" as the individual who supervises the work of directors, plans the productions, etc., not in the broader sense used elsewhere.) He kept to the demanding schedule of those days without waste of money or time. He continued a strong production role at Reliance and Majestic and was supposed to be head of production at Triangle–Fine Arts, but his interest in that function apparently lessened as he involved himself more in his own major feature films. While the industry as a whole invested in a specialized system and divided up and limited the functions in the studio, Griffith, preferring his intuitive working methods and full creative control, became more or less an outsider.[14]

Thomas Ince, on the other hand, began to withdraw from directing to give his talents to production management. By November 1913 Ince was vice-president, manager of Western production, and chief producer, and was setting up new efficiency systems for the studio. The New York Motion Picture Company, it was reported, "even now has a system whereby the director only directs. That is to say, he only supervises the dramatic work of the players. He enters the studio to find his sets all ready, his act players all made up, and his script fit to use. So all he has to do is rehearse and take a scene."[15]

This was to be the basis of the Hollywood studio system, but Ince should not receive sole credit for introducing it: it was already the tendency among most of the producers of the Patents Company group. Earlier that year it was announced that Lubin was dividing the functions of the scenario editors and the directors, and that directors would have to film the assigned scripts whether they appealed to them or not. "The fact is," noted William Lord Wright, "Lubin is falling into line with Edison and Vitagraph. It has been the policy of these two latter concerns to put a working script up to a director with strict orders to produce it."[16]

By 1914 Mutual had to its credit some important feature films: THE BATTLE OF GETTYSBURG (June 1913, directed by Thomas Ince, five reels), THE WRATH OF THE

GODS (June 1914, directed by Reginald Barker, six reels), HOME, SWEET HOME (May 1914, directed by D. W. Griffith, six reels), and THE AVENGING CONSCIENCE (August 1914, directed by D. W. Griffith, six reels). Harry Aitken, it would seem, had enough of the cards to survive in competition with Carl Laemmle at Universal.

The first president of Universal was Charles Baumann of the New York Motion Picture Company; Carl Laemmle was the treasurer, and Fred Balshofer was to be the general manager. The stormy beginnings of Universal would be a good subject for another version of Kurosawa's RASHOMON, with each participant having a different version to tell. For lack of space, we will look only at David Horsley's account in a letter of May 1914 to Robert Grau, because there is some value in its closeness to the events. David Horsley owned Centaur Films and stayed to become part of Universal; thus we should not expect to find objectivity in his account:

> The class of men now in control of the film business were always ready to take a long chance legally and otherwise. They were all individualists who do not work well together. "Lucky" Laemmle, "Foxy" Powers, "Erratic" Swanson, "Suave" Brulatour, "Road-Roller" Baumann and myself were thrown in one basket, and the cover put on. These men are all dynamos accustomed to generating their own power, and did not work well as motors, as they refused to receive their power from an aspiring leader; this brought on friction, including the affable Brulatour to retire, followed by Baumann and Kessel. Laemmle was in Europe, Swanson in California, and Pat Powers and myself sat on the lid in New York. Things went along fairly smoothly until Laemmle and Swanson returned to New York, when began a struggle for control of the Universal Company, with Laemmle on one side and Powers on the other, with the polished Mark Dintenfass, the holder of a small block of stock, also holding the balance of power and fully aware of the fact (quoted in Robert Grau, *The Theatre of Science*, pp. 39–41).

As Horsley explained it, Laemmle and Swanson purchased Dintenfass' stock, and then Powers sold his holdings, leaving Horsley a hopeless minority. Powers then joined in again with Swanson against Laemmle and both sides quarreled over Horsley's stock. In 1913 Horsley purchased another block of Universal stock, which just happened to be owned by his brother William, who had built a factory with P. A. Powers in Bayonne, New Jersey. This brought Horsley back into a position of power in Universal, but in his view, "Laemmle will eventually win out, because it will be recognized that he is the most capable." Horsley's forecast was accurate. Powers' stock was purchased by Laemmle and Swanson, and Powers was out of Universal by February 1913.[17]

Another picturesque story of the struggle that began immediately after the forming of Universal in 1912, from the point of view of Fred J. Balshofer, is recounted in Balshofer and Miller's *One Reel a Week*. The end result in this case was the complete split between the New York Motion Picture Company and Universal. Balshofer gives the details of the struggle when Pat Powers tried to take forcible possession of the New York Motion Picture Company's studios on the grounds they belonged to Universal. In the course of the legal battles that followed, Universal came out with the right to use the "101" Bison brand name, which the New York Motion Picture

Company, with the help of Thomas Ince, had endowed with its reputation for high-quality Westerns. The last "101" Bison from the New York Motion Picture Company was THE COLONEL'S WARD (October 1912, directed by Ince). The production unit at New York Motion Picture Company was retained, but the trademark was changed to "Broncho". Later "101" Bisons were all produced by a new group at Universal.[18]

In 1914 the companies brought together in Universal added up to an impressive empire. IMP, Victor, and the Animated Weekly had studios in New York on Eleventh Avenue, near Universal headquarters; the Crystal studio was in the Bronx at the corner of Park and Wendover; American Eclair was in Fort Lee, New Jersey, and Victor had another studio in Coytesville, New Jersey. At Universal City in Southern California there were eight production companies at work: "101" Bison, Nestor, Rex, Gold Seal, "Universal Ike," Joker, Powers, and Sterling. In March 1914 Universal bought a ranch in the San Fernando Valley and moved there from Hollywood. Universal's Special Features branch began production of four-to-six-reel features. The first one, ABSINTHE, actually made in late 1913 in Paris by "the European branch of the IMP Company," was produced by Herbert Brenon and featured King Baggott and Leah Baird. (There were also a couple of three-reel features in 1913 under the name of Powers/Universal films.) The most celebrated of these first Universal Special Features was NEPTUNE'S DAUGHTER (1914), an extravaganza featuring the swimming celebrity Annette Kellerman in a shockingly form-fitting tank suit. Only a very tiny fragment of this spectacle film survives, preserved by the Soviet state film archive, Gosfilmofond, in Moscow.[19]

In November 1913, when Jacques Berst of Pathé was testifying in the federal suit against the Trust, he acknowledged three groups of independents: Mutual, Universal, and Film Supply. It was just about at the time of his testimony that Mutual began to replace Film Supply. But these independent firms were no longer the source of the major competition for the Trust. Berst reported that the last twelve months had seen the growth of competition between the licensed program and the special-feature films. New companies and combinations had been formed to produce and distribute these.[20]

The outlines of the new industry began to take shape in 1913–1914, with the formation of the new feature-production companies that would change the methods of distribution and exhibition. When the feature fever swept through the entertainment world in this period, there were more new companies founded than we can name, but most were short-lived. Some were formed to distribute only one feature film. But this was also the beginning of a limited number of major production companies that would end up with greater control of distribution and exhibition than the Trust companies had ever achieved. That discussion will have to be left for a later volume, but here we will just mention the major companies founded before 1915.

Pat Powers, after leaving Universal, went on to become president of Warner's Features, Inc., organized on 1 August 1913, with Albert Warner as vice-president. However, this company already existed under the same name at least as early as April 1912, with Albert Warner at its head. It was then an importer of features, and by October 1912 it owned a chain of fifteen exchanges, which grew to twenty-three by 1913. The Warners had established the Pittsburg Photoplay Company in 1905, and Albert Warner was well known as a distributor in 1912. Although the company had little success as a producer in these beginning years, some films were made. The first was the three-reel PERIL OF THE PLAINS, with Dot Farley, produced in St. Louis and released in September 1912. At the end of that year, Warner's took on the distribution of the Gene Gauntier Feature Players productions, and Albert Warner acted as business manager for the newly formed company. In 1913 Warner's Features also distributed the films made by the Helen Gardner Feature Players, Marion Leonard Features, and numerous other small companies. The Warner brothers also had "close connections," it was later said, with the St. Louis Motion Picture Company. This company's first release was A GYPSY'S LOVE, in May 1912, and perhaps not coincidentally, it also featured Dot Farley. In October 1912 Harry Warner went to St. Louis to take care of his brother's agency there.[21]

Warner's Features of 1913 opened a "new epoch," according to Robert Grau, because they found a way to get their product to the exhibitor, through the system of exchanges they had established. By 1914 Warner's, renamed United Film Service at the end of the year, was releasing three feature films a week, each a three-reeler, an exclusive service that was supposed to restrict the showings to one theater in an area. As Pat Powers observed, "At present, there seems to be a demand for melo-dramatic and sensational subjects."[22]

Theatrical producer Daniel Frohman, innocent of the ways of the motion-picture establishment, tells of being sent by the wily Adolph Zukor in 1912 to talk to Thomas

Mary Pickford and Owen Moore in CAPRICE *(Famous Players, 1913). Directed by J. Seale Dawley.*

Edison about motion-picture uplift. Frohman may have pointed out that Bernhardt's CAMILLE in two reels and Réjane's MADAME SANS-GÊNE in three reels were being offered independently on a states rights basis by the French-American Film Company. As a consequence of that visit, Bernhardt's QUEEN ELIZABETH was sold as "the only states-right production licensed by the Motion Picture Patents Company in over a year." That is how the Trust companies assisted in establishing their own competition, the Famous Players Company, in the fall of 1912. In his autobiography, Frohman reports that Zukor had the letters that had been extracted from Edison photographed. Daniel Frohman was managing director of the new company formed with Zukor, the former fur dealer who had become a successful exhibitor and distributor, and Edwin S. Porter, who was their first director.[23]

In November 1912, Frohman signed up Minnie Maddern Fiske to perform her famous role as Becky Sharp for the camera, but for some reason, perhaps the discovery that Helen Gardner had already played the role in Vitagraph's VANITY FAIR not quite a year earlier, this film was not made until 1915, and at that time, it was produced by the Edison Company rather than Famous Players. Mrs. Fiske's first film was TESS OF THE D'URBERVILLES (Famous Players, September 1913). In February 1914 Famous Players signed with Henry W. Savage to film the productions he owned, and theatrical producer Charles Frohman (Daniel's famous brother) joined the fast-growing company the following month. By July the slogan "Famous Players in Famous Plays" had been coined. According to Zukor: "The idea of putting out different grades of pictures we abandoned as impractical; there was not a strong

Famous Players' first studio, on West Twenty-sixth Street in New York City.

enough demand for the three-reel pictures with stock companies, and only the big four- and five-part productions proved successful. We have now reached a stage where film plays must be treated as other plays and not as merchandise containing so many feet." Thus began the systematic distribution of thirty pictures a year, a yearly service available to exhibitors. As examples of exhibition practices in an earlier chapter have shown, at this time a theater might contract for a regular short-film service with, say, General Film, and with Famous Players for a feature to show on Sunday night.[24]

In January 1913 Hobart Bosworth formed Bosworth, Inc., on the basis of an exclusive contract with Jack London to produce features based on his novels. Other productions, including the Lois Weber/Phillips Smalley films, were later added to strengthen this company.[25]

Jesse Lasky, the vaudeville producer, headed another new company founded at the end of 1913 with feature production in mind. His partners included his brother-in-law, Samuel Goldfish (later known as Samuel Goldwyn), and the playwright and stage manager Cecil B. DeMille. By November of the following year the Lasky Feature Play Company had grown to five directors and cameramen, eighteen "stars," and eighty stock members, traveling by train to Hollywood. When they reached Chicago, Dustin Farnum and Winifred Kingston left the company to go to New Orleans, where CAMEO KIRBY was in the midst of location shooting. Stars Marguerite Clark (loaned to Lasky for just one film) and Edith Taliaferro were among those continuing on to California.[26]

In May 1914 came the affiliation of Famous Players, Lasky, and Bosworth, Inc., with distribution to be provided by the newly organized Paramount Pictures Corporation. Paramount's president, W. W. Hodkinson, planned to distribute the features on a percentage basis, which signaled an important change in the distribution system. For the right to distribute, Paramount received 35 percent of the proceeds; in exchange, it provided cash advances for production costs and guaranteed a minimum return to the producer. The Hodkinson system pointed the way to the future organization of the major companies.[27]

Although William Fox was active and well known in the motion-picture field as exhibitor and distributor from the early days, he was late to get into feature production. In fact, his Box Office Attraction Company, organized in January 1914, was begun with the idea of specializing in the distribution of features, but he then decided to attempt production also. As president of the new company, Fox expressed a firm belief that features would dominate in the future.[28]

The World Special Films Corporation was announced in November 1913, with E. Mandelbaum, a former exchange man, as president and Lewis J. Selznick (father of David O. Selznick) as general manager. Six months later it was called World Film Corporation and offered a list of foreign films, and by July 1914 World was "a three-million-dollar company," distributing exclusively the photoplay features to be produced from plays owned by the Shuberts, William A. Brady, Charles E. Blaney, Owen Davis, and the Thomas McEnnery Syndicate. More than 160 features were going to be listed in their catalogue, they indicated. In another unusual proceeding, World Film sold stock openly to the general public: there had always been some highly speculative wildcat stock available, but the major production companies all existed as closed corporations.[29]

Kinemacolor

The history of one company that was born and died in this period provides a good example of the course of the uplift movement and the changes in distribution patterns. The special place that American Kinemacolor occupied in the industry is signaled by the fact that the reviews in the trade papers were divided into three groups: the licensed, the independent, and the Kinemacolor productions. The *New York Dramatic Mirror* sometimes carried news of Kinemacolor in its theatrical section instead of in the moving-pictures section. Kinemacolor was important to the cause of uplifting the industry and attracting a middle-class audience. Operating outside the organized distribution system of the movie theaters, it carried special prestige and offered serious competition to the shows of Lyman Howe and Burton Holmes. Like those traveling companies, it played in legitimate theaters, auditoriums, opera houses, and similar high-class venues and was not licensed by the Patents Company.

During the trial of the U.S. government versus the Patents Company in 1913, Kinemacolor's exclusion from the licensed companies was invoked as an example of illegal restraint of trade. William Fox testified that he wanted to be able to show the Kinemacolor films in his licensed theaters but was forbidden by the Patents Company rules. Arthur H. Sawyer, Kinemacolor's general manager, explained that the films were more expensive than ordinary ones, and that the company needed bigger theaters, such as the Keith circuit, one of the big vaudeville chains, which could pay the rental. Kinemacolor was not for the nickel houses. The Keith managers, however, had been told they would lose their licenses if they showed any unlicensed pictures.[30]

Undoubtedly as a result of the courtroom testimony, the Kinemacolor Company was finally granted a license in August 1913, the only addition that Patents Company had permitted since its founding in 1909, except for the belated acknowledgment of Méliès' American production company in 1909, the exchange of Cines for Gaumont among the foreign films imported by Kleine at the beginning of 1912, and the short-lived Kinetograph distribution company. Moreover, Kinemacolor's agreement said that it could deal with both licensed and independent exhibitors, which was unique. As it turned out, however, the licensing was too late to be of much help to either Kinemacolor or the Patents Company.[31]

Kinemacolor was the most successful of the pre-Technicolor systems for mass production of color films. The color was "additive," depending on a system of color filters during filming and also during projection, with additional frames (two images for one) projected through alternate color filters. To allow for the extra frames, the film was twice as long as normal and had to be projected at twice the normal speed. Like the Kinemacolor camera, the projector required to show Kinemacolor was quite different from the ordinary one. Massive and motor-driven, it required extra-brilliant illumination for two reasons: the speed of projection and the color filters revolving just in front of the aperture.

To show Kinemacolor, an exhibitor rented a traveling company, with a manager and staff, the special projector, and a program of films. Charles Urban, American by birth but now head of the parent British firm of Kinemacolor, and G. Albert Smith, the inventor, demonstrated the system to the industry in New York on 11 December 1909 in the hope of selling the American rights. According to Terry Ramsaye, Urban negotiated with the members of the Patents Company at that time but without success. It is probable that those working to stabilize and standardize the industry in 1909 decided Kinemacolor would not be very practical for wide use in moving-picture theaters, as indeed time proved.[32]

The American rights were purchased by two men without previous experience in the film industry, Gilbert H. Aymar and James K. Bowen, both of Allentown, Pennsylvania. They founded American Kinemacolor in April 1910 with the intent of exploiting the device in the big variety theaters rather than in motion-picture houses. Their Allentown plant was to be used for the manufacture of the special apparatus, and they planned to sell territorial rights for exploiting the projection system and the films. They did not produce film themselves, or if they did so, the output was negligible. Indeed, the American Kinemacolor Company got off to a slow start, owing in part, no doubt, to the exploiters' lack of experience in show business. The company began by exhibiting the British productions, consisting of travel and educational films in color and films of important topical events, since the British company made relatively few dramatic films.[33]

There were technical problems from the outset. The American company tried to adapt ordinary projectors to show their films, but that experiment was not successful. Reporting on private screenings held in Chicago in July 1910, one reviewer complained that a haze hung over REVIEW OF TROOPS BY GEORGE V, and that all through the show, red and green were dominant, although he did grant that REBEL'S DAUGHTER showed lifelike flesh tones.[34]

The first public exhibition of Kinemacolor in New York took place in January 1911 at the Eden Musee, where it attracted a lot of attention and enjoyed an extended run. But three months later, the *World* was saying that Kinemacolor had not yet caught on.[35]

In April came the announcement that J. J. Murdock, "well known in the theatrical and vaudeville world and formerly identified with the first independent movement, the International Company of Chicago," had purchased the company. In reporting Murdock's advent into Kinemacolor, the *Mirror* optimistically told its readers that "the new Kinemacolor Company appears to be the most important development that has taken place in motion picture affairs since the organization of the Sales Company as a competitor of the Patents Company." According to the account that followed, the new Kinemacolor corporation had some $6 million in backing from "capitalists of both New York and Chicago and a prominent New York trust company," and it had already purchased the Urban-Smith patents for the United States from Charles Urban. With Murdock "placed in full charge," Arthur H. Sawyer was the only executive holdover from the old Allentown operation.[36]

The "avowed purpose" of the new Kinemacolor enterprise, reported the *Mirror*, was to "broaden the field of the motion picture," to which end:

> It will produce not only colored films but will also produce [sic] black and white films. The process will be rented to manufacturers who affiliate with the corporation but to none outside. . . . They propose to exhibit only in the best and higher class theatres superior subjects. . . . The English factory and the American will act in unison and exchange prints. . . . The special release of the coronation of King George in colors will be handled by a special company (*New York Dramatic Mirror*, 3 May 1911, p. 34).

Kinemacolor's coronation pictures turned out to be a sellout at the Herald Square Theater in New York that August and added greatly to the prestige of the American company. It was this event that caused Robert Grau to ask, "Is the Two-Dollar-a-Seat Picture Theater in Sight?"[37]

American Kinemacolor went through endless changes in management, with Sawyer remaining the only constant. During 1911, the company ambitiously undertook an adaptation of *The Clansman*, a play by Thomas Dixon that had been touring the country for the past six years. Filmed by arrangement with the author and under the supervision of George Brennan, manager of the traveling company, it was produced in the South with members of the original company in the principal roles. The shooting on THE CLANSMAN was completed by January 1912, and the ten-reel film (actually the equivalent in running time of five reels because of the double speed of projection) was announced for release as soon as the current big attraction, the British company's Delhi Durbar films, had completed its run. However, since THE CLANSMAN never appeared, and there was no explanation given, it must be that the completed footage was not found to be good enough. In December 1912 THE CLANSMAN was also announced as one of the projects of the Famous Players Lasky Company, but that version too failed to appear. Frank Woods (the *Moving Picture World's* "Spectator"), very briefly employed as a Kinemacolor director, later suggested the project to D. W. Griffith, who was to transform it into THE BIRTH OF A NATION (1915).[38]

Despite the fiasco with THE CLANSMAN, which must have lost a lot of money for the company, by the fall of 1912 American Kinemacolor declared itself finally ready to set up an ambitious production program. A studio was put into operation in Whitestone, Long Island, but because Kinemacolor's shooting speed of thirty-two pictures a second required more light, only the brightest sunshine would do, and winter darkness soon provided a motive for the company to go to California instead. A site at 4500 Sunset Boulevard in Hollywood (then still referred to as "a suburb of Los Angeles") was leased for ten years. Film pioneer David Miles was the chief director, supervising the work of two others, Frank Woods and Jack Le Saint. Each director was to turn out one film of two reels or more every week. Linda Arvidson, formerly of Biograph (and still Mrs. D. W. Griffith, though separated from her husband by this time), and Mabel Van Buren were hired as players.[39]

The company was intent on finding a way to expand their market. That same October they advertised a Kinemacolor Film Service with American productions, which could be rented exclusively in small towns. The first release was a two-reel Western, directed by David Miles on his way to California and shown to the press that month under the title EAST AND WEST. This may have been the same film that, reviewed in the *Mirror* four months later as FIFTY MILES FROM TOMBSTONE, earned the following scant recognition: "The best that can be said of this picture is that it gives the producer a chance for some wonderful color effects. . . . But there are many scenes which would tax the credulity of an audience." On 25 November 1912, however, Kinemacolor kept up its prestigious reputation by screening one of its films—about the building of the Panama Canal—for President Taft.[40]

Early in 1913, the famed but aging beauty Lillian Russell spent two weeks at the Kinemacolor studio in Los Angeles making a physical-culture film called HOW TO LIVE 100 YEARS. On 24 February she launched a lecture tour with the film at the Orchestra Hall in Chicago, then went on to New York. At the end of her tour,

The director Gaston Bell and his star, the famed beauty Lillian Russell (now over fifty), at the Kinemacolor studio in Los Angeles, February 1913.

ownership of the film reverted to Kinemacolor. Russell was scheduled to follow this venture by playing Lady Teazle in a film version of Sheridan's play *The School for Scandal*, which was to be directed by David Miles under a contract that called for his exclusive services as her director, but this was apparently never made.[41]

In April 1913 the company was announcing the development of a new filter that needed much less light in projection and that was being fitted onto every Kinemacolor machine. "Far more important to the picture patron," they claimed, "is the improvement in the blending of the colors. The jarring effect of the reds and greens is done away with, and the colors blend perfectly, giving a remarkably soft effect to the picture and making a wonderful improvement to the eye." Whether the new filter corrected the problem or not, the announcement attests to the earlier problems.[42]

Six months after the new filter, Kinemacolor began offering a new, cheaper service. Under the former system, it had been necessary to transport the heavy projector to the site of each film showing. Now the projector was to be sold outright at what the company claimed to be a low price. It was adapted for screening black and white as well as color, they said, and exhibitors were supposed to be able to use it as their regular machine and to show Kinemacolor at the same time. But in order for this scheme to succeed, the new projector would have had to be as good as, if not better than, the others that theaters were using, and it was not.[43]

The technological complications that haunted exhibition must have added to the burden of making films as well. Indeed, none of the directors remained at Kinemacolor any length of time; Frank Woods, for example, went over to IMP in April. According to *Motography's Hand Book and Film Record*, between 1 October 1912 and 30 September 1913, Kinemacolor released only twelve multireel dramas, eight multireel comedies, and thirteen films classed as educational, scenic, and topical, most of them about one reel or less (and at least some of them British productions). A few other Kinemacolor releases reviewed in the trade periodicals in the early months of 1913 are not listed there, but in any event, it is clear that production was too small to support the company without the addition of the British films. By June 1913 the Los Angeles studio was closed, permanently, it was said, and the staff was reported to be looking for other jobs. At the end of that year, theatrical managers Cohan and Harris bought American Kinemacolor with the intention of producing films of the plays they owned, for screening in their own theaters in both black and white and Kinemacolor.[44]

The Urban patents ran out in 1914, and American Kinemacolor did not last much longer. In an article called "Demise of Kinemacolor: Technological, Legal, Economic, and Aesthetic Problems in Early Color History," Gorham Kindem assigns blame to a combination of all the items listed in his title. My opinion is that the largest factor in Kinemacolor's failure was technological. If, as it seems, the projection equipment could not be made practical for the many ordinary moving-picture theaters, the market was not big enough to justify the high cost of production. In his courtroom testimony, Sawyer claimed that Kinemacolor felt limited in output and could not expand because the market was not broad enough. At that time, early in 1913, he admitted that Kinemacolor had played in very few of the smaller cities. Among other factors contributing to its demise were the incredible number of changes of management Kinemacolor underwent during its brief history, and the company's failure to lease its technical facilities to other producers, as Technicolor was to do later on.[45]

By 1914, America's film exports were becoming important to the national economy. The year ending 30 June 1912 was the first for which the U.S. consular reports included statistics relating to the motion-picture industry. That year, over fourteen million feet of positive film were imported, while eighty million feet were exported. During the period ending March 1914, motion-picture exports were four times those of the same nine-month period in 1912. When war started in Europe in 1914, it abruptly cut off a substantial part of this export market from those companies now heavily dependent on it (although it also led to the development of the Latin American market as compensation for this loss). European exchanges and theaters closed, at least temporarily, when the adult males who had operated them marched off to war. This was an economic blow for Edison, Lubin, and Vitagraph, and especially for Kleine, with his big new studio under construction in Italy. It may also have been one of the strongest factors in bringing about the demise of some of the licensed companies, coming as it did in the midst of the government's action to disband them. Among the independents, the Mutual Company also had important European markets.[46]

By 1914 the center for European distribution of American films was London, and most of the established companies maintained offices there. The newest feature-film production companies and combines, however, had not yet established a dependence on the European market, except those that needed Europe as a source for their film supply. On the whole, they did not suffer as big a blow, and they were ready to fill a gap left when fewer foreign feature films were available. Even before the war broke out, a fall-off in European feature-film production was noticed, giving support to the conservatives who believed that the feature film was a passing craze of 1913.[47]

14

Refining the Product

The novel effects in pictures, such as the unique dissolves and multiple
exposures, have an immeasurable bearing on their popularity. Titles run in
over the scene, as in "Footprints of Mozart," recently released, and "The
Cricket on the Hearth," in which the style of type used was in conformity
with the spirit and locale of the story, are of greater importance than would
appear to the casual observer, and they really supply the little touches that
make up the "finished" product.

> —S. S. Hutchinson, president of the American Film Manufacturing
> Company, in *Moving Picture World*, 11 July 1914, p. 183

*I*mprovements in lighting and special lighting effects were among the first refinements that began to preoccupy producers (and critics) in the newly structured
motion-picture industry of 1909. Although the art and science of photography were
at hand to provide models of lighting skill when the motion picture began, and some
of the moving-picture cameramen had experience as still photographers prior to
getting into film, the transformation of the lighting techniques of still photography to
lighting for moving images was slow. One reason was probably the expense: the early
outdoor production crews could not wait for the best natural conditions, and the
more subtle aspects of using artificial light required the construction of enclosed
studios and installation of lighting equipment. These developments came later, with
the stabilization of the industry and more investment in the film plant. It would not
have cost much, to be sure, to improvise reflectors and diffusers and modify the
effects of sunlight, if there had been enough interest. But in the beginning, producers were satisfied as long as the image was clear. It was only with the new dominance
of the story film that the need for illusionistic and expressive lighting grew stronger.

When the producers first formed themselves into an organized group, Vitagraph,
Edison, and Pathé had just built large studios of glass, and Lubin was about to do the
same. The glass-enclosed studios made it possible to film in cold weather and to avoid
the problems of wind and rain on the sets. The newer companies or smaller ones
continued to do most of their filming out-of-doors. The Biograph studio in the brownstone building at 11 East Fourteenth Street in New York, in operation from 1903 to
1913, was unusual in being lit entirely by artificial light. These were the banks of
mercury-vapor tubes known as Cooper-Hewitts; they were also available in the glass
studios, but there, they were usually combined with natural light. At best, the
Cooper-Hewitts gave a diffused and even lighting, while the sun was apt to create
harsh shadows (although these shadows could be softened with diffusers made of

special kinds of glass or sheets of muslin and hung overhead). Certain effects could be obtained with small spotlights beamed from outside the camera range or inserted into furniture and objects. As early as 1905 Edwin S. Porter had used a spotlight comng from a fireplace to simulate firelight, and G. W. Bitzer had created similar effects for Biograph films. All kinds of special effects were certainly well known in theatrical lighting too and therefore would have been familiar to the new generation of filmmakers, many of whom had theatrical backgrounds. After 1908 there was increased attention to illusionism; from 1911 onward the expressive uses of light were explored; and by 1913 there was also an interest in pictorialism.[1]

Then, as now, lighting served to increase the illusion of reality by giving depth to settings and dimension to people and objects. This is accomplished by providing a variety of light sources, from the back and the sides as well as the front, so that one side of the figure or object receives additional light. Naturalistic effects are further enhanced by placing light sources where they would appear in actuality—in windows and doors, and especially in lamps and candles—and by changing the amount of light in the image as such sources are lit or extinguished.

Good or poor photography was a frequent topic of comment in the early film reviews, but very often only from the viewpoint of clarity and sharpness. Thus, in comments on Biograph's ROMANCE OF A JEWESS in the fall of 1908, a writer implicitly chided lightning defects with the remark that "One cannot help noticing in this film the superior photographic quality in the scenes that are taken outdoors over those that are photographed with the glare of the electric arc light."

By 1911, however, it was in the name of realism that Louis Reeves Harrison

LOVE MICROBES (Biograph, 1907). The image has been extended beyond the Biograph one-hole negative perforations in order to show the lights in use in this studio.

PIPPA PASSES (Biograph, 1909), directed by D. W. Griffith. Gertrude Robinson as Pippa.

The Biograph studio in the Bronx, 1913, during the Klaw and Erlanger regime, showing the Cooper-Hewitt lights. Production shot from an unidentified film, Linda Arvidson in the armchair.

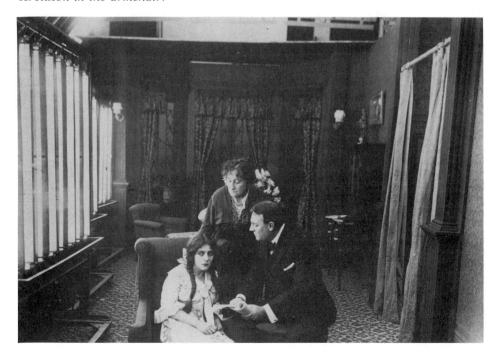

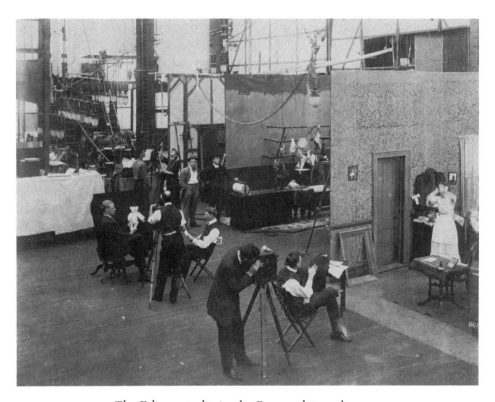

The Edison studio in the Bronx, date unknown.

praised Rex's FIVE HOURS: "A notable feature of this photoplay is the light. It comes from where it should come from. This is a most desirable feature in moving pictures; the high lights and shadows are so carefully adjusted as to perfectly mold the figures, bringing them out in clear relief from the background. They are human beings, not photographs." Remarks on other films praised "figures in full relief" and the fact that "the light is so good that practically every branch, not to say every leaf, is seen in relief, nothing flat—a picture full of depth."[2]

It was similarly in the name of realism that in OLIVER TWIST (Vitagraph, May 1909), when Nancy Sykes lit a candle, the room was lighted, and in THE POWER OF THE PRESS (Vitagraph, December 1909), when a lamp was broken, the light went out, and in THE CAT'S-PAW (Essanay, December 1912), when Eva turned on the light, the room went from semidarkness to light. Such touches were for the big studios with the facilities to execute them, but by 1911, if a character carried a candle or a lantern without an effect of light coming from it, the failure would be criticized. It was not "realistic."[3]

Another motivation for developing lighting skill was to add to the means of expression. Lighting, it was discovered, could be used to enhance a psychological mood, point up a moral, clarify a narrative, or deepen an emotion. The expressive qualities of selective lighting had already been noted in SUFFER LITTLE CHILDREN (Edison, 1909), a film about child labor: "Some very beautiful lighting effects are introduced, effects which emphasize the faces while subordinating everything else." A reviewer of Biograph's THE PUNISHMENT (April 1912) asked his readers to "note especially the soft lights cast upon the faces of the actors to bring out the slightest detail of facial expression."[4]

A more dramatic use of lighting contrasts began to appear in American films from 1911 onward, especially in mystery and horror films. The extreme contrast of light and dark created an atmosphere of emotion, drama, and mystery, as noted in this review of AT SWORD'S POINT (Reliance, March 1911), which suggested that an unusual lighting effect had its motivation in the plot:

> One of the most striking features ever introduced in motion pictures is the duel in the dark between the young king's mother, impersonated by Miss Marion Leonard, and the assassins who had come to murder him. The only light comes from the clashing of steel as sword strikes sword in the darkness. The audience sat as though rooted to the spot while this life and death struggle was in process. It is impossible to convey to those who have never seen it the strange, weird fascination which makes this scene one of the most notable ever seen on the screen (*Moving Picture World,* 1 April 1911, p. 728).

Essanay made use of similar lighting contrasts in GHOSTS (October 1912) and again in THE SHADOW OF THE CROSS (December 1912). In the latter, a candle is dashed to the floor, the room left in darkness, and slowly "a shaft of light penetrates the gloom and falls upon the crucifix," and saves the hero from committing murder.[5]

By the fall of 1912, however, at least one observer thought that special lighting effects could be overdone. Calling attention to this "struggle for effect and atmosphere, or what might be called tone," for "bringing out certain impressions of moment to the story," the *Mirror*'s critic cautioned that "[they] may be used indiscriminately in such a way as to detract from the drama itself."[6] At the time, expressive lighting was attracting attention in the theater, especially in the work of Max Reinhardt in Germany, although when the low-key and dramatic lighting of THE CHEAT (Famous Players–Laksy–Paramount, directed by Cecil B. DeMille) came along in 1915, in keeping with the loftier aspirations of the producers the inspiration was attributed to Rembrandt.

When filmmakers began to aspire to high art, they looked first to pictorialism—that is, to beautiful images, such as might be found in nineteenth-century paintings and photography. One much-admired pictorial lighting effect was the "open door." Derived from still photography, it entailed posing the subject inside an open door, looking out. The figure inside would be seen nearly in silhouette, with a little sidelighting, while the exterior would be very bright. This was a popular and easy way to obtain strong contrast lighting without artificial light and in some instances may well have occurred only as an accident of a real location. In addition to its pictorial qualities, the effect could also serve to highlight action occurring in two different spatial areas within the same shot. The *World* critic first noted its appearance late in 1909 with an Italian film known in English as A BROKEN LIFE (Roma, Turin):

> There are some effects . . . such as we have never seen before, notably the simultaneous exposition of an exterior street scene with an interior and with movement taking place in both. Then another part of the picture shows the figure of a woman almost silhouetted against a very bright

The "open door" shot (or open-window in this case), in an unidentified Vitagraph film.

Side lighting adds to the dramatic effect in this scene from an unidentified Vitagraph film.

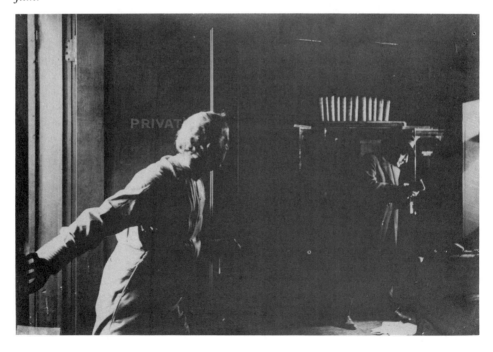

"Night lighting" for THE HOUSE OF FEAR (IMP, 1915), directed by Stuart Paton, cinematography by Eugene Gaudio.

exterior scene—an open-air effect very popular in stationary photography (*Moving Picture World*, 13 November 1909, p. 648).

The "open door" effect was subsequently admired by the critics in Essanay's A BANDIT'S WIFE (June 1910) and in GAY, GAY, LET US BE MARRIED (January 1911). It is not difficult to find examples of this kind of pictorial shot, which may also be used quite expressively, in surviving films. In POWER OF THE PRESS (Vitagraph, December 1909), there is a strikingly dramatic composition in which a girl at the left side of the image eavesdrops at a door, while the rest of the frame is shrouded in darkness. In THE DEERSLAYER (Vitagraph, May 1913), an impressive pictorial shot looks through a wide door onto water, with this central panel of water and its bright light reflections bordered by two panels of darkness of about equal size. In A MODERN NOBLE (Domino, February 1915), there is a similar interior shot of the open door, at the beer garden in Heidelberg, where the central panel is bright, and the actors in the dark side panels are nearly in silhouette.[7]

Still other examples use the effect to more explicitly narrative ends. In THE DREAM (Republic, March 1912), a deranged mill worker, in near silhouette, looks out the door to see his daughter meeting the mill owner's son in the snow and light outside. In a kind of waking dream or nightmare that is the "working of a distorted mind," he kills the man, then enters the door of his house in semi-silhouette, with sharp side light from the window. The lighting creates the dramatic mood of the scene; the mill worker, standing at the window, fists clenched, thinks he hears the dead man call.[8] Similarly, a shot in THE ARMY SURGEON (Kay-Bee, November 1912, directed by

Francis Ford) uses combined light sources at a window to highlight a dramatic choice. The hero, standing outside, looks through a window at a party scene; the interior light shines on him on one side, and the softer light of a dying sun on a hillside filters behind him. The scene is meant to be emotionally expressive, because at that moment the hero is giving up his chance to win the hand of the girl at the party in order to go and do his duty.

In the fall of 1912 Essanay brought out "a powerful battery of searchlights" to do some night shooting on the big sets of their three-reel feature KING ROBERT OF SICILY (August 1913), based on the Longfellow poem. According to a viewing of the test results, the experiment was a success and achieved "a photographic effect unusual in lighting schemes." At the end of 1914, new Panchrome Twin Arcs, powerful and portable arc lamps, were used for a night-shooting sequence for THE HOUSE OF FEAR (IMP, January 1915). This time, the use of the lamps also served as a publicity device, as Kristin Thompson points out, because the press was invited to attend the shooting. The sequence that was filmed that night (by Eugene Gaudio) might be described as a "reverse angle" of the open-door effect. The lights were placed inside the house and the camera was outside; technically, therefore, it was night shooting out-of-doors. According to the *World*, the new lamps were bright enough "to make clear not merely the outlining of the figures, but their faces." The use of arc lamps to light specific areas of the image was not at all news at this time, but the particular value of the new lamps, it was explained to the press, was their portability. When the heroine rushed out the front door of the house, another of the brilliant portable arcs placed up in a tree lit her face, as though the moon had come out from under a cloud just at that moment to reveal her fearful expression.[9]

Artificial light was used much more rarely in California, where the brilliant sunshine could be tapped for similar special effects. For example, Karl Brown describes such an effect in the filming of THE BIRTH OF A NATION: a mirror reflection of sunlight was used to make a "follow spot" for Lincoln's assassin as he crept through the crowds in the re-creation of Ford's Theater. According to Brown, this was not a realistic use of a spotlight, but one that transformed the black-clad figure into a symbol of death.[10]

It was only at the very end of this period that there began to appear some examples of artificial lighting for filming at night. Normally the scenes were made in daylight and the prints tinted blue in dye baths to indicate night. Because the tint was applied after printing, it was easy enough for some prints to slip out without the blue color, as evidenced by the complaints of C. H. Claudy: "The time is past when you can take a picture in broad sunlight and call it midnight and get away with it. . . . They won't stand for such crudities now." At that time, prints were still assembled by hand, individually, shot spliced to shot. In the long run, the separate tinting of scenes for every print that was released was not very practical, especially given the growing numbers of prints needed, and it is difficult to understand why the practice lingered as long as it did. In the name of efficiency and mass production, it would later become preferable to complete editing in the negative and make release prints that did not need to be individually spliced together. (Indeed, since this is the case today, most modern prints of early films are without the tinting bath, which accounts for scenes such as that in THE LONEDALE OPERATOR where Blanche Sweet pretends that a wrench is a gun and fools the burglars. It does not look very plausible until the blue tint is added.)[11]

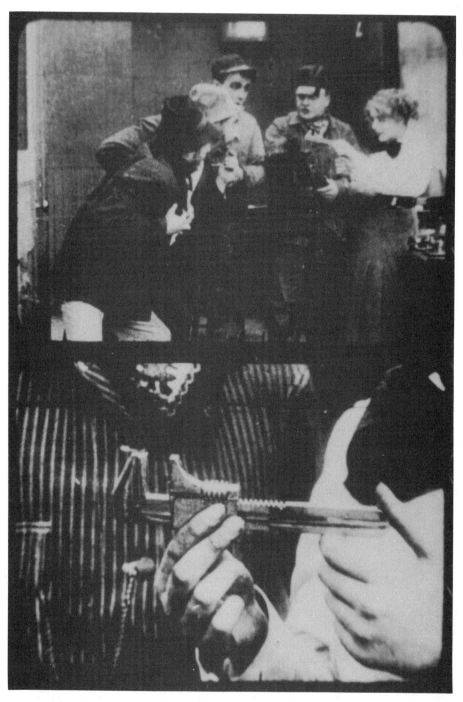

Two frames from THE LONEDALE OPERATOR *(Biograph, 1911). Filmed in black-and-white, the scene was tinted blue for night. The close-up shows the audience (but not the thieves) that Blanche really has no gun. The Museum of Modern Art has restored a print with the original tint, making the deception believable as it was to the first audiences.*

Other refinements increasingly employed from 1911 on were the "fade-in" and "fade-out" (gradually darkening or lightening a scene) and the "iris-in" and "iris-out" (opening or closing the camera's iris so that a round framing device becomes smaller or larger). These were used for beginning and ending shots or scenes, and one reason for their popularity might have been a lingering unease about continuity in cutting to a new scene. Like the style of alternate editing that depended on interrupting one line of action and resuming another, the fade and the iris called attention to the rupture between shots, but these devices softened it, making the change less abrupt. The iris could also function in the role of a close-up, directing attention to a detail without risk of the disorientation that was then felt, or feared, when cutting to a close-up. Later, however, when emphasis was placed on making cuts as inconspicuous as possible, by such means as cutting on action, the use of these early devices lessened.

Both the fade and the iris served to refine the product: they made the finish more "smooth." Judging by surviving films, there seems to have been no particular consistency in their use. In WENONA'S BROKEN PROMISE (Bison, November 1911), a fade-out is used to end a film. It becomes a transition between present and past in THE OLD GUARD (Vitagraph, 22 February 1913), in which the last "Old Guard" of Napoleon dreams of the past days of glory; each of the old soldier's mental visits to the past is faded in and faded out, or faded out and additionally faded in to the present. In THE WARNING (Majestic, September 1914), an iris closes as a transition to a new scene. An iris opening to begin a film was quite a popular device, as seen in THE TRAGEDY THAT LIVED (Selig, October 1914), which is actually a good example of the varied uses of all these devices within a single film: a fade-out followed by an iris opening serves as a transition to the past; then, after an iris closes on the scenes set in the past, there is a straight cut to the present. In this sequence, an iris opens as a transition to another scene, and finally, an iris closes to end the film. In Vitagraph's THE MAN THAT MIGHT HAVE BEEN (November 1914), fades signal the end of memories. Following the long introductory sequence of DAMON AND PYTHIAS (December 1914, Universal), an opening iris signals the beginning of the story, then in several places marks the beginning of another scene, while a fading iris ends one.

Discussing these refinements in his column for aspiring photoplaywrights, William Lord Wright discouraged their use on economic grounds (note that he also defines a fade incorrectly):

> When one scene dissolves into another it is termed a fade. However, this fade and trick stuff frequently mitigates the sale of a story. Trick effects mean a lot of work. Visions are also annoying to handle and the writers who persist in submitting the "dream stuff" soon become unpopular in many studios. Effects will never save a weak idea or pull up the necessary threads of a story (*Motion Picture News*, 8 November 1913, p. 23).

In fact, the economic argument may be applied in reverse. In the 1913–1914 period the cost of production was one of the reasons why a feature film was worth the extra price, to rent or to see. Expensive refinements added to the value of the film. However, Wright's column was directed to the amateur scenarists who were expected to write for the one-reel film, and therefore he was giving sound advice to his readers.

Another addition to the list of refinements was the great revival of interest in the double exposure beginning about 1912. This had been one of the devices of the early trick film: it could be done in the camera, either by exposing two images on the same frame with a neutral background or by masking part of the image and then winding back the film to expose that part, or alternatively, it could be done in the printer by the double printing of two films, one over the other. Such effects might destroy the illusion of reality, especially if they were not executed with care and skill, and they were therefore rejected by some filmmakers at the beginning of this period. The most frequent use of the double exposure in the story film was to show a vision, a memory, or a thought. In AN ALPINE ECHO (1909, Vitagraph), for example, the immigrant from Switzerland remembers a childhood scene when he hears a familiar music box and raises his arms to a vision of his past, which appears on the wall.

The more modern system used other forms—alternate scenes and inserts, closer views, a more intimate acting style—as embodied, in Tom Gunning's term, in the "narrator system." Nevertheless a number of producers continued to prefer double exposures as a narrative device, and in this period perfected the techniques for making them. As pointed out in chapter 4, some people considered it "more realistic" to show a character's memory on the wall of the set than to cut to another shot. The coming of the feature film with its greater narrative complexity drew producers to a renewed emphasis on such devices. Then, as we will discover, the double exposure became quite attractive as a novelty in a period when producers sought means to hold the spectator's interest during longer films.

According to Barry Salt, the Bell and Howell studio camera available in 1912 not only offered greater steadiness and improved image viewing but came equipped with a built-in frame counter "which facilitated the making of accurate dissolves and other special effects." Finding "no definite mention" that any cameraman had acquired the new device before 1914, Salt concluded that the high price probably discouraged immediate sales. However, there is evidence that the camera was indeed acquired by the Essanay studio and used for the special effects in SUNSHINE (October 1912). Given the great emphasis on double-exposure scenes at this time, it seems probable that the camera was employed by other studios as well. The growing use of the Bell and Howell camera at this particular time would surely have owed something to the court decisions of the same year that declared the Latham loop patent to be invalid and thus freed independent producers to use openly whatever camera they wished without fear of lawsuits.[12]

The renewed interest in the use of double exposures in 1912 manifested itself most strongly in the fad for playing double roles, where one actor would appear in the same scene with himself. In Edison's THE CORSICAN BROTHERS (January 1912), for example, both of the brothers were played by George Lessey. The same month, the Selig Company released a double-role film with Hobart Bosworth playing both the tramp and the millionaire in MERELY A MILLIONAIRE.

As a reviewer explained in the case of THE CORSICAN BROTHERS, "This is done by means of a trick of photography that is well understood in all studios, the distinctive point of this example is that it is so well done as not to be apparent. For instance, in the scene pictured below, in which the two brothers are seated at the table, the mother pours coffee on the hand of one brother, and both flinch at the same moment."[13]

The double exposure in THE CORSICAN BROTHERS *(Selig, February 1912), directed by Oscar Apfel and J. Searle Dawley. George Lessey is the duplicated figure.*

The use of double roles required a considerable degree of advance planning in the production stages in order for the illusion to work properly, but the results were not always successful, as can be seen in Kalem's THE PARASITE (September 1912). A man has stolen the identity of a "look-alike" from what he thinks is a dead body on the battlefield, but the supposed corpse reappears, alive, and faces the fake. During this very brief confrontation, the body of the authentic character is insubstantial, transparent, but as soon as the fake leaves the scene, there is a cut (supposed to be invisible) and the real figure appears to be more solid. The scene lasts such a short time, however, that it betrays the producer's awareness of its weakness.

Wilbur Crane appeared on the same screen with himself in Pathé American's THE COMPACT (November 1912), and Porter announced plans to use the device in order for James Hackett to play the double role of the King and Rudolph in THE PRISONER OF ZENDA.[14]

In 1913 such scenes grew in popularity. In THE TWIN BROTHERS (Edison, June 1913), Augustus Phillips is shown shaking hands with himself: the publicity claimed that "this is the first double-exposure picture in which a player, appearing in two roles, seems to come into contact." Marion Leonard played a double role in THE DEAD SECRET (April 1913), as did James Cruze in THE PLOT AGAINST THE GOVERNOR (Thanhouser, October 1913). In BREED OF THE NORTH (Lubin, October 1913), twin brothers are played by the same man in double exposure. Edwin August wrote and directed and played both roles in A STOLEN IDENTITY (Powers-Universal, November 1913), where his special achievement was said to be filming the two men he played walking and talking together along a sidewalk. As the film has not survived,

Lillian Gish and Henry B. Walthall in the allegorical scene that ends HOME SWEET HOME *(Mutual, 1914), directed by D. W. Griffith. In this sequence, Walthall, as the composer John Howard Payne, struggles against Lust and Greed to rise to heaven with his sweetheart, now become an angel.*

DAYDREAM OF A PHOTOPLAY ARTIST *(Essanay, ca. 1912). Francis X. Bushman in one of a series of double exposures used in this film.*

it is not known whether that might have meant a tracking shot, which would indeed have complicated the trick. Paul Wegener's double portrayal in the German film THE STUDENT OF PRAGUE (1913) arrived on American shores at about the same time, while Grace Cunard outdid everyone by making the leap from double to triple exposure with THE TWIN'S DOUBLE (Universal–Gold Seal, November 1913, directed by Francis Ford), a film for which she wrote her own scenario, calling for her to appear in the same scene as three different women.[15] A year later, King Baggott found a way to go further still. He played six parts in one scene for SHADOWS (IMP, October 1914), necessitating six exposures of the film. This trick undoubtedly required the Bell and Howell frame counter for accuracy.[16]

The double—or sextuple—role, always a challenge to the ego of an actor, by no means represented all the varied uses of double exposure from 1912 onward. It is clear that the multiple exposure was appreciated as a special effect, something to add to a film's interest, admired by the viewers for its cleverness. Such uses of the device departed from the notion that a double exposure is more "realistic" because less disruptive of the narrative flow than a cut to another scene; on the contrary, the device was now calling attention to itself, breaking the illusion that the screen represents reality. American Eclair won "especial praise" for "a bit of double exposing wherein is shown a moving picture screen projection. The register of action is . . . perfect." It is a particular loss to the history of film exhibition that the film described, THE TRANSGRESSION OF DEACON JONES (November 1912), no longer survives, as it showed a nickelodeon in a small town, and the actions of a "Purity League" that wanted to close it. Edison brought out THE THIRD THANKSGIVING (November 1912) in time for the holiday, with "a pretty double exposure" to contrast two celebrations. Kinemacolor claimed to have succeeded in doing a double exposure for the first time in a Christmas film for the 1912 season (A CHRISTMAS SPIRIT); this was previously believed impossible to do with the Kinemacolor process. Edison's AN UNSULLIED SHIELD (December 1912) won high praise from Louis Reeves Harrison for its double exposures showing the dreams of a degenerate scion as his ancestors step out of their portraits one after another to relive their achievements in the same image with the sleeping man. But shortly afterward, Harrison marveled over Thomas Ince's double exposures to show the heroine's thoughts in A SHADOW OF THE PAST (Kay-Bee, January 1913), as though no one had ever done it before.[17]

In Essanay's THE WARNING HAND (October 1912), a mysterious painting of a jeweled hand suspended from a sword by a chain appears at times of moral crisis to guide the hero on the right path. THE PHANTOM SIGNAL (Edison, October 1913), in two reels, was an attack on corporate heads of an unnamed railroad in New England, who are at fault for train wrecks resulting from the long hours and exhausting work of men at signal stations. A double-exposure animated skeleton forecasts each of several tragedies, while another shows two trains approaching on a V switch. In another double exposure, in THE GHOST (Domino, November 1913), a drunkard, in a dream, thinks he is dead and wanders among his friends as a ghost.[18]

The new skill in handling multiple exposures also yielded a variation on the telephone theme already discussed in chapter 4, as Essanay returned to the example of Porter's 1907 film COLLEGE CHUMS in THE BATTLE FOR LOVE (December 1914):

> In this scene Francis X. Bushman is discovered in his office at the telephone on one side, and Ruth Stonehouse, his sweetheart, at the phone on

the other side. In the center is a picture of a street with the telephone wires. From these wires flash out the message on the screen letter by letter. This requires a fourth exposure to work the letters into the central picture, making it practically a quadruple exposure to finish the picture (*Motion Picture News*, 19 December 1914, p. 113).

The more complex the use of multiple exposures, the more publicity value it had. In its description of THE STOLEN BIRTHRIGHT (Eclectic, December 1914), filmed by the Whartons at the Ithaca studio, the *Motion Picture News* told readers:

> Near the close of the picture there is a particularly fine series of double exposures. These show the two principal male characters hurrying to their homes. One is rushing west and the other east. The two are shown boarding different trains, and the trains are seen on their respective tracks in this series of double exposures. As a climax to this photographic effect the two men are seen on opposite sides of the screen, one clasping his wife and the other his sweetheart in his arms (*Motion Picture News*, 19 December 1914, p. 60).

Another important development toward the end of this period was the return of camera movement. The moving camera, while not frequent in pre-1907 cinema, was not unusual either. The mounted moving camera, or traveling shot, was extremely popular as a novelty around the turn of the century, when train- and ship-mounted cameras thrilled the spectators with movement for its own sake. After 1907, however, the camera rarely moved. Where a far-reaching camera pan was previously found useful in carrying the scene of action to another location, now a cut accomplished the same end.

For the most part, any camera movement that was employed between 1908 and 1912 remained unobtrusive, with the camera shifting only slightly on occasion to keep significant action in the center of the shot: for example, when an actor sits down or gets up. Even in such a case, many producers did not object to large areas of unused space left over when the camera position remained static. At this time, when symmetry was important in compositions, such unused areas are often unintentional clues that someone is about to enter the space, or that a double-exposure vision is about to appear in it. In this respect, the long panoramic shot that begins and ends THE COUNTRY DOCTOR (Biograph, July, 1909) was quite unusual for its time. But even so, while the panning at the beginning and end of the film forms a lyric circular frame, it should be noted that this movement does not interrupt the formal editing pattern of the interior of the film. If one accepts a technological explanation for film history, it might be argued that cameras seldom moved in this period because a smoothly panning shot was too difficult to achieve with existing equipment. However, the more overpowering reason was the need to discard pre-1907 techniques, including panning shots, while trying out new methods, such as editing. The technique would have seemed old-fashioned to the new generation of filmmakers.

The moving camera began to be found useful, however, for the horseback chases of Westerns and any other far-ranging movement that could not be precisely controlled out-of-doors. The camera moved in order to keep the action within the frame and centered as much as possible. The lengthy panning shot to follow action began to be more fully exploited in 1911–1912. It is especially noticeable in films from the American Film Company, which was making a specialty of Westerns: the posse going after an outlaw in THE RANCHMAN'S NERVE (July 1911), a horseback chase in THEIR HERO SON (September 1912), an unusually extended camera movement in THE FEAR (September 1912), probably influenced to some extent by the California terrain. In this last film, the camera follows a group of cowboys riding a diagonal line down a hill, pans with them as they cross a stream, and ends with a reverse-angle cut to show the back view as the cowboys break through to the beach.

While the moving camera did not become a strong factor in the dominant style (compared to later developments in the twenties), in 1912 it was being reintegrated into the narrative system that had been built on alternate editing. The tracking shots of the train in THE GIRL AND HER TRUST (Biograph, March 1912) added a dynamic element to the "ride to the rescue." Biograph's THE MASSACRE, filmed in November of the same year, made dynamic use of traveling shots, combined with fluid editing.[19] In January 1913 the American Film Company used a smooth traveling shot to follow a horseback chase after kidnappers in THE TRAIL OF CARDS. This shot enables the spectator to see the kidnapping victim drop cards to leave a trail. After the capture, the hero and heroine ride toward the camera, which now pulls back to mark the end of the film on a slow fade. Here one cannot help but think that the filmmakers were so intrigued with making these traveling shots that they did not consider using a close-up to show the cards being dropped, although this might have made the event clearer to the spectator.

The camera is mounted on the moving handcar for this thrilling scene in THE GIRL AND HER TRUST *(Biograph, 1912), directed by D. W. Griffith. Dorothy Bernard is the heroine.*

In 1913 many productions employed occasional moving-camera shots, but they were still the exception. According to William Christy Cabanne, Griffith didn't use the dolly shot (the "traveling" shot) much because he thought the movement attracted the attention of the audience.[20] In THE COUNT OF MONTE CRISTO (Famous Players, November 1913, directed by Edwin S. Porter), so old-fashioned in style as to permit James O'Neill (in the role he made famous onstage) to look at the audience and gesture what he intends to do, the action of a walking couple is followed by the same type of long camera pan used in the early days to avoid a cut.

On 1 June 1914 the big Italian spectacle film by Pastrone, CABIRIA, made a sensational American debut at the Knickerbocker Theatre in New York. The fluid camera movements in this film gave a three-dimensional depth and solidity to the enormous sets that had been constructed for it, and they brought scenes forward to the spectator by traveling into the depth of a shot. They were not quite the same kinds of camera movements that had been used in American films, where the purpose was more apt to be that of following action and centering the actors. In any case, the traveling-camera style of CABIRIA appeared so unusual to the industry that they dubbed it the "Cabiria movement." Lionel Barrymore later recalled going to see CABIRIA with D. W. Griffith, who remarked, "I wonder how they do that goddamn thing?"[21]

While CABIRIA probably encouraged the increasing use of a moving camera, the most visible evidence of a new trend in American films during 1914–1915 was another kind of camera movement: the traveling shot that functioned as the camera following or pulling back, to maintain a constant distance between the camera and the action. This device has already been mentioned in connection with THE TRAIL OF CARDS, made in January 1913. In THE MAN ON THE BOX (Jesse Lasky, July 1914), there is a camera pulling back as a carriage races down street toward camera, followed by mounted policemen. A camera pullback in IN THE DAYS OF THE THUNDERING HERD (Selig, November 1914) manages to be extremely smooth while showing fast-galloping horses on rough terrain.

These shots, still unusual in the production practice and therefore apt to call attention to themselves, sometimes appear like bravura gestures. In JIMMY (Domino, October 1914, directed by Scott Sidney), the opening shot features a very lengthy camera pullback that keeps ahead of Jimmy the newsboy as he runs toward camera on a busy street, crossing intersections and passing many people; this is intercut several times with static shots of the household that depends on him for its support, and interrupted by a fight with another newsboy, after which the camera continues to pull back and Jimmy to run. The unusual shot sequence is placed at the beginning of the film in order not to distract the spectator from the narrative. It serves as a dynamic introduction to the main characters, after which the story can continue. By contrast, however, pans are used fluidly and unobtrusively in DAMON AND PYTHIAS (Universal, December 1914), where the camera moves across spectators at the stadium, tilts down to include the gladiators, and continues to pan. The traveling camera pullback is also used to film the chariot race, but unlike in CABIRIA, it is not used to explore the big sets in depth.

THE BARGAIN (New York Motion Picture Company, December 1914) opens with a prolonged, slow pan over a magnificent landscape, and later, when William S. Hart first looks around the saloon and gambling hall near the Mexican border, there is another long, slow pan, this time around the room, an almost completely circular movement that takes in all the details of the busy scene. This is a subjective shot, from the point of view of the character. Some months into 1915, this same type of movement was used objectively for the opening shot of Lois Weber's SUNSHINE MOLLIE, with a very high-angle view of far-stretching oil fields, full of countless derricks pushing upward as far as the eye can see, and a very slow, circular panorama that ends up with the small figure of Lois Weber standing in the road with her suitcase. The interest in new kinds of camera movements continued actively through 1915.

Chapter 4 described the general tendency toward centering the action on the screen as a factor in the new narrative systems. Centering the action guided the spectator to find the significant elements of the image and was generally reinforced by movements of the actors toward the center from the edge of the frame. For interior shooting in particular, the centering of the camera level as well, at the actor's face or the upper part of the body, created a kind of shallow stage area with balanced amounts of space around it; again, a careful arrangement of several actors also worked toward this balance. The change to the "nine-foot line," or "American foreground," in 1909–1910 very slightly unbalanced this symmetry, gently "distorting" the image in such a way as to emphasize the actors, bringing the camera closer and lower at the same time, and reducing the amount of "unused" space above the actors' heads and below their knees. A modern viewer does not think of this as distortion, but remember that the *World* critic Thomas Bedding felt it strongly. It was an actor-centered universe.

Changes from this standard type of shot usually occurred first in outdoor shooting. The differences in composition are particularly striking in the case of the Biograph films, whenever the action moves from the cramped interior sets of the brownstone building on Fourteenth Street to an exterior.

Some of the unusual compositions in this period might well be only the result of an accident. In a film known as MARGHARITA (IMP, 1911)—I think this is probably not the original title), the sets are flimsy painted flats that a wind threatens to tear down. The compositions of the interior scenes are quite undistinguished. But suddenly there is an exterior shot on a city street, and a woman walks toward the camera down a sidewalk that extends into a perspective of great distance; she finally meets her lover at a street corner in the left foreground—a scene with all the depth and strange atmosphere of a De Chirico painting.

In a period when spectators were well accustomed to the practice of centered action and symmetrically balanced compositions, the occasional use of an unbalanced image was found to be very expressive. Diagonal compositions increase dramatic tension in some exterior shots showing Jekyll, the monster, in Thanhouser's DR. JEKYLL AND MR. HYDE (January 1912). The "vampire" films indicated the off-center nature of the sensual, self-serving woman by placing her in the corners of the frame, her head down on a pillow or on her arms, distorted in relation to her body. She also smoked cigarettes and dressed alluringly to underline her immorality, but her position in the image, when it shifted attention from the center screen, could be as good an indication as any of her tainted character. A similar off-centering served to make an audience experience fright or thrills. One example described in an earlier chapter is the terror-filled image of a threatening face in the corner of the screen in THE MUSKETEERS OF PIG ALLEY (1912). Another startling image appeared in Lois Weber and Phillip Smalley's SUSPENSE (Rex, 1913), which is off-balance in quite another

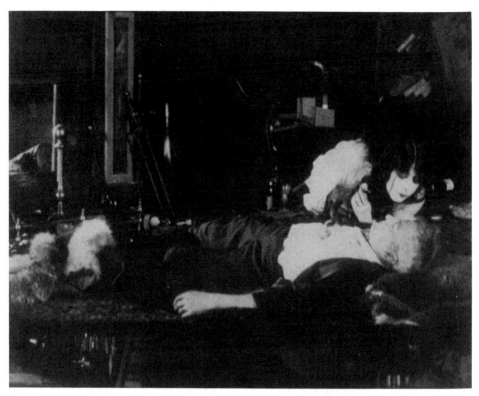

Theda Bara and Edward Jose in A FOOL THERE WAS (Fox Film Company, 1915), directed by Frank Powell.

way. When the heroine looks out of her window to find the source of a noise, her downward glance is followed by an unexpected overhead-angle shot showing the upturned face of a threatening tramp. Such extreme overhead angles are rare in this period, and therefore all the more startling when they do occur.

There is a distinct though subtle change in the look of a number of films at the end of this period, as they go from a classic, balanced composition to a disturbing asymmetry. The occasional breaks from the centered and balanced composition and the depth emphasis of traveling shots together contributed to a change from the boxlike stage space. Spaces in the more modern films are apt to have indefinite boundaries, and action flows in all directions. George Blaisdell noted the interiors of "marked depth" in reviewing THE PORT OF DOOM (Famous Players, November 1913). Vachel Lindsay commented that in JUDITH OF BETHULIA (Biograph, 1913–1914), "though the people seem to be coming from everywhere and going everywhere, when we watch closely, we see that the individuals enter at the near right-hand corner, or enter at the near left-hand corner and exit at the near right-hand corner." The *Variety* critic who reviewed THE AVENGING CONSCIENCE in 1914 observed that Griffith "somehow makes his studio scenes of immense proportions in an oblong way."[22] Similarly, in THE PERILS OF PAULINE (March–December 1914), in interiors as well as exteriors, the action moves from the camera into great depth and forward again. Pearl White as Pauline throws herself energetically through this deep space, showing her youthful eagerness for life to the point of becoming a distraction, because she is never in repose, even when she is not supposed to be the focus of attention.

The expressive use of lighting effects, the intriguing double exposures, and the use of traveling camera shots were all refinements noted and admired by trade-press critics. Eventually, all these refinements became less obtrusive in the way they were used, and they were incorporated into the expressive techniques available to the filmmaker. The changing spatial concepts created by off-center compositions, diagonal movements, and movements in depth—the apparently limitless space continuing outside the range of the camera's view—were more subtle and less observed at the time, but nonetheless contributed as much to the changes in film style in the mid teens.

15

Scene Dissection, Spectacle, Film as Art

The making and showing of moving pictures seems to constitute what I have
taken the liberty of terming the "New Art."
—Louis Reeves Harrison, *Moving Picture World,* 28 June 1913, p. 1336

*T*he coming of the feature film brought changes in film form once again. The
longer film created problems similar in some ways to, if not as extreme as, the
narrative crisis of the nickelodeon days. Among the first multireel Vitagraph films,
THE LIFE OF NAPOLEON and THE LIFE OF MOSES reflected the renewed narrative
problems by reverting to the tableau style of pre-1908. When the stories to be told
grew longer and more complex, clarity again became an issue. There was a renewed
demand for lecturers to go out on the road with big special features such as DANTE'S
INFERNO. There were also several revived attempts to provide mechanical "talking"
devices with the film, including the new version of Gaumont's system that was
demonstrated in New York on 10 June 1913; Hepworth's Vivaphone, which was
brought from Britain; and the prestigious presentation of Edison's long-awaited Kinetophone in early 1913. However, the now well-established mass-production system of the film industry gave even greater preference to a self-sufficient product than
had been the case in 1909. Lecturers could not easily be provided for every film
showing, and the experimental sound systems depended on separate sound mecha-
nisms. When Warner's Features imported Eclair's three-reel REDEMPTION in the
spring of 1912 for sale on the states rights plan, their advertising stressed that it was
"understandable to any audience—no lecture necessary."[1]

When a higher-paying audience came to see films in the more palatial theaters,
there was a renewed call for respectable film fare and uplift. The social and educational goals of the earlier period were still important, but now there was a new
emphasis on the need for a higher degree of art and intellect in keeping with this new
audience. When the manager of the People's Theater in Sunbury, Pennsylvania,
expressed his annoyance that Kleine's big production QUO VADIS? was going to
non-film theaters instead of to the regular picture shows that rented the less-
important Kleine releases, the *World* explained that QUO VADIS? was bringing in
people who would not go to the nickelodeons. After seeing such features, it was
argued, they would become regular patrons of the moving picture.[2]

Suitable fare for the higher-class audience was found in part through a reversion to the classics of theater and literature. At a much earlier time, before the development of the narrative systems that made a feature-length film possible, similar subjects were chosen because familiar stories would be recognized by audiences that shared a cultural heritage. Now the filming of classics assured the intellectual level of the works to be seen by an upward-striving middle-class audience. Of course, it was of equal importance that acknowledged classics provided pretested material on which higher production costs could be risked. Many of these early features, such as THE LIFE OF MOSES, FROM THE MANGER TO THE CROSS, QUO VADIS?, and DAMON AND PYTHIAS, were of a religious or historical nature and took place in ancient times, subjects that reassured the newer audiences about the respectability and the intellectual level of the motion picture.

As features became more common, producers more often dared the production of modern plays or novels. However, original stories, written for the screen, were rare in the early years of the feature film. (TRAFFIC IN SOULS, November 1913, was one of the few exceptions.) An invaluable index of the literary sources tapped during this period is the list published by the *World* in July 1915 under the title "Books and Plays in Pictures: A Comprehensive List of Authors and Titles of Their Works That Have Been Produced in Motion Pictures Since 1910." Composed mostly of feature films, the list takes up five double-columned pages of the journal. Both classic and modern authors appear prominently, but the largest numbers of films are based on older works. Fifteen films are based on Dickens, thirteen on Shakespeare plays, eleven on Alexandre Dumas, nine on Henry Wadsworth Longfellow, and nine on Washington Irving (but five of these are versions of *Rip Van Winkle*, which seems to have exercised a particular appeal for filmmakers, as there were also versions before 1910). Six films each are based on the works of Scott, Schiller, and Clyde Fitch; five films each on Jules Verne, Charles Reade, and Victorien Sardou, and four films each on Victor Hugo and Wilkie Collins. Tennyson, Dion Boucicault, and Charlotte Brontë (four versions of *Jane Eyre*) are also well represented, as are the modern authors William C. DeMille and Richard Harding Davis, whose works are associated with seven films each. Likewise, Bosworth had produced film versions of six of Jack London's novels by that time.[3]

It must be admitted that an enormous number of the short films produced from 1907 to 1912 had also used well-established works as sources, but in the all-consuming daily search for new subjects, original stories had often been filmed as well. Writing for films was a new craft, having little to do with established literary forms. Production in the days of the one-reeler depended on the work of hundreds of amateurs. It was not only that the price paid for scripts was beneath the dignity of an established writer, but the craft itself was not in the professional writer's realm. An elegant turn of phrase was of no use in a silent-movie script (unless it appeared as an intertitle). The plot and the visual ideas were what mattered. The Edison Company hired "name" writers for their publicity value, but most companies advertised widely for scripts, and the scenario editor on the staff read, selected, and adapted the submissions. Out of the hundreds of journalists, magazine story writers, actors, and amateurs who submitted scripts, a handful developed into professional scriptwriters and were hired as the scenario editors of production companies. With the coming of the feature film, scenario editors more often prepared the shooting scripts of the established works in-house.

As discussed in previous chapters, the distribution and exhibition practices of the first multireel films had imposed certain requirements on the film structure, notably that of providing a sense of climax and completion for each reel. At the same time, there was less need for story compression in the feature film, and consequently, there was less of the compression of fast cutting. There was more time to build up atmosphere and more time to portray character and add psychological depth, and therefore less place for the shorthand of ideological editing in which Griffith had become a specialist. Editing rhythms tended to slow down and crosscutting to be used less extensively. The advice given in a 1914 manual for structuring a scenario is encapsulated by the subtitle for one of the chapters: "Sequence and Consequence; Logical Cause and Complete Solution; Sustained Climax; All Expectations Fulfilled."[4] In those few words are outlined what was considered the ideal structure for the feature film. In the early days of the feature-film craze, there was also quite a lot of "padding," by those producers who lacked sufficiently large ideas or who were saving money by reusing footage shot for another purpose. (Nonetheless, it is sometimes difficult to know from the mangled and incomplete prints that survive whether an original film was really lacking in a coherent structure.)

Feature films also brought changes in the use of intertitles. The longer, more complex narratives of the feature films called once more for the help of titles to make the story clear to the spectator. On the other hand, titles that might take away from the suspense created by new narrative systems, by announcing what was to happen, were no longer desirable. It was felt that expository titles should be kept to a minimum. Dialogue titles, however, could supply exposition in what now began to be considered a more realistic manner and at the same time supplant, to some degree, the explanatory elements such as lecturers, actors behind the screen, and mechanical reproductions of talking. There was another reason, however, for the increasing use of dialogue titles: they came closer to the theatrical model. Dialogue lines formed the basis of the play script in the theater, and as we saw in chapter 9, dialogue titles in 1913–1914 sometimes even followed the procedures of the play script by naming the character who spoke. The procedure that had been rejected for the short film, that is, dialogue titles cut into the shot at the place where they were spoken or immediately after, was now found right for the feature film. The unassailable integrity of the single shot was giving way. From now on, dialogue titles began to appear more frequently than narrative titles and to carry more of the burden of narration.

The feature was required to hold the interest of the audience over a long period of time. In the earlier film program composed of short films, illustrated songs, and vaudeville acts, variety in the fare could be counted on to hold the spectator, who would be willing to wait through a less-successful offering because the next one might be better. As the feature replaced the variety show, it was found that some variety elements could still be incorporated. The most important at this time would prove to be spectacle. This could be provided in many ways: by impressive landscapes, enormous and expensive sets, large numbers of actors and period costumes, sweeping action in great depth, "big scenes," or special effects. Film spectacle far surpassed anything that the stage could offer, and audiences responded accordingly.

The popularity of the double exposure for scenes showing an actor meeting himself is an indication of how the process of making films fascinated audiences. Such effects were occasionally given a slight precedence over the principle of not breaking the illusion of reality: admiring the novelty, or wondering how it was achieved, might make audiences remember that they were watching a moving picture and not the real world. However, the most spectacular special effects, it was felt, should appear at the beginning or at the climax. As we have seen, when the producers of JIMMY (October 1914) used a bravura traveling shot, they placed it at the beginning of the film, where it would not distract once the narrative was under way. Such increasingly elaborate introductory sequences appeared before the story began, offering spectacle but in advance of the narrative. An additional motive for the introduction of actors at the beginning of the film is made clear in a review of THE PRISONER OF ZENDA (Famous Players, February 1913), where the critic applauds "the idea of showing each of the principal characters on the screen prior to the first reel, and giving a good purpose in making identities clear." The introductions, then, could not only add spectacle and exploit star value; they could also serve to clarify a complex plot.[5]

The foreign imports that pushed the development of features in America were historical-spectacle films. The bigger the spectacle—that is, the more battle scenes, the larger the sets, the greater number of actors employed in such films as DANTE'S INFERNO, QUO VADIS? and CABIRIA—the more sensational the appeal to the Americans. Ambitious producers in the United States followed this lead. Griffith's first feature (longer than two reels), JUDITH OF BETHULIA, was a spectacle film, and his greatest success, THE BIRTH OF A NATION, was first of all seen as spectacle. THE BIRTH OF A NATION would not have been so successful if it were not for the intricate interweaving of more intimate scenes, the small scale that balances the large-scale scenes, but at that moment, the beginning of 1915, it was the size of the spectacle that counted most. Ince's production of THE WRATH OF THE GODS depended on such big, spectacular scenes as "Lava flowing! Houses crumbling! Villages burning! The typhoon at sea!" With all that to look forward to, a spectator could certainly sit patiently through six reels. To a certain degree, spectacle in the feature film revived some of the fascination felt by the earliest movie audiences.[6]

Two methods exploited big spectacle scenes to the greatest advantage: (1) a moving camera, as in CABIRIA, offered a sense of great depth and solidity in enormous sets, or followed action over a broad geography; or (2) large scenes were dissected in editing, providing through a variety of details an otherwise inexpressible sense of a larger whole. Both methods were used during this period.

In 1911–1912 Griffith's Biograph films came in for some sharp criticism for the increasing number of shots. Frank Woods thought that FATE'S INTERCEPTION (April 1912) overdid it: "There seems to be too frequent a change of scene with a rapidity that destroys a full continuity of thought by too much change in action of scenes." In August, when the Reverend Dr. Stockton took a pocket counting machine and stopwatch in hand to make an actual tally of the images flashing across the screen in a week's releases, he targeted THE SANDS OF DEE as the outstanding "horrible example" with 68 shots.[7] (Tom Gunning counted 75 shots in this film when he examined it on a viewing table.) That same month Stockton could have counted, but didn't, 107 shots in MAN'S LUST FOR GOLD. And even that was far from the largest number per reel, which could be found in some of the 1913 films. By 1915 the *New York Times* critic (undoubtedly Alexander Woollcott), reflecting on THE BIRTH OF A NATION, contended:

> The film director, flushed with the realization that he could move about
> with a freedom unknown to the stage, has been so delighted with this

Fleeing the volcanic eruption in THE WRATH OF THE GODS *(Mutual, 1914), supervised by Thomas H. Ince and directed by Reginald Barker.*

liberty that he has indulged himself incontinently, without pausing to consider that he might be playing havoc with that precious element called tension. It is easy to predict that the cut back, and similar evidences of restlessness, will fade gradually from the screens, to be used only on special occasions (reprinted in George Pratt, *Spellbound in Darkness*, p. 208).

Many other producers followed Griffith's lead, but none went to such lengths as he did. The reaction to this development marks one of those turns in film history that shock and unsettle their first audiences and later are taken for granted, such as the effect of the moving camera in L'AVVENTURA (1960) or the jump cuts in À BOUT DE SOUFFLE (1960). To be sure, mainstream or classical Hollywood cinema followed the prediction of the *Times* critic. Griffith was an individualist who tested extremes, who had an enormous impact on the construction of narrative systems at the base of classical Hollywood cinema, but who in the end drifted outside the dominant cinema, just as he remained something of an outsider in the industrial production system after he left Biograph.

The increasing number of shots in the Griffith Biograph films (and to a lesser extent in the work of other filmmakers) in the same years when the multireel film was appearing in growing numbers may have indicated Griffith's restlessness with the limits of the form, which he seemed always to be testing. However, the rapid cutting in these films was rarely due to the breaking up of the scene into details: the high number of shots in a Biograph film reflected an emphasis on alternate editing: the dividing of the action into numerous separate locations and cutting between them;

when the producer returned to the same scene, he usually employed the same camera position. With the exception of occasional inserted close-ups, the integrity of the single scene was still important even in these rapidly cut films, although the concept was in process of change.[8]

To maintain perspective on the narrative systems in use at this time, let us remember that some films were still being made in one shot, from one camera position, and in full-figure shot. In THE BORROWED FLAT (American, 1911), for example, the one shot is interrupted only by titles, some of them announcing time lapses. Two men play practical jokes on each other, just as they did in comedy films in the days before 1907. And as Robert Grau observed at the time, director Thomas Ricketts' claim to fame in 1914 was dependent on

> the famous one-thousand-feet-no-stop pictures, that is, one entire scene of a thousand feet without a stop or a sub-title. Motion picture followers will recall the earlier Essanay releases, "Justified," "Gratitude," "The Adventuress," "A Woman's Wit," and similar productions, produced, written and acted in by Ricketts, in which there was no change of scene for one thousand feet of film (*The Theatre of Science*, p. 366).[9]

Many other films of the 1907–1915 period used simple linear cutting, progressing from one scene, one shot, to the next for most of their length. We really cannot say with certainty, on the basis of surviving films, that the newer narrative systems we have been describing—and which are most evident in the work of D. W. Griffith at Biograph, of Thomas Ince at "101" Bison, and of Reginald Barker, Ralph Ince, Herbert Brenon, Sidney Olcott, Lois Weber and Phillips Smalley, and a handful of others—were dominant in this period.

Now, simultaneously with the growth of the multireel film, some producers, at least, increasingly began to employ elements of what we now call "scene dissection." This is the editing of shots taken from different positions and angles in the same scene, where previously only one position, one shot, would have been used. Such editing further increases the fragmentation of film space. Its use is justified on the grounds that in reality the spectator looks at only one part of a scene at a time, glancing from one person to another; therefore scene dissection may lend itself to (1) a greater illusion of reality, and (2) more control over the spectator's thoughts and feelings. The new use of the moving camera, asymmetrical compositions, and the cutting-in of dialogue titles signaled a shift in space perception. Such a shift affected the dissection of the scene as well. Producers of the spectacle film, with its immense sets, huge crowds, and big sweep of action, also found it useful to dissect scenes into smaller details.

One reason for the increase in scene dissection was the need for diversity within the film itself, previously supplied by a variety of short films. This motive finds some support in a scriptwriting manual of 1914, which explains that "the close-view has no equal for breaking dangerously long scenes." Now that it was necessary to hold spectator interest over a longer time span, the change in position would save tedium. A stronger motive, however, may be found in the growing complexity of narratives in feature films and the desire to portray psychological depth.[10]

Cuts to close views of the same scene, called "inserts," are probably the earliest manifestation of scene dissection. They required a physical cut in the film material to place the insert in the scene. Close-view inserts were no longer rare in 1912 (and, as we pointed out earlier, they were not unusual before 1907). Many close views in intervening years were achieved by having the actor move closer to the camera without breaking up the shot. Earlier, when the close-ups were inserted, they were apt to be filmed at just the same position as the larger scene, on the same axis to the camera, but closer. Probably there was a fear of disorientation for the spectator if the angle was not preserved when the close-up was cut in. In Vitagraph's NAPOLEON, THE MAN OF DESTINY (April 1909), there is a cut to mid-shot on the scene in which Napoleon, in a crowded room, is holding a child on his lap. At that time, when children appeared in a film, it was not uncommon to place the camera closer than was done for adults. The closer view of Napoleon and child is photographed from the same angle as the previous shot, but the background figures and objects in the closer view are different, either out of carelessness or, more likely, because the filmmaker did not think of the two shots as continuous in time. When cuts to close views became more common in the next few years, however, most such cuts would be carefully matched, in order to make them appear spatially and temporally related.

The newer way to handle a cut to a close-up may be seen in American Eclair's FILIAL LOVE (September 1912), in which there is a three-shot sequence showing a little boy writing a note. The cut goes from a medium shot to a close-up and back to the medium shot. The cut is on action and perfectly matched. The medium shot is at an almost frontal angle, while the close-up is over the boy's shoulder. This sequence of shots signifies a radical change in approach from the cut to closer view in the Napoleon film. There was no longer the feeling that the viewer must be eased into the change of proportion. Now the intervening space could be eliminated with a cut, and the spectator could easily accept another angle. The users of the new narrative system showed confidence in being able to lead the spectator through these changes without disorientation.

Another important factor in the development of scene dissection is the shot motivated by a character's point of view. This editing of shots occurs in a few cases in the pre-1907 period as well, in the two-shot sequences consisting of a character looking at or hearing something out of the frame, followed by the shot of what the person sees or hears. These sequences would normally be shown in reversed angles, such as the point of view of people attending the theater in THE DRUNKARD'S REFORMATION (Biograph, April 1909) and many other films with "spectator" sequences. One shot shows the spectators looking more or less in the direction of the camera; the next shows the stage frontally as they see it.

A newer version of reverse-angle editing appears in BILLY'S STRATAGEM (Biograph, February 1912), showing two children pursued by Indians and running toward the safety of the stockade. The sequence is cut in a series of alternate shots, representing each group's point of view of the other. Here, however, not all of the angles are quite frontal to the camera as the film cuts from one point of view to the other, since filmmakers had discovered that continuity could be held while varying the shots, as long as there was careful attention to screen direction. The added implication of a change of angle is that it is no longer necessarily the point of view of one of the characters: it may be a privileged point of view, that of the "narrator" or the film's spectators.

Attention to screen direction was a "rule" of editing that was only now beginning to be considered important. Today referred to as the "eye-line match," the rule dictates that when cutting from one person's gaze to another, the camera should maintain an angle that seems to remain "in front" of the scene. If the angle to which one cuts is too extreme, the spectator will have a feeling of having jumped to a new position, behind the actors. Once again, the purpose is to keep the spectator oriented from one shot to the next. Most spectators would not realize why they experienced disorientation, but they would probably feel it anyway, and even more strongly once they became accustomed to this guidance from the producer. The film historian Barry Salt reports that in tests conducted with film-school students in recent times, the spectators were totally unconscious of mismatched eyeline direction. Nevertheless, if filmmakers were concerned enough about the problem to make it into an editing "rule," it must have affected them as spectators, and presumably their contemporaries as well. The growing complexities of the feature film demanded more guidance for the spectator as more drastic changes in form were taking place.[11]

Point-of-view shots may be one of the most common elements of scene dissection, showing as they do groups of people talking and reacting to each other. Yet, when there are shots within the same scene and location that do not depend on a character's point of view, I think we can mark the beginnings of a more modern kind of scene dissection, and one that follows in the same direction as earlier developments in the creation of a narrative system, where the "narrator" is built into the film.

This may be illustrated with a sequence from the Vitagraph film RED AND WHITE ROSES (March 1913, probably directed by Ralph Ince). The sequence deals with a plot to ruin the reputation of a political candidate and takes place in a restaurant. It begins with a title:

Title: "Murray of the opposition notes that Lida's brilliance makes an impression on Andrew."

1. Andrew and his wife sit at a foreground table, with a merry group at another table behind them. Andrew seems to be looking at Lida at the other table.
2. Similar camera angle but close enough to exclude the foreground couple while showing a closer view of the vivacious Lida and her friends.
3. Return to first shot: Lida may be noticing Andrew, maybe not.
4. At a third table, seen in the background of shot one, two men are observing Andrew's gaze toward Lida.
5. Return to second shot: Lida laughing, a man leaves the table.
6. Return to first shot: Andrew gazing at Lida.
7. Return to fourth shot: the man from Lida's table now joins the two men, and they exchange confidential whispered remarks.
8. Return to the first shot: the group at Lida's table gets up to leave; one man comes forward to greet Andrew and his wife and then introduces Lida to Andrew at the left of the image. She meets Andrew's gaze and smiles.

In this example all the shots take place within the same location, the restaurant. The first cut is motivated by a gaze and is at much the same camera angle. The cut from shot 3 to shot 4, however, does not appear to be any character's point of view. It does involve a gaze, of course, inasmuch as the two men have been watching the other people, but this is only apparent after the cut. The point may seem minor, but in fact it marks the significant shift in the way of filming a scene that was taking place in this period. There is a much more complex narration than would have occurred if, as in the earlier system, this sequence had been filmed as one shot.

Instances of scene dissection may be found in a considerable number of films from 1913 to 1914.[12] The gambling sequence in THE SPOILERS (Selig, July 1914), for example, shows the conventions of scene dissection to be established in a way quite close to the future Hollywood style:

1. Master scene showing the gambling table.
Title: "My share of the Midas against . . ."
2. Close-up of hero looking down to the right.
3. Semi-close-up of the "good-bad" woman facing camera.
4. Semi-close-up of the dealer looking to the left.
5. Reduced view of master scene, in which the above three characters dominate the scene, although others crowd around.
6. Extreme close-up of the dealer's hands and the cards.
7. Master scene as in shot 1: the hero reacts.

D. W. Griffith also turned to scene dissection when he began to make feature films, and, as in the case of rapid cutting, he used the device in a way unique to himself, more extreme, if you will. Louis Reeves Harrison had noted a new film trend in the summer of 1914 (probably influenced by popular interest in the work of Sigmund Freud):

> There is another form of visualized story, which may be called "intense drama." . . . It dissects . . . some mysterious working of the human mind. . . . We are far from being what we think we are and there are many exciting adventures yet to be made into the dark realms of mental change, adventures which can be used to awaken high suspense and, at the same time, fascinate us by startling revelations concerning our personal relations to the forces directing our careers (*Moving Picture World,* 11 July 1914, p. 208).

RED AND WHITE ROSES sequence. The actors are Earle Williams (Andrew), Edith Storey (his wife), Julia Swayne Gordon (Lida), and Harry T. Morey (Murray).

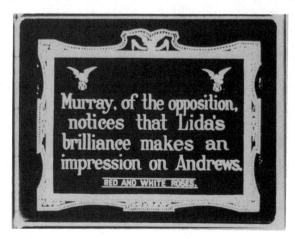

Shot 1, last of 37 frames.

Shot 2, frame 5 (of 49).

Shot 3, frame 47 (of 61).

Shot 4, frame 14 (of 54).

Shot 5, frame 2 (of 105).

Shot 6, frame 90 (of 90).

Shot 7, frame 2 (of 78).

Shot 8, frame 2 (of 358).

Shot 8, frame 23.

Shot 8, frame 123.

Shot 8, frame 160.

Shot 8, frame 239.

He was referring specifically to THE NORTHERN LIGHTS and THE ESCAPE, both known as "psychological dramas," but he could have been describing Griffith's THE AVENGING CONSCIENCE (Reliance-Majestic, August 1914) as well. The celebrated sequence showing the detective's questioning of Henry B. Walthall, who is being driven to madness by his guilt feelings, consumes nearly fifty shots. The sequence includes only about three or four shots that might be considered master shots: medium shots of the two sitting together in Walthall's study. There is one exterior shot showing two men waiting and several "vision" shots showing Walthall's mental torment—an owl in a tree ruffling his feathers and hooting (two shots), and the demons of hell (two shots). The remainder (approximately forty shots) consists of a variety of close-ups, most of them extreme close-ups; Walthall's clasped hands on his knees, thumbs twisting; the detective's hand tapping a pencil on the desk, the swinging of the pendulum of the clock, the detective's foot under the desk, tapping; Walthall's nervous smiles, his darting eyes. In the cutting, rhythms are picked up from the content of the shots, and a title underlines the metaphor: "Like the beating of the dead man's heart."

Another factor in the growth of the feature was an increasing perception of film as art. In the words of Jesse L. Lasky, "Features . . . provoked the word art in connection with the moving picture."[13] As early as 1909, the aesthetic qualities of some films were being singled out. THE LITTLE SHEPHERD OF TUMBLING RUN from the Edison studio in the spring of 1909 was praised in the name of artistic achievement. It was poetic, one critic wrote, the tones and lighting sublime. In October 1909 PIPPA

Henry B. Walthall and friend in THE AVENGING CONSCIENCE.

PASSES, from Biograph, drew the attention of the *New York Times*, which at that time largely ignored the nickelodeon fare. The reviewer compared the lighting effects in PIPPA PASSES to those achieved by the Secessionist photographers. As it happens, Alfred Stieglitz's Gallery of the Photo-Secession, where this movement had its center, was on Fifth Avenue, around the corner from Biograph's Fourteenth Street studio. Stieglitz was dedicated to obtaining recognition for photography as a fine art, and in its early days, the Secessionist group had strongly emphasized the pictorial qualities of photography, which were influenced by nineteenth-century painting. (By 1911 and 1912, however, the Stieglitz gallery was also exhibiting the latest in modern painting and sculpture.)[14]

The idea that film might be considered an art form appeared at first in a similar search for pictorial elements. As Frank Woods wrote at the end of 1910:

> There is increasing evidence that film manufacturers are becoming thoroughly awake to the great value of making their scenic backgrounds, together with the groupings of the characters, conform to artistic ideals, so that the scenes and the players will stand out as attractive pictures, as well as having dramatic or story values, and all this is very much as it should be. The French have been very successful in this respect, and have had the advantage of the wonderful scenery and architecture of the old world to make their selections less difficult. But the American producers are improving to a gratifying extent. In a film production last week by the Selig Company, A Tale of the Sea, there were several well studied scenes, and in recent films produced by the Essanay Company, the Edison Company, the Kalem Company, the Reliance Company, the Vitagraph and the Biograph companies there have been notable instances of artistic effect. It is a point that film producers should bear constantly in mind (*New York Dramatic Mirror*, 21 December 1910, p. 29).

In search of the pictorial, producers every now and then took to the reproduction of well-known paintings. Biograph proudly called attention to "an animated reproduction of Jean François Millet's Masterpiece, 'The Sowers,' " in their description of A CORNER IN WHEAT (December 1909). A reporter noted that in Lubin's THE IRISH BOY, released on St. Patrick's Day in 1910, "One of the settings showing a cabin in Ireland is from a famous painting, one of the poses reproducing that painting entire."[15]

The link between painting and film was also taken up in early film criticism and theory. In a 1913 editorial, the *World* suggested that aspiring scenarists might visit the picture galleries for inspiration:

> One of the recent successes of the art world in Europe was a problem picture, if we may so call it, entitled "The Fallen Idol." This picture was by the Honorable John Collier, a well-known painter who has made a specialty of problem pictures. . . . The majority of great paintings, display incidents: historical, dramatic, and so forth. Modern art, however, is turning more and more to the problematical. As in the play, so in the picture. . . . Writers and painters of advanced methods of thought think it the right thing to leave you guessing. Now in this picture (there were

reproductions of it in the New York Times and other papers in this country last summer) . . . we see a man seated, as it were, at his study table with a troubled expression on his face. At his feet kneels in suppliant attitude a beautiful girl, presumably his wife. . . . Now we see that a film maker in Europe has taken this picture as the kernel of a film story. . . . To the best of our recollection, this is the first instance in which a single picture has formed the inspiration of a film play. (*Motion Picture News*, 8 November 1913, p. 14).

In an article in Stieglitz's magazine *Camera Work*, the film theorist Sadakichi Hartmann recommended "short episodes in which all the laws of composition, color and chiaroscuro are obeyed, just as in a painting," and proposed such romantic paintings as Böcklin's *Villa at the Sea* as sources of films:

—Old Roman architecture, with waving pinions, and the approach of a coming storm. The wave would caress the shore, the leaves would be carried away by the wind, and into this scene of melancholy and solitude would enter a dark draped figure who in a few superb gestures, would express the essence of grief ("The Esthetic Significance of the Motion Picture," in *Camera Work*, April 1912, p. 21).

The scenarist Maibelle Heikes Justice had already followed the recommended method of visiting the art galleries, but her reaction was quite different. The famous Armory Show of the spring of 1913 presented a more radical version of modern art than the Honorable John Collier's "problem picture" in the 1912 season. Maibelle Heikes Justice was a very successful scriptwriter and representative of popular culture. When she visited the International Cubists' Exhibition, she, like countless other witnesses, found it to be a great inspiration for comedy, and she wrote a new scenario the next day. Selig promptly produced it as THE POST-IMPRESSIONISTS (May 1913, directed by Hardee Kirkland), "a rip-roaring comedy on the Futurists and Cubists. There is a 'cube to a cupful' and then some." Noted the approving reviewer, "It is the silly season of the Cubists and we have been watching and waiting for something to freak."[16]

In a more serious vein, Louis Reeves Harrison called attention to characteristics of "modern art" that he found in a feature film called AFTER DEATH (NACH DEM TODE, Germany, October 1913, distributed in the United States in November). I think he may have been referring to French impressionism, but it is difficult to be sure. What is significant is that films might now aspire to be works of art in themselves:

There is an expression, even more important than beauty, that affects the emotions, a new and rather rare thing in moving pictures, though a highly-prized characteristic in modern paintings of rhythmic intensity. It was though one sat watching a series of expressionist pictures in exquisite tints, where ordinarily hard lines, glaring lights and smudges instead of soft shadows make outdoor effects and those indoors as well almost as repulsive as old-fashioned wall paper. [It] is a work of art (*Moving Picture World*, 22 November 1913, p. 873).

Henry B. Walthall in THE BIRTH OF A NATION *(Epoch, 1915), directed by D. W. Griffith.*

If a film were to be considered as art, then there must be an artist, and, according to the nineteenth-century romantic tradition, an artist who is a creative genius. The title of artist in this sense was awarded to D. W. Griffith by Louis Reeves Harrison when Griffith left Biograph in 1913. When Griffith entered films at the end of 1907, the publicized creator of the film was the production company, and films were sold by the brand. Now, at the end of 1913, Harrison set forth the myth of Griffith as the dreamer-artist opposed to practical businessmen who tried to hold him back. In a publicity story subtitled "The Art Director and His Work" (the term "art director" for the one who designs the film was not yet in use), Harrison wrote that "his efforts" were "hindered by the traditions of the studio," but the absence of the chief director for a few days in the summer of 1908 gave Griffith the chance to stage a picture as he wanted. Just a few weeks earlier, W. Stephen Bush had written, "[Griffith] has introduced many rules of moving picture stage craft which are recognized as absolutely essential to the art today and he possesses a power to tell 'a story in pictures' which almost amounts to genius." It is almost impossible, however, to find any contemporary published reference to Griffith's important contributions to the art of editing in this period. In 1914 Harry Aitken acknowledged them in a general sense, when he credited Griffith with "new ideas of . . . scenic arrangement or 'cutting' as we call it." he added, "Proper editing of the film should be a matter of weeks, not of minutes," explaining Griffith's system of tryouts in theaters before the real public, which allowed him to study the effect on the audience. "On that foundation," he explained, "we make the final cutting."[17]

Only a few people of culture at this time were really prepared to think of films as art, however. Others would say that such an idea was unrealistic, in the light of film's nature as a product of a major industry. Nonetheless, it was a time of high ideals in the years before World War I, and artistic ferment was in the air all over the world, even if the breath of the latest movements in the fine arts did not always reach the moving-picture people. There were still some parallels to be drawn between the expression of the new film art and the ideas bursting forth in other forms. One of the tenets of the modern-art movement as it was to develop in the following years was that the motion picture is the new art medium of the twentieth century. One of the earliest to begin to consider this possibility was Sadakichi Hartmann, a supporter of modern art who was struck, as were other intellectuals of the day, by the great popularity of the moving picture. He wrote, in the *Camera Work* article cited above:

> It contains some element that appeals to the masses, and whenever I see one of these auditoriums packed to standing room only, I become conscious that I am in the presence of something that touches the pulse-beat of time, something that interests a large number of people and in a way reflects their esthetic taste (p. 19).

At the same time, he declared that he did see traces of art in the movies:

> I know that most cultivated people feel a trifle ashamed of acknowledging that they occasionally attend moving picture shows. . . . To my mind there is not the slightest doubt that these performances show much that is vivid, instructive and picturesque, and also occasionally a fleeting vision of something that is truly artistic. Of course, it is generally not the story which interests me but the representation of mere incidents, a rider galloping along a mountain path, a handsome woman with hair and skirts fluttering in the wind, the rushing water of a stream, the struggle of two desperate men in some twilight atmosphere. These fragmentary bits of life, or merely of scenery, with the animating spirit of motion as main attraction, contain all the elements of pure esthetic pleasure (pp. 20–21).

Hartmann exemplified the current approach to the artistic qualities of film when he added, "Only when poetic and pictorial expression become the main object will it develop in esthetic lines."[18]

George Soule, writing of the drama and the new ballet of Pavlova and Folkine in the *Little Review* in May 1914, thought that the masses might be led to these higher forms by their experience with the movies, and went on, in a later issue, to express his gratitude that the films created a crisis for the stage, which he considered to be in a low state: "It is but a step from a moving picture such as D'Annunzio's *Cabiria* to a spectacle such as Reinhardt's *The Miracle*." The older and more conservative literary journal *The Dial* devoted an editorial in February 1914 to "The Cinematograph Craze," admiring the recent film illustrations of two literary masterpieces, LES MISÉRABLES and DANTE'S INFERNO.[19]

George Pratt has some incisive observations to make on the cinematic parallels of the time with other modern-art movements:

> Griffith's bold juggling with, and breakneck pacing of film editing in 1912 and 1913—his use of motion continually intercepted, and continually resumed—exactly coincided with the American public's growing awareness in those years of a restless "crisis which threatens all the arts." Reports from abroad described the "hysterical yelling" of the singer in Schönberg's revolutionary composition "Pierrot Lunaire," a work which seemed to be "strung together at random," and sounded "like madness." In his quarterly, *Camera Work*, Stieglitz published the baffling Gertrude Stein on "Henri Matisse" and "Pablo Picasso," asserting that this was "the Post-Impressionist spirit . . . expressing itself in literary form." Miss Stein herself, in later years, explained that in these two pieces she was "doing what the cinema was doing": building up each portrait with statements superficially the same, but subtly different, like the successive frames of a strip of film, but to one enraged reader, she was inexcusably tearing words loose from their meanings, applying an egg-beater to the brain (*Spellbound in Darkness*, p. 105).[20]

In a 1914 interview, J. Searle Dawley, a former Edison director now directing for Famous Players, offered a definition of film art as what he called "the drama of silence":

> The drama of silence is human emotion conveyed by the poetry of movement. . . . The art of the drama of silence is movement prompted by emotions, not emotions represented by movement, as in the art of pantomime. The sequence of events and method of constructing a story give us an opportunity to eliminate what is called pantomime. An actor may stand motionless, gazing into a lighted window, and convey to the mind all the depths of love or hate. The intelligence of his position is carried to the spectator by what has gone before or by what may come afterwards. . . . It is the sequence of movement and scenes that is really the essence of this new art.

What is particularly interesting about his definition is the underlying notion that the spectator now participates in the film:

> The universal appeal which the drama of silence has for the entire world lies in the fact that each auditor is creating his own emotions and language for the characters before him on the canvas, and they are according to his own mental and spiritual standard. Therefore, the spectator is supplying the thoughts and words of the actor and becomes a part of the performance itself. This, I fully believe, is the reason for the phenomenal popularity of the drama of silence throughout the world today (*Moving Picture World*, 31 January 1914, pp. 547–548).

The following year saw the publication of Vachel Lindsay's *The Art of the Moving Picture* and William Morgan Hannon's *The Photodrama: Its Place Among the Fine Arts*. Lindsay pronounced his thesis in capital letters: "THE MOTION PICTURE ART IS A GREAT HIGH ART, NOT A PROCESS OF COMMERCIAL MANU-FACTURE." "It is not a factory-made staple article," he insisted, "but the product of the creative force of one soul, the flowering of a spirit that has the habit of perpetually renewing itself." Hannon, meanwhile, argued that the motion picture "is a *representative* fine art, like sculpture and painting, rather than a *presentative* one, like architecture or music" (emphasis in original). For both authors, film was related to painting, sculpture, music, and architecture. The idea that it should be thought of as "canned" theater, still held by some studio executives and theatrical impresarios, was now out-of-date. Only in an age of idealism could Lindsay so boldly challenge reality as to deny the motion picture its commercial basis. Most producers might have granted Lindsay his "poetic license" and continued to try to find ways to run a profitable business. Nevertheless the appearance of Vachel Lindsay's book provides some indication of the distance traveled since 1907, when an industry was struggling to mass-produce a factory product. It reflects some of the excitement felt by intellectuals when, in 1915, they began to look at the extraordinary phenomenon of the motion picture.[21]

322 South Adams Street, Peoria, Illinois, January 1916.

List of Abbreviations

FREQUENTLY CITED PERIODICALS

MPW   Moving Picture World
NYDM   New York Dramatic Mirror

CASE CITATIONS

US v. MPPC   United States of America v. Motion Pictures Patent Company et al.

Notes

CHAPTER 1. The Nickelodeon

1. *MPW*, 16 January 1909, p. 57.
2. *MPW*, 15 October 1910, p. 848.
3. Frank Howard, *US* v. *MPPC* 3:1849 (19 November 1913). See also testimony of Aaron Brylawski (exhibitor in Washington, D.C.), *US* v. *MPPC* 6:3243–3244, and that of Arthur Talmadge (exhibitor in Brooklyn, N.Y.), 6:3251–3252 (March–April 1914).
4. *The Willimantic Journal*, cited in *MPW*, 4 July 1908, p. 6.
5. *MPW*, 29 May 1909, p. 711 and 31 December 1910, p. 1541.
6. Joseph Medill Paterson, "The Nickelodeons: The Poor Man's Elementary Course in the Drama," *Saturday Evening Post*, 23 November 1907, pp. 10–11, 38.
7. Patterson, "The Nickelodeons"; *MPW*, 9 July 1910, p. 92. The word "subtitles" was in use throughout this period, although today we often reserve this term for the titles printed on the image of sound films and use the more descriptive "intertitles" for silent films.
8. The nickelodeon was located at the Tompkins Square Vaudeville, 103 Avenue B in New York, and the Herr Professor was Dr. Lamberger. He lectured with ROMEO AND JULIET on 12 May 1908, THE SCARLET LETTER on 13 May, JUDITH AND HOLOFERNES on 14 May, and RIP VAN WINKLE on 15 May.
9. *Variety*, 26 January 1907, p. 12; *MPW*, 4 May 1907, p. 140; Patterson, "The Nickelodeons," p. 46; *Oakland Tribune* (California), cited in *MPW*, 11 July 1908, p. 2.
10. *MPW*, 15 May 1909, p. 631; *US* v. *MPPC*, vol. 4, Defendant's Exhibits 154 and 155; Robert Grau, *The Theatre of Science* (New York: Broadway, 1914), pp. 116–117.
11. *MPW*, 1 August 1908, p. 83, and 3 June 1911, p. 1248.
12. *MPW*, 25 July 1908, p. 63 (Grand Rapids); 31 July 1909, p. 163 (Philadelphia); 11 September 1908, p. 195 (Lubin); 7 August 1909, p. 189 (Rochester).
13. *MPW*, 9 October 1909, p. 732 (Chicago) and 26 October 1912, p. 329; *US* v. *MPPC* 4:2236 (testimony of Ike Van Ronkel, manager of the Chicago branch of General Film, 8 December 1913).
14. *MPW*, 15 August 1908, p. 121 (New York); Robert C. Allen, "Motion Picture Exhibition in Manhattan, 1906–1912: Beyond the Nickelodeon," in John L. Fell, ed., *Film Before Griffith* (Berkeley: University of California Press, 1983); *MPW*, 4 June 1910, p. 934; report of Raymond B. Fosdick to Mayor William J. Gaynor of New York, 22 March 1911, cited in *MPW*, 20 April 1911, p. 879; *An Ordinance Relating to Motion Picture Theatres*, Mayor's Bureau of Licenses, New York City, adopted 1 July 1913 (it defines a motion-picture theater as one where capacity does not exceed 600 and there is no stage or scenery); *MPW*, 15 May 1909, p. 631 and 11 June 1910, p. 986.
15. Russell Merritt, "Nickelodeon Theaters, 1905–1914: Building an Audience for the Movies," in Tino Balio, ed., *The American Film Industry* (Madison: University of Wisconsin Press, 1976), pp. 59–79; Allen, "Motion Picture Exhibition in Manhattan."
16. According to Frank L. Dyer, in *US* v. *MPPC* 3:1502 (10 November 1913): "The usual price of admission then, and at the present time is five cents. In some localities the price is ten cents or more, where the theatres are very large, or where the program is so long that the audience cannot be changed often." *Motion Picture News*, 19 December 1914, p. 31; *MPW*, 2 January 1915, p. 103.

17. Lary May, *Screening Out the Past* (New York: Oxford University Press, 1980), p. 3.

18. Charles Musser with Carol Nelson, *High Class Moving Pictures: Lyman H. Howe and the Traveling Exhibitor* (Princeton, N.J.: Princeton University Press, 1990).

19. *MPW*, 25 October 1913, p. 363.

20. *MPW*, 30 July 1910, p. 249

21. "Notes from Chicago," *MPW*, 5 February 1910, p. 170, mentions several very poor places that were showing films without any musical accompaniment. *MPW*: 14 January 1911, p. 75. (Evansville); 3 December 1910, p. 1293 (New England); 9 November 1912, pp. 564, 566 (musicians' strikes).

22. *MPW*, 20 November 1909, p. 717, and 4 June 1910, p. 945.

23. *MPW*, 2 October 1909, p. 447, and 23 October 1909, p. 559.

24. Fred J. Balshofer and Arthur C. Miller, *One Reel a Week* (Berkeley: University of California Press, 1967), p. 3; Norma Talmadge, "Close-ups," *The Saturday Evening Post*, 12 March 1927, reprinted in Balio, ed., *The American Film Industry*, pp. 83–101.

25. *Motion Picture News*, 13 June 1914, p. 108 (advertisement for Imperial Singing Pictures: "Animated Songs"); *ibid.*, 13 June 1914, p. 107 (ad for Renfax Musical Motion Pictures: "The latest song hits and vaudeville acts on the screen, our pictures require no singer").

26. *MPW*, 19 October 1912, p. 220.

27. *MPW*, 22 April 1911, p. 877; Robert C. Allen, *Vaudeville and Film, 1895–1915: A Study in Media Interaction* (New York: Arno Press, 1980).

28. Marcus Ravage and others cited in Irving Howe and Kenneth Libo, eds., *How We Lived: A Documentary History of Immigrant Jews in America, 1880–1930* (New York: Richard Marek, 1979), pp. 279–280.

29. *MPW*, 23 May 1908, pp. 459–460, and 4 July 1908, pp. 28, 428. The "crisis in film narrative" has been well described in two 1986 Ph.D. dissertations completed at New York University: Tom Gunning, "D. W. Griffith and the 'Narrator-System': Narrative Structure and Industry Organization in Biograph Films, 1908–1909," and Charles Musser "Before the Nickelodeon: Edwin S. Porter and the Edison Manufacturing Company." The latter is to be published by the University of California Press in 1990.

CHAPTER 2. A Game of Freeze-Out

1. William Swanson on cross-examination, *US* v. *MPPC* 1:492–493 (23 January 1913).

2. Figures are estimated on basis of films released in last ten months of 1907 as recorded in the *Moving Picture World*. See Lawrence Karr's introduction to Rita Horwitz, *Index to Volume I, 1907, Moving Picture World and View Photographer* (Washington, D.C.: American Film Institute, 1974); Musser, *Before the Nickelodeon*; Jon Gartenberg, "Vitagraph before Griffith: Forging Ahead in the Nickelodeon Era," *Studies in Visual Communication* (Fall 1984), pp. 7–23; Pathé Frères catalog, 1907.

3. Jeremiah J. Kennedy on cross-examination, *US* v. *MPPC* 6:3235 (17 March 1913); Terry Ramsaye, *A Million and One Nights* (1926 reprinted; New York: Simon and Schuster, 1964), pp. 468–470; Albert Smith, *Two Reels and a Crank* (Garden City, N.Y.: Doubleday, 1952), p. 77; "Our Man About Town," *MPW*, 29 April 1911, p. 942 (internal evidence shows that Richard Hollaman of the Eden Musee is "Our Man About Town").

4. Ralph Cassady, Jr., *Monopoly in Motion Picture Production and Distribution, 1908–1915* (Los Angeles: Bureau of Business and Economic Research, University of California, 1959); Albert E. Smith (of Vitagraph), *US* v. *MPPC* 3:1714 (14 November 1913); J. A. Berst (of Pathé Frères), *US* v. *MPPC* 3:1761 (18 November 1913); *Ciné-Journal* 60 (11–18 October 1909), pp. 3–4.

5. Charles Musser, "The American Vitagraph," in Fell, *Film Before Griffith*; Eileen Bowser, "Preparation for Brighton: The American Contribution," in Roger Holman, ed., *Cinema 1900–1906: An Analytical Study* (London: Fédération Internationale des Archives du Film, 1982): vol. 1, pp. 3–29.

6. Musser, *Before the Nickelodeon*; Karr, introduction to Horwitz, *Index to Moving Picture World* (production figures); Frank L. Dyer, *US* v. *MPPC* 3:1497–1525 (10 November 1913).

7. Samuel Long (of Kalem), *US* v. *MPPC* 4:1898–1899 (20 November 1913); Gene Gauntier, "Blazing the Trail," unpublished manuscript, Museum of Modern Art Film Study Center, Special Collections, pp. 4–16 (published in part in *Women's Home Companion*, 1928–1929); Samuel Long, *US* v. *MPPC* 4:1899 (20 November 1913) (he replaced Kleine as president of Kalem in 1908); Musser, *Before the Nickelodeon*, p. 516. Note that this account differs from that of Robert Jack Anderson, "The Motion Picture Patents Company," Ph.D. diss. University of Wisconsin, Madison, 1983, p. 82. Anderson's statements are contradicted by the dates of Kalem's founding and licensing.

8. Frank L. Dyer, *US* v. *MPPC* 3:1502 (10 November 1913); *MPW*, 6 November 1909, p. 638; George Spoor (of Essanay), *US* v. *MPPC* 5:2986–2984 (10 March 1914); *Variety*, 15 February 1908, p. 10; letter of William T. Rock to Albert Smith (31 January 1908) in Albert Smith Collection, University of California, Los Angeles, cited in Musser, "Before the Nickelodeon," pp. 516–518 (*re* Essanay's license).

9. J. Stuart Blackton, *US* v. *MPPC* 4:1880 (20 November 1914) (on Kleine's role); memorandum of 29 July 1908, in Kleine collection, Museum of Modern Art Film Study Center.

10. *Variety*, 29 February 1908, p. 10; Jacques Berst, *US* v. *MPPC* 3:1776 (18 November 1913); Armat-Jenkins agreement of 21 March 1908, *US* v. *MPPC* 4:2166.

11. Petitioner's Exhibit No. 9, Edison license agreement of 15 February 1908, *US* v. *MPPC* 1:350–356.

12. *MPW*, 4 July 1908, p. 18.

13. Frank Dyer, *US* v. *MPPC* 3:1497–1525 (10 November 1913); William Swanson, *US* v. *MPPC* 1:293–323 (21 January 1913).

14. *MPW*, 14 March 1908, p. 205.

15. Kleine Collection, Museum of Modern Art Film Study Center.

16. Carl W. Ackerman, *George Eastman* (Boston & New York: Houghton Mifflin Co., 1930).

17. *Ciné-Journal* report reprinted in *MPW*, 5 December 1908, p. 447, and 12 September 1908, p. 191 (Pathé's New York office).

18. Harry N. Marvin (of Biograph), *US* v. *MPPC* 1:7–257 (15–17 January 1913) (on establishment of *MPPC*); Petitioner's Exhibits 1–78, *US* v. *MPPC* (agreements, bulletins to exchanges and exhibitors, etc.); *MPW*, 26 December 1908, p. 519, and 9 January 1909, p. 29 (editorial).

19. *MPW*, 26 December 1908, p. 519 (Méliès listed as one of licensees); 31 July 1909, p. 152 (G. Méliès advertisement announces Patents Company license granted); 9 October 1909, p. 487; 23 October 1909, p. 561; *Views and Film Index*, 16 January 1909, p. 5 (Gaston returns from Europe) and 24 July 1909, p. 2 (hearing on trial postponed); James L. Lodge, *US* v. *MPPC* 2:1171–1205 (10 July 1913); Defendants' Exhibit No. 39, opinion of U.S. Circuit Court of Appeals, *Georges Méliès Company* v. *MPPC*, *Edison Manufacturing Company, Georges and Gaston Méliès* (October 1912); Petitioner's Exhibit No. 217, *US* v. *MPPC* 3:1642; Georges Méliès letters to Merritt Crawford (8 December 1930 and 8 April 1931) in the Merritt Crawford Collection), Museum of Modern Art Film Study Center; Jacques Malthête, ed., *Le Voyage autour du monde de la G. Méliès Manufacturing Company* (Paris: Association "Les Amis de Georges Méliès," 1988), pp. 10–11; *Views and Film Index* 7 August 1909, p. 12 (plans for Brooklyn studio and McCutcheon named); *ibid.*, 4 September 1909, p. 2 (new Méliès studio completed and first picture finished on Saturday, 21 August); *ibid.*, 11 September 1909, p. 12 (first films completed); "Méliès Releases Temporarily Suspended," *ibid.*, 18 December 1909, p. 4. Note that Robert Anderson (in *The Motion Picture Patents Company*, pp. 120–122) is in error in saying Méliès was never licensed and operated as an independent.

20. Frank Dyer, *US* v. *MPPC* 3:1497 (10 November 1913); Ackerman, *George Eastman*, pp. 220–227; Petitioner's Exhibit No.. 267, the case of "The Goodwin Film Camera Company v. Eastman Kodak Company" (1913), *US* v. *MPPC* 6:3294.

21. Marvin to Kleine, 23 November 1908, Kleine Collection Museum of Modern Art Film Study Center; *US* v. *MPPC* 1:242; Agreement of 1 January 1909, between MPPC, Edison, and Eastman, Petitioner's Exhibit No. 133, *US* v. *MPPC* 1:558–582; Petitioner's Exhibit No. 134, 15 June 1909, *US* v. *MPPC* 1:582–604 (agreement amended to include N.I. stock).

22. Petitioner's Exhibit No. 135, Agreement of 14 February 1911, *US* v. *MPPC* 1:632–637 (amending agreement of 1 January 1909, to permit Eastman to sell to unlicensed manufacturers); Cassady, *Monopoly in Motion Picture Production* (case of Hannibal Goodwin).

23. *MPW*, 17 July 1909, pp. 81–84 (retrospective look at the Patents Company at six months old).

24. J. J. Kennedy, *US* v. *MPPC* 6:3156–3206 (March 1914).

25. J. J. Robinson (letter), *MPW*, 4 February 1911, pp. 236–237, and 15 April 1911, p. 820.

CHAPTER 3. The Recruiting Stations of Vice

1. *MPW*, 17 July 1909, p. 81, and 16 January 1909, p. 57.

2. *MPW*, 2 October 1909, p. 447; *New York Evening World*, quoted in *MPW*, 12 March 1910, p. 370; *MPW*, 11 June 1910, pp. 982, 984. The effects on society of new freedoms for women are discussed by Lary May in *Screening Out the Past*.

3. *MPW*, 4 June 1910, p. 922.

4. Will Hemsteger in *MPW*, 13 August 1910, p. 359; Russell Merritt, "Nickelodeon Theaters, 1905–1914: Building an Audience for the Movies," in Balio, ed., *The American Film Industry*.

5. *MPW*, 25 July 1908, p. 63, and 5 December 1908, p. 451. (Jane Addams); *NYDM*, 2 May 1908, p. 17 (Armitage Chapel); Musser and Nelson, *High Class Moving Pictures: Lyman H. Howe and the Traveling Exhibitor*; *MPW*, 24 October 1908, p. 319; 4 June 1910, p. 928 (Mayor Seidel).

6. *NYDM*, 2 May 1908, p. 4, and 2 May 1908, p. 6; Patterson, "The Nickelodeons: The Poor Man's Elementary Course in the Drama," p. 46.

7. *MPW*, 7 August 1909, p. 191; *NYDM*, 2 November 1910, p. 34; *MPW*, September 1910, p. 572.

8. *MPW*, 22 April 1911, p. 878.

9. *MPW*, 2 October 1909, p. 443.

10. *MPW*, 29 August 1908, p. 153; *Variety*, 20 April 1907, 14 March 1908, 21 March 1908; *US v. MPPC* 4:1936 (December 1913), cross-examination of upstate New York exhibitor George Cohen; *MPW*, 2 July 1910, pp. 31–32. The letter describes nearly all scenes of Au Bagne in detail, and a postscript lists films banned by the D.C. police, including some of Griffith's Biograph films.

11. *MPW*, 2 January 1909, p. 32.

12. *MPW*, 15 August 1908, p. 121. I suppose The Unwritten Law to be the film meant by "the old Thaw-White trial pictures." Films got "old" very quickly in those days.

13. W. Stephen Bush, *MPW*, 29 August 1908, p. 153, and 24 July 1909, p. 124.

14. *MPW*, 20 February 1909, p. 200.

15. Musser and Nelson, *High Class Moving Pictures*.

16. *MPW*, 9 July 1910, p. 77; *US v. MPPC* vol. 4 (contains testimony of many exchange men and exhibitors on dislike of the educational film); *MPW*, 6 November 1909, p. 641 (announces preparation of Kleine's first catalogue of educational films).

17. Edison and Biograph *Bulletins* for the films mentioned; *MPW*, 27 April 1912, p. 305 (The Cry of the Children). The Price of Human Life, Edison's Red Cross Seal story for 1913, debunked the fake tuberculosis cures (*MPW*, 6 December 1913, p. 1128).

18. *MPW*, 31 July 1909, p. 165.

19. *MPW*, 25 March 1911, p. 641; Frank Dyer (resident of Montclair), *US v. MPPC* 3:1630 (13 November 1913); *MPW*, 16 November 1912, p. 674. In Wilmette they had made the license fee a prohibitive $10 a day.

20. *MPW*, 4 June 1910, p. 947 (female ushers), and 15 October 1910, pp. 859–860 (woman exhibitor in Boston).

21. Female exhibitors in *MPW*: 16 November 1912, p. 611; 30 November 1912, p. 889; 14 December 1912, p. 1072; 21 December 1912, p. 1192; 13 October 1913, p. 250; 22 November 1913, p. 860; 6 December 1913, pp 1137–1139.

22. *MPW*, 9 January 1909, p. 30.

23. "Our Man About Town," *MPW*, 30 December 1911, p. 1066, credits William Fox as leader of the exhibitors.

24. *MPW*, 6 March 1909, p. 264 and 20 March 1909, p. 335.

25. *MPW*, 27 March 1909, p. 365.

26. The rejection of The Heart of an Outlaw was discovered by Tom Gunning, when he was looking through the early reports of the Board, some of which survive among the Edison Papers at the Edison Historic Site in East Orange, New Jersey.

27. "A Year of Censorship," *Motion Picture News*, 13 June 1914, pp. 39–40; *MPW*, 8 November 1913, pp. 598, 657. The dance film was a demonstration of the latest steps by the young Wallace McCutcheon of the New York musical-comedy stage, son of the former director for Biograph, Edison, and the Georges Méliès Company.

28. *MPW*, 6 December 1913, p. 1133.

29. "A Year of Censorship," *Motion Picture News*, 13 June 1914, pp. 39–40.

30. *Motion Picture News*, 13 June 1914, p. 96.

CHAPTER 4. The Films: Alternate Scenes

1. Gaudreault, "Detours in Film Narrative: The Development of Cross-Cutting," and Charles Musser, "Early Cinema and Edwin Porter," in Roger Holman, ed., *Cinema, 1900–1906: An Analytical Study* (Brussels: FIAF, 1982), pp. 181–200, 261–280.

2. Musser, *Before the Nickelodeon*.

3. *MPW*, 10 October 1908, p. 176; 22 August 1908, p. 13; 7 November 1908, p. 358.

4. Eric Barnouw, *The Magician and the Cinema* (New York: Oxford University Press, 1981); May, *Screening Out the Past*, pp. 250–253.

5. Frank Dyer, *US* v. *MPPC* 3:1538 (11 November 1913); *MPW*, 19 September 1908, p. 211 (Summers).

6. *MPW*, 31 July 1909, p. 151.

7. Grau, *The Theatre of Science*, p. 147. Grau submitted the question to Thomas Edison himself, who quite agreed with him (*MPW*, 4 September 1909, p. 312).

8. Gunning, "D. W. Griffith and the 'Narrator-System.' "

9. John Fell, "Motive, Mischief, and Melodrama: The State of Film Narrative in 1907," in his *Film Before Griffith*, pp. 272–283; Tom Gunning, "Non-Continuity, Continuity, Discontinuity," *Iris* 12 (1984): 102–112.

10. André Gaudreault, "Temporality and Narrativity in Early Cinema, 1900–1906"; Tom Gunning, "The Non-Continuous Style of Early Film, 1900–1906"; and Charles Musser, "Early Cinema of Edwin Porter," in Holman, ed., *Cinema, 1900–1906*, pp. 201–230, 261–280.

11. Alfred Capus, quoted in the *New York Times* (8 March 1908); Thomas Bedding, *MPW*, 13 March 1909, p. 294; F. W. Richardson, *MPW*, 20 February 1909, p. 196, and 20 November 1909, p. 711.

12. *MPW*, 5 November 1910, p. 1043.

13. David Bordwell, Janet Staiger, and Kristin Thompson, *The Classical Hollywood Cinema* (New York: Columbia University Press, 1985), pp. 48, 210.

14. Biograph *Bulletin* No. 162 (18 August 1908) (THE FATAL HOUR); in Kemp Niver, ed., *Biograph Bulletins, 1896–1908* (Los Angeles: Locare Research Group, 1971) p. 377; Biograph *Bulletin* No. 217 (25 February 1909) (AT THE ALTAR); in Eileen Bowser, ed., *Biograph Bulletins, 1908–1912* (New York: Farrar, Straus, and Giroux, 1973), p. 67; *MPW*, 6 March 1909, p. 268.

15. "The Drama of the People" (editorial), *New York Independent*, reprinted in *MPW*, 15 October 1910, p. 865.

16. *MPW*, 10 December 1910, p. 1345; 31 December, p. 1531; 15 July 1911, p. 32.

17. *MPW*, 29 November 1913, pp. 1064–1065.

18. Harold Weston, *The Art of Photo-Play Writing* (London: McBride, Nast, 1916), pp. 35–36.

19. Epes Winthrop Sargent, "Techniques of the Photoplay," *MPW*, 26 August 1911, p. 525.

20. Eileen Bowser, "Toward Narrative, 1907: *The Mill Girl*," Fell, *Film Before Griffith*, pp. 330–338.

21. Frank Woods, " 'Spectator's Comments," *NYDM*, 8 March 1911, p. 29. For a more extended analysis, see Charles Harpole, *Gradients of Depth in the Cinema Image* (New York: Arno Press, 1976).

22. Biograph's ROMANCE OF A JEWESS (October 1908), a story of New York's Lower East Side immigrant population, sold forty-seven copies; THE SALVATION ARMY LASS (March 1909), with a similar setting, sold eighty-four. Each of these films established records for Biograph at the time they appeared. There are other factors, however, which may have influenced the number of copies sold, such as the change from selling direct to exhibitors to selling to the distributors (1 January 1909), the number of exchanges, efficiency of distribution, or sale to foreign countries. (See the Biograph print order book, September 1908–June 1909, Museum of Modern Art Film Study Center, Special Collections.)

23. Eileen Bowser, " 'Old Isaacs the Pawnbroker' et le raccordement d'espaces éloignés," in Jean Mottet, ed., *David Wark Griffith* (Paris: L'Harmattan, 1984), pp. 31–43.

24. Gunning, "D. W. Griffith and the 'Narrator-System.' "

25. Biograph *Bulletin* No. 169 (11 September 1908) (BEHIND THE SCENES), in Bowser, *Biograph Bulletins, 1908–1912*, p. 18.

26. Biograph *Bulletin* No. 135 (8 May 1908) (THE MUSIC MASTER), *Biograph Bulletins, 1896–1908*, p. 349; *MPW*, 26 October 1912, p. 322, and 6 May 1911, p. 1020.

27. Bowser, "Le coup de téléphone dans les films des premiere temps," *Les premiers ans du cinéma français* (Perpignan: Institut Jean Vigo, 1985), pp. 218–224. I am indebted to Elaine Burrows of the National Film Archive, London, for a description and illustrations of ARE YOU THERE? In the 16-mm reduction print of COLLEGE CHUMS, the man at the left is invisible at least part of the time, accounting for a mistaken description in the article mentioned above. As the frame reproduced from the film shows, he is present in the shot. See illustration on p. 65.

28. The Pathé film released in the United States as A NARROW ESCAPE in 1908 is preserved in the National Film Archive in London as THE PHYSICIAN AND THE CASTLE, *ca.* 1907, original French title unknown. Jay Leyda discovered this film as a possible source for THE LONELY VILLA, and Cooper Graham found the U.S. release record. This film and other precedents for THE LONELY VILLA are extensively discussed in Gunning, "D. W. Griffith and the 'Narrator-System.' "

29. Biograph *Bulletin* No. 226 (29 March 1909) (THE MEDICINE BOTTLE), "a thriller which demonstrates two things, the efficacy of that time-saving agent . . . the telephone, and the importance of that movement to enforce a differential form of bottle, in which to hold poisonous liquids." In Bowser, *Biograph Bulletins, 1908–1912, p. 76.*

30. *MPW,* 19 June 1909, p. 834.

31. I am indebted to Jon Gartenberg for his description of the shot sequence of THE TELEPHONE, from his work in progress on the Vitagraph Company.

32. Thompson, in Bordwell *et al., The Classical Hollywood Cinema,* pp. 210–211.

CHAPTER 5.   General Flimco and the Pushcart Peddlers

1. Tom Gunning told me about a fad that existed at this time for a doll called "Billiken": this is a pun on the Bianchi camera.

2. *MPW,* 20 February 1909, p. 223; 3 April 1909, p. 423; 8 May 1909, p. 592.

3. *MPW,* 9 January 1909, p. 40 (letter from Ingvold Oes of Great Northern); *MPW,* 4 July 1908, p. 18.

4. *MPW,* 20 February 1909, p. 220.

5. *MPW,* 16 January 1909, pp. 58–59, 63; 30 January 1909, p. 119; 17 April 1909, p. 467.

6. *MPW,* 30 January 1909, p. 116; 6 February 1909, p. 137; 4 July 1908, p. 3.

7. *MPW,* 2 April 1910, pp. 501–504 and 23 April 1910, pp. 636–637; Balshofer and Miller, *One Reel a Week,* p. 52.

8. *MPW,* 25 September 1909, pp. 410–412 (report on Alliance).

9. On N.I. stock, *MPW:* 19 June 1909, p. 827; 10 July 1909, p. 47; 24 July 1909, p. 127; 25 September 1909, p. 406; 23 October 1909, p. 574; 30 October 1909, p. 603; 8 January 1910, p. 89; 12 February 1910, pp. 210–213; 4 June 1910, p. 940; 11 June 1910, p. 982; 9 July 1910, p. 137; 20 August 1910, p. 399; 3 December 1910, p. 1287; 8 July 1911, p. 1597 ("The Cleveland Press indulged in a howl nearly a column long, because it heard that the N.I. film stock is no longer used"); 26 August 1911, p. 527 (MPPC sent information to exhibitors that after 1 June the exchanges could specify which stock was wanted).

10. *MPW,* 27 May 1911, p. 1047, and 26 October 1912, p. 332.

11. *MPW,* 25 September 1909, pp. 410–412.

12. *MPW,* 5 February 1910, pp. 163–165 (*re* Murdock in *Ciné-Journal*); 20 February 1909, p. 193; 24 April 1909, pp. 512–513; 9 October 1909, p. 479.

13. *MPW,* 8 May 1909, p. 590.

14. There is conflicting evidence about the first release: it may have been THE JUSTICE OF SOLOMON on 8 January. *MPW,* 12 September 1908, p. 194; 19 September, p. 225; 8 January 1910, p. 38. I am indebted to George Pratt for the references, which conflict with *MPW,* 27 March 1909, p. 365.

15. Balshofer and Miller, *One Reel a Week,* pp. 24–29; *MPW,* 15 May 1909, p. 632.

16. *MPW,* 2 October 1909, p. 444; 23 October 1909, p. 563; 30 October 1909, p. 608.

17. *MPW,* 27 March 1909, p. 365; 15 May 1909, 653; 27 November 1909, pp. 779, 795; 25 December 1909, p. 922. The first release of Exclusive American was announced as A ROMANCE OF THE SOUTH.

18. *MPW,* 31 December 1909, p. 946, advertisement.

19. *MPW,* 27 November 1909, p. 764; 30 October 1909, p. 601; 4 December 1909, p. 793; 11 December 1909, p. 843.

20. *MPW,* 5 February 1910, p. 177; 12 March 1910, pp. 363, 374; 28 May 1910, p. 876.

21. *MPW,* 7 May 1910, p. 732 (Motograph, Philadelphia, soon renamed Electragraff); 14 May 1910, p. 787 (Motograph, Baltimore); 21 May 1910, p. 861 (Whyte Film Co.); 11 June 1910, pp. 982 (Defender and Atlas releases), 992 (Motograph), 996 (Electragraff release, A MESSAGE FROM THE EAST), 1003 (A CHILD OF THE REGIMENT); 18 June 1910, p. 1073 (Dandy Films, A MESSAGE FROM THE EAST); 26 November 1910, p. 1223 (Owl).

22. *MPW,* 30 July 1910, p. 286.

23. *MPW,* 17 September 1910, p. 637, and 23 September 1910, p. 683.

24. *NYDM,* 1 October 1910, p. 726 (adv.) and 8 October 1910, p. 786 (Reliance).

25. *MPW,* 1 October 1910, p. 742; 8 October 1910, p. 817; 15 October 1910, p. 864; 29 October 1910, p. 1060 (American). For a detailed history, see Timothy James Lyons, *The Silent Partner: The History of the American Film Manufacturing Company, 1910–1921* (New York: Arno Press, 1974).

26. *MPW,* 8 October 1910, p. 812 (Solax).

27. *MPW*, 9 April 1910, p. 549; 16 April 1910, pp. 582, 589–590, 595, 596; 7 May 1910, p. 724 (Sales Co. revised structure).
28. *MPW*, 21 May 1910, pp. 822–823 (editorial); 29 October 1910, p. 985 (National Film Mfg.); 7 January 1911, p. 55 (Revier advertisement).
29. *MPW*, 11 June 1910, p. 992; 16 July 1910, p. 134; 21 January 1911, p. 115 (Sales Co.).
30. *MPW*, 10 June 1910, p. 949; *US* v. *MPPC* vol. 1, Original Petition; *New York Times*, 17 August 1912.
31. William Fox, *US* v. *MPPC* 2:659–665 (11 July 1913); Frank Howard for the defense, *US* v. *MPPC* 3:1843 (19 November 1913).
32. Defendant's Exhibit No. 46, *US* v. *MPPC* 3:1308 (summary of cancellations and reinstatements of Fox's customers 1910–1913); William Fox, *US* v. *MPPC* 2:658–797 (13–28 February 1913); Louis Rosenbluh (general manager of the Greater New York Film Exchange), *US* v. *MPPC* 1:357–387, 420–479 (22–23 January 1913) and 2:700–734 (13 February 1913). William H. Swanson had some scurrilous gossip about anti-Semitic remarks by General Film Company executives, but his hostility must be taken into account and weighed against the success of Sigmund Lubin, a Jew who was one of the insiders in the Trust. Anti-Semitism no doubt existed, but was not permitted to interfere with business prosperity. See Swanson in *US* v. *MPPC* 1:323 (January 1913).
33. Jeremiah J. Kennedy on direct examination, *US* v. *MPPC* 5:3156–3206 (17 March 1914) (Mandelbaum of Detroit was the talkative distributor); *MPW*, 22 October 1910, p. 920.
34. *MPW*, 5 November 1910, p. 1063.
35. *MPW*, 24 December 1910, p. 1470.
36. *MPW*, 1 April 1911, pp. 702, 720.
37. *MPW*, 17 June 1911, pp. 1368–1369; 1 July 1911, pp. 1504, 1583; 15 July 1911, p. 114. Latham loop Patent overthrown: *MPW*, 17 February 1912, p. 560, and 24 August 1912, p. 747.
38. *MPW*, 22 October 1910, p. 927.
39. *MPW*, 15 April 1911, p. 827, and 17 June 1911, p. 1466.
40. *MPW*, 25 March 1911, p. 643, and 12 March 1910, p. 379 (in Chicago).
41. *MPW*, 17 June 1911, p. 1466, and 25 March 1911, p. 645.
42. *MPW*, 26 August 1911, p. 522, and 26 August 1911, p. 530 (Moving Picture League).
43. *MPW*, 4 November 1911, p. 357. Figures for 1912 are based on a count of the releases listed in *Motography's Hand Book and Film Record* (April 1913).

CHAPTER 6. Acting: The Camera's Closer View

1. *MPW*, 22 January 1910, pp. 84–85.
2. *MPW*, 7 November 1908, p. 358; 14 November 1908, pp. 378–380; 30 January 1909, p. 120.
3. *MPW*, 26 August 1910, p. 405.
4. *MPW*, 26 November 1910, pp. 1239–1240.
5. *NYDM*, 9 April 1910, p. 17.
6. *MPW*, 20 May 1911, pp. 1120–1121.
7. *MPW*, 22 April 1911, p. 881; *NYDM*, 13 August 1910, p. 28.
8. *MPW*, 3 September 1910, p. 511.
9. Gunning, "D. W. Griffith and the 'Narrator-System,' " pp. 756–760.
10. *MPW*, 19 October 1912, p. 239. George Pratt has reminded me that Bernhardt had injured her leg sometime before in the leap from the parapet at the end of *La Tosca* and would lose the leg by amputation in the next year or so. In the filming of QUEEN ELIZABETH, the producers wanted to ease her fall to the floor.
11. *MPW*, 25 October 1913, p. 356.
12. William Christy Cabanne later indicated that they used the terms "knee figure," "waist figure," "bust figure," and "big head." In the same interview, he recalled D. W. Griffith saying, "The feet can't act." Noted in the "Interviews" file of the Braverman Collection, D. W. Griffith Papers, Museum of Modern Art Film Study Center.
13. Salt, *Film Style and Technology*, pp. 106–108; *MPW*, 3 July 1909, p. 11.
14. *MPW*, 14 May 1910, p. 791; *NYDM*, 31 January 1912, p. 56.
15. Thomas Gunning, "Le récit filmé et l'idéal théâtral: Griffith et 'les films d'Art' français," in Pierre Guibbert, ed., *Les premiers ans du cinéma français* (Perpignan: Institut Jean Vigo, 1985), pp. 123–132. LA MORT DU DUC DE GUISE is referred to in the film histories as L'ASSASSINAT DU DUC DE

GUISE, but a recent restoration of the film shows LA MORT . . . to have been the original title, as observed by Pierre Jenn and Michel Nagard in *L'Avant-Scène Cinéma* (November 1984): 58.

16. I am indebted to George Pratt and Andrew Eskind of the International Museum of Photography at George Eastman House for identifying "Dunkoop" as Rudolph Dührkoop (1848–1918), a German portrait photographer whose work was widely exhibited. He was called "the pioneer of artistic portrait photography on the Continent" in 1909.

17. *MPW*, 26 February 1910, pp. 303–304.

18. *MPW*, 19 September 1908, p. 211.

19. Mae Marsh, *Screen Acting* (Los Angeles: Photo-Star Publishing Company, 1921), p. 99.

CHAPTER 7. Brand Names and Stars

1. *MPW*, 20 March, 1909, 328.

2. *US* v. *MPPC*, 4:2442; *MPW*: 26 November 1910, p. 1219; 11 February 1911, p. 308; 13 May 1911, p. 1070; 14 December 1912, pp. 1061–1062; 8 February 1913, pp. 553–554 (New Zealand); 17 May 1913, pp. 687–688 (Australia); 21 June 1913, pp. 1234–1235 (Java); 20 June 1914, p. 1839 (Méliès "G" brand comedies); 24 April 1915, p. 532 (delayed announcement of Gaston's death).

3. *MPW*, 19 November 1910, p. 1158.

4. *MPW*, 27 March 1909, p. 363; 29 May 1909, p. 712; 9 April 1910, p. 561; 16 April 1910, p. 607; 27 August 1910, p. 498.

5. *MPW*, 5 November 1910, p. 1062.

6. *MPW*, 3 April 1909, p. 405; *Denver Post*, reprinted in *MPW*, 4 December 1909, pp. 801–802.

7. "Spectator's Comments," *NYDM*, 10 July 1909, p. 15.

8. *MPW*, 12 September 1908, p. 196; 3 April 1909, p. 317; 31 July 1909, p. 166; 7 August 1909, p. 225; 28 August 1909, p. 278.

9. *MPW*, 4 December 1909, p. 802.

10. *MPW*, 5 October 1912, pp. 34, 56.

11. *Motion Picture News*, 19 December 1914, p. 34.

12. George Pratt has called my attention to the date that the Biograph Company first issued a photograph identifying members of its stock company; see *NYDM*, 19 March 1913, pp. 26–27, and *MPW*, 5 April 1913, p. 59. It appears that names and photographs of Biograph actors may have been supplied in England a year earlier than this; see "Inquiries," *MPW*, 27 April 1912, p. 327.

13. *MPW*, 19 November 1910, p. 1161.

14. *MPW*, 26 August 1911, p. 523, and 18 November 1911, p. 548.

15. Balshofer and Miller, *One Reel a Week*, p. 40.

16. Linda Arvidson, *When the Movies Were Young* (New York: Dutton, 1925), p. 31.

17. Gunning, "D. W. Griffith and the 'Narrator-System,' " p. 540; *MPW*, 24 April 1909, p. 515, and 29 May 1909, p. 712.

18. *MPW*, 19 February 1910, p. 256.

19. *MPW*, 15 January 1910, p. 50 (Kalem stock company photo); 5 February 1910, p. 167; 5 March 1910, p. 342.

20. Ramsaye, *A Million and One Nights*, pp. 523–524; *MPW*: 18 December 1909, p. 866 (advertisement); 29 January 1910, p. 134 (advertisement); 25 February 1910, p. 323. George Pratt gave me two of these citations.

21. *MPW*, 12 March 1910, p. 369.

22. *MPW*, 26 March 1910, p. 468.

23. *MPW*, 2 April 1910, p. 517; 23 April 1910, p. 643; 21 May 1910, p. 825; *NYDM*, 18 June 1910, p. 17; *MPW*, 23 July 1910, pp. 187–188; 8 October 1910, p. 817; 12 November 1910, p. 1123; 7 January 1911, p. 37; 31 December 1910, p. 1521; 26 November 1910, p. 1223.

24. *MPW*, 24 December 1910, p. 1462; 7 January 1911, p. 26; 14 January 1911, p. 60; 11 February 1911, p. 352 (Johnson and Lawrence at Lubin).

25. *MPW*, 26 March 1910, p. 472 (Thanhouser policy), and 8 April, 1911, p. 763 (Frank Crane).

26. *NYDM*, 13 December 1911, p. 30.

27. *MPW*, 2 April 1910, p. 515, and 23 September 1910, p. 682.

28. *MPW*, 9 April 1910, p. 559.

29. *MPW*, 22 April 1911, p. 916, and 29 April 1911, p. 940.

30. *MPW*, 23 September 1911, p. 879; *Motion Picture News*, 19 December 1914, pp. 53–54. "At the

Moving Picture Ball," music by Joseph Santly, lyrics by Howard Johnson, was published by Feist *ca.* 1921. I am indebted to Charles Turner for the information.

31. Herbert Reynolds (in conversation with the author) notes a Kalem film released a week earlier, ON THE WAR PATH, which used a similar credit title, and among Kalem "lost films" he finds that IN OLD FLORIDA, released on 12 April 1911, was reported to have cast listings on the screen. *MPW*, 3 May 1911, p. 34 (fan letter); 20 May 1911, p. 1140 (AIDA); 29 July 1911, p. 216; 30 April 1913, p. 29; *NYDM*, 4 June 1913, pp. 32–33 (review of THE WISHING SEAT).

32. *MPW*, 27 May 1911, p. 1172.

33. *MPW*, 25 February 1911, p. 415.

34. *NYDM*, 8 January 1913, p. 27.

35. *MPW*, 29 November 1913, pp. 1026–1027, and 22 November 1913, p. 874.

CHAPTER 8. Movie Palaces

1. *MPW*, 5 February 1910, p. 16, and 16 September 1911, p. 808.

2. *MPW*, 14 January 1911, pp. 82–83.

3. *MPW*, 3 September 1910, p. 528.

4. *MPW*, 25 September 1909, pp. 406, 412, and 9 April 1910, p. 557.

5. *MPW*, 23 October 1909, pp. 570, 574.

6. *Kansas City Star*, quoted in *MPW*, 29 October 1910, p. 925.

7. *MPW*, 5 November 1910, p. 1043.

8. *NYDM*, 13 November 1912, pp. 25–26.

9. *NYDM*, 24 January 1912, p. 40.

10. *MPW*, 19 August 1911, p. 368.

11. *MPW*, 30 October 1909, p. 599 (Philadelphia), and 31 July 1909, p. 160 (New York).

12. May, *Screening Out the Past*, pp. 147–166.

13. *MPW*, 28 August 1909, p. 307, and 30 October 1909, p. 599.

14. *MPW*, 28 August 1909, p. 307.

15. *MPW*, 5 February 1910, p. 170; 23 April 1910, p. 651; 17 September 1910, pp. 627–628; 5 November 1910, p. 1053; 30 September 1911, p. 959.

16. *MPW*, 22 October 1910, p. 928; 30 April 1910, pp. 684–685 (report by Bedding of a visit to this region); 3 June 1911, p. 1243.

17. *MPW*, 13 March 1909, p. 300, and 6 August 1910, p. 299.

18. *NYDM*, 2 April 1910, p. 19 (advertisement); *MPW*, 23 April 1910, p. 634 and 30 April 1910, p. 697.

19. *MPW*, 7 May 1910, p. 723.

20. *MPW*, 17 September 1910, p. 640, and 22 October 1910, p. 927.

21. *MPW*, 11 February 1911, pp. 296–7.

22. *MPW*, 14 January 1911, pp. 70–71, and 15 April 1911, p. 832.

23. *MPW*, 13 May 1911, p. 1069.

24. *MPW*, 16 September 1911, p. 784; 29 April 1911, p. 947; 6 May 1911, p. 945.

25. *Motion Picture News*, 21 February 1914, p. 13.

26. *MPW*, 9 April 1910, p. 548.

27. *MPW*, 12 February 1910, p. 202; 26 February 1910, pp. 289, 297; 30 December 1911, p. 1055 (as reported by Jas. S. McQuade).

28. *MPW*, 15 November 1913, p. 714; *New York Times*, 12 April 1914.

29. *MPW*, 5 August 1911, p. 299.

30. *MPW*, 26 October 1912, p. 324; 7 December 1912, p. 957; 9 November 1912, p. 538.

31. *MPW*, 14 December 1912, p. 1058.

32. *MPW*, 25 October 1913, p. 366, and 8 November 1913, p. 616.

33. *MPW*, 25 October 1913, p. 384, and 8 November 1913, p. 595.

34. *Motion Picture News*, 19 December 1914, p. 18, and 2 January 1915, p. 116 (advertisement).

35. *MPW*, 30 December 1911, p. 1081.

36. *NYDM*, 2 April 1910, p. 16.

37. *MPW*, 29 November 1913, p. 999. I remember that when I was a child in the thirties, my grandmother, who disapproved of all vulgar slang, objected to the word "movies."

38. *MPW*, 12 March 1910, p. 372.

CHAPTER 9. **Trademarks, Titles, Introductions**

1. A print of an American film recovered from the Netherlands was first thought to be SWEETHEART OF THE DOOMED, a Vitagraph production of 1910, because the end title had the company name and trademark on it. A closer look and further research showed it to be the Kalem film BY A WOMAN'S WIT (released April 1911) because the Kalem trademark appears on the wall. End titles could be changed, but it is more difficult to get rid of a trademark photographed within the scene. This print is at the Library of Congress. On the evidence of a Vitagraph trademark, a charge of illegal duping was proved against R. G. Bachman in the case of *Vitagraph* v. *20th Century Optiscope Company*, Equity No. 28856, 1907. "How to Prevent Duping," *MPW*, 1 October 1907, p. 519.
2. *Agreements of the Motion Picture Patents Company*, Copy No. 7, in the collection of the Museum of Modern Art Library.
3. Balshofer and Miller, *One Reel a Week*, p. 5.
4. George Rockhill Craw, *MPW*, 4 February 1911, p. 229; C. H. Claudy, *MPW*, 4 February 1911, p. 231, also criticizes lack of verisimilitude when trademarks appear in film.
5. *MPW*, 24 June 1911, p. 1427.
6. William Lord Wright, *Moving Picture News*, 11 January 1913, p. 14.
7. *MPW*, 17 October 1908, p. 298, and 27 February 1909, p. 235.
8. *MPW*, 4 February 1911, p. 248; 13 May 1911, p. 1057; 3 June 1911, p. 1237.
9. *NYDM*, 12 February 1913, p. 31. A print of AS IN A LOOKING GLASS *with* intertitles survives in the collection of the International Museum of Photography at George Eastman House. Jan-Christopher Horak, curator, kindly examined it for me.
10. Everett McNeill, *MPW*, "Outline of How to Write a Photoplay," 15 July 1911, p. 27; 18 November 1911, p. 534; 30 December 1911, p. 1062.
11. *MPW*, 12 August 1911, p. 363.
12. *MPW*, 19 October 1912, p. 241.
13. *NYDM*, 10 January 1912, p. 26, and 24 December 1910, p. 1471. Note that the practice of adding the main title to the intertitles may also help to date those films which did not follow it. For example, a Vitagraph film of the period with no main title on the intertitles would probably be no later than 1911.
14. *NYDM*, 24 January 1912, p. 32.
15. *MPW*, 15 July 1911, p. 42.
16. Scripts, title lists, assembly sheets in the collections of the Museum of Modern Art and the Library of Congress. Further research needs to be done in the LOC copyright records, but these must be copied for preservation before they are fully available for research.
17. *MPW*, 3 June 1911, p. 1259, and 6 March 1909, p. 12.
18. *MPW*, 24 June 1911, p. 1434.
19. *MPW*, 11 November 1911, p. 459.
20. *MPW*, 16 January 1915, p. 374.
21. *MPW*, 2 January 1915, p. 59.

CHAPTER 10. **Detours on the Way to Hollywood**

1. Balshofer and Miller, *One Reel a Week*, p. 41.
2. Report of Charles A. Buckbee of the Buckbee Detective Service (24 June 1910), *MPPC* v. *NYMPC*, Equity No. 12,037, Eastern District of New York; McCoy's Reports, Edison National Historic Site; *MPW*, 3 June 1911, p. 1282, and 24 June 1911, p. 1432; *MPPC* v. *Fred Siegert & P. H. Berg*, Equity No. 1618, Southern District of California, 1911.
3. *MPW*, 18 November 1911, p. 542. The words are those of the reporter and not direct quotes from Dintenfass.
4. *MPW*, 27 June 1908, p. 541; 18 September 1909, p. 381; "The Essanay Company Out West," 4 December 1909, pp. 801–802.
5. *MPW*, 4 December 1909, p. 801; *NYDM*, 13 August 1910 (advertisement on back cover).
6. *MPW*, 15 February 1908, pp. 121–122; Marc Wanamaker, "Historic Hollywood Movie Studios," part 1, *American Cinematographer* (March 1976): 280–283, 286–288, 297. On Boggs in California in 1907, see also Balshofer and Miller, *One Reel a Week*, pp. 55–57; Ramsaye, *A Million and One Nights*, pp. 532–533; *NYDM*, 2 October 1912, p. 25; *MPW*: 15 April 1911, p. 826; 27 April 1911, p. 889; 5 August 1911, pp. 276–277; 9 September 1911, p. 697; 11 November 1911, p. 455 (Boggs's murder).

7. *MPW*, 29 January 1910, p. 120, and 30 April 1910, p. 679; *Los Angeles Examiner*, cited in *MPW*, 19 February 1910, p. 256.

8. Gene Gauntier, "Blazing the Trail," p. 22.

9. "Far Afield," *NYDM*, 2 November 1910, p. 29.

10. *NYDM*, 3 May 1911, p. 33; *MPW*: 3 June 1911, p. 1242; 18 November 1911, p. 560; 16 December 1911, p. 880; 30 December 1911, p. 1059; *NYDM*, 10 January 1912, p. 30.

11. *MPW*: 5 November 1910, pp. 1044–1045; 10 December 1910, p. 1350 (Selig); 19 October 1912, p. 244 (Lubin); *NYDM*: 2 October 1912, p. 17; 14 December 1910, p. 28; 8 January 1913, p. 20 (Gauntier); 19 February 1913, p. 33 (Majestic).

12. Richard Alan Nelson, *Florida and the American Motion Picture Industry, 1898–1980* (New York and London: Garland, 1983).

13. *MPW*, 28 May 1910, p. 887; 3 September 1910, p. 510; 31 July 1910, pp. 287–288 (reply to "Spectator").

14. *MPW*, 5 March 1910, p. 341, and 9 July 1910, p. 89; *NYDM*, 23 April 1910, pp. 20–21.

15. *San Antonio Daily Express*, quoted in *MPW*, 15 January 1910, p. 93; *MPW*: 26 March 1910, p. 471; 11 February 1911, p. 308; 13 May 1911, p. 1070; 14 December 1912, pp. 1061–1062.

16. *MPW*, 6 November 1909, p. 765 (Vitagraph); 12 February 1910, p. 203; 25 November 1911, pp. 619–621 (Eclair); *NYDM*, 9 April 1910, p. 21 (Pathé). Pathé began to distinguish its European product from the American by printing the letters "C.G.P.C." (for "Compagnie Générale Pathé Cinématographique") along the edge of the prints; see *MPW*, 2 December 1911, p. 738.

17. *MPW*, 5 February 1910, p. 160, and 10 December 1910, p. 1360.

18. *NYDM*, 5 March 1910, p. 19 (Lubin); 5 March 1910, p. 20 (Selig and Edison); *MPW*: 19 March 1910, p. 429; 25 June 1910, p. 110 (Essanay); 26 March 1910, p. 473 (Lubin).

19. *MPW*, 8 October 1910, p. 843 (advertisement).

20. *MPW*, 21 January 1911, p. 146, and 28 January 1911, p. 168.

21. *MPW*, 8 April 1911, p. 765.

22. *MPW*, 25 March 1911, p. 665 (advertisement).

23. *MPW*, 1 April 1911, p. 704, and 6 May 1911, p. 1019.

24. *Motion Picture News*, 11 January 1913, p. 13.

25. Raoul Walsh, *Each Man in His Time* (New York: Farrar, Straus and Giroux, 1974), pp. 85–112.

26. *Los Angeles Times* cited in *MPW*, 5 November 1910, pp. 1044–1045.

27. *NYDM*, 21 December 1910, p. 29; *MPW*, 7 January 1911, p. 30.

28. *MPW*, 11 March 1911, pp. 520, 524, and 25 March 1911, p. 701 (photograph and story on the Liberty Theatre).

29. *MPW*, 7 January 1911, p. 36; 21 January 1911, p. 137; 4 February 1911, p. 253; 18 February 1911, p. 360.

30. *MPW*, 30 December 1911, p. 1065 (Nestor in Hollywood), 3 June 1911, p. 1244 (ten companies at work), 9 July 1911, p. 1576 ("picture mad"); *Motion Picture News* 3 April 1915, p. 173.

CHAPTER 11. The Genre Film

1. *MPW*, 10 June 1911, p. 1285; 17 June 1911, p. 1385; 24 June 1911, p. 1429.

2. *MPW*, 12 December 1908, p. 472; 6 February 1909, p. 143; 3 April 1909, p. 397; 14 May 1910, p. 793; 15 April 1911, p. 832; 11 February 1911, p. 294. "Industrials" are films about manufacturing processes and systems.

3. *NYDM*, 13 August 1910, p. 25.

4. *MPW*, 19 October 1912, p. 221, and 22 November 1913, pp. 844–845.

5. *MPW*, 19 February 1910, p. 246, and 11 February 1911, p. 314.

6. Charles Silver, *The Western Film* (New York: Pyramid, 1976), p. 37.

7. *MPW*, 8 April 1911, p. 779, and 27 April 1911, p. 882.

8. Balshofer and Miller, *One Reel a Week*, p. 40.

9. *MPW*: 6 August 1910, p. 299; 19 February 1910, p. 256; 22 April 1911, p. 872; 6 May 1911, p. 999.

10. *NYDM*, 8 March 1911, p. 29; *MPW*, 29 July 1911, p. 192.

11. *MPW*, 17 June 1911, p. 1365.

12. *MPW*, 13 October 1913, p. 258.

13. Statistics based on Paul C. Spehr, *The Civil War in Motion Pictures: A Bibliography of Films Produced in the United States Since 1897* (Washington, D.C.: Library of Congress, 1961).

14. *NYDM*, 2 April 1913, p. 25.

15. *MPW*, 17 April 1909, p. 477; 24 July 1909, p. 129; 28 May 1910, p. 883; 18 June 1910, p. 1041.

16. *MPW*, 22 May 1909, p. 672.

17. *MPW*, 22 November 1913, p. 877.

18. *MPW*, 20 February 1909, p. 202. According to the Biograph production records in the Museum of Modern Art Library Special Collections, there was an unusually long delay of about four months between the production of the film and its release.

19. *MPW*, 20 February 1909, p. 126.

20. *MPW*, 4 December 1909, p. 837.

21. Statistics from "Production Patterns at the Biograph, 1907–1918," a paper delivered by the author at the Society for Cinema Studies annual conference (New York, 22–24 April 1981), based in part on an analysis of the Biograph production records.

22. *MPW*, 25 November 1911, p. 622 (Bunny), and 22 July 1911, p. 102 (Drew).

23. *MPW*, 18 June 1910, p. 1045; 7 January 1911, p. 37; "The Dearth of Comedy," 10 June 1911, p. 1292.

24. *MPW*, 10 September 1910, p. 569.

25. *MPW*, 25 September 1912, p. 29; 5 October 1912, p. 43 (THE WATER NYMPH and COHEN COLLECTS A DEBT); 9 November 1912, p. 598; 23 November 1912, p. 769 (THE DEACON'S TROUBLES); 25 January 1913, p. 300 (FOR LIZZIE'S SAKE); 18 January 1913, p. 229 (THE BATTLE OF WHO RUN); 1 March 1913, p. 930 (FORCED BRAVERY); Kalton C. Lahue, *Kops and Custards* (Norman: University of Oklahoma Press, 1967).

26. Theodore Huff, "The Early Work of Charles Chaplin," *Sight and Sound*, March 1945: pp. 1, 11.

27. Jay Leyda, "Defining California Slapstick," in *The Slapstick Symposium*, edited by Eileen Bowser, (Brussels and New York: Fédération Internationale des Achives du Film–Museum of Modern Art 1988).

28. *NYDM*, 8 March 1911, p. 34 (Hank and Lank, played by Augustus Carney and Victor Potel) and 7 February 1912, p. 36. See also chapter 10, note 19 (Hotaling, Punch); *Motion Picture News Studio Directory*, 21 October 1916, p. 26 (Oliver Hardy), pp. 107, 164–165 (Al Christie), p. 153 (Hal Roach), p. 197 (Ham and Bud), and 29 January 1916, p. 11 (Ham and Bud).

29. Raymond Fielding, *The American Newsreel, 1911–1967*, (Norman: University of Oklahoma Press, 1972); *MPW*, 29 July 1911, p. 283 (Vitagraph's "Current Events"). I am indebted to George Pratt for additional information about the dates and issues of newsreels, based on his research in the trade periodicals.

30. *Our Mutual Girl Weekly* (January 1914–January 1915).

31. *MPW*, 5 June 1909, p. 755; 8 October 1910, p. 831; 11 March 1911, p. 54; 11 November 1911, p. 451.

32. *Motion Picture News*, 19 December 1914, p. 33.

33. *MPW*, 8 November 1913, p. 620.

34. *MPW*, 27 August 1910, p. 471.

35. *MPW*, 5 October 1912, p. 57.

36. *MPW*, 28 December 1912, p. 1284; *Motion Picture News*, 11 January 1913, p. 23; *MPW*, 8 November 1913, p. 627, and 15 November 1913, p. 741.

37. *MPW*, 26 November 1910, p. 1236.

38. *MPW*, 30 October 1909, p. 599; 11 September 1909, p. 346; 24 July 1909, p. 164; *St. Louis Times*, cited in *MPW*, 19 November 1910, p. 1185. George Pratt provided the information about the opening of the play *Drink*.

39. *MPW*, 12 February 1910, p. 220; 2 April 1910, p. 509; 10 April 1910, p. 551.

40. *MPW*, 13 May 1911, p. 1082; 27 May 1911, p. 1185.

CHAPTER 12. The Feature Film

1. *MPW*, 21 May 1910, p. 838.

2. Letter to Motion Picture Patents Company from W. H. Clune, T. L. Tally, W. E. Krantz (22 November 1909), Defendant's Exhibit No. 104, *US v. MPPC* 3:1465.

3. *NYDM*, 8 January 1913, p. 27.

4. *MPW*, 11 July 1914, p. 272.

5. *NYDM*, 13 November 1912, p. 11.

6. *MPW*, 17 April 1909, p. 477.

7. *MPW*, 24 April 1909, p. 515, and 1 May 1909 (advertisement).

8. *MPW*, 8 January 1910, p. 18.

9. *MPW*, 30 April 1910, p. 697.

10. *MPW*, 30 October 1909, p. 599.

11. *MPW*, 27 November 1909, p. 751.

12. *MPW*, 12 February 1910, pp. 210–213; 13 August 1910, p. 366 (advertisement); 22 October 1910, pp. 940–941; 13 October 1913, p. 131 (editorial).

13. *MPW*, 9 July 1910, p. 140.

14. *MPW*, 9 July 1910, p. 136, and 12 November 1910, p. 1104.

15. *MPW*, 22 July 1911, p. 105; "Thanhouser Advocates Natural-Length Films," *MPW*, 5 October 1912, p. 47; *MPW*, 18 November 1911, p. 523 (advertisement).

16. *MPW*, 17 June 1911, p. 1367. American rights for this film were secured by P. P. Craft of the Buffalo Bill and Pawnee Bill Film Company, and it was sold by states rights.

17. *Christian Science Monitor*, cited in *MPW*, 19 March 1910, p. 421; *NYDM*, 12 February 1913, p. 30.

18. *MPW*, 29 April 1911, p. 935; 13 May 1911, p. 1065; 20 May 1911, p. 1124; 15 July 1911, pp. 14–16 (review), 44 (advertisement, World's Best Film Company).

19. James S. McQuade, *MPW*, 4 November 191, pp. 362–365.

20. *NYDM*, 2 April 1910, pp. 16, 18.

21. *MPW*, 25 June 1910, p. 1097; 9 July 1910, p. 89 (Rock making the deal); 2 July 1910, p. 17 (overseeing the filming).

22. *MPW*, 9 July 1910, pp. 133, 135 (national attention on the film); July 23, 1910:190–191 (moving picture interests at stake and the fear of race riots), 195 (banned in D.C.), 200–201 (opinions on showing film); 30 July 1910, 240 (showings in Brooklyn).

23. *MPW*, 20 August 1910, p. 398 (advertisement of Johnson in vaudeville, on Cinephone); Jim Jacobs, in conversation with the author; Ramsaye, *A Million and One Nights*, pp. 693–694.

24. *MPW*, 16 July 1910, p. 133.

25. *US* v. *MPPC* 3:1539 (November 1913).

26. *MPW*, 9 September 1911, p. 699 (filming THE COMING OF COLUMBUS); 4 May 1912, pp. 407–410 (James McQuade review); 11 May 1912, pp. 521–522 (presentation to pope).

27. *NYDM*, 13 November 1912 (back-cover advertisement).

28. *NYDM*, 19 February 1913, p. 15; *Motion Picture News*, 8 November 1913, p. 10.

29. *NYDM*, 8 January 1913, p. 27.

30. *MPW*, 29 June 1912, p. 1212 (WHAT HAPPENED TO MARY), and 8 November 1913, p. 594.

31. *NYDM*, 19 December 1914, pp. 26, 33 (the two Pathé serials and ZUDORA). George Pratt has generously provided some of the specific dates for the beginnings of serials.

32. *NYDM*, 26 August 1914, pp. 24, 25.

33. *NYDM*, 30 April 1913, p. 28.

34. *NYDM*, 4 June 1913, p. 31 (advertisement).

35. Contract between Ambrosio and the Photo-Drama Company, 20 June 1913, quoted in Rita Horwitz, "George Kleine and the Early Motion Picture Industry," in *The George Kleine Collection of Early Motion Pictures in the Library of Congress: A Catalog*, edited by Rita Horwitz and Harriet Harrison (Washington, D.C.: Library of Congress, 1980), p. xvii.

36. *Motion Picture News*, 8 November 1913, pp. 42, 43 (report of Chicago premiere); Horwitz, "George Kleine and the Early Motion Picture Industry," p. xvii.

37. *US* v. *MPPC* 4:1947, 2002 (December 1913).

38. *Ibid.*, 4:2057.

39. *Ibid.*, 4:2238–2239; *Motion Picture News*, 22 November 1913, p. 25.

40. *MPW*, 4 July 1914, p. 21.

41. *New York Times*, 12 June 1914, and 27 December 1914.

42. *MPW*, special number, 11 July 1914, pp. 181–182, 185, 197–198.

CHAPTER 13. The Lid Comes Off

1. *MPW*: 2 December 1911, p. 709 (Latham loop in court); 17 February 1912, p. 560; 24 August 1912, p. 747; *New York Times*, 17 August 1912; *US* v. *MPPC* vol. 1, Original Petition; *MPW*, 25 July 1914, p. 574 (MPPC gets a temporary injunction against Universal's use of the Warwick camera).

2. *NYDM*, 21 August 1912, p. 27.

3. *NYDM*, 2 April 1913, p. 34 (importing LES MISÉRABLES); "The Growth of Eclectic in a Year," *Motion*

Picture News, 13 June 1914, p. 69. Les Misérables was clearly identified as a Pathé film when reviewed from London in "British Notes," *MPW*, 11 January 1913, p. 146.

4. *NYDM*, 9 April 1913, p. 27, and 19 February 1913, p. 25 (beginning of Kinetograph's regular exchange service); *MPW*, special number, 11 July 1914, pp. 175–180 (account of Kinetograph); Kennedy on cross-examination (17 March 1914), *US* v. *MPPC* 6:3235.

5. *Motion Picture News*, 22 March 1913, pp. 4–5 (advertisement), and 21 June 1913, p. 12.

6. Kemp Niver, *Klaw & Erlanger Present Famous Plays in Pictures* (Los Angeles: Locare Research Group, 1976); *Variety* reviews: 23 January 1914 (Fatal Wedding); 27 February 1914 (Classmates); 10 April 1914 (Seven Days); 17 April 1914 (Strongheart, "filmed last May when Walthall was on the payroll"); 29 May 1914 (The Billionaire); 10 July 1914 (Man's Enemy); *MPW*, 4 July 1914, p. 91 (advertisement); Biograph Production Records, Museum of Modern Art Library Special Collections. I think that Niver's theory about limited projection, based on the nonstandard perforations, is in error, since the original Biograph negatives of the same period (in the Museum of Modern Art collection) have nonstandard perforations, but release prints with standard perforations can be made on the Biograph printer.

7. *MPW*, 27 April 1912, p. 322.

8. *NYDM*, 3 April 1912, p. 27; *MPW*, 6 April 1912, p. 34 (Mutual founded), and 13 April, p. 122 (Chicago meeting).

9. *MPW*, 12 August 1911, p. 191 (rumor that Cochrane, formerly manager of IMP and lately connected with Lubin, had signed to produce for the Keith and Proctor circuit exclusively), and 25 November 1911, pp. 619–621 (review of The Courting of Mary); Grau, *The Theatre of Science*, pp. 54–60 (Aitken); *MPW*, 14 October 1911), p. 136, and 27 April 1912, p. 322 (Baumann).

10. *MPW*: 21 October 1911, p. 215; 16 March 1912, pp. 946–947 (Crystal); 25 November 1911, pp. 619–621 (review of Hands Across the Sea); 20 April 1912, p. 207 (Hite buys Thanhouser). Hite was killed in a car accident on 22 August 1914; see "Last Moment Addenda," in Grau, *The Theatre of Science*, p. 2.

11. *MPW*, 11 July 1914, p. 175 (summary of breakup of Sales Company, founding of Mutual and Universal).

12. Based on trade-journal release charts. Mutual had a separate release listing by the time of a 29 November release, with Kaybee, Keystone, and Broncho. Ammex had a separate listing by 4 December. See also *NYDM*, 12 February 1913, p. 29 (Blaché interview), and 2 April 1913, pp. 26–27 (Exclusive Supply Co.). In *Motography Handbook* (1 April 1912–31 March 1913), Mutual Film Corporation lists thirty exchanges and Film Supply only two.

13. Grau, *The Theatre of Science*, pp. 54–60.

14. Iris Barry and Eileen Bowser, *D. W. Griffith: American Film Master* (New York: Museum of Modern Art, 1965), pp. 9–11, 44, 49.

15. *Motion Picture News*, 8 November 1913, p. 18.

16. *Motion Picture News*, 21 June 1913, p. 16.

17. *NYDM*, 19 February 1913, p. 26 (Powers); Robert Grau, *The Theatre of Science*, pp. 39–41.

18. Balshofer and Miller, *One Reel a Week*, pp. 83–93; *MPW*, 5 October 1912, pp. 12, 32; Steven Higgins, "I film di Thomas H. Ince" (filmography), in *Thomas H. Ince*, special issue of *Griffithiana* (October 1984): 155–194.

19. Grau, *The Theatre of Science*, p. 41.

20. *US* v. *MPPC* 3 (18 November 1913) 1780; *NYDM*, 25 September 1912, p. 31 (release listings divided into Licensed, Universal, and Film Supply, but not Mutual.)

21. *MPW*, 6 April 1912, p. 13 (advertisement, Warner's Features, 145 W. 45 Street); 6 April 1912, p. 48; 12 October 1912, p. 130 (St. Louis); 19 October 1912, p. 212 (Warner's fifteen exchanges); 21 December 1912, p. 1169 (founding of Gauntier Co.); 15 November 1913, p. 781 (advertisement).

22. Grau, *The Theatre of Science*, pp. 62–63; *MPW*, 4 October 1913, p. 50, and 11 July 1914, p. 262.

23. *NYDM*, 21 February 1912, p. 29 (advertisement for Camille and Madame sans Gêne); Daniel Frohman, *Daniel Frohman Presents* (New York: Kendall & Sharp, 1935), pp. 277–280; *MPW*, 12 October 1912, pp. 154, 167 (advertisement).

24. *NYDM*, 13 November 1912, p. 11 (Mrs. Fiske; new company is called Prominent Players Motion Picture Company here); *MPW*: 4 January 1913, pp. 26–28; 21 February 1914, p. 955; 28 March 1914, p. 1659; 11 July 1914, p. 186; 6 June 1914, p. 1394 (Zukor statement). Charles Frohman died on the *Lusitania*, 7 May 1915.

25. *MPW*, 8 January 1913, p. 17.

26. *MPW*, 20 December 1913, p. 1417; 3 January 1914, p. 35; 22 November 1914, p. 921; 5 August 1916, p. 929.

27. *MPW*, 30 May 1914, pp. 1268–1269.

28. *MPW*, 4 July 1914, p. 43, and 11 July 1914, pp. 260–261.

29. *Motion Picture News*, 8 November 1913, p. 16; *MPW:* 4 April 1914, pp. 26–27 (advertisement); 20 June 1914, p. 1700; 21 July 1914, p. 264. Alco, begun in 1914, was the predecessor to Metro.

30. *US* v. *MPPC* 2:699–700 (27–28 February 1913) (Fox); *ibid.*, 736–741 (Sawyer).

31. *New York Times*, 8 August 1913.

32. *MPW*, 17 December 1910, p. 1406 (photo, diagram, description); 11 December 1909, p. 831; 18 December 1909, pp. 873–874; 25 December 1909, pp. 912–917 (demonstration at Madison Square Garden); 31 December 1909, p. 959 (problems); 15 July 1911, p. 23 (technical). Ramsaye, *A Million and One Nights*, pp. 566–571.

33. *MPW*, 16 April 1910, p. 605, and 17 December 1910, p. 1406.

34. *MPW*, 16 July 1910, p. 146; 23 July 1910, p. 182; 6 August 1910, p. 291.

35. *MPW*, 14 January 1911, p. 61; 11 February 1911, p. 295; 11 March 1911, p. 529.

36. *NYDM*, 3 May 1911, p. 34; 10 June 1911, p. 1307.

37. *MPW*, 12 August 1911, p. 363; 30 September 1911, p. 959.

38. *NYDM*, 24 January 1912, p. 33, and 31 January 1912, p. 53; *MPW*, 19 October 1912, p. 231, and 14 December 1912, p. 1217 (advertisement).

39. *NYDM*, 4 September 1912, p. 27, and 2 October 1912, p. 34.

40. *MPW*, 12 October 1912, p. 16; 19 October 1912, pp. 231, 234; 26 October, 1912, p. 340; 16 November 1912, p. 650; *NYDM*, 12 February 1913, p. 34; *MPW*, 14 December 1912, p. 1090 (Taft screening).

41. *MPW*, 21 December 1912, p. 1175; *NYDM*, 12 February 1913, p. 30.

42. *NYDM*, 30 April 1913, p. 26; see also the illustration of THE SCARLET LETTER, same page.

43. *MPW*, 4 October 1913, p. 138; Grau, *The Theatre of Science*, pp. 61–62; *MPW*, 25 October 1913, p. 391; *Motion Picture News*, 8 November 1913, p. 46.

44. *NYDM*, 2 April 1913, p. 26, and 4 June 1913, p. 26 (Woods); *Motography's Hand Book and Film Record* (October 1913); *MPW*, 21 June 1913, p. 1238; *New York Times*, 20 December 1913.

45. Gorham Kindem, "Demise of Kinemacolor: Technological, Legal, Economic, and Aesthetic Problems in Early Color History," *Cinema Journal* (Spring 1981): 3–14; *US* v. *MPPC* 2:827–830 (1 March 1913); *MPW*, 2 January 1915, p. 105.

46. *MPW*, 19 October 1912, p. 224; "Big Figures on Films," *New York Times*, 9 May 1914; *MPW*, 11 July 1914, pp. 175–198.

CHAPTER 14. Refining the Product

1. G. W. Bitzer: *Billy Bitzer: His Story* (New York: Farrar, Straus and Giroux, 1973), pp. 45, 91 (1905 photograph, interior of studio); Biograph *Bulletin* No. 6, 1 June 1903 (electricity in studio), see Porter's THE SEVEN AGES (February 1905) and Bitzer's THE MUSIC MASTER (1908) for side-lit fireplace effects and Bitzer's silhouette effects for THE FOUR SEASONS (January 1904), in Niver, ed., *Biograph Bulletins, 1896–1908*.

2. *MPW*, 31 October 1908, p. 338; 1 April 1911, p. 699 (FIVE HOURS); 14 January 1911, p. 71.

3. See prints of the films mentioned. C. H. Claudy, *MPW*, 27 May 1911, p. 1177, complains about a lantern that sheds no light.

4. *MPW*, 11 September 1909, p. 347 (SUFFER LITTLE CHILDREN), and 20 April 1912, p. 217 (THE PUNISHMENT).

5. *MPW*, 5 October 1912, p. 53 (GHOSTS), and 14 December 1912, p. 1091 (IN THE SHADOW OF THE CROSS).

6. *NYDM*, 11 September 1912, p. 24.

7. *MPW*, 25 June 1910, p. 1102 (A BANDIT'S WIFE), 14 January 1911, p. 71 (GAY, GAY, . . .). George Pratt has supplied a reference that seems to date filming of THE DEERSLAYER much earlier than its release: reports of the movie company's arrival for location work appear in the Cooperstown, New York, *Otsego Farmer* on 8, 15, and 29 September 1911.

8. The quoted phrase is an intertitle in the film, THE DREAM.

9. *NYDM*, 11 September 1912, p. 26 (ROBERT OF SICILY); *MPW*, 5 December 1914, pp. 1388–1389 (HOUSE OF FEAR); Bordwell *et al.*, *The Classical Hollywood Cinema*, p. 263. KING ROBERT OF SICILY

may have encountered other problems, however, since it did not appear until a year later, and then only in two reels.

10. Karl Brown, *Adventures with D. W. Griffith* (New York: Farrar, Straus and Giroux, 1973), pp. 74–75, 90. The shot Brown described does not survive in the existing prints, although the spotlight effect created by a mirror may be seen in the scenes on the stage of the theater.

11. *MPW*, 20 May 1911, pp. 1116–1117, and 27 May 1911, p. 1177.

12. Salt, *Film Style and Technology: History and Analysis*, p. 151; *MPW*, 26 October 1912, p. 322; Thompson, "Initial Standardization of the Basic Technology," in Bordwell *et al.*, *The Classical Hollywood Cinema*, pp. 266–269.

13. *NYDM*, 24 January 1912, pp. 33, 38.

14. *MPW*, 9 November 1912, p. 534; 14 December 1912, p. 1084.

15. *NYDM*, 4 June 1913, p. 28 (Phillips), and 30 April 1913, p. 26 (Marion Leonard); *MPW*: 4 October 1913, p. 161; *MPW*, 11 October 1912, p. 113 (Lubin); *MPW*, 29 November 1913, p. 989 (Wegener); p. 1009 (Edwin August), p. 1017 (Grace Cunard).

16. "King Baggott," *Variety*, 10 April 1914.

17. *MPW*, 19 October 1912, p. 252; 2 November 1912, p. 461; 16 November 1912, p. 638; 30 November 1912, p. 870; 28 December 1912, p. 1278; 29 December 1912, p. 1277.

18. *MPW*, 15 November 1913, p. 738 (GHOST).

19. The example of THE MASSACRE, however, could not have been influential on American style because it was one of those films shelved by Biograph and not released until 1914, except in Europe.

20. W. Christy Cabanne, "Interviews" file, Braverman Papers, in D. W. Griffith Papers, Museum of Modern Art Film Study Center, undated (1940s).

21. Lionel Barrymore file, Braverman Papers, in D. W. Griffith Papers, Museum of Modern Art Film Study Center, undated (1940s).

22. *MPW*, 29 November 1913, p. 989 (THE PORT OF DOOM); Vachel Lindsay, *The Art of the Moving Picture* (New York: 1915; reprint by Liveright, 1970), p. 188; *Variety*, 6 August 1914.

CHAPTER 15. Scene Dissection, Spectacle, Film as Art

1. *MPW*, 28 June 1913, pp. 1346, 1347 (sound systems), and 6 April 1912, p. 13 (Warner's advertisement).

2. *MPW*, 1 November 1913, p. 488.

3. Margaret I. MacDonald, *MPW*, 17 July 1915, p. 491–496. The Charles Dickens Centenary was celebrated in 1912.

4. Henry A. Phillips, *The Photo-Drama* (Larchmont, N.Y.: Stanhope-Dodge, 1914), p. 146.

5. "D.," *NYDM*, 26 February 1913, p. 28.

6. *MPW*, 18 July 1914, p. 380 (advertisement).

7. These quotations and others, evidence of the criticism of fast cutting, are reprinted in Pratt, *Spellbound in Darkness*, pp. 100–105.

8. As Jay Leyda pointed out to me, it may be necessary to explain that the "return to the same camera position" is not a literal return, since it was normally the efficient practice of Griffith and other filmmakers of the time to film all the shots at the same location at one time, out of order of the continuity. The practice is clearly demonstrated by the surviving original negatives because they were usually left unassembled, in the order of the shooting, while the prints would be edited individually. The "return" I refer to is in the editing.

9. The "earlier Essanay releases" were from 8 and 22 September 1909, 5 January 1910, and 20 October 1909, respectively.

10. Phillips, *The Photo-Drama*, p. 60.

11. Salt, *Film Style and Technology: History and Analysis*, pp. 164–165.

12. Some other films of interest for a study of the developments in scene dissection in 1913–1914 include: THE CAT'S PAW (Essanay, December 1912), AUNTIE'S AFFINITY (Lubin, February 1913), THE GIRL OF THE CABARET (Thanhouser, August 1913), THE HOUR AND THE MAN (Essanay, January 1914), THE WARNING (Majestic, 1914), THE TRAGEDY THAT LIVED (Selig, October 1914), THE HOOSIER SCHOOLMASTER (Masterpiece Films, October 1914), THE EGYPTIAN MUMMY (Vitagraph, December 1914).

13. *MPW*, 11 July 1914, p. 214.

14. *MPW*, 1 May 1909, pp. 553–555, and 16 October 1909, p. 529; "Browning Now Given in Motion

Pictures," *New York Times*, 10 October 1909. Rodin and Matisse were shown at the Stieglitz Gallery as early as 1908.

15. *Biograph Bulletins, 1908–1912*, p. 150; *NYDM*, 5 March 1910, p. 19.

16. *Motion Picture News*, 24 May 1913, p. 16.

17. *MPW*, 22 November 1913, pp. 847–848 (Harrison on Griffith); 8 November 1913, p. 589 (Bush); 11 July 1914, p. 211 (Aitken).

18. Sadakichi Hartmann, "The Esthetic Significance of the Motion Picture," *Camera Work*, April 1912, pp. 19, 20–21, 479. Karl Struss, the future cinematographer, was the photographer whose work appeared in this issue.

19. "New York Letter," *Little Review*, May 1914: pp. 36–37, September 1914: 40; *Dial*, 16 February 1914: pp. 3–4.

20. Pratt credits the sources for his quotations: "The Riddle of America," Guglielmo Ferrero, *Atlantic Monthly* 112:707 (November 1913); foreign dispatches to the *Musical Courier from Hamburg* 65: (6 November 1912) 19:22; *Dresden* 65: (27 November 1912) 22:8; "Editorial," *Camera Work*, special number (August 1912):3; Gertrude Stein, *Lectures in America* (New York: Random House, 1935), p. 176.

21. Lindsay, *The Art of the Moving Picture*, p. 45. William Morgan Hannon, *The Photodrama: Its Place Among the Fine Arts* (New Orleans: The Ruskin Press, 1915), p. 17.

Bibliography

The most frequently used sources for this volume are trade periodicals from the period 1907–1915, especially the *Moving Picture World*, often referred to in the text as the *World*, and the *New York Dramatic Mirror*, often shortened to the *Mirror*; and to a lesser extent, such periodicals as *Motion Picture News, Motography, Nickelodeon, Variety, Motion Picture Story Magazine, Ciné-Journal, Views and Film Index*. The articles cited from these periodicals are found in the notes and are not repeated here.

When a film is described in the text without any reference to a written source it should be understood that a copy of the film is the source of the information. The film described is held by one of the following film archives: International Museum of Photography/George Eastman House (Rochester); Library of Congress (Washington, D.C.); Department of Film/The Museum of Modern Art (New York); National Film Archive/British Film Institute (London). For the location of surviving short silent fiction films in general, see Ron Magliozzi, ed., *Treasures from the Film Archives* (1988).

BOOKS

Ackerman, Carl W. *George Eastman*. Boston and New York: Houghton Mifflin Company, 1930.

Allen, Robert C. *Vaudeville and Film, 1895–1915: A Study in Media Interaction*. New York: Arno Press, 1980.

Allen, Robert C., and Douglas Gomery. *Film History: Theory and Practice*. New York: Alfred A. Knopf, 1985.

Anderson, Robert Jack. "The Motion Picture Patents Company." Ph.D. diss., University of Wisconsin (Madison), 1983.

Balio, Tino, ed. *The American Film Industry*. Madison: University of Wisconsin Press, 1976.

Balshofer, Fred J., and Arthur C. Miller. *One Reel a Week*. Berkeley and Los Angeles: University of California Press, 1967.

Barnouw, Eric. *The Magician and the Cinema*. New York: Oxford University Press, 1981.

Bitzer, G. W. *Billy Bitzer: His Story*. New York: Farrar, Straus and Giroux, 1973.

Borde, Raymond, ed. *Le Cinéma français muet dans le monde*. Perpignan: Cinémathèque de Toulouse and Institute Jean Vigo, 1989.

Bordwell, David, Janet Staiger, and Kristin Thompson. *The Classical Hollywood Cinema: Film Style and Mode of Production to 1960*. New York: Columbia University Press, 1985.

Bowser, Eileen, ed. *Biograph Bulletins 1908–1912*. New York: Farrar, Straus and Giroux, 1973.

Brion-Guerry, L., ed. *L'Année 1913: Les formes esthétiques de l'oeuvre d'art à la veille de la première guerre mondiale*. Paris: Klincksieck, 1971.

Brown, Karl. *Adventures with D. W. Griffith*. New York: Farrar, Straus and Giroux, 1973.

Cassady, Ralph Jr., *Monopoly in Motion Picture Production and Distribution: 1908–1915*. *Southern California Law Review* 32:4 (1959). Reprint. Los Angeles: Bureau of Business and Economic Research, University of California, 1959.

Chanan, Michael. *The Dream That Kicks*. London: Routledge and Kegan Paul, 1980.

Cherchi Usai, Paolo, ed. *La Vitagraph e la nascità del langometraggio: Vitagraph Company of America*. Pordenone, Italy: Edizioni Studio Tesi, 1987.

A Compilation of Legal Agreements Between the Motion Picture Patents Company and the Major Film Companies, 1898–1913, New York: Motion Picture Patents Company, 1913. Copy no. 7 is in the Library of the Museum of Modern Art, New York.

Conant, Michael. *Antitrust in the Motion Picture Industry: Economic and Legal Analysis*. Berkeley and Los Angeles: University of California Press, 1960.

Cook, David. *A History of Narrative Film*. New York: W. W. Norton and Company, 1981.

Crafton, Donald. *Before Mickey: The Animated Film, 1898–1928*. Boston: MIT Press, 1982.

Cripps, Thomas. *Slow Fade to Black: The Negro in American Film, 1900–1942*. London: Oxford University Press, 1977.

Davis, Michael. *The Exploitation of Pleasure: A Study of Commercial Recreations in New York City*. New York: Russell Sage Foundation, 1911.

Dench, Ernest. *Making the Movies*. New York: Macmillan, 1915.

Dyer, Frank Lewis, and Thomas Commerford Martin. *Edison: His Life and Inventions*. New York and London: Harper and Brothers, 1910.

Fell, John L. *Film and the Narrative Tradition*. Norman: University of Oklahoma Press, 1974.

———, ed. *Film Before Griffith*. Berkeley and Los Angeles: University of California Press, 1983.

Fielding, Raymond. *The American Newsreel, 1911–1967*. Norman: University of Oklahoma Press, 1972.

———. *A Technological History of Motion Pictures and Television*. Berkeley and Los Angeles: University of California Press, 1967.

Fosdick, Raymond B. *Report on the Conditions of Motion Picture Shows in New York*. New York: Office of the Commissioner of Accounts, 1911.

Frohman, Daniel. *Daniel Frohman Presents: An Autobiography*. New York: Claude Kendall and Willoughby Sharp, 1935.

Graham, Cooper C., Steven Higgins, Elaine Mancini, and João Luiz Vieira. *D. W. Griffith and the Biograph Company*. Metuchen, N.J.: Scarecrow Press, 1985.

Grau, Robert. *The Theatre of Science*. New York: Broadway Publishing Company, 1914.

Griffith, Linda Arvidson. *When the Movies Were Young*. New York: E. P. Dutton, 1925.

Guibbert, Pierre, ed. *Les Premiers Ans du cinéma français*. Perpignan: Institute Jean Vigo, 1985.

Gunning, Thomas R. "D. W. Griffith and the 'Narrator-System': Narrative Structure and Industry Organization in Biograph Films, 1908–1909." Ph.D. diss., New York University, 1986.

Hannon, William Morgan. *The Photodrama: Its Place Among the Fine Arts*. New Orleans: The Ruskin Press, 1915.

Holman, Roger, ed. *Cinema 1900–1906: An Analytical Study*. London: Fédération Internationale des Archives du Film, 1982.

Horwitz, Rita. *Index to Volume I, 1907, Moving Picture World and View Photographer*. Introduction by Lawrence Karr. Washington, D.C.: American Film Institute, 1974.

Horwitz, Rita, and Harriet Harrison. *The George Kleine Collection of Early Motion Pictures in the Library of Congress: A Catalog*. Washington, D.C., Library of Congress, 1980.

Howe, Irving, and Kenneth Libo, eds. *How We Lived: A Documentary History of Immigrant Jews in America, 1880–1930.* New York: Richard Marek, 1979.

Hulfish, David Sherill. *Cyclopedia of Motion-Picture Work.* 1911. Reprint. *Motion Picture Work.* Chicago: American Technical Society, 1915.

———*The Motion Picture: Its Making and Its Theater.* Chicago: Electricity Magazine Corporation, 1909.

Kleine, George. *Catalogue of Educational Motion Picture Films.* Chicago: Kleine Optical Company, 1910.

Lahue, Kalton C. *Continued Next Week.* Norman: University of Oklahoma Press, 1964.

Lahue, Kalton C., and Terry Brewer. *Kops and Custards.* Norman: University of Oklahoma Press, 1967.

Lahue, Kalton C. *Motion Picture Pioneer: The Selig Polyscope Company,* Cranbury, N.J.: A. S. Barnes, 1973.

Leyda, Jay, and Charles Musser, eds. *Before Hollywood: Turn-of-the-Century Film from American Archives.* Catalog for the touring film exhibition. New York: American Federation of the Arts, 1986.

Lindsay, Vachel. *The Art of the Moving Picture.* New York: Macmillan, 1915. Reprint. Liveright, 1970.

Lyons, Timothy James. *The Silent Partner: The History of the American Film Manufacturing Company, 1910–1921.* New York: Arno Press, 1974.

Magliozzi, Ron, ed. *Treasures from the Film Archives: A Catalog of Short Silent Fiction Film Held by FIAF Archives.* Metuchen, N.J.: Scarecrow Press, 1988. A publication of the Fédération Internationale des Archives du Film.

Malthête, Jacques, ed. *Le Voyage autour du monde de la G. Méliès Manufacturing Company.* Paris: Association "Les Amis de Georges Méliès," 1988.

Marsh, Mae. *Screen Acting.* Los Angeles: Photo-Star Publishing Company, 1921.

May, Lary. *Screening Out the Past: The Birth of Mass Culture and the Motion Picture Industry.* New York: Oxford University Press, 1980.

Mottet, Jean, ed. *David Wark Griffith.* Paris: L'Harmattan, 1984.

Mottram, Ron. "The Danish Cinema, 1896–1917." Ph.D. diss., New York University, 1980.

Musser, Charles. *Before the Nickelodeon: Edwin S. Porter and the Edison Manufacturing Company.* Berkeley: University of California Press, forthcoming.

———, with Carol Nelson. *High Class Moving Pictures: Lyman H. Howe and the Traveling Exhibitor.* Princeton: Princeton University Press, 1990.

Nelson, Richard Alan. *Florida and the American Motion Picture Industry, 1898–1980.* New York: Garland, 1983.

Niver, Kemp, ed. *Biograph Bulletins, 1896–1908.* Los Angeles: Locare Research Group, 1971.

———.*Klaw & Erlanger Present Famous Plays in Pictures.* Edited by Bebe Bergsten. Los Angeles: Locare Research Group, 1976.

An Ordinance Relative to Motion Picture Theatres. New York: Mayor's Bureau of Licenses, 1913.

Parsons, Louella O. *How to Write for the "Movies."* Chicago: A. C. McClurg, 1915.

Phillips, Henry A. *The Photo-Drama.* Larchmont, N.Y.: Stanhope-Dodge, 1914.

Photoplay Arts Portfolio of Eclair Moving Picture Stars with Biographies and Autographs. New York: Photoplay Artists Company, 1914.

Photoplay Arts Portfolio of Kalem Moving Picture Stars with Biographies and Autographs. New York: Photoplay Artists Company, 1914.

Photoplay Arts Portfolio of Thanhouser Moving Picture Stars with Biographies and Autographs. New York: Photoplay Artists Company, 1914.

Pratt, George, ed. *Spellbound in Darkness.* Greenwich, Conn.: New York Graphic Society, 1973.

Ramsaye, Terry. *A Million and One Nights*. New York, 1926. Reprint. New York: Simon and Schuster, 1964.

Richardson, Frank Herbert. *Motion Picture Handbook: A Guide for Managers and Operators of Motion Picture Theatres*. New York: Moving Picture World, 1910.

Salt, Barry. *Film Style and Technology: History and Analysis*. London: Starword, 1983.

Sargent, Epes Winthrop. *Picture Theatre Advertising*. New York: Moving Picture World, Chalmers Publishing Company, 1915.

———. *The Technique of the Photoplay*. New York: Moving Picture World, 1913.

Screen Club First Annual Ball. New York: Screen Club, 1913.

Slide, Anthony. *Aspects of American Film History Prior to 1920*. Metuchen, N.J.: Scarecrow Press, 1978.

Smith, Albert E. *Two Reels and a Crank*. Garden City, N.Y.: Doubleday, 1952.

Spehr, Paul. *The Civil War in Motion Pictures: A Bibliography of Films Produced in the United States Since 1897*. Washington, D.C.: Library of Congress, 1961.

———. *The Movies Begin: Making Movies in New Jersey, 1887–1920*. Newark: Newark Museum–Morgan and Morgan, 1977.

Talbot, Frederick A. *Moving Pictures: How They Are Made and Worked*. Philadelphia: Lippincott, 1912. Revised edition, 1914.

———. *Practical Cinematography and Its Applications*. Philadelphia: Lippincott, 1913.

Thompson, Kristin. *Exporting Entertainment: America in the World Film Market*. London: British Film Institute, 1985.

The United States Government v. The Motion Picture Patents Company. Equity No. 889, District Court, Eastern District of Pennsylvania. The transcript of the court case in six volumes, 1913–1914, in the Library of the Museum of Modern Art, New York.

Vardac, A. Nicholas. *From Stage to Screen: Theatrical Method from Garrick to Griffith*. Cambridge, Mass.: Harvard University Press, 1949.

Wagenknecht, Edward. *The Movies in the Age of Innocence*. Norman: University of Oklahoma Press, 1962.

Walsh, Raoul. *Each Man in His Time*. New York: Farrar, Straus and Giroux, 1974.

ARTICLES

Allen, Robert C. "Motion Picture Exhibition in Manhattan, 1906–1912." *Cinema Journal* 8, no. 2 (Spring 1979): 2–15.

Anderson, Robert. "The Role of the Western Film Genre in Industry Competition, 1907–1911." *Journal of the University Film Association* (Spring 1979): 19–27.

Bowser, Eileen. "Le Coup de téléphone dans les films des premiers temps." In *Les Premiers Ans du cinéma français*, edited by Pierre Guibbert. Perpignan: Institute Jean Vigo, 1985. Pp. 218–224.

———. " 'Old Isaacs the Pawnbroker' et le raccordement d'espaces éloignés." In *David Wark Griffith*, edited by Jean Mottet. Paris: L'Harmattan, 1984. Pp. 31–43.

Burch, Noel. "Un Mode de représentation primitif?" *Iris* 2, no. 1 (1st semester 1984): 113–123.

Currie, Barton. "The Nickel Madness." *Harper's Weekly*, August 24, 1907: 1246–1247.

Czitrom, Daniel. "The Redemption of Leisure: The National Board of Censorship and the Rise of Motion Pictures in New York City, 1900–1920." *Studies in Visual Communication* 10 (Fall 1984): 2–5.

deCordova, Fred. "The Emergence of the Star System in America." *Wide Angle*, Spring 1985: 5–13.

Fisher, Robert. "Film Censorship and Progressive Reform, 1909–1922." *Journal of Popular Film* 4, no. 2 (1975): 143–156.

Gartenberg, Jon. "Vitagraph Before Griffith: Forging Ahead in the Nickelodeon Era." *Studies in Visual Communication* 10 (Fall 1984): 7–23.

Gauntier, Gene. "Blazing the Trail." *Woman's Home Companion* (October 1928–March 1929). References in this volume are to the unpublished MSS in the Special Collections of the Museum of Modern Art Film Study Center, New York. The manuscript contains much material not in the published version, according to a comparison made by Steve Higgins (Higgins to author).

Gaudreault, André. "Detours in Film Narrative: The Development of Cross-Cutting." *Cinema Journal* 19 (Fall 1979): 39–59.

———. "Temporality and Narrativity in Early Cinema, 1900–1906." In *Cinema 1900–1906*, edited by Roger Holman. Brussels: FIAF, 1982. Pp. 201–218.

Gunning, Thomas. "Non-Continuity, Continuity, Discontinuity," *Iris* 1 (1st semester 1984): 102–112.

———. "The Non-Continuous Style of Early Film, 1900–1906." In *Cinema 1900–1906*, edited by Roger Holman. Brussels: FIAF, 1982. Pp. 219–230.

———. "Le Récit filmé et l'idéal théâtral: Griffith et 'les films d'art' français." In *Les Premiers ans du cinéma français*, edited by Pierre Guibbert. Perpignan: Institute Jean Vigo, 1985. Pp. 123–132.

Hartmann, Sadakichi. "The Esthetic Significance of the Motion Picture." *Camera Work*, April 1912: 19–21.

Higgins, Steve. "I film di Thomas H. Ince." *Thomas H. Ince*, special issue of *Griffithiana* (October 1984): 155–194.

Jenn, Pierre, and Michel Nagard. "*L'Assasinat du duc de Guise*." *L'Avant-scène* (November 1984): 58.

Jowett, Garth S. "The First Motion Picture Audiences." *Journal of Popular Film* (Winter 1974): 39–54.

Karr, Kathleen. "The Long Square-Up: Exploitation Trends in the Silent Films." *Journal of Popular Film*, Spring 1974: 107–128.

Kindem, Gorham. "Demise of Kinemacolor: Technological, Legal, Economic, and Aesthetic Problems in Early Color History." *Cinema Journal* 20, no. 2 (Spring 1981): 3–14.

Lawrence, Florence, and Monte M. Katterjohn. "Growing Up with the Movies." *Photoplay*, November 1914: 28–41; December 1914: 91–100; January 1915: 95–107; February 1915: 142–146.

Leyda, Jay. "Defining California Slapstick." In *The Slapstick Symposium*, edited by Eileen Bowser. Brussels and New York: Fédération Internationale des Archives du Film Museum of Modern Art (New York), 1988.

McDonald, Gerald. "United States Filmmaking Abroad." *Films in Review* 5 (1954): 257–262.

Merritt, Russell. "Nickelodeon Theaters: Building an Audience for the Movies." In *The American Film Industry*, edited by Tino Balio. Madison: University of Wisconsin Press, 1976. Pp. 83–102.

Mitchell, George. "Sidney Olcott." *Films in Review* 5 (1954): 175–181. See also letter from George Geltzer, p. 251.

Musser, Charles. "Early Cinema of Edwin Porter." In *Cinema 1900–1906*, edited by Roger Holman. Brussels: FIAF, 1982. Pp. 261–280.

———. "The Nickelodeon Era Begins: Establishing the Framework for Hollywood's Mode of Representation." *Framework*, Fall 1983: 4–11.

Patterson, Joseph Medill. "The Nickelodeons: The Poor Man's Elementary Course in the Drama." *Saturday Evening Post*, 23 November 1907.

Slide, Anthony. "The Evolution of the Film Star." *Films in Review* 25 (December 1974): 591–594.

———. "The Thanhouser Company." *Films in Review* 26 (November 1975): 441–445.

Staiger, Janet. "Seeing Stars." *Velvet Light Trap* 20 (1983): 10–14.

———. "Combination and Litigation: Structures of U.S. Film Distribution, 1896–1917." *Cinema Journal*, Winter 1983: 41–71.

————. "The Eyes Are Really the Focus: Photoplay Acting and Film Form and Style." *Wide Angle* 6, no. 4 (1985): 14–23.

————. "Mass-Produced Photoplays: Economic and Signifying Practices in the First Years of Hollywood." In *Movies and Methods*, vol. 2, edited by Bill Nichols. Berkeley: University of California Press, 1985. Pp. 144–164.

Talmadge, Norma. "Close-Ups." *Saturday Evening Post*, 12 March 1927. Reprinted in *The American Film Industry*, edited by Tino Balio. Madison: University of Wisconsin Press, 1976. Pp. 83–101.

Wanamaker, Mark. "Historic Hollywood Movie Studios." *American Cinematographer*, May 1976: 280–283, 286–288, 297. Part 1 of a series of articles.

SPECIAL COLLECTIONS OF THE MUSEUM OF MODERN ART LIBRARY

The first item is held by the Museum Library. All the others are in the Special Collections of the Film Study Center.

The Biograph Production Records
The Bartlett Collection
The Biograph Collection
The David Wark Griffith Collection*
The Edison Collection
The Merritt Crawford Collection*
The George Kleine Collection
Personality and subject clipping files

---

* Available on microfilm from University Microfilms.

Picture Sources

The World wants to protest now and forever against the use of still photos
as illustrations or advertisements of the motion picture. That is, unless it is
taken with a specific camera at the same time and from the same point of
view as the motion picture itself. Specially posed still pictures of moving
picture scenes do not interest us. An enlargement from the film itself always
does.

—Moving Picture World, 6 August 1910, p. 352

The illustrations are from The Museum of Modern Art/Department of Film Stills
Archive, with the following exceptions:

Illustrations on pages 16, 34, 115, 124, 130, 131, 193, 214, and 215 are from the
Bartlett Collection; page 116 from the Horburgh Collection; page 141 from the
Edison Script Collection; page 212 from the Film Poster Collection; all in the De-
partment of Film's Film Study Center, Special Collections.

The illustration on page 138 is reproduced from *Moving Picture World*, 19 June
1915, p. 1906; page 231 from *New York Dramatic Mirror*, 12 February 1913, p. 30;
page 246 from *New York Dramatic Mirror*, 24 January 1912, p. 33.

The photographs on pages 5, 9, 11, 14, and 127 are from the collection of Q. David
Bowers and first appeared in his *Nickelodeon Theatres and Their Music* (New York:
Vestal Press, 1986). The song slides reproduced as frontispiece and on page 17 are
from the John W. Ripley Collection. The photographs on pages 263–265 were specially made for this book from the film by the kindness of Patrick Loughney of the
Library of Congress. The photograph on page 236 is a frame enlargement from the
film made by James Williams.

General Index

Italic numerals signify illustrations.

Index of Films

About the Author

Eileen Bowser was Curator in the Department of Film at the Museum of Modern Art, responsible for the growth and care of the film collection and its long-term preservation from 1976 to 1993. In her more than thirty-five years at the Museum she organized film programs and exhibitions on various aspects of film history, including two major retrospectives on D. W. Griffith, in addition to touring shows that have traveled the world. She has lectured in many countries, including China, France, Britain, Bulgaria, and the USSR. In 1989 she was awarded the first Prix Jean Mitry by the Giornate del Cinema Muto of Pordenone, Italy. Her publications include *The Movies* (with Richard Griffith and Arthur Mayer), *D. W. Griffith* (with Iris Barry), *Film Notes, Carl Dreyer, The Slapstick Symposium, A Handbook for Film Archives,* and numerous articles on aspects of film history, research, and archival work.